Thinking Things Through

Thinking Things Through

CRITICAL THINKING FOR DECISIONS YOU CAN LIVE WITH

Dianne Romain

Sonoma State University

MAYFIELD PUBLISHING COMPANY

Mountain View, California
London · Toronto

Library of Congress Cataloging-in-Publication Data

Romain, Dianne Elise.
    Thinking things through : critical thinking for decisions
you can live with / Dianne Romain.
      p.   cm.
    Includes index.
    ISBN 1-55934-175-0
    1. Critical thinking.   2. Reasoning.   3. Decision-making—Moral and
ethical aspects.   I. Title.
BC177.R65   1996   96-8152
160—dc20   CIP

Manufactured in the United States of America

10   9   8   7   6   5   4   3   2

Mayfield Publishing Company
1280 Villa Street
Mountain View, CA 94041

Sponsoring editor, James Bull; developmental editors, Christine Freeman, Kathleen
Engelberg; production editor, Julianna Scott Fein; manuscript editor, Sally Peyrefitte;
art director, Jeanne M. Schreiber; text and cover designer, Claire Seng-Niemoeller;
cover art, José Ortega; art manager, Robin Mouat; illustrators, Larry Daste and Joan
Carol; manufacturing manager, Amy Folden. The text was set in 10/12 Usherwood
Medium by G&S Typesetters, Inc., and printed on 50# Ecolocote by Malloy Litho-
graphing, Inc.

To Sterling, who encourages me to write
and reminds me to play

Preface

I first took critical thinking thirty years ago, the summer before my junior year at the University of Missouri at Kansas City. The text we used, *Logic: An Introduction* by Lionel Ruby, was divided into three sections: language and logic, deductive logic, and scientific methodology.

I loved the class. I'd always enjoyed working on math and word puzzles with my siblings, so I found the short exercises at the end of the chapters fun to do. Also, I had more to contribute to discussions after taking that class. I no longer looked at an essay and wondered what in the world I could say about it. I could identify the author's main point, and I had labels to use to evaluate the author's reasoning. By learning the language of critical thinking, I became more articulate in describing the moves that newscasters and advertisers make to get audiences to believe and do what they want.

I've still got the textbook from that class. It's by my side now as I write. And I'm asking myself again the question I've asked myself over and over in the decade it has taken me to research and write this book: why? Why—when I clearly had such a positive experience with critical thinking—why write another book? Why not use the book that introduced me to this wonderful subject? Or why not use one of the many other fine critical thinking books that have been published since that time? Why do I sit in my study writing on a Sunday afternoon instead of going Greek dancing with my love?

GENERAL GOAL OF THIS BOOK

I've written this book because I believe a critical thinking class can give students even more than I received from mine. A critical thinking class can empower students to sort through complex, multifaceted issues, find solutions to problems, and resolve conflicts. In short, a critical thinking class can teach students how to make decisions they can live with.

To achieve this goal, critical thinking must include a study of topics traditionally taught in critical thinking classes. Students need to learn to clarify meaning and analyze and evaluate arguments. They also need to identify and compensate for slanting in the media. But in order to put these skills into use in their daily lives, students need to study topics not traditionally taught in critical thinking classes. They need to become aware of and reflect on their emotions. They also need to learn how emotion and the traditionally taught thinking skills fit into the processes of deciding how to act and resolving conflicts. Most important, students need plenty of practice in the range of activities useful for making and implementing their decisions.

This book includes chapters on emotion and decision making. It links the traditionally taught thinking skills to understanding emotion, decision making, and conflict resolution. And it offers multiple opportunities for students to put these thinking skills into practice with real-life exercises and writing assignments.

ORGANIZATION

The first two chapters of this book, "Questioning Emotions" and "Deciding How to Act," serve to motivate the study of the traditionally taught thinking skills.

Chapter 3, "Breaking Up Arguments," introduces argument analysis, and the following two chapters, "Deciding on Definitions" and "Attending to Language," help students produce clearly and engagingly written arguments. Chapter 6, "Slanting for Fun and Profit," teaches students to recognize and remodel slanted arguments and information.

The final four chapters of the book focus primarily on argument evaluation. The first of these provides an overview of how to evaluate inductive and deductive arguments, and the last three chapters provide more detailed study of analogies, statistical reasoning, and causal reasoning.

Instructors who prefer can teach Chapter 2, "Deciding How to Act," and/or the chapters on language and slanting after teaching the chapters on argument evaluation.

KEY FEATURES

Key features of this book are as follows:

- Coherency achieved by linking the many diverse concepts and distinctions of critical thinking to the overall goal of making decisions.
- Emphasis on the constructive use of critical thinking by placing its traditional concepts and distinctions, including common fallacies, in the context of problem solving and conflict resolution.
- Integration of the study and practice of writing and critical thinking.
- Inclusion of thinking and writing skills and concepts most useful in everyday life.
- Readable writing that keeps technical language to a minimum.
- Pedagogy that invites students to participate in the teaching and learning of critical thinking at each step along the way.

- A "Your Thoughts About . . ." section at the beginning of each chapter asking students to examine their pre-existing ideas about the topic of the chapter.

- "Your Turn" exercises in the body of each chapter that give students an opportunity to check their understanding of concepts and offer their own ideas about the subject.

- Paper topics at the end of each chapter that invite students to write about their additional ideas on the topic of the chapter.

- Ample short exercises at the end of each chapter to allow students to practice applying key concepts.

- Advertisements with visual images for students to analyze and evaluate.

- Readings, often from several different points of view on the same topic, that give students a chance to delve more deeply into subjects they are analyzing and writing about.

- Readings and short passages selected from a wide range of disciplines and contexts, including advertising, anthropology, editorials, ethnic studies, everyday dialogues, history, law, literature, news, philosophy, psychology, medical science, sociology, and women's studies.

- Glossary of key concepts.

INSTRUCTOR'S MANUAL

The instructor's manual includes summaries of the chapters, sample answers to questions in the book, sample quizzes with answers, additional ideas for assignments, suggestions for classroom activities, and advice about how to respond to common student questions.

ACKNOWLEDGMENTS

I am grateful to my students, teaching assistants, and research assistants for challenging me to find more effective ways to teach and write, including especially Lorraine Barnes, Sui Barnet, Corrinne Bedecarre, Jill Binker, James Cantor, Rocky Dubenmeier, Tim Jones, Sachiko Kawara, Robert Lally, Ron Lisky, Carol Paoli, and Pamela Rosada.

Many faculty members read parts or all of various drafts of this book, and some of them tested my ideas in their classes. For their advice and support I want to thank David Averbuck, Melinda Barnard, Cathy Charmaz, Philip Clayton, Lynn Cominsky, Bill Dorman, Susan Gevirtz, Bernice Goldmark, Ralph Johnson, Ardath Lee, Deborah Mathieu, Edward F. Mooney, Gillian Parker, Richard Paul, Jonah Raskin, Michael Scriven, Philip Temko, Francisco Velasquez, and Carole Wade. I am especially grateful to Victor Daniels for helping with last-minute revisions. Karen Peterson and Michael Schwager explored cover ideas with me. I want to thank Ann Garry, Helen

Heise, Ann Kerwin, Rita Manning, Wanda Teays, Mary Anne Warren, and other members of the Society for Women in Philosophy for encouragement and constructive criticism. I am also indebted to a number of anonymous reviewers for their suggestions and to the many authors who gave me permission to use their words and images.

I am grateful to many others: the Affirmative Action Faculty Development Program for partial support of my work; Arthur Hoffman for guiding me in developing emotional awareness; Jan Beaulyn, Pat Damery, Elizabeth Evans, Elizabeth Herron, Jimalee Plank, and Judy Temko of Thursday Night Writers for making a warm nest for hatching ideas; Barbara Shearer for inspiration and hope; Elizabeth Atwood Taylor for editorial advice; Barbara Donecker for proofreading; and Julie Thompson for copyediting, research, Socratic questioning, and good humor when I most needed it.

Many people at Mayfield added their own special touches to this project, including Kate Engelberg, Julianna Scott Fein, Robin Mouat, and Pam Trainer. I'm grateful to them for their work and laughter, and I'm especially grateful to Jim Bull for allowing me to take the time I needed to complete this book and for his continued support and encouragement. Others who helped bring this book to life include Christine Freeman, Cristi A. Grider, and Sally Peyrefitte.

For continued support and inspiration I want to thank my parents, Virginia Graebner Flakne and Earl J. Flakne, the rest of my large extended Midwestern family, and my California family, Laura Sandoval and Dylan, Markus, and Sterling Bennett.

Brief Contents

Contents

4 ✍

Deciding on Definitions   104

5 ✍

Attending to Language   134

6 ✍

Slanting for Fun and Profit   164

7 ✍

Evaluating Arguments:
An Overview   196

8 ✍

Thinking through Analogies   237

9 ✍

Generating Generalizations   265

Where Do We Begin?

Have you ever been told to think something through but weren't quite sure how to do that? Many people call this way of thinking **critical thinking**. You may be reading this book for a class called "Critical Thinking." The book is designed to give you ideas about how to think critically so that you can make decisions that are less likely to go awry.

WHAT IS CRITICAL THINKING?

Some of my students worry about taking a critical thinking class because they think of critical thinking as negative thinking. They do not want to be unfavorably criticized, nor do they want to learn how to criticize others unfavorably. Good for them. I agree totally. I don't want to teach this destructive way of thinking. In fact, I want to help people learn how to stop being unfavorably critical of themselves and others.

Critical thinking, as I define and teach it, consists of those activities of the mind that are indispensable to making decisions we can live with. The processes involved in critical thinking include becoming aware of our emotions and reflecting on them, identifying our values, assessing information and the authorities who provide it, analyzing and clarifying language, imagining solutions to problems, evaluating alternative solutions, and assessing and producing arguments.

After reading this short definition of critical thinking, you may still be puzzled about what, exactly, critical thinking *is*. Don't worry. You can't understand critical thinking just by learning a definition; you understand critical thinking by practicing it. And you'll get plenty of practice from this book.

What do you think this person should do?

ABOUT THIS BOOK

The following sections summarize what you'll be reading in this text and provide some advice about how to get the most from your reading.

A Quick View of Chapter Contents

What is this book going to teach you? Let's run quickly through the chapter contents.

Chapter 1, "Questioning Emotions," describes emotion as the interplay of perception, thought, feeling, and motivation. It teaches how to become aware of emotions and emotional alternatives—to help you discover your values and develop emotions that guide you to actions that are in your best interest. The remaining chapters provide additional practice in the thinking skills you need to increase your emotional awareness and choice.

Chapter 2, "Deciding How to Act," introduces steps for making thoughtful decisions and resolving conflicts—to help you define problems, generate and decide among solutions, and resolve conflicts with others when making decisions. The remaining chapters provide more practice in the skills you use when making decisions and resolving conflicts.

Chapter 3, "Breaking Up Arguments," teaches how to identify arguments, break them into their parts, and distinguish them from disputes—to help you structure your reasons for your decisions into argumentative essays or speeches and to prepare you for evaluating them. Learning to distinguish arguments from disputes also improves your ability to resolve conflicts.

Chapter 4, "Deciding on Definitions," teaches methods for defining words, recommends resources to use to develop definitions, and introduces ways to critique definitions—to help you explain novel or ambiguous language in your decisions and arguments. By becoming aware of the ambiguity of words, you will be more likely to avoid conflicts that result from misunderstanding, and by learning to define your words, you will be able to resolve those misunderstandings when they arise.

Chapter 5, "Attending to Language," describes language used to produce double meanings, distinguishes language that awakens the senses from language that dulls them, and identifies language that evokes positive and negative associations—to help you select language for precise and engaging communication and to help you avoid being misled and controlled by the language of others. This chapter also prepares you for a study of slanting, the topic of the next chapter.

Chapter 6, "Slanting for Fun and Profit," explains the uses of slanting, shows how to determine the dominant slant of a medium, describes basic techniques of slanting used in advertising and the news, and recommends ways to compensate for slanting—to help you see beyond one-sided reports, arguments, and decisions.

Chapter 7, "Evaluating Arguments," provides an overview on how to tell better from worse arguments—to help you develop a healthy skepticism. It includes ideas about how to question expert and witness testimony, and it introduces the distinction between inductive and deductive arguments.

The final three chapters of the book go into more detail on how to evaluate three of the most common types of reasoning used in decision making: reasoning from analogy, reasoning about generalizations, and reasoning about causes.

Chapter 8, "Thinking through Analogies," introduces the roles analogies play in explaining complex or abstract subjects and in supporting predictions, evaluations, and legal decisions—to help you communicate effectively and support and critique predictions and evaluations used in decisions. Understanding analogies is also central to an understanding of reasoning about generalizations, the topic of the next chapter.

Chapter 9, "Generating Generalizations," explains how to identify questionable generalizations and how to produce reliable ones—to help you recognize misleading or damaging stereotypes, avoid jumping to questionable generalizations, and question polls and surveys.

Chapter 10, "Causal Reasoning," introduces ways to generate causal hypotheses, methods of testing them, and societal constraints on achieving scientific certainty—to help you question experts and improve your own causal reasoning.

How You Will Learn from This Book

By this stage in your education, you probably have developed some good ideas about how to learn from a text. Here are some of my ideas. Are any of them similar to yours?

Read, Review, Respond   Critical thinking is an activity. As with learning how to swim, to play music, or to ride a horse, you learn how to think critically by doing it as well as by reading about it, watching others do it, and reviewing what you have read or seen.

To help you get into the habit of reviewing and responding, this book poses questions to you in "Your Turn" sections throughout the chapters and in additional exercises at the end of each chapter. These questions ask you to respond to what you've read in a variety of ways:

1. To apply what you have read to different situations.
2. To evaluate what you have read.
3. To identify any confusions you have about what you have read.

Although you can respond by thinking or speaking, I emphasize writing because writing helps us clarify our ideas. We can also use writing to generate ideas, especially when we turn off our internal critics. Because generating ideas is crucial to thoughtful decision making, many of the "Your Turn" sections ask you to do a "freewrite" or to "jot down some ideas."

To do a **freewrite,** just put your fingers on your keyboard, or put your pencil to paper, and take off. Don't stop to question or critique what you write. Don't scratch out or edit. Just keep writing. You can guide your freewrite by starting with a topic or question, but watch out for trying to come up with the "right" answer to the question or "right" position on the topic. Searching for the right response turns a freewrite into a confined exercise.

You can time your freewrite, if you like. Ten-minute freewrites can be quite productive. Use a timer if you find yourself stopping to look at your watch every minute.

Willingly Admit Confusion and Ignorance   Sometimes we feel embarrassed about admitting confusion and ignorance. But we shouldn't be embarrassed; admitting our confusion and ignorance moves us to creativity and wisdom.

FROM CONFUSION TO CREATIVITY   Sensitivity to confusion is a key to creativity and learning. When you identify your confusions, you begin to make discoveries and reach new depths of understanding. So I encourage you to practice admitting confusion, attending to confusion, listening to confusion, thinking about confusion, valuing confusion, welcoming confusion, courting confusion, playing with confusion, resting on confusion, and sleeping on confusion.

Once I begin courting confusion, I find it everywhere. Sometimes I feel confused when I read something the first time, sometimes not until the second time. Sometimes I think I understand something perfectly but become confused when I try to apply it. Sometimes my confusion appears when I try to explain what I know to someone else. I get confused at least once an hour when writing this text. All in all, I find countless occasions for confusion. I can't say that I like confusion, but because I know that admitting to it will take me closer to understanding, I take a deep breath and face it.

If you try to be aware of your confusion as you go along, it is less likely to pop up at an inopportune time—say, on the day of an exam or deadline.

Here are some questions to ask yourself:

1. Is there anything I am unclear about, confused about, do not understand the meaning of, cannot make sense of? Is it something that does not jibe or seems inconsistent with something else in the text or elsewhere?

2. Can I begin to clarify the confusion? Can I locate its source in a word, phrase, or paragraph?

3. Who can help me with my confusion? Another student? A tutor? The teacher?

FROM IGNORANCE TO WISDOM   In ancient Greece, in the sacred city of Delphi, an oracle (a priest who could speak with the gods) declared that there was no one in Athens wiser than Socrates. Not feeling unusually wise, Socrates was confused at the oracle's pronouncement. He decided to question the men of Athens to find out how wise they were. Socrates discovered that the political leaders, artists, and other prominent persons all thought they knew things they did not know, whereas he, Socrates, recognized his ignorance. Socrates decided that the oracle meant that Socrates was wise because he recognized his ignorance.

Ann Kerwin, a contemporary philosopher, gave me some help in learning how to recognize ignorance. She describes the concept of a **world of ignorance,** which includes the following:

1. Things you realize that you do not know.

2. Things you have not yet thought of.

3. Things you assume you know but in fact do not know.

Once we see the world of ignorance in this way, we need not be too threatened by our ignorance, for luckily we can make progress. For example, we can think of something new but realize we do not know anything about it. This happened to me when watching a television program about subatomic particles. I heard about quarks for the first time on that show, but I still did not know much about them. Nonetheless, I made some progress in my world of ignorance. I moved from 2 to 1 in the above list. We can also move from 3 to 1. We can discover that we do not know something we assumed we knew and thereby (according to Socrates) gain a little wisdom.

When reading this text and doing the exercises, ask yourself these questions to check your progress in your world of ignorance:

1. Have I heard of something I had not thought of before?
2. Have I come to question something I assumed I knew?

The further you are able to progress in your world of ignorance, the more you are able to learn, because each step gives you new questions to explore. Now that I have heard of quarks I can ask what they are. Once I question something I assumed to be true, I can prepare for further inquiry into my assumption. The world of ignorance is a fascinating place. And it is infinitely greater than the world of knowledge.

YOUR TURN A

1. Select one of the following to guide a ten-minute freewrite:

   a. Does recognizing the importance of courting confusion and identifying ignorance help you feel more comfortable about your confusion and ignorance?

   b. Do you think a wise person is one who recognizes his or her own ignorance?

2. Identify a change you have made in your world of ignorance after reading this far.

3. What ideas did you have about critical thinking before reading my definition on page 1?

Relate Critical Thinking to What Matters to You   Some of you are required to read this book in conjunction with a required course. Your university thinks you should learn critical thinking, but you may not have thought about why *you* want to learn critical thinking. Do not let the university think for you; look at what matters to you and consider how critical thinking can help you meet your goals. One of my students, for example, once practiced critical thinking skills to help her decide whether to tell her parents that she was living with her boyfriend. Critical thinking became more meaningful to her because she found a way to relate it to her own concerns. When you relate the material in this text to what you care about, you will learn more and be happier learning.

Turn Your Resistance into an Opportunity to Learn   Many students resist learning critical thinking; maybe you're one of them. Some students report feeling threatened about questioning their values. Others worry that they will find out that they cannot think critically. Others think they already know how to think critically and resent being required to take a course on it. If you can identify what threatens or annoys you about learning critical thinking, you will have the opportunity to face your resistance and get beyond it.

One of my students returned to college to finish his bachelor of arts degree after supporting himself as a journalist for years. He recognized that he was resisting the critical thinking section of an interdisciplinary course he was taking from me. He became annoyed whenever we began to discuss critical thinking even though he was an unusually enthusiastic student. Eventually he spoke with me about his feelings. He decided that his strong reaction indicated that he needed to look more carefully at critical thinking, so he arranged to take an independent study course focusing on critical and creative thinking the next semester. He turned his resistance into an opportunity to learn.

Maintain Hope A while ago, I told my piano teacher that although I had practiced in every way I could think of, I still could not play a piece I had been working on. She gave me some new ways to practice, then later in the lesson told me that my original attitude was immature: I could have said that I had done everything I could think of but that I had not *yet* discovered a solution to my problem. If I had added the word "yet" I would have shown hope rather than discouragement.

We need hope to learn. If we have no hope, we will not keep looking or recognize what is right in front of us. And we need to learn how to renew hope when we get tired and discouraged. Luckily, my teacher knew how to renew my hope when I got discouraged. If you have trouble maintaining hope in yourself, find a tutor, teacher, or friend who can help you.

Replace Frustration with Play Pay careful attention to your moods when you are reading, answering the "Your Turn" questions, or doing the end-of-chapter exercises. If you are feeling frustrated, stop immediately. You cannot learn when you are frustrated. Take a deep breath, do a cartwheel, tell yourself a joke, take a break for one full minute. Then start again. Look at the question in a new way, reread a relevant section of the book aloud in a silly accent, or ask someone who has faith in you for help. Do anything that turns the exercise into play, and you will learn.

YOUR TURN B

1. List several personal, academic, or career goals that critical thinking can help you achieve.

2. Use one of the following to guide a ten-minute freewrite.

   a. Do you have any resistance to learning critical thinking?

   b. Do you get frightened, frustrated, pleased, or excited at the thought of trying something new or different?

   c. What is the most playful class you have taken?

Questioning Emotions

CHAPTER GOALS

- To understand emotion as the interplay of perception, thought, feeling, and motivation.
- To develop emotional awareness and to understand the constraints on the emotions you experience.
- To learn ways to modify your emotions.
- To learn ways to use your emotions as a guide to actions that are in your best interest.

YOUR THOUGHTS ABOUT EMOTIONS

What comes to mind when you think about emotions? Jot down your ideas; then read this story and answer the questions that follow.

One day a teacher was giving tests back. She had just explained the test scores when a student pointed to his test and said in a grating tone of voice, "I can't understand these numbers." She interpreted his tone of voice as accusatory and thought, "He is accusing me unjustly. I just explained the scores. At least he could use a more gracious tone of voice with me, one less blaming." She got annoyed with the student and marched over to his desk to explain the numbers to him. "100 minus 34 equals 66," she said. "That is a D."

As soon as she heard the words come out of her mouth and saw the look on her student's face, her anger turned to sorrow. She realized she had made her student uncomfortable by saying his grade out loud. She had acted quickly, without thinking, and she regretted her action.

Later, she reflected on her beliefs about this student. She had inferred from his tone of voice that he was accusing her, and she had assumed he could figure out the numbers on his own if he had tried. On reflection, she discovered another interpretation of his tone of voice. She considered the possibility that his grating tone of voice expressed anxiety. She also considered the possibility that he genuinely had difficulty figuring out what the numbers meant, even though she had just explained them. She reminded herself that he had a learning disability and that he was having a hard time learning critical thinking. With her new interpretation of her student's tone of voice and behavior, she felt compassionate toward him. She became motivated to give him the clear, slow directions he needed to succeed in her class.

By thinking again about the events of the day, she developed emotions that helped her be a more effective teacher. Later, she and the student talked over what happened. She apologized for calling attention to his grade, and he agreed to take more responsibility for learning critical thinking. They worked together more effectively from that time onward.

Questions

1. In the above story, the teacher first acts from emotion and regrets her action; later, she acts from emotion and is pleased with the outcome. What difference do you find between the first time she acted from emotion and the second time she acted from emotion?

2. Do you have a story to tell about a positive or negative outcome of acting from emotion? What is it?

On the one hand, we worry about letting emotion guide our decisions. Students sometimes say, "I'm so glad I'm taking critical thinking. I've always been told I was too emotional. I want to make more rational decisions." On the other hand, noted neurologist Oliver Sacks highlights the importance of emotion in decision making. He tells the story of a judge who resigned after a frontal lobe injury because "he could no longer enter sympathetically into the motives of anyone concerned, and that since justice involved feeling, and not merely thinking, he felt that his injury totally disqualified him."[1] Thus, contrary to popular belief, ridding ourselves of emotion does not make us better decision makers.

Yet people who worry over the possible negative effects of emotion do have cause for concern. Emotions, like the weather, have mixed effects on our decision making. Sometimes our emotion sails us safely to shore. Our anger at injustice, for example, can motivate us to protect a young child from a bully. Another time—as in the story you read earlier—emotion can sink us in a sea of regret.

The goal of this chapter is to help you develop emotions that guide you to action you can live with. How can you achieve that goal? The title of this chapter gives my answer: "Questioning Emotions." By questioning and, if necessary, changing or modifying your emotions, you are more likely to make choices you can live with.

This chapter recognizes the roles that perception, feeling, and motivation play in emotion and focuses on the role that thinking plays in emotion. You will learn to question your emotions by becoming aware of and questioning your thinking. With its focus on thinking, this chapter forms a backdrop for the rest of the book; that is, the concepts introduced in the remaining chapters—which help you question your thinking—will in turn help you question your emotions.

Also, you will be more likely to benefit from the other chapters once you have begun to appreciate the place of thought in emotion. By recognizing the role of thought in emotion and—most important—by becoming aware of what you're thinking when you're experiencing an emotion, you will be able to put the rest of the chapters to positive use in your own life.

EMOTION: THE INTERPLAY OF PERCEPTION, THOUGHT, FEELING, AND MOTIVATION

Let's start with an example.

> It's the first day of class, and the critical thinking teacher has just announced that each student will be making an oral presentation sometime during the semester. José's face lights up with joy. He remembers students complimenting him on a presentation he made in a previous course. He expects to have a good time making a presentation in this class as well and pictures the other students applauding him. His ears perk up, and he listens attentively when his teacher offers to talk with the students individually about their presentations. His heart feels as if it's beating a little more quickly in anticipation, and he plans to ask the teacher for an appointment right away.

José's **emotion** of joy or happiness at giving an oral presentation involves the interplay of **perception, thought, feeling,** and **motivation.** He starts out hearing (perceiving) the teacher announce the assignment. He thinks about this information: he expects his experience to be similar to one in the past and judges that the experience will be positive. At the same time, he has some internal sensations (feelings). He feels his heartbeat quicken. His thoughts and feelings together motivate him to act: he plans to make an appointment with the teacher.

José's story also illustrates several other common aspects of emotion: imagistic thinking and changes in attentiveness. He engages in imagistic thinking when he pictures other students applauding him. He becomes more attentive and listens carefully to the teacher's offer to help.

Let's look at another example.

> After hearing the teacher's announcement, Sam casts his eyes away from the teacher. He remembers being scolded by his high school speech teacher in front of the class. He feels his stomach drop at the thought of everyone's eyes on him once again. He's so preoccupied with his last awful experience that he doesn't hear the teacher offer to meet with the students individually. He thinks there's nothing he can do to give a successful presentation and decides to see whether he can drop the class.

Notice that Sam starts out hearing the same thing that José heard. But their emotions are very different. Sam becomes anxious or fearful at the news. Like José, Sam interprets the coming oral presentation to be like his previous one, but he judges it differently. Because Sam expects to have another bad experience, he's motivated in a different direction: instead of trying to get help, he wants to drop the class.

José and Sam experience different emotions and are motivated to act differently when their teacher announces an oral presentation assignment.

Notice also that although Sam and José start out hearing the same thing, they do not end up hearing the same thing. José hears the teacher offer to help; Sam, who has become less attentive, does not.

In everyday conversation people frequently use the words "emotion" and "feeling" interchangeably. But, as you see above, I use the word "feeling" to refer to the inner sensations (heart pounding, stomach dropping) of emotions, and the word "emotions" to refer to a complex assortment of perceptions, thoughts, feelings, and motivations.

In the examples above, Sam's and José's feelings differ; frequently, however, people who are experiencing different emotions have very similar internal sensations. Thus, emotions are typically differentiated on the basis of the thoughts and motivations to act that are associated with them, not on the basis of the internal sensations that are associated with them.

Emotions differ not only in kind but also in intensity. Some people become a little anxious when they are required to make an oral presentation; others, like Sam, become so anxious they look for ways to avoid it. The degree of intensity of emotion affects the change in perceptual attentiveness. When emotions become very intense, perceptual attentiveness drops. People who become just a little anxious when hearing about an oral presentation will, like José, perk up their ears to hear more. But when people become very anxious, like Sam, they become less attentive to what's happening. We can also distinguish emotions from **moods**. Emotions tend to be intense and brief, whereas moods tend to be less intense, less focused on particular thoughts, and more protracted.

Emotions frequently come in clusters. Some students who are assigned an oral presentation will be happy and anxious at the same time. They are happy to have a chance to improve their speaking skills but anxious that they will make a mistake in front of people. Many other occasions offer opportunities for mixed emotions. Hearing of the death of a long-ailing friend triggers sadness at the loss of the friend and relief that the friend no longer suffers; being offered a new job leads to happiness about a new challenge and sadness about leaving present co-workers.

YOUR TURN A

Note: Sample answers to the questions marked with a diamond are located in the answer section at the back of the book.

◆ 1. What perceptions, thoughts (interpretations and judgments), and motivations did the teacher have when she became annoyed with her student?

Does the story describe the teacher's feelings?

2. Many people believe that emotion is something very different from thought. Is that what you thought before reading the above section? What do you think now?

Developing Emotional Awareness

Why develop **emotional awareness?** First, we must develop emotional awareness to put the task of this chapter—questioning emotions—into effect in our own lives. We can't begin to question our emotions until we become aware of them.

Second, awareness of our emotions leads to awareness of our values, because we respond emotionally to things we care about. We are joyful at the thought of having things that matter to us—our health, our jobs, our friends, our family, our successes, our prized possessions. We experience fear at the thought of losing them. We become sad when we realize we have lost someone or something we care about. And we become angry when we think the loss was unjust. Thus, by becoming aware of our emotions, we become aware of our values. And knowledge of our values forms an important part of self-knowledge. The familiar Socratic dictum "Know thyself" could be rewritten "Know thyself, know thy emotions."

Some people will have difficulty following this dictum. They identify emotion with feeling and separate it from thought. Some identify themselves as "thinkers" and scorn "feeling types." Others admire feeling and dismiss thinking as irrelevant to the good life. These self-identified thinkers and feelers will have to broaden their views to become aware of their emotions. The thinkers will have to begin to recognize their feelings, and the feelers will have to pay attention to their thoughts.

Even those of us who are ready and willing to develop emotional awareness find the task daunting. It's hard to catch hold of thoughts that go in and out of our consciousness like driftwood sinking and bobbing up again in the surf. Nor do we find it easy to keep in touch with feelings that die down to nothing after flaming with intensity.

Also, we frequently do not know what emotion we are experiencing. Thoughts and feelings do not—like servers in a fast-food restaurant—come with a name tag: "Hi, I'm Anger. How may I serve you?" So even when we become aware of our thoughts and feelings, we may still have difficulty labeling them.

For the purpose of this book, it's not so important that you label your emotions precisely, distinguishing, for example, fear from anxiety or panic. It's more important that you become aware of your perceptions, thoughts, feelings, motivations, and emotional intensity.

The guided freewrite provides a way to develop emotional awareness. When freewriting, remember not to judge yourself. Allow whatever thoughts come to mind to find a way to your paper, without censoring them. You may use the following starting points to guide emotion awareness freewrites:

1. When . . . happened, I got emotional (joyful, afraid, sad, angry . . .)

2. I got emotional (joyful, afraid, sad, angry . . .) because I (saw, heard, tasted, touched, smelled . . .)

3. I became emotional (joyful, afraid, sad, angry . . .) because I thought . . .

4. I got emotional (joyful, afraid, sad, angry . . .) because I care about . . .

5. When I became emotional (joyful, afraid, sad, angry . . .), I kept picturing . . .

6. When I became emotional (joyful, afraid, sad, angry . . .), I thought over and over that . . .

7. The event that's making me emotional (joyful, afraid, sad, angry . . .) reminds me of this event from my past . . .

8. When I became emotional (joyful, afraid, sad, angry . . .), my (stomach, heart, breath, pulse . . .) began to . . .

9. When I became emotional (joyful, afraid, sad, angry . . .), I wanted to . . .

10. When I became emotional (joyful, afraid, sad, angry . . .), my voice sounded like . . .

11. When I became emotional (joyful, afraid, sad, angry . . .), my (eyes, mouth, jaws, shoulders . . .) began to . . .

12. I didn't want to become emotional (joyful, afraid, sad, angry . . .) because . . .

To begin developing emotional awareness, you might want to start at the point that is the easiest or most comfortable for you. If you think of yourself as a "feeling type," begin with number 7 or number 11. If you think of yourself as a "thinking type," begin with number 3 or number 4. Gradually add other starting points to increase the breadth of your emotional awareness.

When you begin to become aware of your emotions, you may find yourself crying or laughing out loud. When you do your emotion freewrites, choose a setting where you feel comfortable with your **emotional expressions.**

Also, take care of your needs for privacy. Think about whether you want to share your emotion freewrites with other persons. Do not share any of your emotion freewrites unless you are comfortable doing so.

YOUR TURN B

1. Do you find yourself resistant to becoming aware of your emotions? Explain why or why not.

2. Pick one of the following situations and do a guided emotion freewrite about it. (Select two or three of the starting points from the list above.)

    a. You have just been told you must make a one-minute speech to the class next week.

    b. Someone has just disagreed with a view you hold dear, for example, that God exists, that a woman has a right to abortion, or that there's nothing wrong with humans killing animals for food.

    c. You received a lower score on an assignment than you expected.

    d. Another student has interrupted you in class discussion for the tenth time.

Reasons for Questioning and Modifying Emotions

Why question our emotions? I gave the basic reason for questioning our emotions in the introduction. Sometimes our emotions sail us safely to our goals and other times they sink us in a sea of regret. So if we want to accomplish our goals, we need to question and be ready to modify our emotions.

Let's look again at the emotions José and Sam experienced when they heard about the oral presentation. Suppose that both José and Sam share the same goals: to succeed in their classes and graduate as quickly as possible. Which student's emotion best serves these purposes, José's joy or Sam's anxiety? José's joy motivated him to get help from the teacher. Sam's anxiety motivated him to consider dropping the class. If Sam can get into another critical thinking class, he might be able to graduate when he wants. But let's suppose that all of the other classes are full. Now Sam's stuck. What can he do?

He can question his emotion. We've already begun to question the act he's motivated to take. We've questioned whether dropping the class is consistent with his goal of graduating on his time schedule. He can consider other actions, such as going to the teacher and telling her of his anxiety about oral presentations. He can question his perceptions. He can ask around and find out whether the teacher said anything he missed. He can question his thoughts: does this experience have to be just like his last experience? Perhaps he will be more successful this time. Perhaps the teacher will be more understanding this time. He can also question his inner sensations: does his chest have to tighten and his mouth go dry when he thinks of giving a presentation, or can he modify those sensations?

In the example above, we imagined Sam being led to question his emotion because dropping the class was inconsistent with his goal of graduating on time. We sometimes start in different places when questioning emotions. Sometimes we question our emotions because we don't like the feelings associated with them. People may crowd into theaters to see a horror film, but fear is less appealing in real life. Few would stand in line to feel the dry-mouth panic of a student giving an oral presentation who looks at the class and can't think of a thing to say. Other times we question our emotions when we are plagued with compulsive, imagistic thinking. Hearing a scolding teacher's voice over and over again when we are trying to prepare for the next oral presentation is just as troubling as having a dry mouth or being motivated to drop the class.

Sometimes we question our emotions because we have come to believe that we have incomplete information because someone else led us astray. Suppose Sam—who wasn't listening to the teacher when she offered help to the students—tells Sue about the oral presentation assignment. Sue becomes anxious at first, but then she questions whether Sam gave her the full information. She questions whether there's as much to be anxious about as she first thought. People frequently give incomplete information when reporting a dispute. After hearing our friend tell about her love's destructive behavior, our compassion for our friend and our anger at her love will be as pure as mountain water, but listening to her love's side of the story will muddy our emotional waters. We'll begin to question our original emotions.

Ways to Change or Modify Emotion

There are ways we can change or modify our emotions: we can change what we perceive, change our thinking about the situation, or change the intensity of our feelings.

Change What You Perceive   We're all familiar with changing our emotions by changing what we perceive. When we're horrified by movie images, we avert our gaze. We can also change what we perceive by changing the external situation.

Here's an example of how we can change the external situation. A friend was annoyed with a neighbor's dog barking whenever he came near. My friend started taking the dog biscuits, the dog stopped barking, and now man and dog are both happy.

Changing the external situation, although it is an effective way to change emotion, is easier said than done. Dogs are hard enough to train, and teachers take a good deal more effort. Bribes are not effective; you've got to give the teacher good reasons. If Sam wants to convince his teacher to drop the oral presentation assignment, he'll need to stay in critical thinking long enough to learn how to give strong reasons.

Change What You Think If you can't change the external situation, you can try to change what you think about it.

CHANGE YOUR INTERPRETATION OF THE SITUATION If the dog hadn't stopped barking, my friend could have tried to reinterpret the dog's behavior. Instead of thinking of the dog as annoying, he could try thinking of the dog as lonely and afraid. Sam, too, could change his thinking. He could replace his view that there's nothing he can do to succeed with the view that there is something he can do, namely, talk with the teacher. He may not rid himself of fear entirely, but he could add a dash of hope.

Changing your thinking is also easier said than done. First, you have to be willing to consider alternative interpretations. Second, you have to come up with alternative interpretations. Sometimes using your imagination will suffice; other times you'll have to do research. When you are having emotions about a dispute, for example, you need to listen to all of the points of view, not just your buddy's. Third, you have to check out the alternative interpretations to see whether one of them fits reality. It won't help Sam to imagine that the teacher will drop the oral presentation requirement if she will not.

We'll learn more about how to change our interpretations later in this chapter, when we discuss how to modify negative thinking. Later chapters in the book provide additional information for questioning our interpretations.

CHANGE THE VOICES FROM THE PAST Some of our emotion thoughts are memories of voices from the past. Students who fear writing or giving oral presentations typically have had one or more painful past experiences. When faced with a new opportunity to speak in public or write, they expect the same painful response they had in the past. Sometimes the most gentle negative response gets reinterpreted as a torrent of abuse through the lens of a negative past experience.

One way to come to terms with the past is to be aware of it and to take charge of it. An excellent writing exercise for this is called "A conversation with my critic." This writing exercise has two stages. First, you describe in detail how your critic looks and sounds. Second, you tell your critic what you want; you educate your critic about how to give you constructive feedback. In other words, you take charge of your critic. You don't ignore the internal voices and whispers that mock and put you down. You address them directly and tell them how to behave.

To quiet troubled nerves before an exam, put your feet flat on the floor, rest your hands, palms up, on your knees, close your eyes, and take in a long slow breath. Hold the breath a moment, then exhale slowly. Repeat several times.

Change the Intensity of Feelings   Suppose you can't change the external situation, and your worst expectations turn out to be true. You can take steps to modify the intensity of your inner sensations. Deep breathing, listening to calming music, meditation, and yoga all work to quiet troubled nerves. You can also avoid stimulants, such as coffee and black tea.

YOUR TURN C

◆ 1. Imagine finding out you have just received a lower grade than you expected on a test. Imagine that this makes you happy. Write down your happy thoughts. Imagine it makes you sad. Write down your sad thoughts. Imagine it makes you angry. Write down your angry thoughts. Imagine it makes you afraid. Write down your fearful thoughts.

2. Describe some music you listen to and its effects on your feelings. What other sights and sounds affect the intensity of your feelings?

CONSTRAINTS ON CHOOSING EMOTIONS

People are often surprised to hear that they can change and modify their emotions. They do not realize they have any choice about their emotions. I understand how they feel. Although we have the capacity to modify our emotions, we can rarely just decide what emotion we want to have and then have it. And sometimes, no matter how much deep breathing we do, we find ourselves flooded with the physical sensations caused by the hormones epinephrine and norepinephrine (commonly known as adrenaline and noradrenaline, respectively). Other times, our bodies are quiet but our thoughts rage, and we cannot seem to rein them in.

The following three sections address a number of common constraints on choosing emotions. By becoming aware of how these constraints operate, we can enhance our ability to choose emotions we can live with.

These sections teach you to question your emotions when (a) others have power over you and ask you to adopt emotions that serve their purposes, (b) you are confronted with a frightful or unjust situation that could lead you to deny your own experience, and (c) you are feeling depressed and unmotivated to act in your best interest.

Pleasing the Powers That Be

This section addresses how our emotional choices are constrained by those who have power over us. On the job, in the army, and in the classroom, people adopt emotional expressions that the boss, sergeant, or teacher want them to adopt.

Pleasing the Boss In *The Managed Heart*, sociologist Arlie Hochschild uses the expression **emotional labor** to describe the task of developing emotional expressions that please the boss. Hochschild uses flight attendants to illustrate her point.

> The flight attendant does physical labor when she pushes heavy meal carts through the aisles, and she does mental work when she prepares for and actually organizes emergency landings and evacuations. But in the course of doing this physical and mental labor, she is also doing something more, something I define as *emotional labor*. This labor requires one to induce or suppress feeling in order to sustain the outward countenance that produces the proper state of mind in others—in this case, the sense of being cared for in a convivial and safe place.[2]

Airline companies want passengers to enjoy flying and feel comfortable. Thus, flight attendants are taught to manage their emotion behavior, especially by smiling. A flight attendant's smile is no longer her own; it belongs to the airline. As Hochschild puts it, "In the flight attendant's work, smiling is separated from its usual function, which is to express a personal feeling, and attached to another one—expressing a company feeling."[3]

Flight attendants are paid to control not only their smiles but also their thoughts. Hochschild relates how flight attendants are informed of appropriate thought processes at the Delta Stewardess Training Center. The instructor asked the class how they alleviate anger at an irate passenger. She provides the answer to her own question:

> I pretend something traumatic has happened in their lives. Once I had an irate that was complaining about me, cursing at me, threatening to get my name and report me to the company. I later found out his son had just died. Now when I meet an irate I think of that man. If you think about the *other* person and why they're so upset, you've taken attention off of yourself and your own frustration. And you won't feel so angry.[4]

Thus Delta flight attendants learn to manage their interpretations of situations—for example, they interpret an aggressive passenger as "having a hard day"—in order to create feelings in themselves and their passengers that are in line with the airline company's goal of making a profit.

In a sense, flight attendants choose their emotions, but their choice is limited by the demands of the airline. They are required to choose emotions that fit the airline's needs and to fabricate interpretations, if necessary, to produce those emotions. According to Hochschild, flight attendants pay a price for their emotional work.

> This deeper extension of the professional smile is not always easy to retract at the end of the workday, as one worker in her first year at World Airways noted: "Sometimes I come off a long trip in a state of utter exhaustion, but I find I can't relax. I giggle a lot; I chatter; I call friends. It's as if I can't release myself from an artificially created elation that kept me 'up' on the trip. . . ."
> As the PSA jingle says, "Our smiles are not just painted on."[5]

In developing a smile that was "not just painted on," this flight attendant diminished her ability to choose emotions that fit her own needs.

An added danger comes from developing the habit of explaining away a bully's aggression. Flight attendants become vulnerable to accepting bullies instead of insisting they change or getting away from them. Instead of saying, "Your behavior is inappropriate. Stop it now," their tendency is to soothe the troubled soul.

Pleasing Our Leaders   Other occupations teach other habits. Military training, for example, teaches recruits to hate "the enemy." Like flight attendants, recruits are taught to think in ways that produce emotions to serve other people's goals. Flight attendants develop emotions to serve the goals of the airlines. During times of war, recruits going into combat develop emotions to serve the goals of U.S. foreign policy. Unlike airline flight attendants, recruits are not free to resign if they disagree with the organization's goals.

Pleasing the Dominant Group   Besides the formal, contractual power relations between employer and employee and between military leaders and subordinates, there are less formal power relations that exist between groups and individuals in our society. Just as persons with formal power establish the appropriate emotions for those with less power, groups with informal power attempt to establish the appropriate emotions for those with less power.

In *Black Lives, White Lives*, Elena Albert, an African-American woman, tells of her experience attending a mostly white school in Montana.

> Once a teacher asked me to stay after school. And he was so embarrassed—he said, "Now we're studying about slavery, and I hope you won't feel hurt when the kids will talk about 'niggers.'" And I was so proud I didn't want him to know that I was hurt, so I said, "Oh, no. I don't mind at all!" But the only time *my* people were mentioned in school were as . . . slaves. And the people who cultivated cotton. . . . Even then I knew that we were not all unskilled. For instance, my father was a blacksmith. And I knew even when I was a very young child about the beautiful ironwork in New Orleans.
>
> This was extremely painful to me. This made me withdraw into myself. I— I, would feel angry and thwarted.[6]

This teacher did not want the child to be hurt by actions that are hurtful or, at any rate, to express hurt. He wasn't successful in keeping the child from recognizing that the situation was hurtful, but she did act as though she were not hurt, saying that she didn't mind.

Elena Albert calls controlling her expressions of emotion "swallowing back." She says her generation thought that education was the key to progress and that those African Americans who had the opportunity to learn had a commitment to learn as much as they could. She saw "swallowing back"— not voicing resentment or anger, not complaining about obvious biases—as necessary behavior modification to get along in a white school.[7]

In a sense, Elena Albert chose not to express her emotions, but her choice was limited by the penalty she would have suffered had she expressed what she really felt. By expecting her to "swallow back," her teachers were asking her to help them maintain the dominant group's assumption that there was nothing wrong with using a denigrating label for African Americans. By asking Elena Albert to control her expression of emotion, her teacher abandoned the opportunity to change unfair behavior.

Elena Albert tried to control her expressions of hurt and anger on hearing the word "nigger," but she maintained her belief that African Americans did not deserve this denigrating label. Others of us accept the limiting interpretations of reality imposed on us by those in power, and as a result we do not try to achieve what we falsely assume we cannot achieve, nor do we try to change a society we falsely assume is fair.

YOUR TURN D

1. Have you ever modified an emotion or emotional expression to please someone in power?

   a. What interpretation, emotional expression, or other aspect of emotion did you modify or feign?

   b. What goal did your modified or feigned emotion serve?

2. Do you think we should modify our emotions to please others? Explain.

Calvin and Hobbes

by Bill Watterson

Avoiding Uncomfortable Emotions

In the last section, we discussed the limits that power imbalances place on our freedom to choose our emotions. We found that people choose interpretations and emotional expressions to serve company, country, and dominant groups. In this section, we look at some psychological strategies that people use to avoid emotions. Although we sometimes deliberately choose these strategies, frequently we are unaware of using them. We can enhance our freedom by becoming aware of these strategies.

Psychologist Carol Tavris describes three strategies we use to maintain our belief that the world is just and safe: denigrating, or blaming, the victim; denial; and reinterpreting an event and its outcome.[8] We use these strategies to protect ourselves from uncomfortable feelings of anger and fear. We don't become angry when we don't recognize that an injustice has been done. We don't get afraid when we don't recognize that something frightening is happening.

Blaming the Victim   Blaming the victim is the strategy of excusing an apparent injustice by saying that the alleged victim was not a victim at all, but asked for or deserved the treatment received. A man who slaps his wife and adds, "She asked for it," blames the victim.

Here's another example of blaming the victim. In Guatemala, all men can be drafted for military service after the age of 18. Periodically the military sends out soldiers to the movie theaters, parks, and other places where young men congregate to round up all of the young men of military age. Some people find this practice unjust and believe that the young men who were taken by the military were wronged. Others blame the victims of the roundup, saying they deserved to be picked up since they were not fast enough on their feet to get away or smart enough to second-guess when the military was coming to town.

Denial   Denial is the strategy of refusing to accept information that would lead us to a conclusion we do not want to hold. Have you ever gone bargain hunting and stopped looking at the prices after you bought your item because you did not want to find a cheaper price? That's denial in action.

Here's a more serious example of denial. A factory moves into town and offers employment to the townspeople, but it uses chemicals that produce toxic waste. People who fail to find out the full extent of the possible hazards are using denial to avoid fear. Citizens also use denial when their country is at war to avoid taking in information that would undermine their faith that young men and women are dying for a just cause.

Reinterpreting the Outcome   We use the strategy of **reinterpreting the outcome** when we find the "silver lining" of the injustice and thus minimize it. Sometimes a person who is oppressed benefits from the experience by developing a deeper understanding of oppression. By focusing on the benefit, the person minimizes the injustice of the oppression.

Len Davis recognizes all three of these strategies at work in the Southern town he grew up in.

> Now the youngsters my age, I think we started the change. I think we started the people to thinking, you know. Right there in the early fifties. But man, anybody that was twenty years old or more, in the early fifties—they were terrible. They had been brainwashed that this white man was really a protector. They *had* to think that way in order to make it. I'm no psychiatrist or anything, but I think that you can just block something out of your mind, you know. And start looking at the good side of it. In other words, I'm not being suppressed, I'm not being discriminated against, I'm just being protected. And I think that's the only way the Negro could have made it back in those days. He couldn't go to bed thinking in the night that, man, this man is treating me like a dog.[9]

In the above quote, Davis describes denial—"block something out of your mind"—and reinterpretation of the outcome—"start looking at the good side of it." In the quote below, Davis relates an example of blaming the victim: the young men's unjust rape conviction and death were excused because the young men should have known better than to be in the presence of a white woman.

> I saw a couple of cases where they took four boys to court—they were caught with a white woman. They didn't rape her, but they were seen with her. So they said all four raped her. They got life sentences. Sheriff Simmons killed a couple of them on the way to prison. I guess I was about fourteen. It was a big thing in my hometown. Everybody was afraid to go out, you know. You just stayed on your side of town. . . .
>
> And what I got out of it, being a kid, was that those guys got out of their place. Even our parents participated in making us think that those boys were wrong for even being in the *presence* of a white woman. Whether they raped her or not. We were brainwashed, in other words.[10]

We frequently use these strategies to maintain a false sense of security. At such times, they prevent us from developing the motivation to change an injustice or remove a threat.

However, if used wisely and economically, these strategies give us needed breaks from a frightening and unjust world. We can rejuvenate ourselves and then get back to work making the world a safer and more just place.

YOUR TURN E

◆ 1. We use the psychological strategies of denial, blaming the victim, and reinterpreting the outcome when we hear bad news and suffer losses: death, the end of a relationship, a poor grade, loss of a job. Show your understanding of each of these strategies by giving an example of each from your own life or from someone you know. Fictionalize your story, if you like, to protect your privacy.

◆ 2. What were some effects of using these strategies?

Leaping to Negative Emotions

In the above section, we discussed psychological strategies used to avoid uncomfortable emotions of fear and anger. We use the same strategies to develop and maintain emotions. Perhaps unsurprisingly, we use these strategies to maintain positive images of ourselves and our activities—in spite of the evidence. We also use them to develop and maintain depression, an emotion that we might expect our minds to protect us from.

As in the case of avoiding emotions, we typically are not fully aware that our minds are using denial and reinterpretation to develop and maintain emotions. Being on the alert for these strategies when we feel depressed gives us the opportunity to choose to feel better. Unfortunately, watching out for these strategies can also bring us down a peg or two in our own evaluation when we have been using them to raise ourselves up!

Psychologists tell us that maintaining a positive view of ourselves helps us to be more productive—even if that positive view is not fully supported by the evidence.[11] Depression, in contrast, undermines our ability to achieve our goals. In the paragraphs that follow, I focus on how we can minimize depression. Let's begin by looking at how we use denial and reinterpretation to develop and maintain depression.

Through denial, we ignore positive experiences of ourselves and our activities. For example, you become depressed about a paper you have written by considering only the parts you didn't fix before you turned it in. You then judge the paper solely in terms of its weaknesses.

Through reinterpreting the outcome, we explain away any positive experiences we do consider. For example, when your roommate tells you that your paper was well written, you say to yourself that she just said that to make you feel good. Thus, in spite of this positive evidence, you conclude that you have not written a good paper. When your teacher turns back your paper with an A on it, you conclude that your teacher does not have very high standards. You explain away all positive evidence.

MODIFYING NEGATIVE EMOTIONS

As we saw earlier, we can change our emotions by changing what we perceive, think, and feel. This section focuses on how we can modify negative emotions by modifying our thinking. But remember that we can also modify negative emotions by other means, such as paying attention to our breathing or listening to relaxing music.

Techniques for Minimizing Negative Thinking

Psychologist A. John Rush suggests confronting negative thinking with his *triple-column technique*. Psychologists Daniels and Horowitz summarize his approach as follows:

> Divide a piece of paper into three columns. Title the first column, "Specific events associated with unpleasant feelings," the second column, "Thought," and the third column, "Evidence for or against the thought." When an event you feel depressed about occurs, fill in the three columns.[12]

We can take this process one step further by labeling the thought patterns we find. Some patterns identified by Albert Ellis, whose "rational-emotive therapy" was the pioneering work in cognitive therapy, include catastrophizing, telling yourself that some things are awful or terrible when in fact they may be only inconvenient; and misreading others, jumping to a conclusion about what someone else is thinking from insufficient evidence.[13]

In *Feeling Good: The New Mood Therapy,* David D. Burns lists these and other categories of mistaken thinking. He defines "all-or-nothing thinking" in the following way: "You see things in black and white categories. If your performance falls short of perfect, you see yourself as a total failure."[14] Burns calls these thinking patterns **cognitive distortions.** Logicians call them **fallacies.** Another phrase that describes this thinking is "jumping to conclusions."

Two more common fallacies that play a role in our emotions are hasty generalization, jumping to a generalization from a single instance; and false fault finding, concluding from wildly insufficient evidence that you (or someone else) is totally responsible for something.

Let's look at some examples of these mistaken ways of thinking.

- *Catastrophizing*: You find out that the bookstore has just sold out the text for your class, and you conclude that that's a disaster.

- *Misreading others*: You hear a woman laughing, and you infer that she is laughing at you.

- *All-or-nothing thinking*: You get a B + on a test, and you label that grade a "failure."

- *Hasty generalization*: When you get a C on your first homework, you infer that you will get C's on all of the rest of your homeworks.

- *False fault finding*: You conclude that you are totally responsible for your father's death because you didn't remind him to fasten his seat belt.

Thinking mistakes look obvious once we become aware of them. But at times the very fact that we're caught up in them means that we don't see what we're doing.

Sometimes talking with another person can help us see what we're doing. Psychotherapist Carl Mitchell devised a technique we can use to help us become aware of our thinking. It's described here by Daniels and Horowitz.

Positive Reframing

Choose a partner you trust and sit near each other. One of you begins by revealing a negative attitude you hold about yourself—some unfavorable evaluation of who you are or how you handle some aspect of your life.

The other person is your reframer. The reframer will guess at the positive intent underlying your behavior, or will look for anything else positive in it he or she can find, and will articulate that for you.

For instance, you say, "I could kick myself for getting angry at my husband and children so much." Your reframer might reply, "Your husband and children are very important to you." You respond by saying either, "No, that doesn't strike home," or "Yes, that's right." If your response was "No," your reframer tries again. If it was "Yes," you reveal another negative attitude for your partner to reframe.

After five minutes, change roles.[15]

By becoming aware of negative thinking and seeking positive evidence you've overlooked, you will have a better chance of avoiding jumping to unsupported negative conclusions. You can take similar steps to challenge questionable positive interpretations. To check for positive illusions, see if you're thinking too positively, and seek negative evidence you may have overlooked.

Don't be too hard on yourself, however, if you find that you can't change your emotions on your own. Some of our emotions are best examined in a therapeutic setting. If your emotions interfere with your school work, try talking with someone in your school's counseling center.

YOUR TURN F

◆ 1. In the examples below, one statement gives evidence, and the other states an interpretation or conclusion. Identify which is which.

   a. I don't have ten hours to work on my paper, so I may as well not work on it at all.

   b. When I called Sara, she said she didn't have time to have tea with me today. She'll never have time to spend with me.

   c. My teacher didn't call on me when I raised my hand. She doesn't respect me.

   d. I was a few minutes late to our group meeting, so it's all my fault that our group didn't finish our homework.

   e. My ride didn't show up for work today. That's the worst thing I can imagine happening to me.

(continued)

YOUR TURN F, *continued*

◆ 2. Discuss whether you find the interpretations or conclusions in the above examples questionable. Consider, for example, whether there could be other evidence the person is overlooking.

◆ 3. Indicate which of the following labels fit the thinking in the above examples: hasty generalization, all-or-nothing thinking, misreading others, false fault finding, catastrophizing. Explain your answers.

A Model Case

One day a student in one of my critical thinking classes came to me to reconsider an emotion she had jumped to. At one point during my lecture the Friday before, I had said with incredulity, "How is it that we can be so unaware of our ignorance that we answer questions we have no knowledge about?" I meant to make a point about humans in general, including myself. But she thought I was directing my incredulity at her and felt humiliated.

When she came to my office, she told me that she had thought over the weekend about what I had said and about how I generally act in the classroom. She remembered that in general I treat students with respect and goodwill, so she considered the possibility that I had not intended to put her down. She decided to tell me what she had felt, to give me a chance to explain what I was doing.

I felt bad that she had felt humiliated but was very grateful that she gave me an opportunity to talk with her. From our talk she learned that I had not intended to single her out for criticism. In fact, I admired her consistently fine performance.

This student exhibited critical thinking at its finest. She checked her interpretation against alternatives and gathered additional information to decide between the alternatives. And she was willing to question even though she was somewhat fearful of what she would find. She had the courage to talk with me, even though she had not yet fully settled in her mind that my comments were not meant as a personal put-down. She was willing to take the risk of being humiliated to find out which of her interpretations was accurate.

This student had the insight to realize that checking her interpretation of my comment was essential to her educational success. If she found that I intended to demean her, she could drop my class. If she found that I was not intentionally putting her down, she could use this information to reestablish trust in me as a teacher she could learn from.

Now that you have studied how to question emotions, you need not feel so much at the mercy of them. If you are more angry or afraid than you would like, you can rethink your interpretations. Later chapters on argument analysis and evaluation give additional information about how to question interpretations to enhance your ability to rethink your emotions.

Nonetheless, even after you have practiced emotional awareness and choice, you will still sometimes act on your emotions without thinking and later regret your action. I sometimes do myself. I was the teacher in the story you read at the beginning of this chapter. Regretting my thoughtless acts motivates me to continue practicing emotional awareness.

Though our emotions sometimes misguide us, they are valuable sources of self-knowledge. By paying attention to our emotions, we can develop insight about what we care about. Thus, becoming aware of our emotions prepares us for decision making, the topic of the next chapter.

EXERCISES

1. Read the following passages and ads. What sensory images, judgments, interpretations, internal sensations, motivations, or other aspects of emotion did you have when reading this passage or looking at the ad? When relevant discuss the emotions of the people in the passages as well as your own emotions.

2. Would you describe your emotional response to these passages and ads as very intense, moderately intense, not very intense?

3. Can you think of a reason to question any aspect of your emotion—or the emotion of the person in the passage or ad? Explain.

   a. The beginning passage from Rebecca Busselle's book about the year she spent taking photographs at Wassaic Developmental Center:

   A boy with an enormous head lay on a bed. I tried to look away out of the politeness I'd spent my lifetime practicing, but the size, the heaviness of his deformity held me. His temples and forehead bulged, his skin stretched tight over the swelling like a polished granite boulder. And how could a neck so thin lift that head? At the end of his small torso lay skinny stick legs with broken ends for feet. At last I turned away. But now he was staring at me, his eyes large and melted at the edges. His lips pulled up over yellow horse teeth.

   "You coming to see me?" he gargled in a voice as brittle as broken egg shells.[16] "You coming to see me?" he croaked as I fled down the corridor.

   b. Elena Albert's description of an incident from her childhood:

   In Montana there were so few of us [African Americans] that we really couldn't support a minister, but we did have a branch of the African Methodist church. Sometimes we didn't have a pastor, so my aunts would persuade us to go to the Presbyterian church [which had a white congregation]. And something happened in my childhood I've never forgotten: there was a church picnic with contests where children would win the prizes. And I always ran so fast that I won the race. I remember no one gave me a prize. Finally the pastor felt he should do something. So he came over and he squatted down and he handed me a box of crackerjacks that had been *opened*. And I—I, I was, when I was a child, I was a . . . well, . . . spoiled, and, and quick-tempered. And I would not accept the box because it had been opened. I realized that this wasn't the prize the other winners got, you know.[17]

c. The following excerpt from an article titled "Fish: How Safe?" published in the *University of California at Berkeley Wellness Letter*.

Shellfish (clams, oysters, mussels) live by filtering 15 to 20 gallons of water a day. If the water they inhabit is polluted, they'll retain bacteria and viruses. Raw shellfish can thus be a source of hepatitis, gastroenteritis, and other diseases. Raw fish, as used in sushi, sashimi, ceviche, and other dishes, may be a source of parasites, such as tapeworms and roundworms, as well as bacteria and viruses. (Marinating raw fish in lemon or lime juice is not the equivalent of cooking—that is, it won't kill all bacteria and parasites.) It's true that a well-trained sushi chef may know how to purchase and handle fish so as to minimize the risk of illness and parasitic infection. But while sushi chefs are licensed in Japan, there's no way to check their credentials in this country. Preparing and eating raw fish at home is definitely not recommended, since home-prepared raw fish is the most common source of parasitic infection from fish in this country. If you make gefilte fish or another dish that uses raw ground fish, remember not to sample it until it's cooked.[18]

d. The following ad from the California Department of Health Services:

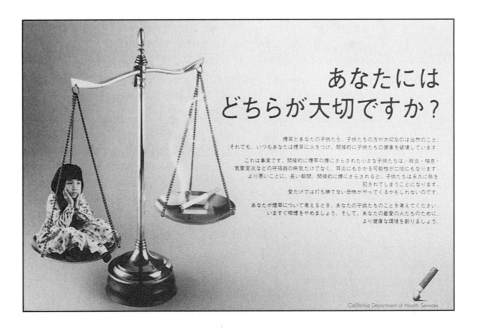

e. The following ad from Children International:

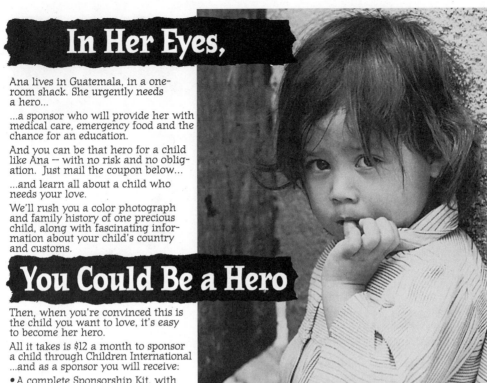

f. The following ad from FEMA:

> **"I Never Thought It Could Happen To Me."**

"I thought I had planned for everything." These are the words of a flood victim—they could be yours. Thousands of people every year find out that it CAN happen.

Are you prepared for a flood? Did you know you don't have to live close to water to become a flood victim? Do you have flood insurance?

You need to know the answers to these questions. Because the terrifying truth is that floods can happen anywhere, anytime. Flood insurance is the best way to protect yourself *before* the flood hits. Flood damage often goes way beyond that of house and home. Flood victims not only lose their homes and treasured possessions, but rebuilding costs also eat up life savings, retirement funds and children's college educations.

You can protect yourself—through the National Flood Insurance Program. We have one mission: to restore the quality of life of flood victims as soon as possible. For more information, call us today.

We can't replace your memories, but we can help you build new ones.

National Flood Insurance Program

4. Identify the following as examples of denial, blaming the victim, or re-interpreting the outcome.

   a. Sam is glad his girlfriend two-timed him because now he knows what that feels like.

   b. Sam deserved to have his girlfriend go out with another man. After all, Sam spent every weekend studying.

   c. Sam stopped calling his girlfriend after 10:00 P.M. because he didn't want to find out she was not at home.

   d. Joyce doesn't attend to her boss's comments about how "sexy" she looks because she doesn't want to confront him.

   e. Joyce's boss fired her because she wouldn't date him, and she's glad because she can now understand other women who have been unfairly fired.

5. In each of the examples below, one statement gives evidence and the other states an interpretation or conclusion. First, identify the conclusion.

   a. "I don't understand what the teacher is saying, but there's no point in asking a question," Sally says. "My confusion is all my own fault."

   b. "I don't have time to do the last question on the 20-item homework assignment, so I haven't done my homework," Tim says. "I may as well not turn it in."

   c. "Maria sounded annoyed when I called," Sabina thinks. "She must have been annoyed with me."

   d. "We forgot to put out the recycling last night," Hal thinks. "That's a disaster."

   e. "The first tutor I talked to at the tutorial center wasn't very helpful," Li thought. "None of the other tutors will be helpful, either."

   f. "I did really well on my first homework assignment without working very hard," Jasmine thinks. "So I'll do really well on the rest of my homework assignments without working very hard."

   g. "No one at the party said I should stop talking when I asked," Jim thought. "So they must not have minded that I talked nonstop for 20 minutes."

6. For each example under question 5, discuss whether you find the interpretation or conclusion questionable. Consider, for example, whether there could be other evidence the person is overlooking.

7. For each example under question 5, do any of the following labels fit the thinking: hasty generalization, catastrophizing, all-or-nothing thinking, misreading others, false fault finding? (If two labels seem equally fitting, explain why.)

Requiem for Mr. Squirrel

Dannie Martin

The following is from Dannie M. Martin and Peter Y. Sussman, *Committing Journalism: The Prison Writings of Red Hog.*

LOMPOC, CALIF. (OCT. 26, 1986)—Convicts always walk around a track counterclockwise, as if to deny time itself, as represented by the clock. It's a losing battle—time always wins. As the years go by, the exercise walks around the track at the prison's perimeter only get more boring.

Four years ago this month, as my walking boredom threatened to become terminal, I met Mr. Squirrel on the yard here at Lompoc penitentiary. Mr. Squirrel was indeed a squirrel and not the nickname of a bushy-haired convict with an overbite.

He was only one of many squirrels that ventured in between the double prison fences and sat upon hind legs in attitudes of supplication, seemingly praying for a morsel. We did throw them food, but mostly all we had was croutons sneaked out of the mess hall.

Most of the croutons fell short of the first fence, as it is hard to throw a small piece of toasted bread more than fifteen or twenty feet. Especially against the wind; and here at Lompoc if you are facing west, which is where the squirrels were, a brisk ocean breeze will almost always be blowing directly in your face.

The squirrels would watch with chagrin and sometimes chatter furiously as our windblown croutons fell short of the fence, only to be swooped on by the ever-present sea gulls and vigilant crows that had no sympathy for squirrels at all. Sometimes those croutons that reached the no-man's-land of rolled razor wire between the fences where the squirrels waited were picked off in the air by diving gulls.

Every day during the noon lunch break, eight or ten of us crouton carriers were beneath the corner gun tower, trying to feed the squirrels. Yet even this diversion was getting boring until the day I met Mr. Squirrel.

Nothing about his looks distinguished him from the others. He looked exactly like a half-grown ground squirrel. His pose was rather striking. While the others ran about frantically chattering at thieving gulls, he sat upright in an attitude of absolute repose.

I chunked a crouton in his direction, and the wind blew it back to a spot about six feet beyond where I stood by a sign that read "Out of Bounds Beyond This Sign," and about twenty feet from where Mr. Squirrel sat between the fences. Three gulls hit the ground in hot pursuit of the crouton, and as I reached for another, a strange and unprecedented tableau unfolded.

Before any of the gulls could snatch the crouton, Mr. Squirrel was right in the middle of them, and they were running in all directions. In my memory it seems that a few feathers flew, but I doubt that; for while gulls are loud, gluttonous, and aggressive, they turn into craven skulking beasts the moment they are confronted by anything larger than a hummingbird.

Mr. Squirrel ate the crouton, and a few more, then left with his jaws stuffed full of the others I had brought. The next day he was waiting, and before I even reached for a crouton, he ran right up to me and sat calmly watching. Before we parted that day, he ate right out of my hand. This squirrel had more nerve than John Dillinger.

Our friendship was born on a note of pure justice. He had rescued me from terminal boredom, and I reciprocated by easing his hunger and teasing his palate with an ever-increasing variety of hoarded edibles.

He was especially fond of peanut butter. I rolled it into little balls, then laughed when he stuffed it in his jaws to save and chattered furiously as it melted in his mouth.

Now that Mr. Squirrel had broken the barriers, most of the squirrels followed his example and sat begging only a few feet from where we walked the track.

Mr. Squirrel would take food from other cons, but he never approached anyone but me. If I had peanut butter or candy-coated almonds, he would sometimes climb up my arm and eat on my shoulder. He left each day with his jaws stuffed. His pantry in the field beyond the fences must have been well stocked.

The day I grabbed him and turned him over to find out if he was a Mr. or a Ms., he clawed me good, bit a chunk out of my arm, jumped down, and chattered at me for a good five minutes. Then forgave and forgot. I never tried that again, but there was no need—he was a Mr.

We met each day at noon for almost a year, except for fifteen days I spent in Isolation for a minor rule infraction. Then he was absent for a while around January.

In early spring that year, he showed up one day followed by two baby squirrels. I don't know if they were his progeny or just admirers, but he led them right up to share my groceries. They never squabbled at all and sat patiently as I fed each in turn. Mr. Squirrel was raising them impeccably, but unfortunately they would never get to grow up.

On a windblown day, as I walked the track to where Mr. Squirrel waited, I noticed outside the fences, at about thirty-foot intervals, a row of little boxes with holes cut in the sides. Squirrels, including Mr. Squirrel's babies, were running in and out of the ominous little boxes and chattering happily.

My heart began to sink as it dawned on me they were being poisoned. Poisoned by a slow-acting agent like arsenic trioxide that would allow them time to crawl to a hole where they would die a slow and agonizing death, thereby leaving the little boxes clear of dead bodies and free of suspicion.

I was a hurt and helpless spectator to the warden's final solution to the squirrel problem. I harbored a dim hope that Mr. Squirrel would be too smart to go for this trick. In the few days that followed I fed him much more than he could eat or carry, and I continually lectured him on the evil that lurked nearby.

The little ones weren't seen again, and after five days Mr. Squirrel was the only one left.

When Mr. Squirrel approached me and pawed listlessly at my peanut butter while looking at me out of reddened and pain-filled eyes, I knew he had been in the box. I knew I would never see him or feed him or play with him again. A most harrowing thought was that he may have wondered if I did it to him.

I walked away knowing that for years to come I would have to pass each day by the place where I fed him, and the justice of our friendship would surely be lost in the bitterness of remembrance.

I haven't seen a squirrel these past three years. Not even on a nearby hill where they used to frolic on good days.

A few gulls were found dead, but all the crows seem to have survived. The vulture population was severely thinned. Two fluffy owls and a beautiful mating pair of red-tailed hawks disappeared about the same time as the squirrels.

The boxes are long gone now, and strange as it seems, not one convict or guard ever said a word about the squirrels or their fate.

Mr. Squirrel was like me in some ways. He disdained the status quo, and gun towers, fences, and razor wire never impressed him much. If he lay in a hole surrounded by peanut butter and croutons while arsenic ate his stomach, I have lain in Isolation strip cells surrounded by vulgar graffiti while the pain of life ate my guts.

My spirit is diminished by the way he died, stunted by the brutal termination of his refulgent soul.

Some days when I walk along the place I used to feed Mr. Squirrel, I am haunted by a verse from an Oscar Wilde poem, "The Ballad of Reading Gaol," where he wrote:

> The vilest deeds like poison weeds
> Bloom well on prison air.
> It is only what is good in man
> That wastes and withers there. . . .

Of course, he never said a word about squirrels. Neither did anyone in here.

Questions

1. Did you feel compassionate, sad, angry, afraid, happy, or another specific emotion when reading about Mr. Squirrel? If you can't name your emotions specifically, can you describe them as positive or negative?
2. Did your emotions change as you read? Explain.
3. Select your most intense emotion, reflect on it, and identify its aspects: any perceptions (or sensory images) that triggered your emotion, any judgments or interpretations connected with your emotion, any internal sensations you felt, and any motivations and emotional expressions your emotion occasioned.
4. Did you approve of the prison warden's solution to the squirrel problem?
5. According to Dannie Martin's editor, "The warden [said] that the prison's squirrels had been a very expensive nuisance, chewing up road and electronic surveillance equipment. He said that poison had been used only after trapping proved ineffective."[19] Does your evaluation of the prison warden change after hearing this information? Explain.
6. What other questions or points would you like to discuss about this reading?

Ordinary People

Jonathan Kozol

The following is excerpted from *Rachael and Her Children: Homeless Families in America.*

He was a carpenter. She was a woman many people nowadays would call old-fashioned. She kept house and cared for their five children while he did construction work in New York City housing projects. Their home was an apartment in a row of neat brick buildings. She was very pretty then, and even now, worn down by months of suffering, she has a lovely, wistful look. She wears blue jeans, a yellow jersey, and a bright red ribbon in her hair—"for luck," she says. But luck has not been with this family for some time.

They were a happy and chaotic family then. He was proud of his acquired skills. "I did carpentry. I painted. I could do wallpapering. I earned a living. We spent Sundays walking with our children at the beach." They lived near Coney Island. That is where this story will begin.

"We were at the boardwalk. We were up some. We had been at Nathan's. We were eating hot dogs."

He's cheerful when he recollects that afternoon. The children have long, unruly hair. They range in age from two to ten. They crawl all over him—exuberant and wild.

Peter says that they were wearing summer clothes: "Shorts and sneakers. Everybody was in shorts."

When they were told about the fire, they grabbed the children and ran home. Everything they owned had been destroyed.

"My grandmother's china," she says, "everything." She adds: "I had that book of gourmet cooking . . ."

What did the children lose?

"My doggy," says one child. Her kitten, born three days before, had also died.

Peter has not had a real job since. "Not since the fire. I had tools. I can't replace those tools. It took me years of work." He explains he had accumulated tools for different jobs, one tool at a time. Each job would enable him to add another tool to his collection. "Everything I had was in that fire."

They had never turned to welfare in the twelve years since they'd met and married. A social worker helped to place them in a homeless shelter called the Martinique Hotel. When we meet, Peter is thirty. Megan is twenty-eight. They have been in this hotel two years.

She explains why they cannot get out: "Welfare tells you how much you can spend for an apartment. The limit for our family is $366. You're from Boston. Try to find a place for seven people for $366 in New York City. You can't do it. I've been looking for two years."

The city pays $3,000 monthly for the two connected rooms in which they live. She shows me the bathroom. Crumbling walls. Broken tiles. The toilet doesn't work. There is a pan to catch something that's dripping from the plaster. The smell is overpowering.

"I don't see any way out," he says. "I want to go home. Where can I go?"

A year later I'm in New York. In front of a Park Avenue hotel I'm facing two panhandlers. It takes a moment before I can recall their names.

They look quite different now. The panic I saw in them a year ago is gone. All five children have been taken from them. Having nothing left to lose has drained them of their desperation.

The children have been scattered—placed in various foster homes. "White children," Peter says, "are in demand by the adoption agencies."

Standing here before a beautiful hotel as evening settles in over New York, I'm reminded of the time before the fire when they had their children and she had her cookbooks and their children had a dog and cat. I remember the words that Peter used: "We were up some. We had been at Nathan's." Although I am not a New Yorker, I know by now what Nathan's is: a glorified hot-dog stand. The other phrase has never left my mind.

Peter laughs. "Up some?"

The laughter stops. Beneath his streetwise manner he is not a hardened man at all. "It means," he says, "that we were happy."

By the time these words are printed there will be almost 500,000 homeless children in America. If all of them were gathered in one city, they would represent a larger population than that of Atlanta, Denver, or St. Louis. Because they are scattered in a thousand cities, they are easily unseen. And because so many die in infancy or lose the strength to struggle and prevail in early years, some will never live to tell their stories.

Not all homeless children will be lost to early death or taken from their parents by the state. Some of their parents will do better than Peter and Megan. Some will be able to keep their children, their stability, their sense of worth. Some will get back their vanished dreams. A few will find jobs again and some may even find a home they can afford. Many will not.

Why are so many people homeless in our nation? What has driven them to the streets? What hope have they to reconstruct their former lives?

The answers will be told in their own words.

Questions

1. Did you feel compassionate, angry, disgusted, or another specific emotion when reading this passage? If you can't name your emotions specifically, can you describe them as positive or negative?
2. Did your emotions change as you read?
3. Can you link your emotions to a particular detail described by Kozol or to something else you were thinking when you read Kozol's words?
4. Select your most intense emotion, reflect on it, and identify its aspects: any perceptions (or sensory images) that triggered your emotion, any judgments or interpretations connected with your emotion, any internal sensations you felt, and any motivations and emotional expressions your emotion occasioned.
5. Can you think of any other information that would change your thinking and your emotion about the people or events in this story?
6. What other questions or points would you like to discuss about this reading?

WRITING IDEAS

1. Do a guided "emotion awareness" freewrite or a "conversation with my critic" freewrite. Edit your freewrite, checking for spelling, word choice, organization, and clarity.
2. Write about a time you modified an emotion or emotional expression to please or appease someone in power. Describe the aspects of emotion (perceptions, thoughts, feelings, or emotional expressions) you modified.
3. Write about a time you acted unreflectively on emotion, then later questioned your emotion and adopted a new course of action.
4. Read or view something that evokes an emotion in you. Become aware of your emotional response, and identify the aspects of emotion (perceptions, feelings, thoughts, motivations, and expressions of emotion) you find.
5. Write about whether this chapter and your class discussions complemented, conflicted with, supported, or left out any of your previous ideas about emotion.

Notes

1. Oliver Sacks, "An Anthropologist on Mars," *The New Yorker* 27 Dec. 1993/3 Jan. 1994: 123.
2. Arlie Hochschild, *The Managed Heart* (Berkeley: University of California Press, 1983) 6–7.

3. Hochschild 127.
4. Hochschild 25.
5. Hochschild 4.
6. Bob Blauner, *Black Lives, White Lives: Three Decades of Race Relations in America* (Berkeley: University of California Press, 1989) 84.
7. Blauner 84.
8. Carol Tavris, *Anger: The Misunderstood Emotion* (New York: Simon & Schuster, 1982) 230–234.
9. Blauner 31.
10. Blauner 31.
11. Psychologists also report that positive illusions promote psychological well-being. See Shelley E. Taylor and Jonathon D. Brown, "Illusion and Well-Being: A Social Psychological Perspective on Mental Health," *Psychology Bulletin* 103 (1988): 193–210.
12. Victor Daniels and Laurence J. Horowitz, *Being & Caring: A Psychology for Living,* 2nd ed. (Mountain View, CA: Mayfield Publishing Company, 1984) 142–143.
13. Albert Ellis and R. Grieger, *Handbook of Rational-Emotive Therapy* (New York: Springer-Verlag) 10.
14. David D. Burns, *Feeling Good: The New Mood Therapy* (New York: William Morrow, 1980) 40.
15. Daniels & Horowitz 218.
16. Rebecca Busselle, *An Exposure of the Heart* (New York: Penguin Books, 1990) 13.
17. Blauner 83.
18. "Is It Okay to East Sushi or Other Raw Fish and Shellfish?" excerpted from "Fish: How Safe?" *University of California at Berkeley Wellness Letter*, July 1992: 4–5.
19. Dannie M. Martin and Peter Y. Sussman, *Committing Journalism: The Prison Writings of Red Hog* (New York: Norton, 1993) 54.

2

Deciding How to Act

CHAPTER GOALS

- To learn how to make thoughtful decisions by defining the problem, generating and choosing among alternative solutions, and taking measures to prevent the same problems from recurring.
- To learn positive, productive ways to resolve conflicts.
- To use your knowledge to evaluate the decision-making and conflict-resolution processes in a variety of contexts.

YOUR THOUGHTS ABOUT DECISION MAKING

What do you find useful for making good decisions and resolving conflicts? Jot down your ideas; then read this essay and answer the questions that follow. "Why I Am Not Going to Buy a Computer" was written by novelist, essayist, and poet Wendell Berry. It was first published in the *New England Review and Bread Loaf Quarterly* and then reprinted in *Harper's*. In a subsequent issue, *Harper's* published a number of letters from readers responding to the essay, along with a reply to the letters by Berry. The original essay is reprinted here. The letters and Berry's reply are reprinted in the "Readings" section later in the chapter.

Why I Am Not Going to Buy a Computer

Wendell Berry

Like almost everybody else, I am hooked to the energy corporations, which I do not admire. I hope to become less hooked to them. In my work, I try to be as little hooked to them as possible. As a farmer, I do almost all of my work with horses. As a writer, I work with a pencil or a pen and a piece of paper.

My wife types my work on a Royal standard typewriter bought new in 1956 and as good now as it was then. As she types, she sees things that are wrong and marks them with small checks in the margins. She is my best critic because she is the one most familiar with my habitual errors and weaknesses. She also understands, sometimes better than I do, what *ought* to be said. We have, I think, a literary cottage industry that works well and pleasantly. I do not see anything wrong with it.

A number of people, by now, have told me that I could greatly improve things by buying a computer. My answer is that I am not going to do it. I have several reasons, and they are good ones.

The first is the one I mentioned at the beginning. I would hate to think that my work as a writer could not be done without a direct dependence on strip-mined coal. How could I write conscientiously against the rape of nature if I were, in the act of writing, implicated in the rape? For the same reason, it matters to me that my writing is done in the daytime, without electric light.

I do not admire the computer manufacturers a great deal more than I admire the energy industries. I have seen their advertisements, attempting to seduce struggling or failing farmers into the belief that they can solve their problems by buying yet another piece of expensive equipment. I am familiar with their propaganda campaigns that have put computers into public schools in need of books. That computers are expected to become as common as TV sets in "the future" does not impress me or matter to me. I do not see that computers are bringing us one step nearer to anything that does matter to me: peace, economic justice, ecological health, political honesty, family and community stability, good work.

What would a computer cost me? More money, for one thing, than I can afford, and more than I wish to pay to people whom I do not admire. But the cost would not be just monetary. It is well understood that technological innovation always requires the discarding of the "old model"—the "old model" in this case being not just our old Royal standard, but my wife, my critic, my closest reader, my fellow worker. Thus (and I think this is typical of present day technological innovation), what would be superseded would be not only something, but somebody. In order to be technologically up-to-date as a writer, I would have to sacrifice an association that I am dependent upon and that I treasure.

My final and perhaps my best reason for not owning a computer is that I do not wish to fool myself. I disbelieve, and therefore strongly resent, the assertion that I or anybody else could write better or more easily with a computer than with a pencil. I do not see why I should not be as scientific about this as the next fellow: when somebody has used a computer to write a work that is demonstrably better than Dante's, and when this better is demonstrably attributable to the use of a computer, then I will speak of computers with a more respectful tone of voice, though I still will not buy one.

To make myself as plain as I can, I should give my standards for technological innovation in my own work. They are as follows:

1. The new tool should be cheaper than the one it replaces.

2. It should be at least as small in scale as the one it replaces.

3. It should do work that is clearly and demonstrably better than the one it replaces.

4. It should use less energy than the one it replaces.

5. If possible, it should use some form of solar energy, such as that of the body.

6. It should be repairable by a person of ordinary intelligence, provided that he or she has the necessary tools.

7. It should be purchasable and repairable as near to home as possible.

8. It should come from a small, privately owned shop or store that will take it back for maintenance and repair.

9. It should not replace or disrupt anything good that already exists, and this includes family and community relationships.

Questions

1. Does this article contain any words or phrases that are unfamiliar to you? Do you know what strip-mined coal is? Can you figure out how Berry thinks strip-mined coal is related to the use of a computer?

2. Do you agree with any of Berry's beliefs about the negative impact of using a computer? Explain.

3. Do you agree with any of Berry's "standards for technological innovation"?

4. Would it be as easy for you to not use a computer as it is for Berry? Does your school require you to have access to a computer, for example? Or do you have someone who could type your papers for you?

Every day we make hundreds, perhaps thousands, of decisions about what to do and how to act. Some of these decisions have little consequence. Whether we get up at 7:00 A.M. or stay in bed until 7:15 does not make much difference most days. We can make up the time by eating our toast on the way to school.

But frequently our decisions have important consequences for ourselves and others. And sometimes we later regret our decision. We marry someone who abuses us, vote for someone who takes the country into economic peril, or take a job that turns out badly.

Are we fated to make decisions we will regret? Yes and no. There is no foolproof method for making decisions we can live with. No matter what we do, we will make some mistakes. But we can reduce the number of mistakes we make by thinking our decisions through.[1]

This chapter introduces a process for thinking through decisions, which I call *thoughtful decision making*.[2] And since disputes with others often arise during decision making, the chapter includes an introduction to conflict resolution. This chapter covers the basic steps of deciding how to act and resolve conflicts. The rest of the book provides skills to help you evaluate information and arguments you consider when taking these steps.

THOUGHTFUL DECISION MAKING

Thoughtful decision making is a real life process that government leaders, business leaders, and others who want to avoid regrettable decisions use. It's also a process we can use to make relatively simple decisions in our every-day lives. Let's begin with a simple example to illustrate the steps of thoughtful decision making.

> *The lost bird.* When sitting in my upstairs study writing an early draft of this chapter, I heard an unexpected sound in my living room below. When I went down to check, I saw a bird flapping against the north window. Apparently it had flown in through the door I had left ajar on that warm June day. I felt worried. I had a cat, and she could clamp her jaws on that bird in no time. Fortunately, my cat was upstairs lazing in my sunny study, so the bird was safe from her for the moment.

Here are the steps I took in deciding what to do:

1. *Defining the problem.*
   a. *Gathering the facts.* I heard a sound in the living room and saw a bird flapping against the north window, which was stuck shut. I noted that my cat, who likes to eat birds, was upstairs sleeping.
   b. *Analyzing the situation.* I inferred that the bird flew in through the open door, and I predicted that it might have a hard time finding its way across the room to the door on its own. I predicted that my cat would try to catch and eat the bird, if it could. I also predicted that the bird would be frightened by me.
   c. *Setting goals.* I wanted the bird to be safe outside, and I didn't want to get pecked in the process.

2. *Discovering alternative solutions.* I thought of closing the door to the upstairs and allowing the bird to find its own way out. I also thought of putting an oven mitt on my hand and helping the bird find the door.

3. *Identifying the pros and cons of the solutions.* If left alone, the bird could hurt itself, and I wouldn't have the fun of taking a break and helping it to the door. By following it around, I could frighten the bird but I would get to take a break from my writing to help it.

4. *Weighing the alternatives.* Taking a break and possibly saving the bird from harm matters more to me than risking scaring the bird. So I put more weight on helping the bird than on leaving the bird alone.

5. *Reviewing and deciding.* I reviewed the situation, considered again the alternatives and their pros and cons, and decided to help the bird find the door. I put on an oven mitt to protect my hand and spoke quietly and in reassuring tones while approaching the bird. To my surprise, the bird stepped onto my hand and stayed there while I crossed the room and went outside into the yard. When I lifted my arm, the bird flew into a tree.

6. *Taking preventive measures*. After the initial crisis was resolved, I considered preventive measures: install a screen door, bell the cat, or leave the door closed or nearly closed.

These steps for thoughtful decision making look fairly straightforward and take very little time when we think through a simple problem, such as the problem of the lost bird. However, when people are facing serious and complicated problems, working with others who have different ideas, and have a limited amount of time and less information than they need, thoughtful decision making becomes more of a challenge.

In the following sections I describe the steps of thoughtful decision making in more detail, developing some of the difficulties each step poses and describing some of the shortcuts people take under pressure.

Defining the Problem

To define the problem, we gather the facts, analyze them, and set our goals. Let's look at these activities in more detail.

Gathering the Facts   Gathering the facts sounds simple and straightforward. All we have to do is look and see what's happening now and find out what happened in the past. But gathering the facts is not quite as simple as it sounds.

We aren't looking for just any facts when we try to solve a problem; we're looking for the facts relevant to the problem before us. And we can't tell merely by looking which facts are relevant and which are not. In the case of the lost bird, for example, there were lots of other facts I could have provided. The bird in the living room, the door open, and my cat upstairs were not the only things I saw; I also saw cobwebs in the corners of the window panes, the blue sofa against the wall, dust on the piano, and a forgotten cup of tea on an end table. The list could go on and on.

To identify the relevant facts, we use our background knowledge to guide us. I know enough about birds and cats and how the world works to realize almost without thinking that the dust on the piano and the forgotten cup of tea were not relevant to the problem before me. But we do not always have the appropriate background knowledge to help us distinguish the relevant facts. Sometimes we need to consult the experts.

When you are feeling sick, you may not be able to identify the facts relevant to your diagnosis. If you don't know that deer ticks carry Lyme disease, for example, you will not see any relationship between your fever and the tick bite you had the week before. And so you won't look on the tick bite as a relevant fact to mention to your doctor.

Though we often need to rely on experts for background knowledge, we don't always. Even when we face a problem we've never faced before, we can sometimes gather the relevant facts, if only we give ourselves the chance. For example, Marvin Levine, author of *Effective Problem Solving*, tells a story about his hesitance to gather the facts about his broken dryer.

When his dryer stopped running, he figured it had worn itself out after many years of use. At first, he didn't even think of looking around for more facts. His dryer was old; it had stopped running. There were new, working dryers at the store. Those were facts enough. He would go to the store and buy a new dryer.

To get more facts, he needed to open the back of the dryer. He'd never done that before, but he decided to give it a try. He unplugged the dryer and opened the back panel. Inside he found lint, just lint, but lots of it. He vacuumed out the lint, put the back panel back on, plugged in the dryer, flipped the on switch, and—voila!—he no longer needed a new dryer.[3]

The moral of Levine's story? We don't always need experts to identify the relevant facts in an unfamiliar problem. If we're willing to try something we've never done before, we can happen onto the relevant facts and solve our problem ourselves.

Here are some questions to ask yourself when you're gathering the facts:

1. Do you lack any background knowledge that you need to determine the relevant facts?

2. Do you need an expert to help you find the relevant facts, or can you try something new and happen onto the relevant facts yourself?

Analyzing the Situation   When we analyze a situation, we try to predict what will happen if we do nothing, and we try to figure out the cause of the problem. Some of this information is common knowledge. We all know that cats like to chase birds, for example. I used common knowledge to make the prediction that my cat would try to capture the bird in my living room.

Other times we consult experts to help us. A woman I know found a patch of her hair growing thin, and she soon became bald in that area. She didn't know what caused her baldness nor what would happen if she did nothing about it. She consulted her doctor, who told her that there were several possible causes, stress being the main one, and that her hair would most likely grow back on its own eventually.

We can also sometimes figure out the causes ourselves. When Marvin Levine saw the lint in the back of his dryer, he figured that the lint might have caused the dryer to stop. He tested his hypothesis by vacuuming out the lint and turning the dryer on.

Here are some questions to ask when developing your **analysis of the situation**:

1. Is the information you need for your analysis common knowledge?

2. Are there any experts who can help you with the analysis?

3. Can you figure out the analysis yourself?

Setting Goals   To identify a situation as a problem, it's not enough to know what is happening and what caused it. You've got to determine what you *want* to happen. Consider a broken dryer, for example. Whether we see this as a problem depends on the **goal** we want to achieve. On the one hand, if we want to dry our clothes as quickly as possible, the broken dryer becomes a problem. On the other hand, if we want to use less electricity, the broken dryer becomes an opportunity to break our habit and find other ways to dry our clothes.

So before moving on to change a situation, it's a good idea to think about whether the situation poses a problem in the first place. To begin setting your goals, think about what you want to be different and what about the present situation works for you.

Sometimes you will find that you have several goals, some of which apparently conflict with each other. We might want to dry our clothes as quickly as possible *and* use less electricity. What can you do then?

Think about *how much* the various goals matter to you. In the case of the dryer, for example, you may find that drying your clothes quickly doesn't matter to you as much as using less electricity. You may also find that these goals *matter differently in different contexts*. During the school year, you may care more about drying your clothes quickly. In the summer, when you have more leisure time, you may care more about saving energy.

Think also about whether the goals *belong to you* or to someone else. Suppose you're shopping for a car and you find you don't have enough money for the one you saw advertised the evening before. Is this a problem for you? That depends on whether you fully endorse buying that particular car. On reflection, you may find that *you* don't really want that car; you had temporarily wanted the car because of the advertisement. The goal of buying that car wasn't so much *yours* as the *salesperson's*. As we saw in Chapter 1, bosses, leaders, and dominant social groups also set goals for others, and we need to be on the alert to decide whether we fully endorse their goals or accept them without thinking.

When reflecting on your goals, ask yourself these questions:

1. What do I want to be different, and what would I like to keep the same about this situation?

2. Do any of my goals matter more to me than others?

3. Will any of my goals matter more or less to me in a different context?

4. Are my goals *mine* or someone else's?

YOUR TURN A

◆ 1. For each of the following situations, interpret the situation as a problem, then interpret it as an opportunity. You may describe the situation more fully and make predictions about the future to support your interpretations. State the goal or goals the situations challenge or support.

a. Your girlfriend (boyfriend) has just told you that she (he) wants to go out with someone else.

b. A friend has just given you a computer for your birthday. (Consider this situation from Wendell Berry's point of view.)

(continued)

2. Review the following goals, filling in the blanks with the particulars of your goals, and answer the questions following:

Goals: graduate from college, have or not have children, have a career in _____, buy a house, achieve and maintain a slim figure, be the best _____, be honest with yourself and others, be independent, be _____.

a. Do any of these goals matter more to you than others? Which ones?

◆ b. Would any of these goals matter more or less to you in a different context? Explain.

◆ c. Are any of these goals not really *yours* but someone else's?

Discovering Alternative Solutions

Why discover alternative solutions to your problem? You only need one. Right, but rarely do problems have only one right solution; instead, they have many solutions, some better or worse than others. The trick comes in finding the solution that works best for you. Frequently you'll have to come up with and think about a second, third, or even hundredth solution before settling on the one you want.

Techniques for Discovering Solutions   What can we do to discover the hundredth solution? Here are some things we can do.

RESEARCH   When seeking alternative solutions, ask other people, read books or articles, watch videos, surf the Internet. For example, when you are seeking solutions for a medical problem, ask your doctor for solutions and look through medical books written for laypersons.

ROLE-PLAY   When others aren't available, try **role-play.** You will find yourself coming up with things you would never have thought of before. Consider again the story of the lost bird. When I "become" my cat, I discover two new responses to the lost bird: take my cat down to the bird, and take the bird up to my cat.

BRAINSTORM   To **brainstorm,** gather a group of people together, describe the problem, and invite everyone to call out any solution, no matter how zany. Do not critique or debate the solutions. Stay playful and nonjudgmental. Ask someone to record the solutions.

TAKE A BREAK   Often, solutions to a problem come only when you *stop* trying to solve it. Go for a walk or take a bath. You can guide your internal problem solver, if you like. For example, before you go to sleep at night remind yourself of a problem; then relax and go to sleep. You may find an answer floating through your mind when you wake in the morning.

Shortcut—Using What's Available   Sometimes, to save time or money, people shortcut research and freeing the mind and seize only on solutions that are immediately available to them. That's fine when the solutions are good ones. Otherwise, they may find themselves committing the fallacy of **false alternatives,** sometimes called **false dilemma.**

We commit this fallacy when we assume that we must take one of a given pool of alternatives, when there are better ones. For example, suppose Sally says:

> I must have a mastectomy. There are only two possible actions for me to take: have a mastectomy or do nothing to save myself from breast cancer.

When Sally reasons this way, she commits the fallacy of false alternatives. She makes a mistake about the number of available alternatives. She may have other options, including removal of the tumor and radiation or chemotherapy treatment. Researching and freeing your mind can save you from making a mistake like Sally's.

YOUR TURN B

◆ 1. Are any of the following false alternatives? If so, list one or more additional alternatives to consider.

    a. When my first-choice university requires that I have access to a computer, I can either buy a computer or go to my second-choice university.

    b. When my roommate is late for the third month paying her part of the telephone bill, I can either pay it myself or ask my roommate to move out.

2. For each of the above, what did you do or whom would you consult to discover additional alternative solutions?

Identifying the Pros and Cons of the Solutions

By now you've come up with a variety of potential solutions to your problem. For any imagined solution to be a genuine solution, it must in fact achieve the goal you originally set. Usually, several of your proposed solutions will do that, but you may need to do some research or further exploration to make sure. You also need to consider the other effects of the solutions, for solutions often create as many problems as they solve. Conversely, some solutions produce benefits you weren't originally looking for. Let's look at an example.

> Jane lives with her family about two miles from campus. She's trying to figure out what transportation to use to get to and from school. She and her mother come up with a variety of solutions: sharing the old family Ford; driving a new, red VW convertible bought for that purpose; riding her bike, tuned up for that purpose; using public transportation; walking to school; driving a car stolen for that purpose.

All of these solutions achieve Jane's goal of getting to and from campus. Some of them, however, create other problems for Jane. Stealing a car could land her in jail. Other solutions offer benefits besides meeting Jane's original goal. Riding her bike and walking not only get Jane to school but also provide her with exercise on the way. Also, Jane's solutions use different resources. New cars cost a bundle. Tuning up Jane's old bike costs relatively little.

Here are four questions to ask when sorting out the pros and cons of alternative solutions:

1. Will the proposed solution meet the goal you established?

2. Will it have other, positive effects?

3. Will it create any problems? Does it conflict with any of your personal values? Does it conflict with any rules, laws, or community values?

4. What resources does the proposed solution use? How much time does the proposed solution take to put into effect and maintain? How much money does it cost to put into effect and maintain?

In the following chart I've listed some answers to these questions for the alternative solutions Jane and her mother came up with.

Family Ford

MEETS GOAL?
Yes

OTHER POSITIVE EFFECTS?
Practice cooperation

PROBLEMS?
Pollution; stodgy looking; need to adjust family schedules

RESOURCES?
$: gas money, insurance for additional driver
Time: 5 min to school

Red VW

MEETS GOAL?
Yes

OTHER POSITIVE EFFECTS?
Looks cool; attracts "friends"

PROBLEMS?
Pollution; need to work extra hours to make the car payment; have less money to spend on other things

RESOURCES?
$: thousands initially, plus gas, tune-ups, and insurance
Time to research the best buy
Time: 5 min to school

Bicycle

MEETS GOAL?
Yes

OTHER POSITIVE EFFECTS?
Exercise; feel the breeze

PROBLEMS?
Cold/wet/hot, depending on weather

RESOURCES?
$: under $100
Time for the tune-up
Time: 10 min to school

Public transit

MEETS GOAL?
Yes

OTHER POSITIVE EFFECTS?
Visit with others or read on the bus

PROBLEMS?
Adjust schedule to bus's

RESOURCES?
$: approximately $2 a day
Time: 7 min to school

Walking

MEETS GOAL?
Yes

OTHER POSITIVE EFFECTS?
Exercise; smell the flowers

PROBLEMS?
Cold/wet/hot, depending on weather

RESOURCES?
$: walking shoes
Time: 30 min to school

Stolen car

MEETS GOAL?
Yes, if not caught

OTHER POSITIVE EFFECTS?
Potential to learn about the criminal justice system first hand; could be a cool-looking car

PROBLEMS?
Air pollution; contrary to law and to personal value of treating others with respect

RESOURCES?
$: gas, tune-ups, attorney's fees, if caught
Time to plan and carry out the theft
Time: 5 min to school
Time in prison, if caught

After looking at the pros and cons of solutions, you may come up with other solutions. For example, Jane might decide to combine some of the solutions: walking or biking and using the bus or the family car, depending on the weather, availability, and how quickly she wants to get to school on any given day.

Keep Long-Range Effects in Mind When listing the effects of various alternatives, people frequently minimize or overlook the long-range effects of the solutions. When using credit, for example, people frequently note the relatively small monthly payments but fail to note the total amount the item costs in the long run, given the interest paid over time. When using credit cards, people even have trouble thinking as long as a month away, when the first monthly payment becomes due. And getting in over one's head with credit leads to other distant troubles, including difficulty getting loans for starting a business or for buying a house.

Some decisions have wide-ranging consequences because they set precedents (establish rules or principles to be followed in the future).

Supreme Court decisions set precedents. So do some decisions in our every-day lives. Suppose Jane's mother decides to buy a car for Jane. If Jane's mother has other children, the other children will also expect a new car when they begin college. So Jane's mother needs to consider not only the cost of Jane's car but also the cost of the other cars her children will ask for.

Other decisions have wide-ranging consequences because they establish addictive behaviors. Smoking, for example, is highly addictive. So once you start the habit, you may have a hard time stopping when you get around to recognizing its long-term health risks.

Consider the Cons of the Preferred Solution   When listing the pros and cons of solutions, people tend to neglect the cons of the solution they prefer. To avoid this, engage others with wide-ranging points of view in the discussion. And listen carefully to all points of view.

Role-Play   If you are concerned that you might not take seriously enough the potential consequences of your alternative solutions, try **role-playing** possible scenarios. By role-playing, you make the future present. When considering taking up smoking, for example, play the role of a patient being informed she has lung cancer. When considering charging something, role-play writing out your bills the next month. By role-playing these effects, you may find it harder to deny them and easier to give them their due.

Role-playing also helps you look more closely at alternative solutions. When you're working with others trying to decide on solutions, ask several people to role-play advocating the alternative solutions. You could also select someone to act as a judge who questions the advocates, weighs the alternatives, and comes up with a tentative decision.[4] Or, after hearing the alternative solutions, the advocates could step out of their roles and continue the decision making as a group.

Calvin is having trouble keeping the long-range effects of his action in mind. Do you see any other problem with Calvin's deliberations about whether to throw the snowball or not?

Calvin and **Hobbes**   by **Bill Watterson**

Shortcut—the Nutshell Briefing   Researching the consequences of solutions takes time, so sometimes people ask others to give a short report, a **nutshell briefing**, of the pros and cons of solutions.[5] On the positive side, the nutshell briefing saves time. On the negative side, when you rely on one person for briefing, you risk getting a one-sided report. Imagine, for example, the different nutshell briefings you would get from Wendell Berry and from a computer salesman about the pluses and minuses of buying a computer.

Sometimes the nutshell briefer will present a weak version of an opposing point of view or argument, point out the weakness, and conclude that the briefer's own point of view is stronger. Instead of boxing with a flesh and blood opponent, the briefer battles with a straw person. He can knock it down easily because it is made of straw, not bone and muscle. This mistake in reasoning is called the **straw person fallacy.**

YOUR TURN C

◆ 1. Suppose you are on a panel of students making decisions about a student photography show. One piece pictures a young man, bare from the waist up, staring straight ahead, and holding a gun to his head. What are some possible pros and cons of including or excluding this photograph?

◆ 2. Is this decision likely to set a precedent?

◆ 3. Are there any predictable long-range consequences to take into account?

◆ 4. Would you ask the student who took the photo for a nutshell briefing? Explain.

5. Think of a time you heard or read about someone presenting a point of view that conflicted with a view you hold dear. Did you find yourself trying to block out, mock, exaggerate, or minimize that conflicting view? Has anyone ever tried to make a straw person of one of your views?

Weighing the Alternatives

Once you have gathered information about the pros and cons of the possible solutions, you are ready to weigh them to make your tentative decision.

To weigh the alternatives, you must think about the relative importance of their effects. Some negative effects may not bother you much; others will give you pause. If you place a high value on treating others with respect, for example, you will avoid stealing a car, even if you think you could get away with it.

The Challenge of Moral Dilemmas   When deciding between alternatives, we sometimes find that two of our deeply held values come into conflict. This is a moral dilemma. For example, suppose a doctor is strongly committed both to saving lives and to patient autonomy. If a thoughtful adult patient refused a life-saving treatment, the doctor would find herself in a moral dilemma. If she overrides the patient's request, she acts against patient autonomy. But if she does not treat the patient, she fails to save a person's life.

The Challenge of Short-Term Self-Interest   Sometimes we have difficulty deciding among solutions because our values conflict with our immediate wants and impulses. When deciding how to respond to an insult, for example, we may find our immediate desire to punish in conflict with our deeply held value of treating others with respect. On other occasions, we may also choose from the impulse to please an authority or a group instead of adhering to our original goals and values.

When faced with a conflict between our impulses and our values and goals, we need to take some time to think about what really matters to us. We might consider, for example, how we will feel about ourselves the next day if we act on our immediate impulse.

Shortcut—Choosing from Impulse   Getting to know ourselves—separating our impulses from our deeply held values—takes time and courage. Frequently, people shortcut this step of decision making and choose on the basis of impulse. This shortcut is particularly troublesome because people frequently do not realize they are taking it. They've convinced themselves, if not others, that they are acting with integrity and in accord with their deeply held values and agreed-upon goals.

"ME FIRST"   When taking the "me first" shortcut, decision makers choose the solution with the best outcome for themselves—regardless of whether they have pledged to take the interests of others into account. Congress voting itself a pay raise in the midst of a failing economy provides one example.

RETALIATING   Decision makers who take the "retaliate" shortcut act from an angry impulse to punish others rather than thinking through the pros and cons of using punishment to achieve their goal. Recently a student told me he had scowled at another student in class when she responded to a comment he made because she hadn't understood what he had been saying. He wanted to shut her up. Intent on retaliation, he hadn't thought about whether scowling at her would in fact shut her up, whether his angry behavior might silence other students, or whether his scowl would help her to understand or hinder her from understanding him in the future.

AVOIDING PUNISHMENT   Sometimes we do not press our values because we fear being punished by some authority. We're all familiar with the impulse to take this shortcut, having had bad experiences with angry teachers, stern parents, or threatening bosses. And sometimes we're even fearful of our peers. Students sometimes tell me they are afraid to speak up in class because they fear the judgment of the other students. Even the relatively powerful succumb to the "avoid punishment" shortcut. Social scientist Irving L. Janis, for example, tells of a national security advisor who did not express his deep concern about a presidential policy because he was afraid of being called "a Commie."[6]

GOING ALONG WITH THE GROUP   People enjoy being part of a cooperative, harmonious group, so they sometimes suppress a concern to avoid "rocking the boat."

Acting from emotional impulse undermines the weighing of alternatives, but being aware of your emotions and thinking carefully about them *helps* you weigh alternatives. By becoming attentive to your emotions, you can get a better understanding of what values you hold dear and of what impulses you need to watch out for.

When solving problems, you can use emotions effectively by continuing to practice the exercises in Chapter 1 for questioning emotions. Leaders can minimize the "avoid punishment" and "go along with the group" shortcuts by reserving room on the meeting agenda for expressing and elaborating on unpopular opinions.

YOUR TURN D

◆ 1. Do any of your values come into conflict when you make the following decisions? Which, if any, of the values do you hold most dearly?

   a. Your girlfriend (or boyfriend) wants to get sexually intimate, but you are not ready to become intimate with her (him).

   b. Someone in your club/sorority/fraternity is having a hard time in her (his) English class, and she's (he's) just asked you whether she (he) can use one of your papers from the class you took.

◆ 2. Would you feel inclined to take any of the impulse shortcuts with respect to any of the following? Explain.

   a. Students in the class you're taking find the class boring, and the teacher doesn't seem to notice.

   b. One of your roommates has just told a homophobic joke, and your other roommates are laughing.

   c. You know your brother would like some of this leftover cake for his lunch, but he'll forget all about it unless you say something to him. And you would like a nice big piece, instead of half as much.

   d. Suzy has left her things lying around this apartment once too often. You're really angry now.

3. If you did act on impulse in response to any of the problems in question 2, would you be acting against any of your values? Explain.

Reviewing and Deciding

Making your final decision can be tough because of the uncertainty you discover when you begin to think seriously about your decisions. You may want to give up altogether.

Indecisiveness and Decision Avoidance   When you are indecisive, keep in mind that putting off a decision is itself a decision—a decision to do nothing. Sometimes that works out, and other times it does not. My companion and

I put off making a decision about what to do about our chimney lined with third-degree creosote, hoping we could wait until we began some foundation work. But we kept using our wood stove—and our chimney—in the meantime, keeping the fire low to minimize danger. One morning the fire got hotter than usual, and the chimney caught fire. Fortunately, a firefighter arrived and put out the fire before it spread from the chimney. But we made an appointment with a chimney sweep that day and have now settled on a solution.

Living with an Uncertain Future To hedge your bets against an uncertain future, you can **implement** your decision in stages and prepare contingency plans.

IMPLEMENT YOUR DECISION IN STAGES You don't always have to jump into your solution with both feet. Sometimes you can stick one toe in first and see what happens. Suppose that Jane wants to buy a car but worries that she won't be able to keep up with the car payments. Jane could put aside the amount of the expected car payment for several months to see whether that will work into her budget as well as she hopes. By implementing her tentative decision to buy a car in stages, Jane gathers more information—and more certainty—about whether her solution will work for her.

PREPARE CONTINGENCY PLANS Very few decisions cannot be overturned or revised once they are put into effect. Preparing yourself for revisions makes the uncertainty of the future easier to face. To prepare yourself, make a list of your uncertainties and settle on a backup plan in case things don't turn out the way you expected.

Even after testing her budget for several months, Jane may still be a little worried about the future. She may wonder if she will always be able to work the hours necessary for the car payments. She may need to drop some hours at work to keep up her grades in school. Or, she may have her hours cut back if her company downsizes. Jane can minimize her concern over buying the car if she develops a contingency plan to sell her car and take public transportation or ride her bike to school. For this contingency to work, Jane will want to buy a car that will hold its value, which—given the rate at which new cars lose value—means that Jane will probably buy a used red VW convertible, not a new one.

Reviewing Your Decision-Making Process Before making your final decision, review your process to make sure you didn't overlook something along the way. Here are some questions to guide your review.

1. Did you explicitly discuss the goals you wanted to achieve?
2. Did you come up with ample alternatives to avoid the fallacy of false dilemma?
3. Did you thoroughly research the original problem and the pros and cons of the alternative solutions?

4. Were you on the alert for one-sided nutshell briefings? Did you look honestly at the cons of your preferred solution? Did you avoid the straw person fallacy?

5. Did you reconsider alternative solutions in the light of additional information gathered during the decision-making process?

6. Was your decision guided by your most deeply held values and the goals you set for yourself?

7. Have you figured out how to put your decision into effect? Have you developed contingency plans in case your chosen solution doesn't work the way you expect?

YOUR TURN E

1. Suppose you wanted to implement the following decisions in stages. What would some of these stages be?

   a. Changing your major to physics

   b. Moving to Africa

   c. Getting married

2. Give an example from your experience in which you developed a contingency plan for a decision you made.

Taking Preventive Measures

Once you have figured out how to respond to the problem in front of you, think about whether it's likely to recur. Have you had the same argument over and over with your roommate? Do you want to keep having that same argument? If not, think about what you can do to prevent the argument from arising again in the future.

Preventive measures are especially important for *problems that have no cure.* Researchers have not yet figured out how to cure AIDS, for example. They continue searching for a cure and inform us that we can prevent the spread of AIDS by avoiding contact with fluids that carry the AIDS virus.

When deciding to take preventive measures, you follow the same steps you took to decide how to respond to the problem. You define the problem, including identifying its causes, discover alternative ways to prevent it from happening again, identify the pros and cons of the preventive measures, weigh the alternative preventive measures, and monitor their implementation.

RESOLVING CONFLICTS WITH OTHERS

"Can't live with 'em and can't live without 'em." That's how I feel about making decisions with others. On the one hand, other people help us see things we wouldn't otherwise see, think up alternative solutions, question our goals, and determine which solutions best achieve our goals. We couldn't live without their help. On the other hand, others sometimes have the audacity

Conflicting goals. Susan would like to free the trapped bird, while her cat would prefer to eat it.

to disagree with us about obvious truths. They even try to further their *own* goals at the expense of ours. How can we live with that?

Consider me and my cat. I wanted to remove the bird from danger. She wanted to catch it for lunch. Even when we agree on our goals, we find things to disagree about in the other steps of decision making. We may disagree about how to define the problem in the first place or disagree about which is the best way to achieve our goal. Here's what we can do to resolve our conflicts.

Understand Each Other

Understanding each other poses a problem for my cat and me, since we don't speak the same language. But that's not so different from what any two humans face—especially disputing humans. Frequently, what one of them says is incomprehensible to the other.

Sometimes practicing **active listening** solves the problem. To actively listen to another, allow that person to speak without interruption, take notes on what the person said, and then repeat back what you heard until the other person agrees that you have heard what he or she said. Sometimes *seeking a translator* helps. Disputing parties can select a third person to listen to and translate what each of them says until the others understand.

Offer Each Other Reasons

Instead of just repeating our disagreement, we can offer each other reasons to find a way to agreement. Let's look at some examples.

We can resolve differences in defining the problem by comparing our reasons. Suppose I say, "We've got a problem. There's not enough pasta for supper," and you say, "No, we have plenty of pasta." We could resolve this disagreement by asking each other to give our reasons. I say, "There's not enough pasta because we've got eight people coming for dinner and there are only four ounces of noodles left in the pantry." You respond, "No we've got only six people coming for dinner—the Lambrinis called to cancel. Besides, I stopped by the market for fresh pasta on the way home. I bought two pounds." Once I heard your reasons, I'd say, "You're right, we do have enough pasta." What started out as a disagreement turned into an agreement when we looked at each other's reasons.

When we dispute our goals, we can discuss the *purposes served by our goals.* For example, my cat's goal of catching the bird for lunch serves two purposes: she gets to play, and she gets nutritious food. My goal of making the bird safe from my cat serves the purpose of prolonging the bird's life.

Brainstorm Alternative Solutions

By taking a minute to brainstorm, I can come up with some alternative ways to meet my cat's purposes: play with my cat myself, get a toy for her to play with, adopt another cat for her to play with, fill her dish with cat food. I could meet my cat's purposes and mine (a win-win solution) by my showing the bird outside and then giving my cat some cat food and a toy to play with.

What if we listen to each other's reasoning, brainstorm solutions, and still can't come to an agreement? What then?

Select a Procedure for Settling the Dispute

Suppose we disagree about which movie to see, even after we've told each other all about the movies and why we want to see them. We could solve our problem by *deciding to take turns.* This week, we'll go to one movie; next week, we'll go to the other. And how will we decide which movie to go to this week? *We could flip a coin:* "Heads you win, tails you lose."

For other disagreements, we might agree to *ask someone we both trust* for their opinion, or we might *go to a mediator* to help us listen to each other more carefully. If there are more than two of us, we might decide to *let the majority rule.*

Whichever way we decide to solve our disagreements, notice that we had to agree on *something.* If we use reasons to help us agree, we have to agree that some reasons (there's two pounds of pasta) are better than others (there's four ounces of pasta). If we used purposes to help us agree, we had to agree that one solution did serve both our purposes. If we use procedures to solve our disagreement, we have to agree on which procedures to use.

Sometimes disputing parties can't agree on anything except to disagree. Married couples get divorced. Employees leave their jobs. Customers walk away from a deal. Countries go to war. And sometimes people agree to disagree without looking carefully at the consequences of *that* decision. It's one thing to walk away from a deal when there's another vendor down the street; it's quite another to take your children away from their only father or mother. You can use the steps of deliberate decision making to help you decide whether to to back to the bargaining table or call it a day.

YOUR TURN F

1. Ask a friend to practice conflict resolution with you. Use a real disagreement you have, or role-play an imaginary dispute between Wendell Berry and his wife, who says she's tired of typing on the old Royal.

   a. Take turns talking and listening to each other's points of view, including repeating back what each other said.

   b. Try to resolve your dispute by exchanging your reasons for your points of view. If you disagree about the problem, ask each other why you see the situation the way you do. If you disagree about your goals, describe the purposes for your goals, brainstorm alternative solutions, and check to see whether one of them serves both of your purposes (a win-win solution).

   c. If you did not settle your disagreement by looking at each other's reasons, see if you can agree upon a procedure for settling your disagreement.

   d. If you agree to disagree, list the consequences of not resolving your disagreement. Are they serious enough to send you back to the bargaining table?

2. Describe what worked for you and what didn't work for you when doing the above exercise.

We study decision making to improve our chances of making decisions we can live with, ones we will not regret later. But as we've seen, some decisions involve moral dilemmas, which means that whatever we choose we will regret. And many decisions rely on uncertain predictions about the future. But even in these cases, thoughtful decision making serves a purpose. We can take some comfort in the thought that we "did our best" by thinking the decision through.

On the other hand, very poor decision-making practices don't always turn out badly. In *The Boat That Wouldn't Float*, Farley Mowat tells of buying a boat practically sight unseen. The boat he bought never did stop leaking, but Mowat found a way to profit from his misfortune: he wrote a hilarious book. So don't worry too much about poor decisions. You can always use them to entertain your friends on a wintry night—if, like Farley Mowat, you're lucky enough to survive.

Once again, remember that this chapter introduces thoughtful decision making. The rest of this book, including Chapter 1, which describes how to question emotions, provides information and exercises designed to help you to clarify your thinking further when deciding how to act. You'll also find future chapters useful for practicing conflict resolution. Chapter 3 introduces you to how to give reasons for the positions you put forward, and Chapter 4 provides tools for translating your words into terms others can understand.

EXERCISES

1. Do you have the facts you need to define the problem in the following situations? If so, what are they? If not, what would you do to obtain them?

   a. Sam has been offered a credit card and has already charged two others to the limit.

   b. Sally's roommates have been asking her to watch a soap opera with them, but she has a test coming up she needs to study for.

   c. Ivan and Rachael want to make love, and neither of them has a condom.

   d. There's a student who talks incessantly in one of Ari's classes, leaving little room for other students to talk.

   e. Suppose you are the editor of your school newspaper and the Institute for Historical Review has asked you to print one of their ads denying the mass killings in German concentration camps in World War II. Before deciding what to do, you read the following editorial:

   > . . . Several campus papers have run full-page ads insisting, for instance, that the gas chambers were only fumigation facilities. The ads have run at the University of Michigan, Cornell and Duke, among others. . . .
   >
   > In explaining the decision of *The Chronicle* at Duke, editor Ann Heimberger wrote, "American newspapers are built on the principles of free speech and free press, so how can a newspaper deny those rights to anyone?" . . .
   >
   > In defending *The Chronicle,* the *Daily Tar Heel* at the University of North Carolina wrote in an editorial:
   >
   > "Once an editor takes that first dangerous step and decides an ad should not run because of its content, that editor begins the plunge . . . toward the abolition of free speech."
   >
   > Not really. Newspapers reject ads on matters of truthfulness or taste, and the principles apply as much to advocacy ads as to ads for hernia aids. Holocaust Revisionism is a lie.
   >
   > The campus ads are sponsored by The Committee for Open Debate

on the Holocaust. It shares some folks with the Institute for Historical Review (IHR), which is a spinoff of the anti-Semitic Liberty Lobby.

In 1980, IHR offered to pay $50,000 [to] anyone who could prove Jews were gassed at Auschwitz. A Holocaust survivor took IHR to court, easily proved the case and IHR was ordered to pay up.[7]

2. For each example under question 1, can you analyze the problem? Do you know what caused it? Do you know what will happen if nothing is done?

3. For each example under question 1, if you were in this situation, what goal would you want to achieve? Are they really your goals, or are they someone else's? Do they conflict with each other or with other goals you have?

4. For each of the following situations, interpret the situation as a problem, then interpret it as an opportunity. You may describe the situation more fully and make predictions about the future to support your interpretations. State the goal or goals the situations challenge or support.

   a. Students in the class you're taking find the class boring, and the teacher doesn't seem to notice.

   b. Your sister is coming to your college, and your parents want her to move in with you.

   c. Robert's teacher has been giving him unwanted sexual attention.

   d. Sara has just found out that her friends each stole something when they went shopping, and they want her to steal something, too.

   e. Every time Paul goes out on a date, his friends ask whether he scored.

5. Are any of the following false alternatives? If, so list one or more additional alternatives to consider.

   a. If your friends want you to go drinking with them, you can either go with them and drink or stay at home.

   b. If your friends want you to go shopping with them, you can either give them a lecture about consumerism or go along and spend money with them.

   c. If you are expected to dissect a frog in biology, you can either dissect the frog or drop the class.

   d. If a teacher gives you a grade that you think isn't fair, you can either talk with the teacher about it or do nothing.

   e. Do you find any false alternatives in the following news report?

   ### Congress Focuses on Teen Moms

   Associated Press

   When Congress takes up welfare reform next year, teen-age mothers will be Exhibit A.

   Critics say the welfare system encourages teen-age girls to have illegitimate babies and allows the fathers to escape responsibility.

   Two reform plans have received the most attention so far.

The House Republicans' "Contract with America" endorses legislation with provisions that:

- Deny welfare benefits and public housing to unwed mothers under age 18; states could ban benefits for all mothers under 21 if they prefer. The money saved would finance orphanages and adoptions.
- Require unwed mothers who qualify for welfare to identify the child's father before receiving aid, and force fathers to pay child support.
- Deny increased benefits for additional children born while a mother is on welfare.

The Clinton administration has its own proposal, which includes provisions to:

- Require mothers under 18 to live with their parents and stay in school to receive benefits.
- Require mothers to identify the child's father before receiving a welfare check, and force fathers to pay child support.
- Restrict welfare recipients to two years of cash assistance, with the clock starting when they turn 18.[8]

6. What are some pros and cons of the alternatives listed in question 5 above? Include the pros and cons of any additional alternatives you came up with when answering question 5.

7. Would any of your values come into conflict if you were making the following decisions? Which, if any, of the values do you hold most dearly?

   a. You're trying to decide whether to use cloth or disposable diapers for your newborn.

   b. You've been saving your money to buy a car. Your mother calls to say that your younger brother has a medical problem and that the family has no insurance or available funds to cover his treatment.

   c. You don't have enough money to finish college. You don't ever want to be in a position of killing another person, but the Army recruiter says the Army will pay your way through school if you join.

   d. Your sixteen-year-old brother has moved out of the house. He's asked you not to tell your parents where he is. Your parents say they'll ground you if you don't tell them where he is.

   e. Should a faithful partner in a long-term relationship insist on practicing safe sex, even when the other partner has given no indication of sexual promiscuity?

8. Would you (or can you imagine that someone would) feel inclined to take any of the impulse shortcuts (me first, retaliating, avoiding punishment, going along with the group) with respect to any of the situations in question 7 above? Explain.

Why I Am Not Going to Buy a Computer: Readers' Letters and Wendell Berry's Reply

The following are letters received by *Harper's* in response to Wendell Berry's essay (reprinted at the beginning of this chapter) and Berry's reply to them.

LETTERS

Wendell Berry provides writers enslaved by the computer with a handy alternative: Wife—a low-tech energy-saving device. Drop a pile of handwritten notes on Wife and you get back a finished manuscript, edited while it was typed. What computer can do that? Wife meets all of Berry's uncompromising standards for technological innovation: she's cheap, repairable near home, and good for the family structure. Best of all, Wife is politically correct because she breaks a writer's "direct dependence on strip-mined coal."

History teaches us that Wife can also be used to beat rugs and wash clothes by hand, thus eliminating the need for the vacuum cleaner and washing machine, two more nasty machines that threaten the act of writing.

Gordon Inkeles
Miranda, Calif.

I have no quarrel with Berry because he prefers to write with pencil and paper; that is his choice. But he implies that I and others are somehow impure because we choose to write on a computer. I do not admire the energy corporations, either. Their shortcoming is not that they produce electricity but how they go about it. They are poorly managed because they are blind to long-term consequences. To solve this problem, wouldn't it make more sense to correct the precise error they are making rather than simply ignore their product? I would be happy to join Berry in a protest against strip mining, but I intend to keep plugging this computer into the wall with a clear conscience.

James Rhoads
Battle Creek, Mich.

I enjoyed reading Berry's declaration of intent never to buy a personal computer in the same way that I enjoy reading about the belief systems of unfamiliar tribal cultures. I tried to imagine a tool that would meet Berry's criteria for superiority to his old manual typewriter. The clear winner is the quill pen. It is cheaper, smaller, more energy-efficient, human-powered, easily repaired, and nondisruptive of existing relationships.

Berry also requires that this tool must be "clearly and demonstrably better" than the one it replaces. But surely we all recognize by now that "better" is in the mind of the beholder. To the quill pen aficionado, the benefits obtained from elegant calligraphy might well outweigh all others.

I have no particular desire to see Berry use a word processor; if he doesn't like computers, that's fine with me. However, I do object to his portrayal of this reluctance as a moral virtue. Many of us have found that computers can be an invaluable tool in the fight to protect our environment. In addition to helping me write, my personal computer gives me access to up-to-the-minute reports on the workings of the EPA and the nuclear industry. I participate in electronic bulletin boards on which environmental activists discuss strategy and warn each other about urgent legislative issues. Perhaps Berry feels that the Sierra Club should eschew modern printing technology, which is highly wasteful of energy, in favor of having its members hand-copy the club's magazines and other mailings each month?

Nathaniel S. Borenstein
Pittsburgh, Pa.

The value of a computer to a writer is that it is a tool not for generating ideas but for typing and editing words. It is cheaper than a secretary (or a wife!) and arguably more fuel-efficient. And it enables spouses who are not inclined to provide free labor more time to concentrate on *their* own work.

We should support alternatives both to coal-generated electricity and to IBM-style technocracy. But I am reluctant to entertain alternatives that presuppose the traditional subservience of one class to another. Let the PCs come and the wives and servants go seek more meaningful work.

Toby Koosman
Knoxville, Tenn.

Berry asks how he could write conscientiously against the rape of nature if in the act of writing on a computer he was implicated in the rape. I find it ironic that a writer who sees the underlying connectedness of things would allow his diatribe against computers to be published in a magazine that carries ads for the National Rural Electric Cooperative Association, Marlboro, Phillips Petroleum, McDonnell Douglas, and yes, even Smith-Corona. If Berry rests comfortably at night, he must be using sleeping pills.

Bradley C. Johnson
Grand Forks, N.D.

WENDELL BERRY REPLIES:

The foregoing letters surprised me with the intensity of the feelings they expressed. According to the writers' testimony, there is nothing wrong with their computers; they are utterly satisfied with them and all that they stand for. My correspondents are certain that I am wrong and that I am, moreover, on the losing side, a side already relegated to the dustbin of history. And yet they grow huffy and condescending over my tiny dissent. What are they so anxious about?

I can only conclude that I have scratched the skin of a technological fundamentalism that, like other fundamentalisms, wishes to monopolize a whole society and, therefore, cannot tolerate the smallest difference of opinion. At the slightest hint of a threat to their complacency, they repeat, like a chorus of toads, the notes sounded by their leaders in industry. The past was gloomy, drudgery-ridden, servile, meaningless, and slow. The present, thanks only to purchasable products, is meaningful, bright, lively, centralized, and fast. The future, thanks only to more purchasable products, is going to be even better. Thus consumers become salesmen, and the world is made safer for corporations.

I am also surprised by the meanness with which two of these writers refer to my wife. In order to imply that I am a tyrant, they suggest by both direct statement and innuendo that she is subservient, characterless, and stupid—a mere "device" easily forced to provide meaningless "free labor." I understand that it is impossible to make an adequate public defense of one's private life, and so I will only point out that there are a number of kinder possibilities that my critics have disdained to imagine: that my wife may do this work because she wants to and likes to; that she may find some use and some meaning in it; that she may not work for nothing. These gentlemen obviously think themselves feminists of the most correct and principled sort, and yet they do not hesitate to stereotype and insult, on the basis of one fact, a woman they do not know. They are audacious and irresponsible gossips.

In his letter, Bradley C. Johnson rushes

past the possibility of sense in what I said in my essay by implying that I am or ought to be a fanatic. That I am a person of this century and am implicated in many practices that I regret is fully acknowledged at the beginning of my essay. I did not say that I proposed to end forthwith all my involvement in harmful technology, for I do not know how to do that. I said merely that I want to limit such involvement, and to a certain extent I do know how to do that. If some technology does damage to the world—as two of the above letters seem to agree that it does—then why is it not reasonable, and indeed moral, to try to limit one's use of that technology? *Of course*, I think that I am right to do this.

I would not think so, obviously, if I agreed with Nathaniel S. Borenstein that "'better' is in the mind of the beholder." But if he truly believes this, I do not see why he bothers with his personal computer's "up-to-the-minute reports on the workings of the EPA and the nuclear industry" or why he wishes to be warned about "urgent legislative issues." According to his system, the "better" in a bureaucratic, industrial, or legislative mind is as good as the "better" in his. His mind apparently is being subverted by an objective standard of some sort, and he had better look out.

Borenstein does not say what he does after his computer has drummed him awake. I assume from his letter that he must send donations to conservation organizations and letters to officials. Like James Rhoads, at any rate, he has a clear conscience. But this is what is wrong with the conservation movement. It has a clear conscience. The guilty are always other people, and the wrong is always somewhere else. That is why Borenstein finds his "electronic bulletin board" so handy. To the conservation movement, it is only production that causes environmental degradation; the consumption that supports the production is rarely acknowledged to be at fault. The ideal of the run-of-the-mill conservationist is to impose restraints upon production without limiting consumption or burdening the consciences of consumers.

But virtually all of our consumption now is extravagant, and virtually all of it consumes the world. It is not beside the point that most electrical power comes from strip-mined coal. The history of the exploitation of the Appalachian coal fields is long, and it is available to readers. I do not see how anyone can read it and plug in any appliance with a clear conscience. If Rhoads can do so, that does not mean that his conscience is clear; it means that his conscience is not working.

To the extent that we consume, in our present circumstances, we are guilty. To the extent that we guilty consumers are conservationists, we are absurd. But what can we do? Must we go on writing letters to politicians and donating to conservation organizations until the majority of our fellow citizens agree with us? Or can we do something directly to solve our share of the problem?

I am a conservationist. I believe wholeheartedly in putting pressure on the politicians and in maintaining the conservation organizations. But I wrote my little essay partly in distrust of centralization. I don't think that the government and the conservation organizations alone will ever make us a conserving society. Why do I need a centralized computer system to alert me to environmental crises? That I live every hour of every day in an environmental crisis I know from all my senses. Why then is not my first duty to reduce, so far as I can, my own consumption?

Finally, it seems to me that none of my correspondents recognizes the innovativeness of my essay. If the use of a computer is a new idea, then a newer idea is not to use one.

Questions

1. Do Wendell Berry or any of the people responding to him define to your satisfaction the problem of owning a computer?
   a. Do they provide the relevant facts you

What do they want to know? What do they include? What do they leave out?

   b. Do they analyze the situation, explaining the causes of the problem and what will happen if nothing is done? What do they include? What do they leave out?

   c. Do they state (or can you easily infer) the goals they want to accomplish? What are the goals?

2. What solutions do these writers offer to the problem of owning a computer? Do they provide false alternatives? (Are there other potential solutions? If so, what are they?)

3. Do any of the writers leave out any important pros or cons of the alternatives they consider? Do they take the long-range consequences of the solutions into account? Do they consider the cons of their recommended solutions?

4. Do they create a straw person of any of the solutions they consider?

5. Is there anyone else you would want to ask for a nutshell briefing about the pros and cons of the solutions they consider? Who? Why?

6. Do any values come into conflict when you try to decide among the alternative solutions? Which ones? Are some of these values more important to you than others?

7. Do you see any difficulties in implementing the solutions the writers recommend?

8. What other question or point would you like to discuss relevant to Wendell Berry and his respondents?

Speech to a Woman Seeking an Abortion

Juli Loesch Wiley

A few years ago, the U. S. Supreme Court upheld most of Pennsylvania's Abortion Control Act, including a provision that requires a woman seeking an abortion to listen to a doctor describe the procedure 24 hours before it takes place. In response to the Court's decision, *Harper's* magazine asked a number of writers to set forth what they would tell a woman requesting an abortion. The following is an answer by Juli Loesch Wiley, a member of Feminists for Life. A different view is expressed in the next selection.

1. You are a complex, easily damaged, and sensitive individual, and so is this newly conceived life. Did you know that some research has found emotional or physical trauma in more than 90 percent of women who abort?

2. Are you aware that your son or daughter is developing beautifully, responds to a variety of stimuli, and is already sensitive to pain?

3. Are you considering abortion because of other people in your life? Your husband? Boyfriend? Parents? Employer? Is it fair that you will be subjected to physical, emotional and spiritual trauma because they possibly have an anti-child attitude?

4. Did you know that it's against the law for anyone to discriminate against you for being pregnant or having a child?

5. Is the father of the baby a responsible and loving person? Does he care about you? Does he care about his baby? Could he rise to the challenge of fatherhood?

6. Is there even one woman in your life whom you love and respect: Grandmother? Sister? Teacher? College roommate? Do you trust her enough to ask her to help you? Would she stand by you and your child during this pregnancy and afterward?

7. (After woman views video interviews with couples eager to adopt her baby.) Do you feel drawn to any of these people? Could

you place your little one in their arms? Are you aware that you're carrying a wanted child?

8. Would you abort if you knew this were the only baby you would ever conceive? If you knew this child were uniquely gifted in some way? If you knew this child were destined to make one other human being supremely happy?

9. Would aborting your baby conflict with other values in your life? A belief in nonviolence? An ethic of "live and let live"? A commitment to natural or holistic living?

10. Do you believe in the Golden Rule, "Do unto others as you would have others do unto you?" Would you want someone to turn against you and physically destroy you because they weren't ready to deal with you at this time?

11. Do you believe in God? And that God made you? Do you believe that God made the baby you are carrying? Did God allow this new human to come into being for some purpose?

12. If your circumstances were different and you didn't have the problems you have now, would you want this baby? If so, can we start there and work backward together, attacking the problems rather than the baby?

13. Do you remember that line from "Desiderata," "You are a child of the Universe, as much as the trees and the stars: you have the right to be here"? Can you say that to your child?

Questions

1. Does Juli Loesch Wiley define the problem of abortion to your satisfaction?
   a. Does she provide the relevant facts you want to know? What does she include? What does she leave out?
   b. Does she analyze the situation, explaining the causes of the problem and what will happen if nothing is done? What does she include? What does she leave out?
   c. Does she state (or can you easily infer) the goals she wants to accomplish? What are they?

2. Do you see abortion as a problem, an opportunity, both, or neither?
   a. If you see it as a problem, which of your goals or values does it undermine?
   b. If you see it as an opportunity, which of your goals or values does it support?

3. What solutions does Wiley offer to the problem of abortion? Are these false alternatives? (Are there other potential solutions? If so, what are they?)

4. Does Wiley leave out any important pros or cons of the alternatives she considers? Does she take the long-range consequences of the solutions into account? Does she consider the cons of her recommended solutions?

5. Does Wiley create a straw person of any of the solutions she considers?

6. Is there anyone else you would want to ask for a nutshell briefing about the pros and cons of the solutions Wiley considers? Who? And why?

7. Do any values come into conflict when you try to decide among the alternative solutions? Which ones? Are some of these values more important to you than others?

8. Can you imagine anyone taking one of the impulse shortcuts ("me first," retaliate, avoid punishment, go along with the group) as a response to the problem of abortion? Explain.

9. Does Wiley or do you see any difficulties in implementing the solutions she recommends?

10. What other question or point would you like to discuss relevant to this essay?

Speech to a Woman Seeking an Abortion

Frederick Turner

This selection is Frederick Turner's response to *Harper's* request (see previous selection). Turner is Founders Professor of Arts and Humanities at the University of Texas at Dallas.

Before we talk, let's get something clear. I'm a doctor, and the facts I'll be mentioning are backed up by my expertise as a doctor. But the intent of the law under which we're going to be talking is basically moral, and I'm no more an expert on morality than you are. That isn't to say morality isn't important, or that you and I can't get it right; in fact, we may be better at it than the authorities.

I'm supposed to give you some facts, so let's get it over with. You're in the early part of the second trimester, so that if we do the abortion, we'll be killing an organism inside you that is potentially human and is shaped like a human baby but has a degree of organized sensitivity and awareness somewhere between that of a sheep and that of your own lower spine. It's pretty small—smaller than your fist—and once it's dead, we'll remove it.

Those are the facts. Now for the difficult part. Suppose your baby were at term and in the birth canal. What you'd have there would be a human being, with rights that need to be protected. Some premature babies can survive when they're three months early. If we killed a preemie, the law would call it murder. They'd be right, wouldn't they? But let's look at the other end of the scale. I'm scratching my hand, as you can see. I just removed, and killed, some hundreds of skin cells. Each of them has a full set of my chromosomes. In a few decades we'll probably have the biotechnology to clone up one of those skin cells into a perfect baby twin of me. So in a sense, I've just killed a potentially viable human life—and yet we both know that it was a completely trivial act.

In the hours after conception, abortion is utterly trivial; nine months later it's as serious a crime as there is. And for all our wishful talk of "trimesters" and "viability," the process between the beginning and the end is completely smooth—there is no dramatic moment of metamorphosis from scrap of human tissue to human being. Many classical cultures abandoned babies even after they were born: They drew the line between what's human and what's not in a different place. And they weren't bad people.

So how do we draw the line? Right now it's up to you. You're the best judge; you're the one on the ground, in the trenches, dealing with the situation.

People sometimes just can't deal with the idea of morality as a gradual slope. They have to draw a line. But I think there is a way to understand it—a way that's helped me, anyway.

See, at some point we have to connect with the rest of nature, and it always involves death. Our immune systems are killing billions of little beasties right now. When we eat, we must kill, even if we're vegetarians. Animals kill and eat one another—the prey is sacrificed to the generally faster metabolism, smarter intelligence, and more sensitive social system of the predator. There's no getting away from the food chain.

That doesn't mean we can't make distinctions. I think most people these days would agree that one wouldn't kill a higher animal—a chimp or a dolphin—without a pretty big reason, like saving human lives. With lower animals, like cows or pigs, most of us feel that it's permissible to eat them, though some of us have qualms and others will eat them only on important or festive occasions, believing that one shouldn't sacrifice them for nothing.

Eating a still lower animal, like a chicken or a fish, doesn't bother most of us, and we feel even less anxiety about eating eggs and milk and vegetables.

In other words, nature—and our own inherited common sense—makes distinctions of value according to how high an organism is on the scale of evolution, and implicitly recognizes that the lower can be legitimately sacrificed to the higher. There's a stage when the human fetus has something like a gill; perhaps it has as much of a soul then as a fish does. Later there's a stage when it's still pretty hard to distinguish a photo of it from one of a chicken embryo. Maybe it's about as important as a live chicken at that point. And so on.

It might help if you think of abortion as a sacrifice—the later the abortion, the heavier and graver the reason had better be, and the more sacred the whole thing is. But just because reproduction is sacred doesn't mean that it's not wasteful.

The male human wastes millions of sperm, and the female wastes a valuable egg every month. Spontaneous miscarriages are wasteful natural sacrifices. If you abort a fetus intentionally for a good reason, you're in accord with nature's own tradition of sacred sacrificial waste.

But the way I look at it, a sacrifice demands respect. It had better be done in a good cause, or it will come back to haunt us. That's why we often make a beautiful communal ritual out of sacrifice, even if it's a highly symbolic one; think of a Buddhist burning a candle or a Catholic priest breaking a bit of bread.

And there's another implication to the idea of abortion as a sacrifice: If it's done right and done in a good cause, it can be something much better than just making the best of a bad situation, a nasty episode to be forgotten as soon as possible. What traditional religious ritual tells us is that sacrifice can be enriching,

creative, evoking powers and values that can contribute great gifts to human existence.

Isn't it possible that abortion, in the right circumstances, for the right reasons and intentions, could be like that?

Our society doesn't provide us much in the way of ritual to deal with this difficult moment you have before you. But maybe you—and I—can take advantage of this blundering, well-intentioned law, and make our little talk into the beginning of a proper rite of sacrifice. Maybe you—and I—can take on a bit more moral and spiritual weight through this work we're doing.

Questions

1. Does Frederick Turner define the problem of abortion to your satisfaction?
   a. Does he provide the relevant facts you want to know? What does he include? What does he leave out?
   b. Does he analyze the situation, explaining the causes of the problem and what will happen if nothing is done? What does he include? What does he leave out?
   c. Does he state (or can you easily infer) the goals he wants to accomplish? What are they?
2. What solution(s) does Turner offer to the problem of abortion? Does he provide false alternatives? Are there other potential solutions? If so, what are they?
3. Does Turner leave out any important pros or cons of the alternatives he considers? Does he take the long-range consequences of the solutions into account? Does he consider the cons of his recommended solutions?
4. Does Turner create a straw person of any of the solutions he considers?
5. Is there anyone else you would want to ask for a nutshell briefing about the pros

and cons of the solutions Turner considers? Who? And why?

6. Do any values come into conflict when you try to decide among the alternative solutions? Which ones? Are some of these values more important to you than others?

7. Does Turner or do you see any difficulties in implementing the solutions he recommends?

8. What other question or point would you like to discuss relevant to this essay?

Options in the Face of Abuse

Nancy Mitchell

At the time of publication, Nancy Mitchell was a doctoral student in Washington at the School of Advanced International Studies of Johns Hopkins University.

The lesson is sad and sobering, just like reality. You can't have it both ways. You can't get the goodies and hope to get justice as well.

Anita Hill moved with Clarence Thomas from one job to what promised to be a better job. She kept in cordial touch with him to maintain a useful contact. There is nothing wrong with that; it is an understandable, and, sadly, even wise choice. You grit your teeth and take it. And you move ahead and dream of justice someday.

But you can't have it both ways. That's the deflating truth of the drama. We sat transfixed and thought "Yes! Once we are secure, we can seek justice!"

I understand and believe Professor Hill's accusations and her behavior. I do not find them, as so many do, inconsistent. She acted with a mixture of paralysis, impotence, ambition, and ambivalence. She probably liked Mr. Thomas. That's a dirty little secret we women have: Sometimes our harassers are, otherwise, likable and even admirable, men. Otherwise. That's the trick to enduring abuse—to focus on the otherwise, to see the man as others seem to see him, to blame ourselves.

Hill is telling the truth, but apparently it was not good enough. That's very sobering. Little children can explain their dependence,

their silence, their affection for their molesters 10, 20, 30 years after the fact. But women are not children. We have responsibilities in this tough world. Yes, we are harassed, touched, mauled, raped, but we cannot collude and still hope for justice. Maybe in a perfect world we could. But not today, not here.

Here, today, when faced with harassment, we have a few, bad choices. Occasionally it is a clear case: We receive unwelcome attention from a man whom we despise *and* we are blessed with financial independence and courage. Then we file a complaint or quit.

Most situations are murkier. Usually the women being harassed—young and junior—lack financial freedom and, furthermore, their every instinct is to compartmentalize the abuse in their thinking, to not let it color their opinion of the otherwise admirable man. It is not easy to think clearly at the time one is being harassed—not even for Yale Law School graduates.

There are several reasons for confusion. First, the man's behavior toward us might not jibe with his reputation. Almost all of us watching the hearings had trouble squaring the image of Thomas with the descriptions of what he said to Hill. Why should it have been easier for Hill?

Second, harassment is "unwelcome attention." Yes, it is unwelcome, but it is also attention. And in a frequently anonymous workplace, it takes more self-confidence than many of us have to flatly reject attention from a man whom we have respected, or from a man who has power over us. It is more likely that we will try to somehow take the "unwelcome" out of the "attention." That we will try to change our behavior, and that we will hope, unrealistically, that the harassment will go away.

I am not blaming the victim, I blame the abusive man. But I am saying that a lesson of the grinding agony of the hearings is that if we want our accusations to be believed, we must think clearly and consider our options when we are being harassed.

We can suffer in silence and do nothing. We can file a complaint. We can tell friends and credible pillars of the community, we can document the abuse, and we can distance ourselves as much as possible from the abuser. Or we can endure the abuse, hoping to bleach the "unwelcome" from it and perhaps eventually turn it to our advantage in a conspiratorial closeness with a powerful man.

What we cannot do is all of the above. We cannot act as though nothing had happened, continue to use the relationship with the man and, at the same time, hope ever to make our accusations stick.

I placed hopes I never dreamt I had on this stoic and credible professor from Oklahoma. But as the hearings droned inexorably on, I realized that being the victim does not absolve us from other responsibilities.

That feels almost too heavy to bear, but it is the truth. Hill was a credible witness but that did not make her story credible to the majority of Americans. For her accusations to have been credible to more Americans, she would have had to have forgone the goodies and the ambivalence. At least then, she might have had a chance. It is a hard lesson, and a useful one.

Questions

1. Does Nancy Mitchell define the problem of unwanted sexual attention to your satisfaction?
   a. Does she provide the relevant facts you want to know? What does she include? What does she leave out?
   b. Does she analyze the situation, explaining the causes of the problem and what will happen if nothing is done? What does she include? What does she leave out?
   c. Does she state (or can you easily infer) the goals she wants to accomplish? What are they?
2. What solutions does Mitchell offer to the problem of unwanted sexual attention? Are these false alternatives? Are there other solutions? If so, what are they?
3. Does Mitchell leave out any important pros or cons of the alternatives she considers? Does she take the long-range consequences of the solutions into account? Does she consider the cons of her recommended solutions?
4. Does Mitchell create a straw person of any of the solutions she considers?
5. Is there anyone else you would want to ask for a nutshell briefing about the pros and cons of the solutions Mitchell considers? Who? And why?
6. Do any values conflict when you try to decide among the alternative solutions? Which ones? Are some of these values more important to you than others?
7. Can you imagine anyone taking one of the impulse shortcuts ("me first," retaliate, avoid punishment, go along with the group) as a response to the problem of unwanted sexual attention? Explain.
8. Does Mitchell or do you see any difficulties in implementing the solutions she recommends?
9. What other question or point would you like to discuss relevant to this essay?

Rape and Modern Sex War

Camille Paglia

Camille Paglia teaches humanities at the University of the Arts in Philadelphia.

Rape is an outrage that cannot be tolerated in civilized society. Yet feminism, which has waged a crusade for rape to be taken more seriously, has put young women in danger by hiding the truth about sex from them. . . .

. . . In our cities, on our campuses far from home, young women are vulnerable and defenseless. Feminism has not prepared them for this. Feminism keeps saying the sexes are the same. It keeps telling women they can do anything, go anywhere, say anything, wear anything. No, they can't. Women will always be in sexual danger. . . .

We must remedy social injustice whenever we can. But there are some things we cannot change. There are sexual differences that are based in biology. Academic feminism is lost in a fog of social constructionism. It believes we are totally the product of our environment. This idea was invented by Rousseau. He was wrong. Emboldened by dumb French language theory, academic feminists repeat the same hollow slogans over and over to each other. Their view of sex is naive and prudish.

The sexes are at war. Men must struggle for identity against the overwhelming power of their mothers. Women have menstruation to tell them they are women. Men must do or risk something to be men. Men become masculine only when other men say they are. Having sex with a woman is one way a boy becomes a man.

College men are at their hormonal peak. They have just left their mothers and are questing for their male identity. In groups, they are dangerous.

A woman going to a fraternity party is walking into Testosterone Flats. If she goes, she should be armed with resolute alertness. She should arrive with girlfriends and leave with them. A girl who lets herself get dead drunk at a fraternity party is a fool. A girl who goes upstairs alone with a brother at a fraternity party is an idiot. Feminists call this "blaming the victim." I call it common sense.

For a decade, feminists have drilled their disciples to say, "Rape is a crime of violence but not of sex." This sugar-coated Shirley Temple nonsense has exposed young women to disaster. Misled by feminism, they do not expect rape from the nice boys who sit next to them in class.

Aggression and eroticism, in fact, are deeply intertwined. Hunt, pursuit and capture are biologically programmed into male sexuality. Generation after generation, men must be educated, refined and ethically persuaded away from their tendency toward anarchy and brutishness.

Society is not the enemy, as feminism ignorantly claims. Society is woman's protection against rape. Feminism, with its solemn Carrie Nation repressiveness, does not see what is for men the eroticism or fun element in rape, especially the wild, infectious delirium of gang rape. . . .

• • •

The only solution to date rape is female self-awareness and self-control. A woman's No. 1 line of defense against rape is herself. When a real rape occurs, she should report it to the police. Complaining to college committees because the courts "take too long" is ridiculous.

College administrations are not a branch of the judiciary. They are not equipped or trained for legal inquiry. Colleges must alert incoming students to the problems and dangers of adulthood. Then colleges must stand back and get out of the sex game.

Questions

1. Does Camille Paglia define the problem of date rape to your satisfaction?
   a. Does she provide the relevant facts you want to know? What does she include? What does she leave out?
   b. Does she analyze the situation, explaining the causes of the problem and what will happen if nothing is done? What does she include? What does she leave out?
   c. Does she state (or can you easily infer) the goals she wants to accomplish? What are they?
2. What solutions does Paglia offer to the problem of date rape? Are these false alternatives? Are there other potential solutions? If so, what are they?
3. Does Paglia leave out any important pros or cons of the alternatives she considers? Does she take the long-range consequences of the solutions into account?
   Does she consider the downs of her recommended solutions?
4. Does Paglia create a straw person of any of the solutions she considers?
5. Is there anyone else you would want to ask for a nutshell briefing about the pros and cons of the solutions Paglia considers? Who? And why?
6. Do any values come into conflict when you try to decide among the alternative solutions? Which ones? Are some of these values more important to you than others?
7. Can you imagine anyone taking one of the impulse shortcuts ("me first," retaliate, avoid punishment, go along with the group) as a response to the problem of date rape? Explain.
8. Does Paglia or do you see any difficulties in implementing the solutions she recommends?
9. What other question or point would you like to discuss relevant to this essay?

WRITING IDEAS

1. Review the two essays titled "Speech to a Woman Seeking an Abortion" in this section, and write the advice you would give to someone who is considering an abortion.
2. Review Camille Paglia's essay, and discuss whether you accept her solution to the problem of date rape.
3. Define a problem of your choice, suggest several alternative solutions for the problem, weigh the pros and cons of these solutions, and indicate which solution you recommend.
4. Write about a time you tried to resolve a conflict with another person, describing what you did and whether you were successful.
5. Write about whether this chapter and your class discussions complemented, conflicted with, supported, or left out any of your previous ideas about decision making or conflict resolution.

Notes

1. For a discussion of the merits of using thoughtful decision making, see Chapter 6, "Are the Main Assumptions about Process and Outcome Warranted?" in Irving L. Janis, *Crucial Decisions* (New York: Free Press, 1989) 119–135.

2. My discussion of thoughtful decision making relies heavily on the work of Irving L. Janis in *Crucial Decisions* and "Causes and Consequences of Defective Policy-Making: A New Theoretical Approach" in *Decision-Making and Leadership*, ed. Frank Heller (New York: Cambridge University Press, 1992) 11–45.

3. Marvin Levine, *Effective Problem Solving*, 2nd ed. (Englewood Cliffs, NJ: Prentice Hall, 1994) 5.

4. Janis, "Causes and Consequences" 40.

5. Janis discusses the problem of the nutshell briefing in *Crucial Decisions* 40–42.

6. Janis, *Crucial Decisions* 47.

7. Tom Teepen, "Lying Holocaust Ads Corrupt the Campuses," Cox News Service, *San Francisco Chronicle* 2 Dec. 1991: A21.

8. "Congress Focuses on Teen Moms," Associated Press, *Marin Independent Journal* 27 Nov. 1994: A9.

3

Breaking Up Arguments

CHAPTER GOALS

- To understand how to recognize an argument and how to distinguish it from a disagreement or a dispute.
- To learn how to identify the parts of an argument—the conclusion, the support statements, and the counterconsiderations.
- To discover how to identify "argument extras"—statements used to enhance arguments or avoid arguments.
- To learn where you are likely to find arguments.
- To use your knowledge to analyze and evaluate arguments, including those embedded in news articles, essays, ads, and everyday conversations.

What comes to mind when you think of arguments? Jot down your ideas; then read these passages and answer the questions that follow.

> The annual Apple Blossom Fair will be held in Sebastopol the first weekend in May. On Saturday morning, the parade starts at 10:00 A.M., rain or shine. There will be displays in the Vets building all day Saturday and Sunday.

> We've got a bushel of apples, and they will spoil before we can eat them all. We both like applesauce. So we should make applesauce with them.

> *Bob*: We've got a bushel of apples. Let's make pies from the apples and freeze them.
> *Betty*: No, we should make applesauce.
> *Bob*: I said I want pies.
> *Betty*: But I want applesauce.
> *Bob*: No, it's pies, you health nut.
> *Betty*: Applesauce, or you can just let the apples rot, for all I care.

> *Juan*: We should eat an apple a day.
> *Stu*: Why?
> *Juan*: An apple a day keeps the doctor away.
> *Stu*: OK.

Questions

1. What do you think of when you hear the word "argument"? Jot down anything that comes to mind.

2. Given your present understanding of arguments, would you say that any of the above passages contain arguments? Explain.

Students frequently tell me that the moment they hear we are going to discuss arguments they get anxious. When they hear the word **argument** they think of heated disagreements. Images of screeching voices and put-downs come to them. They remember feelings of panic and humiliation.

Some years ago, there was a "Monty Python" sketch in which a man enters an argument clinic hoping to have an argument with somebody. After paying his money to the receptionist, he goes to the first desk, where a man starts calling him names. After a few moments of this, the argument seeker explains that he has come to have an argument, and the man behind the desk apologizes and explains that his job is to give abuse. He directs the argument seeker to the next desk. The man behind that desk disagrees with whatever the argument seeker says. Finally the argument seeker points out that the man behind the desk is merely contradicting him, not offering an argument. The seeker explains that he's looking for a series of statements intended to support a conclusion.

This sketch highlights several different senses of the word "argument." Sometimes the word "argument" is used to mean abuse; other times, disagreement. Still other times—in this chapter, for example—we use "argument" to mean a statement or statements offered to support (establish the truth or acceptability of) another statement.

This chapter teaches you how to break arguments into their parts, how to distinguish supporting a conclusion from enhancing the communication of arguments, and how to distinguish argument from abuse and disagreement. It also directs you to places where you are most likely to find arguments. After reading this chapter, you'll be in a better position to go in search of an argument and come back with one. You'll also have a better grip on presenting your reasoning to others. You'll be able to produce arguments with the requisite parts, and you'll be able to defuse distracting disputes and get back to the business of argument.

YOUR TURN A

◆ 1. Do any of the passages at the beginning of the chapter contain arguments—that is, a series of statements intended to support another statement?

2. Has your understanding of "argument" changed since you read the definitions given above?

ELEMENTS OF ARGUMENT

To understand an argument as a statement or series of statements that is intended to support another statement, it helps to learn how to break arguments into their parts, or elements. Taking an argument apart is called **argument analysis.**[1]

As you can see from the definition of "argument," arguments have two main elements: the statement or statements offered as support *and* the statement that is being supported. The supporting statements are called **support** (premises, evidence, reasons), and the statement being supported is called the **conclusion** (claim). In an argumentative essay, the conclusion is also called the *thesis.* Many arguments also contain **counterconsiderations,** statements that go against the conclusion, and the author's response to them.

Here's an example of an argument from the beginning of the chapter.

> We've got a bushel of apples, and they will spoil before we can eat them all. We both like applesauce. So we should make applesauce with them.

"We've got a bushel of apples," "They will spoil before we can eat them all," and "We both like applesauce" are offered to support the conclusion "We should make applesauce."

Here's another example:

> *Tabatha*: Oh no, I've got poison oak again!
>
> *Jeremy*: Are you sure?
>
> *Tabatha*: See these red bumps on my arm? They itch just like the bumps the doctor diagnosed two months ago as poison oak. And remember, we walked right through a patch of poison oak on our hike last weekend.

In this dialogue Tabatha is offering Jeremy support for her conclusion that she has poison oak. She supports her conclusion with the statements that she has red bumps on her arm, that they itch like the bumps the doctor previously diagnosed as poison oak, and that she and Jeremy walked through poison oak the weekend before.

Identifying Conclusions

To break up an argument, you need to be able to find its conclusion. When searching for a conclusion, ask yourself, *What is the main point the author is trying to establish, show, or prove?* When you find an answer to that question, you have found the conclusion.

Let's look at an example:

> Tabatha should be more careful where she walks in the future. She is susceptible to getting poison oak.

What is the main point the author is trying to establish, show, or prove in the above argument? *Tabatha should be more careful where she walks in the future*. Thus, "Tabatha should be more careful where she walks in the future" is the conclusion of the above argument.

When looking for conclusions, look for conclusion clue words and pay attention to statement placement.

Conclusion Clue Words   The following is a list of **conclusion clue words**:

thus	points to the conclusion that
therefore	proves that
so	gives us reason to believe that
consequently	establishes
hence	justifies
accordingly	supports
demonstrates that	we can conclude that
it follows that	

These words and phrases often precede conclusions. But notice that Tabatha's conclusion is *not* preceded by one of these words or phrases. Often there is no clue word to tip you off; you have to identify the relationship among statements to tell whether one of them is a conclusion.

Think about the definition of "argument" above. For a statement to be a conclusion, it must occur in conjunction with one or more statements that are intended to show, establish, or prove it.

Conclusion Placement   In argumentative essays, such as newspaper editorials, you will often find the conclusion (thesis) in the first or second paragraph and/or in the final paragraph.

You might be surprised to learn that conclusions can come at the beginning of arguments. You may think that conclusions must come last. This is a natural assumption, because the word "conclusion" sometimes means "last" or "final." In the context of an argument, however, "conclusion" has a different meaning. A statement becomes an argument's conclusion (thesis) *not* by its spacial or temporal position, but by its *relation* to other statements. If other statements are offered to support it, it is a conclusion. Otherwise, the statement is not an argument's conclusion (thesis), no matter where it occurs.

Conclusions of Subarguments   In the last few pages, I presented simple arguments, each of which had one stated conclusion. Many arguments are not so simple. Some arguments have several conclusions. Frequently, when offering a support statement for a conclusion, an author will offer support for the support statement. To help distinguish between these arguments, I will call supported support statements **subarguments.** I will call the argument as a whole the **main argument,** and its conclusion the **main conclusion.**

When you are reading an argument that contains subarguments, you will find more than one conclusion: the main conclusion of the main argu-

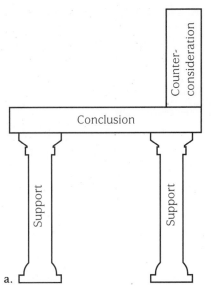

a.
Supports try to hold conclusions up. Counter-considerations try to push conclusions down.

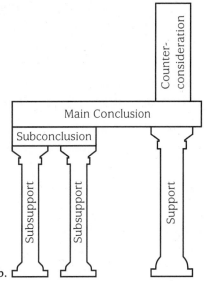

b.
Subconclusions support main conclusions and are themselves supported by subsupport.

ment and the **subconclusions** of the subarguments. The subarguments' conclusions have a dual role. They are *conclusions* of the subarguments and they *support* the main conclusion. Let's look at an example:

> Mrs. Wright was most likely the one who killed Mr. Wright. After all, she was acting strangely after his death. Also, Mrs. Wright had a motive for killing Mr. Wright. He had treated her harshly for years, and just before he was found dead, he had killed the one thing that gave her joy, a sweetly singing canary. Finally, Mrs. Wright had the opportunity to kill her husband. She was at home with him on the day of his death.

This argument contains one unsupported support statement:

Support 1:   Mrs. Wright was acting strangely after Mr. Wright's death.

and two subarguments, which include their **subsupports:**

Support 2 (Subconclusion):   Mrs. Wright had a motive for killing Mr. Wright.

Subsupport a: Mr. Wright had treated Mrs. Wright harshly for years.

Subsupport b: Mr. Wright killed Mrs. Wright's sweetly singing canary.

Subsupport c: Mrs. Wright's canary was the one thing that gave her joy.

Support 3 (Subconclusion):	Mrs. Wright had the opportunity to kill her husband.
Subsupport a:	She was at home with him on the evening of his death.

Supports 1, 2, and 3 offer support for the argument's main conclusion:

Mrs. Wright was most likely the one who killed Mr. Wright.

Notice that you can summarize the main argument by leaving out the support for the subconclusions. Here's what the main argument's summary looks like:

Conclusion:	Mrs. Wright was most likely the one who killed Mr. Wright.
Support 1:	Mrs. Wright was acting strangely after Mr. Wright's death.
Support 2:	Mrs. Wright had a motive for killing Mr. Wright.
Support 3:	Mrs. Wright had the opportunity to kill her husband.

Same Support, Different Conclusions   Sometimes authors use the same support to support two different conclusions. Let's look at an example.

Juanita earned the highest grade average in her graduating class. She'll most likely be offered a job at a good law firm, and she deserves that trip we promised her for good grades.

This argument has one support and two conclusions.

Conclusion 1:	She'll most likely be offered a job at a good law firm.
Conclusion 2:	She deserves that trip we promised her for good grades.
Support 1:	Juanita earned the highest grade average in her graduating class.

The Case of the Missing Conclusion   Sometimes the conclusion is just too obvious to state. Advertisers, for example, seek to convince their audiences of the conclusion "You should buy our product," but rarely do they state it. They rely on their audiences to figure it out.

Let's look at an example:

More people eat Yum Yums than any other snack on the market. They taste great, they're loaded with vitamins, and you can eat as many as you like without worrying about your waistline. Yum Yums have no calories.

Conclusion:	Buy Yum Yums.
Support 1:	More people eat Yum Yums than any other snack on the market.
Support 2:	They taste great.
Support 3:	They are loaded with vitamins.
Support 4 (Subconclusion):	You can eat as many as you like without worrying about your waistline.
Subsupport a:	Yum Yums have no calories.

Here's another example of an argument with a conclusion too obvious to state:

> *Cathy*: Mom, there's a party over at Jane's tonight. May I go?
>
> *Mom*: I warned you that the next time you stayed out late, I would ground you. You were an hour late last night.

What do you think Mom's answer to Cathy is?

No Conclusion Because No Argument   Remember, not everything is an argument. People frequently give each other information without intending that information to support a conclusion. The passages at the beginning of the chapter contain one such example:

> The annual Apple Blossom Fair will be held in Sebastopol the first weekend in May. On Saturday morning, the parade starts at 10:00 A.M., rain or shine. There will be displays in the Vets building all day Saturday and Sunday.

This passage provides information about the Apple Blossom Fair. It doesn't provide support for a conclusion.

Providing support for conclusions is only one purpose of communication. Some of the other purposes are discussed later in this chapter in the sections "Communication Enhancers" and "Support Avoidance."

Once again, if you're in doubt about whether you have an argument or some other form of communication in front of you, ask yourself whether the author intends to support a conclusion. If the answer is clearly yes, you have an argument. If not, then chances are you've got something else.

YOUR TURN B

◆ 1. Do you find any conclusion clue words in the following passages? What are they?

   a. There are big black clouds in the sky, and the air is turning cooler. Consequently, it's likely to rain soon.

   b. Children play more roughly after watching violent images on television. So, watching violent images causes children to play roughly. As a result, children should not be allowed to watch violent images on television.

   c. You want to go to Heidi's cabin? OK. Take a left at the next block, then go two more blocks and turn right. When you get to the end of that street, park your car. Look for the path between the two tallest redwoods at the end of the street. Follow that path past the pond, then go to the left when the path forks. The house will be on your left just past the blackberry patch.

◆ 2. List the conclusions you found in the passages above. Are any of them sub-conclusions?

Identifying Support

Webster's Third New International Dictionary defines "support" as "to serve as verification, corroboration, or substantiation."[2] "Support" has a similar meaning in this text. The support in an argument is the statement or statements *intended to verify, corroborate, or substantiate* the conclusion. In other words, the support answers these questions: What evidence, reasons, or premises does the author provide to *attempt to* establish, show, or prove the conclusion? Why does the author accept the conclusion? How does the author know the conclusion?

Notice the italicized phrase "attempt to." I am using "support" in this text to include statements that do in fact establish conclusions, as well as statements that are offered with the intention of establishing a conclusion but do not succeed. Consider the following passage:

Jim: John won't be coming to the movies with us tonight.

Steve: Why do you think that?

Jim: Because he's got too much homework.

Steve: Are you kidding? John never lets his homework stand in the way of seeing a good movie. He'll be there.

In this dialogue, Jim and Steve each offer support for a conclusion:

Jim's conclusion:	John won't be coming to the movies with us tonight.
Jim's support:	He has too much homework.
Steve's conclusion:	John will be coming to the movies with us tonight.
Steve's support:	John never lets his homework stand in the way of seeing a good movie.

Both Jim and Steve offer evidence in support of a conclusion. However, if Steve is right about John, Jim's support does not succeed in establishing his conclusion. Yet it is support nonetheless: Jim does *intend* his statement "He has too much homework" to provide evidence for his conclusion.

As with conclusions, when you look for support statements pay attention to certain clue words and to placement.

Support Clue Words   Key **support clue words** include the following:

follows from	may be inferred (deduced, derived) from
in as much as	for
after all	because
as shown by	since
for the reasons that	as indicated by

In a dialogue, the support sometimes follows the word "why." Consider an example from the passages at the beginning of the chapter:

Juan: We should eat an apple a day.

Stu: Why?

Juan: An apple a day keeps the doctor away.

Stu: OK.

The clue words listed here frequently introduce support statements, but not all support statements are introduced by a clue word.

Support Placement   In an argumentative essay, the middle paragraphs (body) of the essay generally contain the support for the conclusion (thesis). However, sometimes an author will introduce the essay with one of the more interesting supports to capture the reader's attention.

Not everything within the body of the essay or argumentative passage is offered as support. As we'll see later in this chapter, authors sometimes switch back and forth between offering support and achieving other goals, such as clarifying the meaning of words or distracting the audience from the author's weak points.

You can't rely on clue words or placement to guarantee you've found support, so you have to test the alleged support. If you can answer yes to one of the following questions, the statements you selected are the real thing.

1. Are the statements offered to show, establish, verify, or prove the truth or acceptability of the thesis (or conclusion)?

2. Do the statements provide answers to the questions, Why does the author accept the conclusion? and How does the author know the conclusion?

Unstated Support   When presenting arguments, we frequently do not state explicitly every support we have for the conclusion. As with conclusions, some of the supports are so obvious that we don't bother stating them. We can expect our audience to fill in these **unstated supports,** or **assumptions,** for themselves. Let's go back to Jim's argument about whether John will come to the movies:

Jim's conclusion: John won't be coming to the movies with us tonight.

Jim's support: He has too much homework.

In this argument, Jim was assuming that John cared more about finishing his homework than about seeing the movie they were going to see.

Unstated support: John cares more about finishing his homework than he does about seeing the movie we're going to see.

Notice that this assumption links Jim's stated support with his conclusion. In other words, Jim moves from his stated support through the unstated support to his conclusion.

We want to avoid being pedantic or simply boring, so we frequently don't spell out every step we take to get to our conclusions. However, sometimes we need to look closely at our assumptions to find the weak point in our argument.

Notice that Steve's support expresses a disagreement with Jim's assumption. Steve says John never lets his homework stand in the way of seeing a good movie. If Steve is correct, Jim's assumption about John was mistaken: John *doesn't* care as much about his homework as about seeing the movie.

Although we constantly rely on assumptions when reasoning from supports to conclusions, indentifying our assumptions and the assumptions of others can be tricky. It helps to have an understanding, first, of how to question the strength of the inference from the stated support to the conclusion. So we'll discuss finding assumptions in later chapters. At this point, just be aware that there's frequently more support for a conclusion than the *stated* support.

YOUR TURN C

◆ 1. Do you find any support clue words in the following arguments? What are they?

   a. Since I feel like kissing Jane, I should go ahead and kiss her.

   b. In as much as Jane turned her head away when I tried to kiss her, and she changes the subject when I try to discuss our becoming romantically involved, Jane probably does not want me to kiss her. Thus, I shouldn't try to kiss Jane again.

   c. John doesn't understand how to read my body language. After all, he keeps trying to kiss me, even though I turn my face away when he comes near. If he understood how to read my body language, he wouldn't keep trying to kiss me.

◆ 2. List the supports you found in arguments (a), (b), and (c) above. Are any of them subsupports?

◆ 3. Do you think there are any unstated supports in either of the arguments above? Write out what you think is being assumed.

Identifying Counterconsiderations

Many times in the process of reasoning toward a conclusion, people weigh evidence or reasons that support a particular conclusion against evidence or reasons that go against the conclusion. We call the evidence or reasons that go against a conclusion "counterconsiderations." Consider the following, for example:

> *Steve*: John will be coming to the movies tonight. True, he has a stack of homework, and he wants to get good grades in his classes. But we're going to see a great movie. And John never lets his homework stand in the way of seeing a good movie.

In this argument, Steve admits two statements that undermine his conclusion:

Counterconsideration 1:   John has a stack of homework.

Counterconsideration 2:   He wants to get good grades in his classes.

Steve then adds additional information to outweigh the undermining information:

Support 1:   We're going to see a great movie.

Support 2:   John never lets his homework stand in the way of seeing a good movie.

From supports 1 and 2, Steve concludes that John will go to the movies. Let's look at another example:

> Jane and I should talk with Professor Velasquez about the student who monopolizes the class conversation. Granted, on the one hand, we're nervous about talking with our teacher. And if we talk with her, we'll have to stay on campus later today than we'd planned. On the other hand, our teacher will be more likely to try to stop the student from monopolizing the conversation if she knows we want to participate but feel left out. And we really should participate more in this class. We learn more from class when we do.

This argument is a little more complex than the preceding one. It has not only counterconsiderations but also a subargument. Here's how it looks.

Conclusion: Jane and I should talk with Professor Velasquez about the student who monopolizes the class conversation.

Counterconsideration 1:   We're nervous about talking with Professor Velasquez.

Counterconsideration 2:   We'll have to stay on campus later than we'd planned if we talk with her.

Support 1:   Professor Velasquez will be more likely to stop the student from monopolizing the conversation if she knows we want to participate.

Support 2 (Subconclusion):   We should participate more in class.

Subsupport a: We learn more from class when we participate.

Support 3 (unstated):   Participating in class is more important to us than avoiding fear at talking with Professor Velasquez and leaving school when we'd planned.

Counterconsideration Clue Words   **Counterconsideration clue words** include the following:

although	in spite of (despite, notwithstanding) the fact that
even though	on the one hand
granted that	

One of the above words or phrases typically precedes a counterconsideration or a list of counterconsiderations. Authors typically introduce support to outweigh the counterconsideration(s) with one of the following words or phrases:

But	on the other hand	yet
still	more importantly	

The Case of the Missing Counterconsideration   For any solution you come up with, there are almost always reasons for it and reasons against it. Thus, you might expect to find counterconsiderations whenever an author presents support for a decision. However, argument authors frequently present no counterconsiderations. First, not all authors realize the full complexity of the problems they face. They leave out counterconsiderations because they don't see them. Second, authors sometimes see no need to state counterconsiderations because they will be obvious to the audience. Third, some authors hope their audiences will overlook counterconsiderations to what they recommend, or at any rate, they certainly don't want to remind their audiences of them. Consider, for example, whether you are likely to find counterconsiderations admitted by advertisers. "Yes, Yum Yums are the most expensive treat on the market, but . . ." And can you imagine a politician saying, "Granted I haven't done a very good job with foreign relations, but I have improved our domestic economy, so you should vote for me anyway"?

Don't expect to find counterconsiderations in every argument. But keep on the lookout for them nonetheless. That way, you'll be less susceptible to the one-sided reasoning of others.

YOUR TURN D

◆ 1. Do you find any counterconsideration clue words in the following arguments? What are they?

a. True, it hasn't rained in July for the last sixty years, which tends to indicate that the July 4 barbecue won't be rained out tomorrow, but there are big storm clouds overhead. We should have a backup plan ready.

b. Yes, eucalyptus are quick growing, they smell wonderful, and there's nothing like the sound of the breeze in their leaves. Still, they spread like weeds, crowding out California natives, and they're a fire hazard. Let's not plant eucalyptus in our pasture.

c. Let's buy a motorcycle instead of the used car your uncle offered us. The motorcycle costs less. It's more fun to ride, and it can get through traffic more easily than the car can.

◆ 2. List the counterconsiderations you found in arguments (a), (b), and (c) above. (**Note:** One of the arguments has no stated counterconsiderations. Can you think of some possible counterconsiderations for that argument?)

3. List the supports and conclusions you find in arguments (a), (b), and (c) above.

ARGUMENT EXTRAS

By now you should find it relatively easy to analyze a short argument into its support, counterconsiderations (if any), and conclusions. However, you may find yourself a little perplexed when reading or listening to longer argumentative essays and speeches, if you expect to find *only* supports, counterconsiderations, and conclusions.

Why? Because argument makers often include **argument extras.**

Communication Enhancers

Argument makers may want to provide the audience some general background about the issue, capture the audience's attention with a joke or story, define technical or vague terms for the audience, and elaborate on the argument's conclusion.

These activities enhance the communication of arguments, so I call them **communication enhancers.** However, though these activities help communicate arguments, they differ from providing support for a conclusion. As a result, when you're trying to identify the supports and conclusions in arguments, you need to put communication enhancers aside.

Consider the following introduction to a paper on capital punishment. Do you find any communication enhancers in this passage?

> What should society do when one person illegally kills another? Many governments have used capital punishment as a response. Executioners have nailed killers to crosses, placed their heads under the guillotine blade, tied nooses around their necks, strapped them into electric chairs, stood them before firing squads, and prepared them to receive a lethal drug dose. Yet illegal killing continues. In this paper, I will describe and analyze the problem of illegal killing, evaluate a range of solutions to the problem, and argue that state-sanctioned killing—whether by guillotine or syringe—is not the best response to illegal killing.

In this introduction you can find several communication enhancers: the statement describing some historical examples of capital punishment and a statement about what the author intends to do to come up with support for this conclusion ("analyze the problem of illegal killing, evaluate a range of solutions to the problem").

You can also find an element of argument: the conclusion the author plans to support ("state-sanctioned killing is not the best response to illegal killing"). And you can find a hint of the direction the author's support will take. You might suspect that the author will offer as one piece of support for the conclusion the fact that illegal killing continues in spite of capital punishment. You might also expect to see this support more explicitly stated as such in the body of the paper, along with additional support for the author's stated conclusion.

Let's look at another example. What argumentative elements and communication enhancers do you find here?

In this essay I will argue against the morality of euthanasia. "Euthanasia" is derived from Greek and originally meant "easy death." For the purposes of this paper, I use one of the contemporary definitions of euthanasia, namely, aiding a terminally ill person to die by withholding or removing a life-prolonging treatment.

I have nothing against dying an easy death. I wish that everyone could die a death without pain. But medical science has not taken us that far. Some people continue to die in great pain. Nonetheless, as I will show in this paper, aiding a person to die, however hard that person's death would otherwise be, is wrong.

Here are the argumentative elements I find:

Conclusion:	Euthanasia is wrong.
Counterconsideration:	Hard deaths are not to be wished for.
Counterconsideration:	Some people die in great pain.

The passage also contains a communication enhancer: clarification. The author gives the etymological definition of "euthanasia" and then stipulates the contemporary meaning of this term the author will use.

Let's look at another example. What communication enhancers and elements of argument do you find here?

Dad: You should clean up after dinner tonight. You said last Saturday you'd clean up every night this week if I gave you an extra $5.00 of allowance. And by the way, when I say "clean up tonight," I mean wash *all* of the dishes. Don't leave the pots and pans for me. Also, get them done *before* bedtime.

Here are the elements of argument:

Conclusion:	You should clean up after dinner tonight.
Support:	You said last Saturday you would clean up every night this week if I gave you an extra $5.00 of allowance.
Unstated support (Assumptions):	I gave you an extra $5.00 of allowance. You should do what you said you would.

The passage also contains a communication enhancer. Besides providing support for his conclusion, Dad is *amplifying* his conclusion: "And by the way, when I say 'clean up tonight,' I mean wash *all* of the dishes. Don't leave the pots and pans for me. Also, get them done *before* bedtime."

Support Avoidance

Sometimes when people offer a claim they want others to accept, they abandon support for their claim. I call this shift **support avoidance**. People use support avoidance for a variety of reasons. They may have only poor support

YOUR TURN E

◆ 1. What communication enhancers do you find in the following passage? What elements of argument do you find?

Should Students Learn a Foreign Language?

For some, the answer to this question is a loud NO. As one governmental official reportedly said, "If English was good enough for Jesus Christ, it's good enough for me." My mother, on the other hand, thinks students should learn a foreign language. She encouraged me to study German and Latin when I had the opportunity in high school, even though languages were not required at that time. Now—at the age of 70—she's studying Spanish on her home computer. I'm with my mother. I think students should learn a foreign language. And I hope to convince you of that in this essay.

Let me begin by telling you more of what I mean by learning a foreign language. Many people think they've learned a foreign language when they can read in that language. That's not what I mean. Of course, it's important to read in a foreign language, but you haven't really learned a foreign language until you can carry on a conversation in it on the complexities of people's lives and the world they live in.

Now let's look at some reasons why students should learn a foreign language. First of all, students cannot understand their own language and culture without knowing a foreign language. . . .

for their claim and hope their audience won't recognize that. They may have support but become impatient with a recalcitrant audience. They may be confused about what they're doing. Or they may just get bored with staying on the straight and narrow path of offering support.

Needless to say, support avoidance does not serve to support a claim. Thus, you need to be aware of the tactics of support avoidance to be better able to identify correctly the supports of an argument. Also, becoming aware of support avoidance can help you break up arguments, in another sense. When things get heated between you and your audience, you can use your understanding of support avoidance to cool things down and get back on the support track.

Repeating a Disagreement (Loudly)   As I've pointed out, there's a difference between giving reasons for a conclusion and disagreeing with another person. Furthermore, contrary to popular belief, people can't change mere disagreement into offering reasons by repeating themselves like two children: "Mommy said I could have it." "No, she didn't." "Yes, she did." "No." "Yes." "No." "Yes." Raising your voice doesn't turn disagreement into argument, either.

You can, of course, disagree in the context of exchanging reasons. People frequently disagree about something and then offer each other reasons in an effort to reach agreement. Also, repetition in the course of giving reasons sometimes enhances communication. When giving a speech, for example, your audience will be able to follow you more readily if you repeat your main support points periodically. Shouting can also enhance communication if you are at some distance from your audience. Nonetheless, repeating and shouting disagreement become support avoidance when they are offered *instead of* support.

Abusing the Audience   Abuse (including name calling, ridicule, and threat) is another common method of avoiding support. As the tongue-in-cheek advice to beginning attorneys goes, "When you've got the facts on your side, argue the facts; when you've got the law on your side, argue the law; when you've got neither the facts nor the law, attack the other attorney." In other words, when you have no legitimate support for your point of view, stop discussing it. Abuse your audience instead.

Let's look at an example from the passages at the beginning of the chapter.

Bob: We've got a bushel of apples. Let's make pies from the apples and freeze them.

Betty: No, we should make applesauce.

Bob: I said I want pies.

Betty: But I want applesauce.

Bob: No, it's pies, you health nut.

Betty: Applesauce, or you can just let the apples rot, for all I care.

In this example, Bob and Betty begin by expressing disagreement: One wants to make pies from the apples, whereas the other wants to make applesauce. When Betty continues to assert that she wants applesauce, Bob switches from repeating himself to abuse, calling Betty a "health nut." Betty retaliates with a threat. Her comment "Applesauce, or you can just let the apples rot, for all I care" expresses the threat that she won't do anything with the apples if Bob doesn't agree with her.

As noted earlier, people sometimes enjoy exchanging abuse during a friendly discussion. For them, abuse becomes a communication enhancer, because it keeps them alert and on their toes. Also, when people exchange reasons in a public setting, sometimes they—like TV wrestlers who stomp on each other for the entertainment value—engage in a bit of bashing for the enjoyment of the bystanders.

Distracting the Audience   In conversations, disputing parties use a number of tactics to avoid exchanging support. They try to distract each other by changing the subject or interrupting.

"My old shoes are killing my feet. I think I should buy these sandals with the lower heels and wider toes. What do you think, Josie?"

"I think your perm is growing out. Why don't you get a new one?"

Josie avoids exchanging support by changing the subject.

So far, I've identified a number of ways that parties avoid giving or receiving support for a claim: repeating the claim; shouting; abusing the audience by name calling, ridicule, or threat; and distracting the audience by changing the subject and interrupting. As you become attentive to the difference between supporting a claim and avoiding support, you'll no doubt discover other tactics speakers and writers use to avoid giving support.

How to Refocus on Support Sometimes people move back and forth easily between avoiding and giving support. Other times, we get derailed from argument by support avoidance. After being ridiculed, interrupted, or shouted at, for example, we have difficulty finding our way back to exchanging reasons. Here are some tips for getting back on the support track.

1. Notice the support avoidance, but do not call attention to it or let it distract you. Take a deep breath. Go back to the last element of argument you recall, and carry on from there.

2. Jokingly agree with the attack, then direct the discussion away from the attack and back to the original point. "You may be right about that. Perhaps I am off my rocker. But that's not what we came here to talk about. Let's get back to that topic." If you prefer a less self-deprecating

response, you could say, "I'm not so sure about your sanity either, but whether you or I, or both of us, need psychiatric care is not the issue here. We came to discuss . . . ." If you're the one who makes the attack, you could try a joke: "Oops, I've done it again. Open mouth, insert foot. Give me a minute to take it out, and I'll try again to tell you why I think we should . . ."

3. Call attention to the support avoidance, and ask the other person to stop. You might say, "I'm having a hard time listening to you when you're shouting at me and calling me names. I want to hear what you say. Could you repeat your point without shouting or name calling?" If you're the one who made the attack, you might try an apology: "I'm sorry. I don't want to offend you. I got carried away because I really care about this issue. Let me phrase that another way. . . ."

4. If the other person continues the support avoidance, suggest taking a break until you're both ready to exchange support. You could say, "I'd like to hear more of what you think about the topic we came together to discuss, but how about taking a break? We don't seem to be getting anywhere right now." If you're the one who keeps introducing support avoidance, you might say, "I'm having trouble concentrating right now. Let's take a break and discuss this later."

The language above may not suit you. Use these suggestions to prime the pump of your imaginations; you don't have to memorize and use them verbatim.

Besides these tips for getting back on the support track, you may find useful some of the techniques of conflict resolution described at the end of Chapter 2.

YOUR TURN F

◆ 1. Identify the elements of argument and tactics of support avoidance in the following examples.

a. A dialogue about capital punishment

Carol: Jed, do you believe in capital punishment?

Jed: Sure. People who commit murder deserve to be killed themselves. You'd have to be a fool or some kind of liberal not to believe in capital punishment.

b. Homework dialogue

Goldie: Gosh, it's almost time to go to class, and I haven't done the CT homework yet. May I look at yours?

Sean: No, Goldie, that wouldn't be right. You'd be giving a false impression to the teacher.

Goldie: Come on, Sean. Don't be such a goodie-two-shoes. I need a good grade in this class.

(continued)

Sean: I understand that, Goldie. You do need a good grade in critical thinking. But you also need to learn how to think for yourself. Copying my answers won't help you learn how to answer them yourself.

Goldie: If you won't give me those answers, I won't give you a ride over to your girlfriend's house tonight.

Sean: Look, Goldie, I understand that you are concerned about your grade. But I just don't think it's right to copy my work. We could both get in trouble that way.

2. You have probably witnessed tactics for avoiding support other than the ones discussed. Can you give some examples?

LOOKING FOR ARGUMENTS

Except in the "Monty Python" sketch, there are no argument clinics, so when you want to find an argument, where should you go? The following are some suggestions about where to look and where not to look. But be wary. These suggestions are *not* formulas for you to apply *without thinking*. You have a good chance of finding arguments in these places, but they'll probably be mixed with communication enhancers and support avoidance. Sometimes you won't find an argument at all.

In other words, the places I recommend are like my lettuce patch, where flowers and weeds grow among the lettuce. You'll have a better chance of finding lettuce there than in the back pasture, but you can't pick indiscriminately, or you might bring in marigolds or dandelions for supper instead of lettuce. And if it's late in the season, there may be no lettuce left at all.

Here are some places where you can expect to find written arguments:

1. Newspaper and magazine editorials, op-ed pages of newspapers, letters to the editor, movie and book reviews (those that do not merely summarize the movie or book but draw conclusions about it)

2. Medical, philosophy, sociology, history, and other scholarly or scientific journals in which scholars and researchers try to convince each other of the truth of their findings

3. Supreme Court decisions

4. Advertisements, requests for contributions, and other written material that is trying to get you to buy or do something

Here are some places where you can expect to find oral (and written) arguments:

1. Contexts in which people are trying to figure out what happened and why: jury room, detective investigations, diagnosing illness

2. Contexts in which people are trying to decide how to evaluate things: art show judging, grading essays, movie reviews

3. Contexts in which people are trying to decide how to act: law courts, legislatures, football huddles, friends deciding which movie or restaurant to go to

Here are some contexts in which arguments are frequently absent:

1. Contexts in which the purpose is to report or summarize events or findings: news articles (although news articles sometimes report excerpts from arguments, they generally are not *themselves* arguments, nor do they typically report complete arguments made by others), self-help books and articles, "how to" books and articles, encyclopedias and textbooks that merely report conclusions about historical happenings or scientific inquiry rather than show the reasoning that led to those conclusions

2. Contexts in which the purpose is to set forth definitions: dictionaries, introductory paragraphs of essays and textbook chapters

This chapter has given you the basic information you need to recognize and write arguments. Now that you have an idea of what an argument is, you are in a better position to exchange reasons with others during conflict resolution and to write arguments in support of your decisions. You are now ready to practice enhancing the communication of your arguments by defining key terms, the topic of the next chapter.

EXERCISES

1. List the main conclusions and subconclusions you find in the passages below. Circle conclusion clue words.

   a. Millions of people and animals have suffered and died from earthquakes, famines, and disease. When you suffer or die, you are harmed. Being harmed is evil. It's not possible to be totally good and cause evil. So either God isn't totally good, or God doesn't cause everything.

   b. No one can know that gods or goddesses exist. The only way to know that something exists is by using your senses. You have to see, hear, taste, touch, or smell something to know it exists. No one can see, hear, taste, touch, or smell gods and goddesses. So no one can know whether or not they exist.

   c. You should believe that a God or Goddess exists. The world looks and feels different to someone who believes in the supernatural. It's a richer, more mysterious place. Also, you'll want to please the God or Goddess. As a result, you'll be more likely to treat others well if you believe a God or Goddess exists.

d. People who believe in a male God should add a female God to their worship. A male God gives men the hope that they can improve themselves spiritually but does little for women. For women could not be formed in a male God's image. Men and women should respect each other as equally God-like, so they should worship male and female Gods.

e. The following excerpt from logician and social critic Bertrand Russell's "Why I Am Not a Christian":

> . . . There is one very serious defect to my mind in Christ's moral character, and that is that He believed in hell. I do not myself feel that any person who is really profoundly humane can believe in everlasting punishment. Christ certainly as depicted in the Gospels did believe in everlasting punishment, and one does find repeatedly a vindictive fury against those people who would not listen to His preaching—an attitude which is not uncommon with preachers, but which does somewhat distract from superlative excellence. You do not, for instance, find that attitude in Socrates. You find him quite bland and urbane toward the people who would not listen to him; and it is, to my mind, far more worthy of a sage to take that line than to take the line of indignation. . . .
>
> You will find in the Gospels Christ said, "Ye serpents, ye generation of vipers, how can ye escape the damnation of hell." That was said to people who did not like His preaching. It is not really to my mind quite the best tone, and there are a great many things about hell [in the Bible]. . . . I really do not think that a person with the proper degree of kindliness in his nature would have put fears and terrors of that sort into the world. . . .
>
> . . . I cannot myself feel that . . . in the matter of virtue Christ stands quite as high as some other people known to history. I think I should put Buddha and Socrates above Him in those respects.[3]

2. List the supports, including subsupports, you find in the passages below.[4] Circle support clue words. (Be on the lookout for passages that contain no arguments.)

a. The phone call

Operator: Will you accept a collect call from Mark?
Dad: OK.
Mark: Hello Dad, I'm running short of cash and need to pay my phone bill. Can you help me out?
Dad: What happened, Mark? Did you lose your job?
Mark: No, I've just had some unexpected expenses, and I'm short.
Dad: What were the unexpected expenses? Have you been sick? Did your car break down?

Mark: No, I met someone I really like. We've been going out to listen to music. Those tickets are expensive.

Dad: Our agreement was that if I paid for your tuition, books, and rent, you would work and pay for the rest from your part-time job. I'm sorry, son. You'll have to call the telephone company and make arrangements to pay them off over time.

Mark: But, Dad, I really want to impress this woman. How can I do that without spending money?

Dad: With your sense of humor, Mark. And by showing her how responsible you are. That's how I impressed your mom.

Mark: (Groan.)

b. The razor case

Jorge: Hey, which one of you has been using my razor? I've told you guys not to use it.

Juan: What makes you think someone's been using your razor?

Jorge: It wasn't where I left it last time.

Juan: Let's see it. . . . Look at this light hair. It's not mine. My hair's as dark as yours, Juan. What about you, Tim?

Tim: Don't try to pin it on me. I'm not the only one with blond hair around here. Your new girlfriend has blond hair, Jorge.

Jorge: Oh, OK, you guys. I'll talk with her about it.

c. In most universities, faculty members go through a process of review, which, if satisfactory, results in their becoming permanent members of the faculty. This process is called the tenure system. The review period typically lasts for six years, and during that time faculty must convince their reviewers that they are good teachers and scholars and congenial members of the university community. Once tenured, faculty cannot be fired, even if the quality of their teaching, scholarship, or good humor deteriorates, unless they have done some egregious wrong. They are, however, occasionally laid off as a result of an unexpected financial crisis.

d. The tenure system should be abolished. It's virtually impossible to fire someone with tenure, regardless of poor productivity. College professors should be judged by productivity, just like everyone else.

e. Communities are more likely to donate funds to support ideas they agree with than ideas they disagree with. In this day of tight budgets, administrators would be inclined to respond to public pressure and rehire only professors who espouse popular views, if professors weren't protected with tenure. Because the unpopular views of today are often the views that prepare us for tomorrow, unpopular views should be taught. The tenure system should continue because professors will be more likely to teach unpopular views if they do not fear getting fired.

3. List the counterconsiderations you find in the passages below. Circle counterconsideration clue words. (Beware: not all of these examples include counterconsiderations.)

    a. Counties should pass domestic partnership laws allowing unmarried persons who live together to share health insurance and other benefits, the way married couples do. After all, lesbian and gay couples need health insurance and other benefits as much as heterosexual couples do. It's unfair to exclude homosexuals and lesbians from receiving social goods, because lesbian and gay people contribute as much to society as heterosexual people. Granted, lesbian and gay couples don't produce children who are biologically related to both members of the couple, but then neither do many heterosexual couples. And lesbian and gay couples help care for the existing children who need care. Gay and lesbian couples should also have the right to get married, if they choose.

    b. True, we haven't graduated from college yet. But we both have jobs, and we love each other. Besides, our parents would like us to get married. So we should go ahead and get married.

    c. I don't think I'm pregnant. I have been feeling a bit sick in the mornings, but I've been staying up late. Besides, I'm using very reliable birth control.

    d. Granted, college professors should teach unpopular views. Nonetheless, they still should not be given tenure. They should have the courage of their convictions.

    e. You should come to class whether you've finished the paper due that day or not. Otherwise, you commit two sins: both missing class and not having your paper done on time.

4. What communication enhancers, support avoidance, and elements of argument do you find in the passages below?

    a. An excerpt from "Comparable Worth, Incomparable Pay":

> When the Equal Pay Act of 1963 prohibited unequal pay for equal work and the broader Civil Rights Act of 1964 set affirmative action into motion, many assumed that the gap between men and women's wages would close. Instead, the average salary for a woman working full-time year-round remained roughly 60 percent of the salary earned by a man. The constancy of the wage gap in the face of antidiscrimination legislation drew attention to the fact that women and men rarely hold the same jobs. Traditional sex roles and outright sex discrimination by employers and workers have had the result of excluding women from most occupations other than homemaking and its labor market exten-

sions. Those paid occupations open to women shared low pay, few opportunities for advancement, and often centered around nurturing and serving others. . . .

The idea of comparable worth was devised to raise women's wages in female-dominated occupations up to the level paid in male occupations of "comparable worth." Also known as pay equity, comparable worth means that jobs deemed to be of "equal value to the employer" should pay the same, regardless of their sex or race-typing. . . .[5]

b. An excerpt from "The Just Wage: From Bad to Worth":

The latest entry on the list of sacred democratic causes is comparable worth. According to that doctrine, it is demonstrable that low-paying female-dominated jobs, like nursing, are worth as much (to employers or society) as "comparable" male-dominated jobs, like plumbing, and that therefore by right and by law they should be paid the same. Comparable worth has become not only *the* women's issue of the 1980s, but also the most prominent civil rights issue not specifically directed at blacks. The Democratic party has warmly embraced it. Every one of its presidential candidates has endorsed it. In the 1984 platform, that sea of well-intended ambiguity and evasion, there are few islands of certainty. Comparable worth is one of them. . . .[6]

c. Kitchen chores

Sue: I cooked dinner tonight. You should wash the dishes. We have an agreement to share kitchen chores.
Jane: I have done all the yard chores. I don't have time to do the dishes. I have homework to do.
Sue: Both of us have homework. That's not the point. We made an agreement to share the kitchen chores, and it's your turn.
Jane: You heartless bitch.
Sue: Please don't scream at me. How about if we study for a while, then discuss the dishes.

d. Affection expected

Julie: I've taken you out and showed you a good time. Now it's payback time.
Dave: You enjoyed yourself, too. I don't owe you anything.
Julie: I've spent money on you, and I deserve a return on my money.
Dave: My affection is not for sale. Take me home.
Julie: Come on, give me a kiss at least. Do you want it to get around that you can't produce?

e. Walking or driving?

Stu: You should drive to school today.
Sid: I prefer walking because it's more healthy.
Stu: But if you drive, you can do some errands we need done.
Sid: OK.

Animals Have No Rights

Jon Margolis

Jon Margolis is a columnist for the *Chicago Tribune*.

CHICAGO—Among the smaller pities of life is that the organized opposition to the "animal rights" movement is being led by furriers and butchers.

Their leadership makes it too easy to dismiss their case as mere greed, and among the larger pities of life is that the ranks of those of us who find greed preferable to earnestness have diminished. The nice thing about people motivated by greed is that you can cut a deal with them. People motivated by earnest conviction are dangerous.

However they are motivated, and however unconvincing some of their slogans (calling mink a "renewable resource" is stretching things a bit), the furriers and the butchers are right. Animals, as all true animal lovers know, can have no rights.

Only human beings can have rights because only human beings can have responsibilities, among the most basic of which is to treat animals with kindness, or at least without cruelty.

Certain animals can be trained to exercise limited, operational responsibilities. There are guide dogs and beasts of burden.

But animals face no moral choices, and therefore exercise no moral responsibility. This is a qualitative difference between them and us.

Seeing a bird hopping about nearby, a cat does not pause to consider the ethics of the situation. He pounces. Nature offers no protection of the bird's right to life, liberty and the pursuit of happiness when weighed against the cat's pursuit of food.

Or, quite often, of fun. Extremists among the animal rightsniks insist that only human beings kill for enjoyment, a proposition which

no minimally observant cat owner can accept. Cats who have just had a full meal will grab a bird or mouse, torment it as long as possible and then proudly bring the not-quite-dead victim to the front door to show what great hunters they are.

• • •

The cruelty done to animals by people pales beside the cruelty one animal commits against another, often of its own species. The bass you fool with your popping bug may not like being caught on your hook. But neither did several thousand of his own children like being his supper just minutes earlier.

Or consider, if you've a strong stomach, chickens. They do not form a harmonious community. Should one of them get a small sore, her flock-mates will be all over her, pecking wildly and tearing at the flesh until the poor thing is dead. Chickens are stupid and despicable creatures, worthless but for being the source of tasty and nutritious meat and eggs.

Animals have feelings, which is why we ought not treat them cruelly. What they lack is consciousness of their own existence.

Those of us who have raised goats know that one method for people who want to milk a goat is to blindfold the doe just before she begins labor, and then to spirit her newborn kid out of her sight. She will not know that she has given birth and will not object when her owner, rather than her offspring, begins milking.

If she sees the kid, the doe will lick off the placenta, nurture her newborn and act in a manner which resembles, and may be, a mother's love. But this is instinct, not consciousness. In a few weeks, when the kid is weaned, its mother will not recognize it as her own.

. . .

A creature which does not know when it will create life does not know that it will die, even if its instinct impels it to fight death. We all know we will die. That's why we created psychiatrists, martinis, meditation, poetry and (perhaps) religion.

Animals are our dependents. It makes no difference whether or not God gave us "dominion" over them, as the Bible says. We have it anyway, by dint of our natural (if not always physical) superiority.

This applies to the lions in the jungle as much as to the kittens and parakeets in the living room. It's another reason we're obligated not to mistreat them, but also another reason why they have no rights. Rights accrue only to the independent, because only the independent can be responsible. All societies restrict the rights of children, who are not yet independent. Animals are like children who will never grow up.

Like most extremist political movements, the animal crusade is as correct in several specifics as it is wrong in general.

To make veal, it is necessary to kill calves.

Until then it is not necessary to chain them so tightly that they cannot move.

Injuring animals or making them sick to find cures for disease is one thing. Blinding rabbits to test cosmetics is quite another.

The animal protection movement performs a service when it points out how frequently people fail to meet their responsibilities to animals. It damages its own case when it tries to invest "rights" in creatures that lack moral sense.

Next time someone calls you a "speciesist," thank him for the compliment.

Questions

1. Do you find a main conclusion in Margolis's essay? If so, what is it? If not, explain why not.
2. Do you find support for a conclusion in Margolis's essay? What is it?
3. Do you find any counterconsiderations in Margolis's essay? If not, write one for him.
4. Do you find any communication enhancers in Margolis's essay?
5. Do you find any support avoidance in Margolis's essay?
6. Is there another question you would like to discuss about Margolis's essay?

Rights for Animals

Serge Etienne

The following is a letter to the editor in response to the above essay.

Editor: Regarding Jon Margolis' March 20 column, "Animals have no rights":

His notion that "Only human beings can have rights because only human beings can have responsibilities" is spurious. We grant rights to infants, the mentally infirm, and comatose individuals. Even those who have proven themselves to be irresponsible due to their criminal behavior have rights.

His attempt to dismiss the cruelty that humans do to animals by attributing the same criticism to fish, cats and chickens, is to commit two errors with one thought.

When cooped chickens turn on one of their own kind and peck it to death it is not out of some preconceived plan to inflict pain and suffering, but rather an abnormal reaction to man's overcrowded confinement practices. Chickens with plentiful range available to them do not behave in that way.

On the other hand, the cruelty that humans inflict on their animal brethren is unforgivable precisely because we do so with full knowledge and aforethought of the pain and suffering that will ensue from our acts.

Margolis shows his true feathers when he writes that "Chickens are stupid and despicable creatures, worthless but for being the source of tasty and nutritious meat and eggs."

In fact, chickens—when allowed to live in a reasonably natural environment—are alert, vivaciously social, and courageous in protecting their young and the rest of their flock. To view them merely as biped protein factories is indicative of great self-centeredness.

Questions

1. Do you find a main conclusion in Etienne's essay? If so what is it? If not, explain why not.
2. Do you find support for a conclusion in Etienne's essay? What is it?
3. Do you find any counterconsiderations in Etienne's essay? If not, write one for him.
4. Do you find any communication enhancers in Etienne's essay?
5. Do you find any support avoidance in Etienne's essay?
6. Is there another question you would like to discuss about Etienne's essay?

Death Penalty No Deterrent

Frances Byrn

The following essay was published in the *Press Democrat* (Santa Rosa, CA), March 29, 1990. At the time Frances Byrn was chairperson of the American Civil Liberties Union of Sonoma County.

On April 3, California will join the Soviet Union, China, Iran, Iraq and South Africa if it executes Robert Harris. No other democratic industrialized country kills its own citizens.

With almost 300 people on death row in California, it is important to understand what's wrong with the death penalty before the bloodbath begins.

The death penalty is not a deterrent. The many studies conducted have proved that the death penalty does not reduce the murder rate. In fact, studies in New York and California (when they were executing people) show that the murder rate actually goes up with each execution. Unstable people react to the publicity surrounding executions with "copycat" crimes or use the state to help them commit "suicide." That is why states without the death penalty have a lower murder rate than states that kill.

The average cost to the taxpayer of each death penalty prosecution exceeds $1 million. A 1988 study by the *Sacramento Bee* concluded that California taxpayers would save more than $90 million a year if the death penalty were replaced with life sentences without the possibility of parole. A jury in a death penalty case has the power to give this sentence.

Not only could the money saved be used to help others, but the person could earn money in prison to pay restitution to the victim's family.

• • •

The death penalty always has been administered in a discriminatory fashion. Studies have shown that it is the poor, uneducated, mentally retarded and people of color who are more likely to be sentenced to death.

Likewise, if the victim is white, middle or upper class, the death penalty is more likely to be given.

This means that it is the IQ, class, and race of the perpetrator—and the race and class of the victim—which determines whether the state will kill, not the act committed.

Robert Harris was born with fetal alcohol syndrome. Brutally beaten while in the womb and as a child, he is brain-damaged. He is an example of those we kill.

Death penalty prosecutions also punish the families of the victim. The long appeal process prevents the family from moving on with their lives. Yet, it is in their name that politicians running for office sponsor law after law that take away rights from all California citizens. These laws increase the likelihood that innocent people will be executed (a Stanford Law Review study documented more than 350 innocent people sentenced to death in America in this century). After an execution, you cannot correct a wrongful conviction.

Worldwide, the number of countries that kill its own citizens is decreasing. Most countries look upon the death penalty as a violation of human rights. Almost all organized religions and human rights groups oppose it.

It is time for California and America to move with the rest of the world and say all killing is wrong. A judicial system based on revenge cannot do justice.

Questions

1. What main conclusion do you find in Frances Byrn's essay?
2. What are some of the main supports for Byrn's main conclusion?
3. Are any of the supports for Byrn's conclusion also subconclusions? If so, identify the subsupport for the subconclusion.
4. Does Byrn provide any counterconsiderations in her essay? If not, do you recommend any? Explain.
5. Do you find any communication enhancers in Byrn's essay? If not, do you recommend any? Explain.
6. Does Byrn use any support avoidance tactics in her essay?
7. Is there another question you would like to discuss about Byrn's essay?

Death and Justice: How Capital Punishment Affirms Life

Edward I. Koch

Edward I. Koch (b. 1924) was mayor of New York from 1978 to 1989.

Last December a man named Robert Lee Willie, who had been convicted of raping and murdering an eighteen-year-old woman, was executed in the Louisiana state prison. In a statement issued several minutes before his death, Mr. Willie said: "Killing people is wrong. . . . It makes no difference whether it's citizens, countries, or governments. Killing is wrong." Two weeks later in South Carolina, an admitted killer named Joseph Carl Shaw was put to death for murdering two teenagers. In an appeal to the governor for clemency, Mr. Shaw wrote: "Killing is wrong when I did it. Killing is wrong when you do it. I hope you have the courage and moral strength to stop the killing. . . ."

Life is indeed precious, and I believe the death penalty helps to affirm this fact. Had the death penalty been a real possibility in the minds of these murderers, they may well have stayed their hand. They might have shown moral awareness before their victims died, and not after. Consider the tragic death of Rosa Velez, who happened to be home when a man named Luis Vera burglarized her apartment in Brooklyn. "Yeah, I shot her," Vera admitted. "She knew me, and I knew I wouldn't go to the chair."

During my twenty-two years in public service, I have heard the pros and cons of capital punishment expressed with special intensity. As a district leader, councilman, congressman, and mayor, I have represented constituencies generally thought of as liberal. Because I support the death penalty for heinous crimes of murder, I have sometimes been the subject of emotional and outraged attacks by voters who find my position reprehensible or worse. I have listened to their ideas. I have weighed their objections carefully. I still support the death penalty. The reasons I maintain my position can be best understood by examining the arguments most frequently heard in opposition. . . .

2. No other major democracy uses the death penalty. No other major democracy—in fact, few other countries of any description—are plagued by a murder rate such as that in the United States. Fewer and fewer Americans can remember the days when unlocked doors were the norm and murder was a rare and terrible offense. In America the murder rate climbed 122 percent between 1963 and 1980. During that same period, the murder rate in New York City increased by almost 400 percent, and the statistics are even worse in many other cities. A study at M.I.T. showed that based on 1970 homicide rates a person who lived in a large American city ran a greater risk of being murdered than an American soldier in World War II ran of being killed in combat. It is not surprising that the laws of each country differ according to differing conditions and traditions. If other countries had our murder problem, the cry

for capital punishment would be just as loud as it is here. And I daresay that any other major democracy where 75 percent of the people supported the death penalty would soon enact it into law. . . .

5. The death penalty is applied in a discriminatory manner. This factor no longer seems to be the problem it once was. The appeals process for a condemned prisoner is lengthy and painstaking. Every effort is made to see that the verdict and sentence were fairly arrived at. However, assertions of discrimination are not an argument for ending the death penalty but for extending it. It is not justice to exclude everyone from the penalty of the law if a few are found to be so favored. Justice requires that the law be applied to all.

6. Thou Shalt Not Kill. The Bible is our greatest source of moral inspiration. Opponents of the death penalty frequently cite the sixth of the Ten Commandments in an attempt to prove that capital punishment is divinely proscribed. In the original Hebrew, however, the Sixth Commandment reads "Thou Shalt Not Commit Murder," and the Torah specifies capital punishment for a variety of offenses. . . .

7. The death penalty is state-sanctioned murder. This is the defense with which Messrs. Willie and Shaw hoped to soften the resolve of those who sentenced them to death. By saying in effect, "You're no better than I am," the murderer seeks to bring his accusers down to his own level. It is also a popular argument among opponents of capital punishment, but a transparently false one. Simply put, the state has rights that the private individual does not. In a democracy, those rights are given to the state by the electorate. The execution of a lawfully condemned killer is no more an act of murder than is legal imprisonment an act of kidnapping. If an individual forces a neighbor to pay him money under threat of punishment, it's called extortion. If the state does it, it's called taxation. Rights and responsibilities surrendered by the individual are what give the state its power to govern. This contract is the foundation of civilization itself.

Everyone wants his or her rights, and will defend them jealously. Not everyone, however, wants responsibilities, especially the painful responsibilities that come with law enforcement. Twenty-one years ago a woman named Kitty Genovese was assaulted and murdered on a street in New York. Dozens of neighbors heard her cries for help but did nothing to assist her. They didn't even call the police. . . .

The death of anyone—even a convicted killer—diminishes us all. But we are diminished even more by a justice system that fails to function. It is an illusion to let ourselves believe that doing away with capital punishment removes the murderer's deed from our conscience. The rights of society are paramount. When we protect guilty lives, we give up innocent lives in exchange. When opponents of capital punishment say to the state, "I will not let you kill in my name," they are also saying to murderers: "You can kill in

your *own* name as long as I have an excuse for not getting involved."

It is hard to imagine anything worse than being murdered while neighbors do nothing. But something worse exists. When those same neighbors shrink back from justly punishing the murderer, the victim dies twice.

Questions

1. What main conclusion do you find in Edward I. Koch's essay?
2. What are some of the main supports for Koch's main conclusion?
3. Are any of the supports for Koch's conclusion also subconclusions? If so, identify the subsupport for the subconclusion.
4. Does Koch provide any counterconsiderations in his essay? If not, can you think of any counterconsiderations relevant to Koch's conclusion?
5. Do you find any communication enhancers in Koch's essay? If not, would you recommend any? Explain.
6. Does Koch use any support avoidance tactics in his essay?
7. Is there another question you would like to discuss about Koch's essay?

WRITING IDEAS

1. Write an argument which contains a main conclusion, at least three supports (at least one of which is a subconclusion), and at least one counterconsideration. Edit your writing, checking for spelling, word choice, organization, and clarity. Write on one of the following topics or a topic of your choice:

   a. Should couples share household tasks?

   b. Should grade-school teachers be permitted to paddle their students?

   c. Should students be required to do community service before they graduate from college?

   After you have typed your argument, take a pencil and underline its conclusions. Put a check by the main conclusion, and number the support statements. Put brackets around your counterconsideration.

2. Write a dialogue of an argument you got into with someone. Write about whether you were exchanging reasons with the other person, avoiding support, or doing a little of each.

3. Look through the letters to the editor in your local paper. Find a letter that states an argument for a position you disagree with. Write a letter to the editor that states an argument for your position.

4. Review an argument you have written previously. Rewrite the argument, adding additional support for your conclusion or a counterconsideration you didn't include before. Edit anything from your argument that you now believe does not help support your conclusion or enhance the communication of your argument. Also edit out repetitive statements.

5. Write about whether this chapter and your class discussions complemented, conflicted with, supported, or left out any of your previous ideas about arguments.

Notes

1. Note that you have already started taking apart arguments. In Chapter 1, you identified interpretations or conclusions and distinguished them from the evidence you had before you.
2. "Support," *Webster's Third New International Dictionary*, 1981 ed.
3. Bertrand Russell, "Why I Am Not a Christian," *Current Issues and Enduring Questions*, eds. Sylvan Barnet and Hugo Bedau (Boston: St. Martin's Press, 1990) 665–66.
4. Ideas for passages (a), (b), and other dialogues below came from Carol Paoli. Passages (c) through (e) were inspired by Margaret Edwards, "Tenure: A Fitting Reward for a Long Apprenticeship," Barnet and Bedau 163–65 and R. Keith Miller, "Tenure: A Cause of Intellectual Cowardice," Barnet and Bedau 161–62.
5. Teresa Amott and Julie Matthaei, "Comparable Worth, Incomparable Pay," Barnet and Bedau 166.
6. Charles Krauthammer, "The Just Wage: From Bad to Worth," Barnet and Bedau 174.

4

Deciding on Definitions

CHAPTER GOALS

- To become alert to the multiple meanings of words.
- To learn to distinguish different types of definitions, including definitions by example, connotative definitions, and expressive definitions.
- To learn how to develop definitions by using resource books as well as your own experience, analytic skills, and imagination.
- To learn how to critique definitions, using such criteria as clarity and scope.
- To use your knowledge to write the definition section of an argumentative essay or speech.

YOUR THOUGHTS ABOUT DEFINITIONS

When do you find it useful to define words? Jot down your ideas; then read this article and answer the questions that follow.

Defining "Sexual Infidelity"

Mary O'Brien

Mary O'Brien is a professor of epidemiology at the University of Illinois at Chicago, where she studies sexual behavior to understand the risks of AIDS to the general population.

. . . Do we . . . agree about what constitutes sexual infidelity? Is intercourse necessary? Fondling? What about watching? What about other forms of involvement: sharing secrets, sharing glances, even sharing intense involvement with work? [Let's look at some examples.]

1. Arthur is happily married to Eunice, and has never pursued another woman outside his marriage. On a business trip to New York, his client, whom he knows well and likes as a friend, takes him to a posh, men-only club in which exceptionally lovely, fresh-faced young women serve drinks topless and perform sexually explicit dances in the nude. One beauty comes on to Arthur, and "dances," naked, on his lap, until he puts a $20 bill in her G-string. Arthur is extremely aroused. . . .

2. Andrea and Jennifer have lived together for five years and have an explicit agreement that they will not have sex of any kind with others. They like to go out to lesbian bars with friends on the weekend, but Andrea's flirtatious behavior always troubles Jennifer. They both acknowledge that bars are generally a scene for picking people up, but they both want to keep going because that's where their friends are, and they want and need to connect with other lesbians outside the straight world in which they otherwise live and work. Andrea's behavior, however, leads to fights when they get home. . . .

3. Co-workers Maria and David are both happily married (not to each other). They are frequently assigned to the same accounts in their ad agency, and their work requires occasional trips out of town together. Maria loves David as a friend—his insights and creativity are a source of inspiration to her. Maria's husband is very jealous of her relationship with David. He would like her to change jobs, but knows that asking her to look for a different job would appear ridiculous—he knows that there is nothing sexual between Maria and David. . . .

4. Jim was out of town, unexpectedly ran into an old girlfriend, had drinks with her, and ended up sleeping with her. As far as both are concerned, it was a one-time, chance event. Neither wants to pursue a relationship, sexual or otherwise. Jim returns home from his trip and doesn't tell his wife, Sharon, about the encounter. In fact, it doesn't even occur to him to tell her. As far as he is concerned, it was a one-time event unconnected to his marriage to Sharon, whom he deeply loves. . . .

5. Renee has been in love with Tony for seven years. They have a clandestine sexual relationship that is extremely fulfilling and important to both of them. Renee is married to Bill, whom she also loves, and with whom she has two children. She feels she has it all. . . .

Questions

1. Are any of these stories clear examples of what you mean by "sexual infidelity"?
2. Explain what you mean by "sexual infidelity."
3. Do any of the people in the stories have meanings different from yours?

Why study definitions, you ask? Because words, as the above passage illustrates, are sometimes **ambiguous** (have more than one meaning). By being attentive to ambiguity and ready to offer definitions when necessary, we enhance the communication of our arguments.

Offering definitions also helps us with the first step of conflict resolution, understanding each other. People who disagree often have different understandings of the same word. When they don't realize that they are using

THE FUSCO BROTHERS

by J.C. Duffy

the same word differently, misunderstanding results. For example, people who disagree about whether abortion should be legal typically have different understandings of "person," "baby," and "life." They can improve their understanding of each other by explaining what they mean by these words.

Ambiguity is not the only problem of communication. Sometimes our audience isn't familiar with our words at all, as when we are talking philosophy with kindergarten students or using 1990s slang with the 1960s generation. We must define our terms or leave our audience in the dark.

Still other times, we may want to introduce a new word to indentify something new that has been discovered, such as a star or a subatomic particle. We may even want to offer a new understanding of an old word, as people do who call cat prints "art."

This chapter provides information about definitions to help us communicate our meanings more effectively. It includes the primary ways to define words, to research, develop, and assess definitions.

YOUR TURN A

◆ 1. Are any of the following words ambiguous? Do you need the speaker to define them to understand which meaning is intended?

   a. "Good" used in "You've got to see the latest Woody Allen Movie. It's such a good movie."

   b. "Bank" used in "Please deposit this check in the bank for me."

   c. "Religion" used in "I know a good class for you to take: Religions of the World."

2. Make a list of words that are important to you in describing who you are (spiritual, activist, artist) or what you care about (integrity, health, courage, patriotism).

   a. Are any of them ambiguous?

   b. Are any of them likely to be unfamiliar to an audience you want to speak with about these things?

   c. Do you have an unusual definition for any of them?

WAYS TO DEFINE WORDS

Once you decide what words you want to define and why you want to define them, you need to think about *how* to define them. There are, it turns out, a number of different ways to define words. I've described some of the most common ones below. As you will see, which ways you choose depend on the word you're defining and the purpose of your definition.

Ostensive Definition

We can define some words ostensively by pointing to the thing they name. If I were sitting by you now, I could point to the book in your hand and define "book." Parents make use of the **ostensive definition** when teaching their children how to talk. "Nose," they say and point to baby's nose.

For some words, ostensive definitions are the best way to explain their meaning. Color words are best taught ostensively, and so are the words for tastes, smells, sounds, and how things feel to the fingertips.

Definition by Example

Ostensive definitions are great, but they work only for words referring to things you can easily point to. We can't easily point to the referents of words like "democracy," "capitalist," or "integrity." But we can give **definitions by example** of these words. We can tell the story of a particular democracy in action, describe the activities of a particular capitalist, or relate the details of a specific person acting with integrity. We can, that is, tell stories to show what we mean by these abstract concepts.

Psychologist Gordon Allport began a talk he gave on prejudice in just this way, telling stories:

> Before I attempt to define prejudice, let us have in mind . . . instances that I think we all would agree are prejudice.
>
> The first is the case of the Cambridge University student, who said, "I despise all Americans. But," he added, a bit puzzled, "I've never met one that I didn't like."
>
> The second is the case of another Englishman, who said to an American, "I think you're awfully unfair in your treatment of Negroes. How *do* Americans feel about Negroes?" The American replied, "Well, I suppose some Americans feel about Negroes just the way you feel about the Irish." The Englishman said, "Oh, come now. The Negroes are human beings." [1]

When giving examples, it is frequently useful to give a number of them. Also, be sure to include examples your audience won't expect you to be talking about. For example, some people would not consider the following to be an example of prejudice. So if you would call it an example of prejudice, you would need to present it to your audience. You might say, for example:

> In my presentation I include the following as an instance of prejudice.
> "I'm going to ask my friend Bob to help me decorate," Jane said.
> "Bob? Are you kidding? I've seen how he decorated his house, and it's a mess. You would hate it," said her friend Peter.
> "I don't care what you say, Peter," Jane said, "Bob is gay, so he must be a good decorator."

You can also give examples that are not actually stories. For example, you could define "animal" by saying, "By 'animal' I mean such things as frogs, gnats, and cheetahs."

Though not all examples are story examples, you frequently need to fill in the story to help your audience know what you mean. Consider, for example, the following definitions by example:

> By "classic novel" I mean such works as Dickens's *Oliver Twist*, Beecher Stowe's *Uncle Tom's Cabin*, and Camus's *The Stranger*.

> By "hero" I mean such people as Albert Einstein, Virginia Woolf, and Anita Hill.

Listing the names of classic novels or heroes isn't enough to clarify the meaning of "classic novel" or "hero." You need to add the specific aspects about these novels that make them classics and the specific acts of these people that make them heroes.

Sometimes your audience will have a number of examples in mind that are not what you mean by the word. You can help your audience focus on your meaning by offering them some examples that you do not mean by the word.

For example, suppose that you do not intend to include positive claims about another person as examples of prejudice, even if those positive claims are based on stereotypes. To make your meaning clear to your audience, you could explicitly exclude Jane's comment as an instance of prejudice. For example, you might say:

> In my presentation I will be *excluding* the following as an instance of prejudice:
> "I'm going to ask my friend Bob to help me decorate," Jane said.
> "Bob? Are you kidding? I've seen how he decorated his house, and it's a mess. You would hate it," said her friend Peter.
> "I don't care what you say, Peter," Jane said, "Bob is gay, so he must be a good decorator."

On the one hand, as you can see, definition by example can be a time-consuming process. You may have to give your audience a number of examples to get them to see the scope of what you are talking about. On the other hand, definitions by example are an excellent way to bring abstract concepts down to earth. Examples are also useful for keeping your audience interested in what you are saying. Your audience will get more involved with what you are saying if you give them some stories to listen to.

Connotative Definition

Sometimes you will not have time or space to tell a sufficient number of stories for your audience to understand fully what you mean by the word or phrase you are defining. In such cases, it is useful to describe what you are talking about in more general terms. You might, for example, set forth several common characteristics of the examples your word or expression refers to. Philosophers typically call this type of definition a **connotative definition**.

Gordon Allport introduces a connotative definition in his talk about prejudice:

> What do these . . . instances have in common? You notice that all of them indicate that somebody is "down" on somebody else—a feeling of rejection, or hostility. But also, in these . . . instances, there is indication that the person is not "up" on his subject—not really informed about Americans, Irish. . . .
>
> So I would offer, first a slang definition of prejudice: *Prejudice is being down on somebody you're not up on*. If you dislike slang, let me offer the same thought in the style of St. Thomas Aquinas. Thomists have defined prejudice as *thinking ill of others without sufficient warrant*.
>
> You notice that both definitions, as well as the examples I gave, specify two ingredients of prejudice. First there is some sort of faulty generalization in thinking about a group. I'll call this the process of *categorization*. Then there is the negative, rejective, or hostile ingredient, a *feeling* tone. "Being down on something" is the hostile ingredient; "that you're not up on" is the categorization ingredient; "thinking ill of others" is the hostile ingredient; "without sufficient warrant" is the faulty categorization.[2]

Notice that Gordon Allport makes explicit that he is giving a connotative definition by pointing out the common features—namely "thinking ill of others" and "without sufficient warrant"—of the instances of prejudice he described.

Many dictionary definitions are connotative definitions. For example, *The American Heritage Dictionary* defines "Madame" as "a married woman in a French-speaking area."[3]

Here are some additional connotative definitions:

Education: the process of teaching how to understand, question, and discover ideas about how the world is and should be.

Indoctrination: the process of imparting the uncritical acceptance of ideas.

Knowledge: a belief or set of beliefs that one has solid evidence for and that is true.

Note: The word "connotation" has a number of meanings. As I've used it, it means the common features of things referred to by a word. It can also mean any thoughts, feelings, words, images, stories, or ideas that come to mind when one hears a word. To avoid confusion, I'll use the word "association" instead of "connotation" in this second instance.

You can also help your audience understand what you mean by distinguishing your meaning from other meanings that may be more familiar to your audience—as I have just done with the word "connotation."

Definition by Synonym

Synonyms are words or phrases that mean (roughly) the same thing. One synonym for "prejudice" is "bigotry." Other synonyms are "intolerance" and "narrow-mindedness." Thus, a **definition by synonym** of "prejudice" is "'Prejudice' means 'bigotry,' 'intolerance,' and 'narrow-mindedness.'" Some other definitions by synonym follow:

"Scholastic" means "academic."

By "pedagogue" I mean "educator."

By "pejorative" I mean "demeaning."

I define "synonyms" as words that are only *roughly* the same, because two different words rarely mean exactly the same thing. It is hard enough to get one word to keep its meaning over time, so naturally we can't expect two different words to follow the same paths of meaning.

As a result, definitions using synonyms are rarely precise. But we do not always need to be precise, at least at the outset of helping someone understand what we are talking about. Sometimes you just want to get your audience into your ball park. A definition using a familiar synonym can serve as a ticket of entry. Later on, you can provide a connotative definition and an example to usher your audience to the precise seat of your meaning.

For example, you could begin to explain to your audience what you mean by "ghoul" by offering them the synonym "monster." And later, clarify your meaning further by offering the following connotative definition: "a legendary evil being that robs graves and feeds on corpses."

You can also help your audience understand what you are saying by distinguishing your meaning from that of a common synonym of the word you're defining. You might say, for example, "By 'education' I don't mean 'indoctrination,'" and then give connotative definitions and definitions by example to explain the difference.

YOUR TURN B

◆ 1. Which ways to define words (definition by example, connotative definition, and definition by synonym) are illustrated below?

   a. By "just law" I mean a law that lifts human personality.[4]

   b. By "unjust law" I mean such laws as the law that African Americans must sit in the back of buses.[5]

   c. By "justice" I mean fairness.

2. Do you find anything confusing about these ways to define words?

Definition by Metaphor

A **definition by metaphor** defines something by equating it with something different. In the following metaphorical definition of "prejudice," prejudice is equated with a lock:

> Prejudice is the lock that keeps a closed mind shut.

Definitions by metaphor are great to use with any abstract concept and are especially useful for defining words whose meaning cannot be captured fully by examples and connotative definitions. "Love" is one of those words. We can tell countless stories and list endless features of love, but sometimes a poetic phrase captures more fully the felt experience of love. Consider the following metaphorical definition:

> Love is mutually feeding each other, not one living on another like a ghoul.[6]

Like definitions by example, metaphorical definitions are useful for creating interest. You can awaken the imagination of your audience with a well-chosen definition by metaphor.

Expressive Definition

As we've seen, when people communicate they frequently use words to refer to things or activities. For example, "poodle" in "Look at that poodle over there" refers to the dog the speaker points out.

People also use words to express their evaluations and/or emotions or to evoke (bring about) evaluations and/or emotions in others. For example, if I say, "Wow, look at that poodle. It just jumped over a six-foot fence," I am using "wow" to express my amazement that the poodle could jump so high. Sometimes people use a word to both refer and express. "Fascism" is one such word; people use it to refer to a type of government and to express strong negative feelings.

An **expressive definition** (sometimes called "emotive definition") sets forth the evaluation and/or feelings or emotions people express or experience when they use, read, or hear words. Here's another expressive definition:

> "Prejudice" expresses and evokes disapproval and negative emotions such as anger and fear.

That is, if I were to say, "You are prejudiced," I would not merely be referring to your attitudes; I would also be expressing my disapproval of your attitudes.

For some words, like "prejudice," there is common agreement about what they express or evoke. Other words express or evoke different things for different people. In fact, even when people agree on the connotative definition of a word, they may disagree on the expressive definition of it.

For example, two people might agree that "capitalism" is defined connotatively as an economic system in which goods are produced for profit. The same two people might disagree about whether producing goods for profit is a good thing.

A person who thinks you can produce profit only by exploiting workers will disapprove of capitalism and have negative feelings about capitalism. This person's expressive/evocative definition of "capitalism" might be:

> "Capitalism" expresses/evokes disapproval and the negative emotions of anger and insecurity.

A person who thinks you can produce a profit and still pay workers a fair wage might have positive feelings about capitalism and value it. This person's expressive definition of "capitalism" might be:

> "Capitalism" expresses and evokes approval and positive emotions such as hope and happiness.

Not all words express evaluations or emotions. Many words, such as "chair," "table," and "desk," are expressively neutral. Synonyms frequently have different expressive definitions. For example, one synonym for "prejudice" is "prejudgment." But people rarely use "prejudgment" to express or evoke disapproval. It has a more neutral sound than "prejudice."

Definition by Association

A **definition by association** sets forth the thoughts, feelings, images, and evaluations that come to mind when one hears a word. Frequently, people have different associations to a word, even when they agree on the word's

Connotative definition of 'ballet': A classical dance form characterized by flowing movement, leaps, and turns.

Same connotative definition; different definitions by association.

connotative definition. Often the associations are stereotypes that are not generally true of the group of people or things the word refers to.

The following are some definitions by association:

These are some associations I have to "student": red eyes from studying late into the night, a pounding heart when waiting to get a paper back, and searching through the bottom of the desk drawer to find enough change to go out to a movie.

These are the associations that some landlords I know have to "student": late with the rent check, holes in the walls, police visits due to loud parties.

These are the associations that some people have to "feminist": doesn't like children, man hater, jumping all over you for no reason.

These are the associations I have to "feminist": unafraid to question authority, supportive of persons who have been badly treated, sensitive to the needs of others.

Describing the associations you and others have to words can help you figure out the expressive meaning of words. List the associations to a word; then consider the evaluations or emotions triggered by those associations. Below are some emotions and evaluations evoked by the associations listed above for "student" and "feminist."

pity, sympathy, compassion

disgust, distrust, disapproval, annoyance

anger, fear, contempt, disapproval

respect, admiration, approval

Learning the associations that other people have to words will help you become aware of words that turn them off. A woman I knew once was not very aware of the strong negative associations that others had to the word "feminist." While giving a public lecture, she mentioned in passing that she was a feminist. A friend of hers reported later that a person sitting next to him said he could not listen to a word my friend said after she described herself as a feminist.

YOUR TURN C

◆ 1. Which ways to define words (definition by metaphor, expressive definition, definition by association) are illustrated below?

   a. "Justice" expresses and evokes approval and positive emotions such as relief and hope.

   b. By "just law" I mean a law that balances the scales of right and wrong.

   c. When I hear the word "injustice," I think of human suffering.

◆ 2. Write an expressive definition of "sexual infidelity." Do you think everyone would have the same expressive definition? Explain.

RESOURCES FOR DEVELOPING DEFINITIONS

When developing definitions, you have two options. You can do some research, consulting word books and readings on your topic. You can also use your own personal experience, your analytic skill, and your imagination.

Word Books

You can begin developing definitions by consulting a standard college dictionary. But to really get to know words, you should explore some of the many other types of dictionaries, ranging in size from a tiny pocket dictionary to the multivolume *Oxford English Dictionary* and ranging in subject from slang to medical terminology. Etymological dictionaries report the original meanings of words. Dictionaries of contemporary usage record present meanings. Standard college dictionaries generally restrict themselves to offering connotative definitions of words. Other specialized dictionaries, like *The Bias-Free Word Finder*, take special care to inform their readers of expressive/evocative definitions. Thesauruses list synonyms.

To help you explain what you are talking about, pocket dictionaries are frequently practically useless; even the largest dictionaries may not list a definition that fully captures what you are talking about. But looking through a large dictionary can be useful. Even if you do not find the definition you are looking for, you might get some ideas about language to use when developing your definition. You also will become familiar with definitions that your audience might have in mind and tend to confuse with what you are talking about. You will want to take special note of these definitions so that you can explicitly contrast them with the definition you present.

When reading through standard college dictionaries, keep in mind that they frequently list many different definitions for the same word. Such dictionaries see their task as reporting as many of the actual uses of a word as they have room for. From their point of view, the more definitions, the merrier. But when you are giving your presentation or writing your paper, you are trying to help your audience see as precisely as possible what you mean by the word(s) you use. So you cannot simply list all of the definitions you find in the dictionary. Many of them do not describe your meaning. Instead, you will need to select a definition (or develop your own definition) that most closely describes what you are talking about.

For example, the following excerpt from *The American Heritage Dictionary* lists three different definitions of "prejudice":

> 1. A strong feeling for or against something formed before one knows the facts; bias. 2. Irrational hostility toward members of a particular race, religion, or group. 3. Harm or injury.[7]

The first definition includes a wider range of feelings than the second: feelings for or feelings against instead of only a feeling against. The third describes something entirely different from the first two: a harm instead of a feeling. Also note that the first definition gives a synonym, "bias," as well as a connotative definition.

Because the meanings of words frequently change over time, an etymological definition (which tells the word's origin) may not capture precisely what you are talking about today. But reading a word's etymology will often give you insight into the word. For example, *A Concise Etymological Dictionary of the English Language* offers the following definition of "prejudice":

> prejudice. (F.—L.) O.F. *prejudice.*—L. *praeiūdicium*, a judicial examination, previous to a trial . . . —L. *prae*, before; *iūdicium*, judgment, from *iūdic-*, a stem of *iūdex*, a judge.[8]

When I read this definition I saw a person standing before a judge, while the judge was trying to figure out on the basis of the available evidence whether the person should stand trial or not. Making a prejudgment of this sort does not strike me as clearly wrong. Sometimes there are good practical reasons for making decisions without all of the possible evidence. We would not necessarily want everyone accused of anything to have to stand trial. Sometimes the available evidence is so great on the defendant's side that it would be unfair to put the defendant through a trial before letting him or her go.

Though "judicial examination" does not capture the common contemporary understanding of "prejudice," it offers an interesting contrast.

When the standard college dictionary or even the *Oxford English Dictionary* does not have the word you are looking for, you have still found out *something* about your word—namely, that it was not frequently found in print when the dictionaries you consulted were being compiled. That itself is useful information. It indicates that the word is a new word, a technical term of a specific discipline, or a word that was not used frequently by those groups who are most likely to get their words published—and their meanings recorded in dictionaries.

So if you are in a group that is less likely to be published, and you are looking for a definition of a word that has a special meaning to people in your group, you may not find an appropriate definition in the standard college dictionary. The word "Chicana" is one such word. A student in my class who wanted to define this word a few years ago searched a number of college dictionaries and found nothing.

Readings on Your Topic

Even when you do find the word you want to define in a dictionary, the definition may not be helpful to you. It may be too vague or abbreviated for your purposes. Or you may be looking for a definition by example, which most dictionaries don't provide.

Look for some readings on your topic. Many authors begin argumentative essays by clarifying key terms on the topic, and sometimes you can find an entire essay devoted to developing the meaning of a term like "integrity," "democracy," or "feminism."

But when you do work on a controversial issue, you will not necessarily want to use the first definition you find. Opposing points of view on an action (for example, abortion) sometimes result from conflicting definitions of the same word. Read definitions offered by persons from several points of view before deciding which one you want to use.

Yourself as a Resource

You can use your own personal experience to develop story examples and your analytic skill to develop connotative definitions from them. You can use your imagination to develop metaphorical definitions.

Your Experience   You can develop a definition by example from your own experience. The woman who wanted to define "Chicana" told a story about herself and others she calls Chicanas to illustrate what she meant by the word. If you are trying to define "friendship," tell stories of your friendships or other friendships you have known.

For any other word you are defining, try to find examples from your own life that illustrate it.

You can also develop examples from things you have read or seen—stories, plays, television programs, movies. You can save space in writing or time in an oral presentation by using a story that you believe is familiar to most people in your audience. You will not need to go into as much detail as you otherwise would. Be careful, though, not to assume that your audience will be familiar with the story you tell; they may not watch the same movies or read the same books that you do.

Your Analytic Skill   After you have found a number of specific examples of what you are talking about, you can develop your own connotative definition by identifying the features your examples have in common. Persons who call themselves "Chicana" have a number of things in common. They are females, of Mexican descent, born in the United States, and committed to social and political change. A connotative definition of "Chicana" could be "a female of Mexican descent who was born in the United States and is committed to social and political change."

When looking for similarities, you will find that sometimes the things you are talking about are not all similar in exactly the same ways. Members of a family do not all look exactly alike, although they may have some resemblances in common, such as the same nose or eyes. Likewise, when we are looking for similarities among the things we are talking about we may find **family resemblances** rather than exact characteristics that everything we are talking about shares. Most chairs have four legs, for example, but some have three. Some have arms, but others don't. Usually they have a back, but not always of the same height. Generally, chairs are for sitting on, but some are works of art and are for looking at.

Your Imagination   Especially when you develop metaphorical definitions, your best resource is your own imagination. Sometimes all you have to do is ask, and your mind will hand over a metaphor. For example, the following are metaphorical definitions of "love":

> Love is the glue that holds polar opposites together.

> Love is a lantern that lights your path.

If nothing comes readily to mind, you can prime your imagination by making a list of things, plants, animals, foods, clothes, machines, places. You may pick things that are related to what you are trying to define, if you like, but you need not. You may develop a more amusing or interesting metaphor by linking your word to something no one would have thought it could be linked to.

After making your list, allow your mind to float from your word to one of the things on your list at a time until something comes to you. You might find it useful to write out "a . . . (your word) is a . . . (one of the things on your list)" and then put whatever comes to you afterward. Your mind will come up with something, including new things to add to your list. All you have to do is sit back and let it happen.

The following is a fairly close record of how I came up with the metaphorical definition "Love is the orchid that grows in the jungle of romance."

> I started by trying to link "love" to "heart," something commonly associated with love. I didn't come up with anything for either "heart" or "heartbeat." So I decided to go in a totally different direction and began linking "love" to animals. For "donkey," I got "Love is the donkey that carries life's burdens." The donkey metaphor made love sound a little stolid, so I tried "salve" and got "Love is the salve that soothes all suffering." Too gooey, I thought, so I tried "chili" and got "Love is the chili that gives spice to life." Better, but a little predictable. I thought of "frog" and got "Love is the frog that emerges from the pollywog of romance." Thinking in terms of development led me to "butterfly" and "worm" and "Love is the butterfly that develops from the worm of romance." I was not happy with worm as a metaphor for "romance," so I looked at the frog metaphor again. Frogs don't exactly emerge from pollywogs, I thought, but they do emerge from swamps. Swamp and romance seemed more fitting for each other. How about "Love is the frog that emerges from the swamp of romance?" I still wasn't happy. The swamp/romance connection had possibility, but I just couldn't see love hopping about snapping up flies. I wanted a more beautiful image, but I didn't know enough about swamps to come up with one. Just when I was ready to give up I got "Love is the orchid that grows in the jungle of romance," which I like.

You may find other ways even more useful for coming up with metaphorical definitions. But whatever you do, do not let your doubts stop your process. Accept whatever you come up with, and keep going until you find a connection that works for your purpose.

◆1. See if you can find any common features of sexual infidelity among any
of the examples in the passage at
the beginning of the chapter. Write a
definition of "sexual infidelity" based
on those features. Does this definition
express what you mean by "sexual
infidelity"? Explain.

2. Make a list of plants, animals, and
objects. Play with ways that these
things relate to the words "success,"
"patriotic," or "friend." Write a
metaphorical definition of one of
these words.

CRITIQUING DEFINITIONS

A number of times I have reminded you that you will have to select the
definition that most closely describes what you are talking about. When
you are writing your own connotative definitions, you will need to select
language that most closely describes the common features of your examples.
This section offers some things to keep in mind to help you make those
decisions.

Clarity

If you want your audience to understand what you mean by your word, your
definition can't be unduly vague or circular.

Vague Definitions   Sometimes a definition does not help us understand the
word in question because it is a **vague definition**—it contains words that are
as imprecise as the word being defined. In the following, James Thurber
comments on the loose or imprecise use of the word "love." Does his
definition tell you precisely what love is?

> The word "love" is used loosely by writers, and they know it. Furthermore, the
> word "love" is accepted loosely by readers, and *they* know it. There are many
> kinds of love, but for the purposes of this article I shall confine my discussion to
> the usual hazy interpretation: the strange bewilderment which overtakes one
> person on account of another person. Thus, when I say love in this article, you
> will take it to mean *the pleasant confusion which we know exists.* When I say pas-
> sion, I *mean* passion.[9]

Thurber's definition of "love" as "the pleasant confusion which we know
exists" would not help anyone who does not already know what love is. But
Thurber doesn't expect it to; he's mocking the human desire to be precise
about love. We are, he implies, befuddled not only when we are in love but
also when we try to define "love."

But sometimes we want our audience to understand precisely what we mean. When sexual infidelity matters to us, for example, we want to give our partner a precise definition, not a vague one. Sometimes we can rewrite a connotative definition to make it less vague. But connotative definitions use general terms, which tend to be vague. We frequently need to add story examples to our connotative definitions to help our audience understand more closely what we are talking about.

Circular Definitions   A **circular definition** uses the word being defined or a form of it in the definition. Thurber's quip "When I say passion I *mean* passion" is a circular definition of "passion." Dictionaries often define a word in terms of itself to save space. For example, *The American Heritage Dictionary* defines the verb "prejudice" as "to cause (someone) to have a prejudice."[10] This definition will not inform someone who does not already understand the noun "prejudice." The dictionary, however, defines the noun "prejudice" also. In general we should avoid circular definitions unless we, too, define the words in the definition (or unless, like Thurber, we are trying, not to inform our audience, but to amuse them).

The following are some more examples of circular definitions:

"Friend" is someone one is friendly with.

"Successful" is having a lot of success.

"Anxiety" is the emotion of feeling anxious.

"Commitment" is the state of being committed.

Useful Distinctions

Some definitions fail to maintain useful distinctions. Consider, for example, the following definitions of "love" and "lust":

Love: (1) a strong feeling of affection for another combined with a strong inclination to act for the other's good; (2) a strong desire to have sex with another.

Lust: (1) a strong desire to have sex with another.

The second definition of "love" fails to make any distinction between love and lust. The first definition of "love," however, maintains a distinction between the two. Defining "love" as "a strong feeling of affection for another combined with a strong inclination to act for the other's good" and "lust" as "a strong desire to have sex with another" helps us see a difference between the two states. And we can then raise questions about how similar or different they are and whether we want to study them separately or together.

In his speech on prejudice, Allport distinguishes what he calls "positive prejudice" from (negative) prejudice:

We can be biased in favor of our children, our neighborhood or our college. Spinoza makes the distinction neatly. He says that *love prejudice* is "thinking well of others, through love, more than is right." *Hate prejudice*, he says, is "thinking ill of others, through hate, more than is right.[11]

When choosing which definition to present to your audience, think about whether the definition maintains a distinction you want maintained. However, once again, it is useful to keep in mind other definitions of the words you are using so you can alert your audience to paths that lead them astray from your meaning. You may see a difference between love and lust, but your audience may not. In such a case, you need to inform your audience that you do perceive a difference and that you will maintain it in your presentation.

Appropriate Scope

Definitions have different scopes; some are broader than others. Let's look again at two of the definitions of "prejudice" from *The American Heritage Dictionary*:

> 1. A strong feeling for or against something formed before one knows the facts; bias. 2. Irrational hostility toward members of a particular race, religion, or group.[12]

The first is broader in scope than the second; that is, it potentially includes more examples of "prejudice" than the second definition, because the first definition includes any strong feeling either for or against as a feature of prejudice. The second definition mentions only the feeling of "hostility," that is, feeling against. You can see that already definition 2 is narrower: it does not include feelings for.

But besides including only feelings against, definition 2 requires that these feelings against be directed toward people. The first definition uses the general word "something." The feeling could be for or against rap music, pit-bulls, or dandelions. The second definition, however, uses the words "members of a race, religion, or group"; it limits the objects of prejudice to persons (unless we understand "group" more broadly).

A definition that indicates a comparatively large range of things when compared with other definitions of the same word is called a **broad definition.** A definition that indicates a comparatively small range of things when compared with other definitions of the same word is called a **narrow definition.**

As with any decision, you need to think about your goals and the restraints on your time when building a definition. Here are a few (of the many possible) reasons to choose a more broad (or narrow) definition.

Expanding Your Understanding   Because the definitions we use affect how we experience things, you can help your audience make new discoveries by offering a broader (or more narrow) definition than they are accustomed to.

Let's look at some definitions of "athlete":

Broad definition of 'athlete': A person who engages in frequent strenuous physical motion.

A broad definition of "athlete" includes a wide range of examples.

1. One who regularly practices a strenuous competitive sport
2. One who engages in frequent strenuous physical motion

Notice that the second definition is broader than the first. The first includes soccer players, football players, tennis players, volleyball players, basketball players—and everyone else who regularly practices a strenuous *competitive* sport. However, the second definition includes these examples and *also* leaves room for noncompetitive exercisers as well as housecleaners, landscapers, and preschool teachers. Thus, the second definition includes more examples and is broader than the first definition.

The second definition is broader than the most common definition of "athlete." And you may choose it for this reason. You may decide that you want to expand the meaning of the word "athlete" beyond its established use in order to point out similarities among tennis players, bike riders, ballerinas, and construction workers that are frequently overlooked or minimized. By expanding the meaning of "athlete," we suddenly see the hard physical work and determination that go into all of these activities as similar. The similarities become salient (stand out), and the differences recede.

However, broad definitions do overlook differences. On college campuses, one primary difference between football players and those who practice yoga is that people will pay money to watch a football team make a first down, but they will not pay to watch someone stand on her head. Thus, on an announcement of athletic scholarships we would expect to find a definition of "athlete" that excludes those who practice yoga.

In the following set of definitions, the first definition is broader than the second.

Religion: (1) any practice of rituals and moral beliefs; (2) a practice of rituals and moral beliefs in which a belief in a supreme deity or deities is important.

Educate: (1) the process of teaching how to read, write, and think as well as teaching how to do such things as play a musical instrument and build a piece of furniture; (2) the process of teaching how to read, write, and think.

Failure to pay attention to the scope of your definition can have painful consequences. For example, your partner may unwittingly engage in a behavior you find unacceptable if you have defined "sexual fidelity" more broadly than you meant to.

Narrowing Your Topic   If you are writing a short paper, you may want to narrow your topic by narrowing your definition. Because your paper is short, there isn't sufficient space for a wider exploration. If you are writing about prejudice, you might focus on one of the narrow definitions of prejudice, such as love prejudice or hate prejudice.

Space and time considerations alone shouldn't dictate the decisions you make in narrowing your topic. You should have another reason to use or explore the narrow definition you offer. For example, you might choose to focus on "hate prejudice" because you think it is the most damaging kind of prejudice. Or you might focus on "love prejudice" because you think people are less likely to be aware of this type of prejudice.

Checking Scope with Examples   When trying to determine whether your connotative definition is appropriately broad or narrow, use your imagination to think of examples that would be included and excluded by your definition. If you think of examples that your definition includes that you didn't mean it to include, then the language of your definition is too broad. If you think of instances that your definition leaves out but you intended to include, then the language of your definition is too narrow.

YOUR TURN E

◆ 1. Are any of the following definitions vague or circular? Do any of them ignore or blur a useful distinction? Are any of them broader or narrower than another of them? Explain.

a. Success is gaining something one values.

b. Success is completing a plan.

c. Health is the state of being healthy.

d. Man is any human being, male or female.

e. Man is a male human being.

f. Man is an adult male.

◆ 2. Suppose that your purpose is to determine whether the following definition of "sexist decision" will guide you in your decision not to make any sexist decisions. Do you find the following definition too broad or too narrow or just right in guiding you?

Sexist decision: A decision made about a person in which a primary consideration is whether the person is male or female.

Instances that are unintentionally excluded or included by a definition are called "counterexamples." They are examples that go against, or counter, the proposed definition. Whenever you propose a connotative definition, think about whether there are any counterexamples to it. If you find any counterexamples, rewrite your definition to include (or exclude) the examples you came up with.

This chapter has shown you a variety of ways to define words and to critique definitions. Now you are better prepared to enhance your arguments with lively metaphorical definitions, precise connotative definitions, and definitions by example. You'll continue to study emotion-evoking language and the associations we have to words in the next chapter.

EXERCISES

1. Identify the types of definitions below.
   a. A house is a structure, usually of wood, rock, metal, stucco, or brick, constructed for the purpose of sheltering and protecting human beings from the elements.
   b. A house is a trap in which the buyer, following her dreams, becomes ensnarled by monthly mortgage payments.
   c. A house is a domicile.
   d. By "house" I mean anything from Henry David Thoreau's cabin to Buckingham Palace.
   e. By "just law" I mean a law that is arrived at by the full participation of everyone who will be governed by the law.
   f. By "law" I mean a rule that carries a penalty if not followed.
   g. By "law" I mean such statements as "An object at rest will remain at rest unless acted upon by an outside force" and "Nothing can go faster than the speed of light."
   h. The following is what I mean by "success": Yesterday morning I decided to finish cleaning the house, then edit a chapter of my book, then prepare for class, then make supper, then practice the piano. It took me all day and into the evening, but I did it.
   i. By "success" I mean the completion of a plan.

2. Do the following examples illustrate the following definitions fully? Explain. Do any of the examples lead you to question whether the definition is adequate to explain the meaning of the word defined, as you understand it? Explain.
   a. *Definition*:   Racism is making a decision on the basis of race.
      Example: My Chinese cousin is racist. He dates only Chinese.
   b. *Definition*:   A family is a group of individuals who live together and share each other's values.

Example: My roommate and I are a family. She's pro-choice and I'm pro-life.

c. *Definition*: Home is a person's primary residence.
   Example: Jill is in jail. She has been living there for a year. Jail is her home.

d. *Definition*: Success is gaining wealth.
   Example: Jim has achieved success. He made a million dollars by selling cocaine.

e. *Definition*: Discipline is acceptance or submission to authority or control.
   Example: Pat's standard poodle is the model of discipline. He comes whenever she calls him, stays by her side on command, and doesn't bark unless she gives him permission.

3. Read the following definitions of "acquaintance rape" and "seduction" and the two stories below.[13] Indicate whether the stories are examples of acquaintance rape. Explain.

Definitions

"Acquaintance rape is forced, unwanted intercourse with a person you know."

"Seduction occurs when a woman is manipulated or cajoled into agreeing to have sex."

Stories

Bob: Patty and I were in the same statistics class together. She usually sat near me and was always very friendly. I liked her and thought maybe she liked me, too. Last Thursday I decided to find out. After class I suggested that she come to my place to study for midterms together. She agreed immediately, which was a good sign. That night everything seemed to go perfectly. We studied for a while and then took a break. I could tell that she liked me, and I was attracted to her. I was getting excited. I started kissing her. I could tell that she really liked it. We started touching each other and it felt really good. All of a sudden she pulled away and said "Stop." I figured she didn't want me to think that she was "easy" or "loose." A lot of girls think they have to say "no" at first. I knew once I showed her what a good time she could have, and that I would respect her in the morning, it would be OK. I just ignored her protests and eventually she stopped struggling. I think she liked it, but afterwards she acted bummed out and cold. Who knows what her problem was?

Patty: I knew Bob from my statistics class. He's cute and we are both good at statistics, so when a tough midterm was scheduled, I was glad that he suggested we study together. It never occurred to me that it was anything except a study date. That night everything went fine at first, we got a lot of studying done in a short amount of time so when he suggested we take a break I thought we deserved it. Well, all of a sudden he started acting really romantic and started kissing me. I liked the kissing but then he started touching me below the waist. I pulled away and tried to stop him, but he didn't listen. After a while I stopped struggling; he was hurting me and I was scared. He was so much bigger and stronger than me. I couldn't believe it was happening to me. I didn't know what to do. He actually forced me to have sex with him. I guess, looking back on it I should have screamed or done something besides trying to reason with him but it was so unexpected. I couldn't believe it was happening. I still can't believe it did.

4. Are any of the following definitions vague and/or circular? What would you do to cure the vagueness or circularity?

   a. "Racism" is unfair discrimination on the basis of race.

   b. "Success" is getting ahead.

   c. "Insecurity" is the state of lacking security.

   d. "Judgmental" is the quality of having strong and unquestioning opinions about almost everything.

   e. "Health" is the state of not being ill.

5. Read the following definitions. Do any of them ignore a distinction you find useful? Explain.

   a. "Gender"

      Denotes sex. It is solely determined by the difference in the physical structure and appearance of the subject, and is used to differentiate male and female.[14]

   b. "Gender"

      [U]nderstanding the difference between sex and gender is crucial to the correct use of language. Sex is biological: people with male genitals are male, and people with female genitals are female. Gender is cultural: our notions of "masculine" tell us how we expect men to behave and our notions of "feminine" tell us how we expect women to behave—but these may have nothing to do with biology. When deciding whether a word is restricted to one sex or the other, the only acceptable limitation is genetic sex. A woman cannot be a sperm donor because it's biologically impossible. It may be culturally unusual for a man to be a secretary, but it is not biologically impossible. To assume all secretaries are women is sexist because the issue is gender, not sex. Gender signifies an individual's personal, legal, and social status without reference to genetic sex; gender is a subjective cultural attitude while sex is an objective biological fact.[15]

   c. "Jealous"

      1. Fearful of losing what one has to another, esp. someone's love or affection. 2. Resentful of another's success, advantages, etc.[16]

d. "Envious"

1. Being resentful of another's success, advantages, and so on.

6. In each of the following sets of definitions, identify the broadest definition. Explain, providing an example that will be included in the broadest definition but will not be included in the other definitions.

a. "Sexism"

- Sexism is making a decision on the basis of sex.
- Sexism is unfair discrimination on the basis of sex.
- Sexism is unfair discrimination against women.

b. "Family"

- A family is a group of biologically related individuals.
- A family is a group of individuals who are biologically related or are related by formal state procedures such as marriage or adoption.
- A family is a group of individuals who live together and care for one another.

c. "Home"

- Home is the place where a person (or family) lives.
- Home is a person or family's primary residence.

d. "Success"

- Success is gaining something one values.
- Success is gaining wealth.
- Success is gaining wealth, status, or knowledge.

e. "Discipline"

- Discipline is self-control.
- Discipline is acceptance or submission to authority or control.

7. Rewrite each of the following definitions to make it broader. Then rewrite each of them to make it more narrow.

a. Love is a strong emotion between family members.

b. An American is someone who lives in the United States.

c. Health is the absence of disease.

d. A friend is a person one knows better than anyone else and is fond of.

e. Trust is the firm belief in another person's honesty.

8. In the following dialogues people are disagreeing about definitions. Which definitions do you find the most acceptable? Explain why.

a. **Freedom From and Freedom To**

- Let's talk very personally, not in grand concepts. When do I feel free? When I get up on a Saturday morning and know I can do anything I want to do. I can lie in bed as long as I please, work in the yard, watch TV. Or, I can leave the house a mess and go to the movies with friends. I'm free because there is no one telling me what to do. I'm left alone—that's the key, isn't it? No interference from others, nobody standing over me.

The freedom to lie in bed on Saturday morning may sound trivial, but I can apply this same understanding to what matters a great deal more to me—the opportunity to strive for any job I want and to move wherever I please. Freedom means no government official or anyone else interfering, telling me which job to take or where to live.

- *Sure, lack of interference from others can enhance my freedom, but not always. If lots of people are out of work and I get laid off, too, no one may be "interfering" with me. And that's my problem. I might be left alone by virtually everyone! But how free am I?*

   If freedom is the opportunity to make something of myself and provide for my kids, then your concept of freedom—freedom from interference—isn't enough.[17]

b. **Affirmative Action: Preference to Qualified Applicants for a Noble Cause vs. Preference to Unqualified Applicants for an Unworthy Cause**

- You focus on possible benefits, but they are far outweighed by the costs. Perhaps the most serious cost of affirmative action that all society is bearing is the lowering of academic and professional standards through obligatory acceptance of weaker applicants.
- *Affirmative action does not suggest that anyone hire or admit an unquali- fied person, but where qualifications are met, to give preference to the underrepresented group. That's all. And where's your consistency? You don't seem too troubled that preferences given to athletes, veterans, and alumni's children are diluting standards. . . .*
- Whatever you say does not change the fact that "affirmative action" means discrimination on racial grounds. To the qualified person passed over, there may be no other equally desirable job opportunity. Whole careers can be at stake. No wonder the white person who is discriminated against is angry. No wonder the whole concept generates a backlash.
- *A critical distinction must be made: Racial discrimination damages people by communicating to them that they are unworthy, lesser human beings. Affirmative action, like my other examples, carries no such message. Yes, the hopes of the person who doesn't get the position are dashed, but no more than if the opening had been eliminated in a budget cut-back or if the employer had decided a midwesterner would be a better sales rep in the Kansas market than the New Yorker who loses out.*[18]

c. **Democracy: Countervailing Powers or Accountability?**

- To talk meaningfully about the market and property, we've already had to touch on many aspects of democracy. Now we need to define what we mean by democracy in the first place.

   This has got to be easier than talking about property! At least there's widespread agreement in this country about what democracy means. It is representative government—leaders elected from among a number of candidates, not just appointed by a single party as in communist states. The essence of democracy is selecting good leaders.

As I pointed out much earlier, the market guarantees our freedom in economic life. And in parallel fashion, the "market" in our political life—competing parties and candidates—guarantees freedom by offering us real choices.

- *But appearances can deceive. Some countries have had dozens of political parties as well as elections, while power remains in the hands of a small group, often of military strongmen. Elections and multiple parties can actually disguise the fact that leadership answers to a privileged minority.*

  So let's not confuse political mechanisms with a core principle of democracy—the accountability of decision makers to all those who must live with their decisions. With this principle, we can cut through appearances. Take a real world example: If in Central America or the Philippines, a government refuses to stand up against the minority interests of wealthy landowners in order to enforce a law allowing idle land to hungry families with no land, then it isn't accountable to the majority who are landless. Elections may have been held. There may be many parties. But we can be pretty sure that the landless weren't fairly represented.

  Let's take another example here at home. Most Americans believe health care should be a citizen's right, but tens of millions of Americans aren't covered, and Washington has yet to come up with a plan to put health care within everybody's reach.[19]

9. Review the dialogues about freedom, affirmative action, and democracy under number 8 (above). Formulate a discussion question for each of these dialogues. (Draft an answer to one of them.)

READINGS FOR ANALYSIS

Sexual Bullying in Schools

Ellen Goodman

Ellen Goodman is a columnist for the *Boston Globe*.

BOSTON—It happens in public, not behind a closed office door. There is no "he said/she said" dispute about the facts. Everybody can see what's going on. Friends, classmates, teachers.

A boy backs a girl up against her junior high locker. Day after day. A high school junior in the hallway grabs a boy's butt. A sophomore in the playground grabs a girl's blouse. An eighth-grade girl gets up to speak in class and the boys begin to "moo" at her. A ninth-grader finds out that her name and her "hot number" are posted in the boy's bathroom.

It's all quite normal, or at least it's become the norm. This aberrant behavior is now as much a part of the daily curriculum, the things children learn, as math or social studies. Or their worth in the world.

• • •

This is the searing message of another survey that came spilling out of the schoolhouse door last week. This one, commissioned by the American Association of University Women, confirmed the grim fact that four out of five public-school students between grades 8 and 11—85 percent of the girls and 76 percent of the boys—have experienced sexual harassment.

That's if sexual harassment means—and it does—"unwanted and unwelcome sexual behavior which interferes with your life." That's if sexual harassment includes—and it does—sexual comments, touching, pinching, grabbing and worse. . . .

A school culture of sexual harassment exists in a wide and troubling social context, but change ultimately rests in the hands of the students themselves. After all, not all boys will be boys. Not all girls follow the leader.

So, these days, when Nan Stein [of Wellesley College] goes into a school, she says, "I talk a lot about courage." She thinks the role that everybody plays, the bystander, is pivotal. "Kids have to learn to speak out, to make moral judgments. I tell them not to be moral spectators."

Sexual harassment is, as Stein says, an older cousin to bullying. Students who understand the dividing line between teasing and bullying can learn the line between sexual play and harassment. They can draw that line.

The most powerful tool for the everyday garden-variety misery of name-calling, body-pinching and sexual bullying that turns a school hallway into a gantlet may not be a lawsuit.

It may be one high school senior walking by who says, "Don't do that, it's gross." It may be one group of buddies who don't laugh at a joke.

In our society, the courts are the last-ditch place for resolving conflicts. The schools must become the place for teaching basics. Like respect and courage.

Questions

1. What methods does the author use to define "sexual harassment"?
2. Does the author succeed in informing you what she's talking about?
3. Are any of the definitions she presents vague or circular? Are any of them too broad or narrow? Do any of them fail to maintain distinctions you think are important?
4. What are some examples of "sexual harassment" as you understand it?
5. Would you suggest an alternative definition to the ones in the above passage?
6. What policy does the author recommend as a way to curtail sexual harassment?
7. What other points would you like to make about the above passage?
8. What questions do you have about Goodman's article?

Bias, Harassment Reports out of Focus: Girls Shortchanged?

Peter Schrag

Peter Schrag is editorial page editor of the *Sacramento Bee*.

Dog-bites-man, according to the cliches of the news business, isn't supposed to be news, but when it comes to politically correct versions of the conventional wisdom, dog-bites-man seems good for a headline every time.

Consider, for example, the . . . report . . . released last week . . . about how schools were dens of sexual harassment. In a survey of some 1,600 11th-graders, fully 85 percent of the girls and 76 percent of the boys reported that they had been sexually harassed.

What was plain from the numbers and the horror stories used to illustrate them, however, was that any nasty remark and a great deal of childish thoughtlessness was evidence of sexual harassment: sexual comments, jokes, gestures, everything counted.

"We were really surprised," said Sharon Shuster, the AAUW [American Association of University Women] president, "how sexual harassment has reached such epidemic proportion in today's schools."

Surprised? If the AAUW had counted other forms of insult—about looks, intelligence, clothes, ethnicity, physical handicap, retardation, eating habits, accents, hairstyles —Sharon Shuster would have been really speechless.

It's not scientifically known how many kids, if any, still call each other dago, wop, mick, kike or polack, because there is no organization currently demanding political correctness on this vocabulary.

But one wonders what illusion about a golden past informed this report that its sponsors should assume that things have so badly deteriorated.

• • •

What has deteriorated is general decorum in speech, dress and behavior and, with the proliferation of rules of due process, the power of schools to enforce reasonable codes of civil behavior.

But that point, lacking any well-organized advocacy group, is rarely made. Perhaps if enough minorities press their separate agendas somehow we will come to realize that the best answer is general civility and mutual respect.

Questions

1. What criticism does Peter Schrag make of the AAUW's definition of "sexual harassment"? Does he ever quote the AAUW's definition of "sexual harassment"?
2. Do you get the same idea of what the AAUW meant by "sexual harassment" from reading Peter Schrag's article as you got from reading Ellen Goodman's article? Explain.
3. Do you agree with Schrag's criticism? Explain.
4. Does Schrag offer his own definition of "sexual harassment"?
5. What policy does Peter Schrag recommend to curtail sexual harassment? Compare his policy with the policy Ellen Goodman recommends in the previous article.
6. What other point or question about Schrag's article would you like to discuss?

Only Approved Indians Can Play: Made in the U.S.A.

Jack Forbes

Jack Forbes is a writer and college professor. His tribal background is Renape, Lenape, and Saponi.

The All-Indian Basketball Tournament was in its second day. Excitement was pretty high, because a lot of the teams were very good or at least eager and hungry to win. Quite a few people had come to watch, mostly Indians. Many were relatives or friends of the players.

A lot of people were betting money and tension was pretty great.

A team from the Tucson Inter-Tribal House was set to play against a group from the Great Lakes region. The Tucson players were mostly very dark young men with long black hair. A few had little goatee beards or mustaches though, and one of the Great Lakes fans had started a rumor that they were really Chicanos. This was a big issue since the Indian Sports League had a rule that all players had to be of one-quarter or more Indian blood and that they had to have their BIA roll numbers available if challenged.

And so a big argument started. One of the biggest, darkest Indians on the Tucson team had been singled out as a Chicano, and the crowd wanted him thrown out. The Great Lakes players, most of whom were pretty light, refused to start. They all had their BIA identification cards, encased in plastic. This proved that they were all real Indians, even a blonde-haired guy. He was really only about one-sixteenth but the BIA rolls had been changed for his tribe so legally he was one-fourth. There was no question about the Great Lakes team. They were all land-based, federally-recognized Indians, although living in a big midwestern city, and they had their cards to prove it.

Anyway, the big, dark Tucson Indian turned out to be a Papago. He didn't have a BIA card but he could talk Papago so they let him alone for the time being. Then they turned towards a lean, very Indian-looking guy who had a pretty big goatee. He seemed to have a Spanish accent, so they demanded to see his card.

Well, he didn't have one either. He said he was a full-blood Tarahumara Indian and he could also speak his language. None of the Great Lakes Indians could talk their languages so they said that was no proof of anything, that you had to have a BIA roll number.

The Tarahumara man was getting pretty angry by then. He said his father and uncle had been killed by the whites in Mexico and that he did not expect to be treated with prejudice by other Indians.

But all that did no good. Someone demanded to know if he had a reservation and if his tribe was recognized. He replied that his people lived high up in the mountains

and that they were still resisting the Mexicanos, that the government was trying to steal their land.

"What state do your people live in," they wanted to know. When he said that his people lived free, outside of control of any state, they only shook their fists at him. "You're not an official Indian. All official Indians are under the whiteman's rule now. We all have a number given to us, to show that we are recognized."

Well, it all came to an end when someone shouted that "Tarahumaras don't exist. They're not listed in the BIA dictionary." Another fan yelled, "He's a Mexican. He can't play. This tournament is only for Indians."

The officials of the tournament had been huddling together. One blew his whistle and an announcement was made. "The Tucson team is disqualified. One of its members is a Yaqui. One is a Tarahumara. The rest are Papagos. None of them have BIA enrollment cards. They are not Indians within the meaning of the laws of the government of the United States. The Great Lakes team is declared the winner by default."

A tremendous roar of applause swept through the stands. A white BIA official wiped the tears from his eyes and said to a companion, "God Bless America. I think we've won."[23]

Questions

1. What definition of "Indian" was used in deciding who was qualified to play in the All-Indian Basketball Tournament?
2. Do you agree with this definition?
3. Do you think the author of this short story, Jack Forbes, agrees with the definition used? Explain. If not, how do you think he would define "Indian"?
4. What other points would you like to make about this story?
5. What questions do you have about this story?

WRITING IDEAS

1. Write two story examples of one of the following words or a similar word of your choice. Then write a connotative definition describing the common features in your examples. Compare your connotative definition with the closest definition to yours you can find in an unabridged dictionary.

   > wise, confident, tolerant, materialistic, idealistic, arrogant, culture shock, discrimination, altruistic, commitment, consumerism, healthy, insecure, judgmental, mature, peace, professional, radical, responsible, selfish, violence

   a. Check the fit between your connotative definition and your examples by linking the common features described in your connotative definition to places where they're illustrated in your example. Here's an example of checking the fit between Allport's definition of prejudice and one of his examples:

Common Features of Prejudice	How Illustrated
Thinking ill of others	"I despise all Americans" said by an Englishman illustrates "thinking ill of others."
Without sufficient reason	"I've never met one I didn't like" illustrates an insufficient reason. The Englishman does not have reason to despise Americans. Quite the contrary. The Englishman has some reason to like Americans.

   b. If it's not possible, or if it's extremely tricky, to provide story examples or a connotative definition of your word, explain why.

2. Find a word that evokes a strong emotion in you. Write a metaphorical definition of the word.

3. The following definition of "racism" was published in *The Bias-Free Word Finder: A Dictionary of Nondiscriminatory Language*, by Rosalie Maggio. Write a letter to Ms. Maggio, telling her whether you agree or disagree with this definition and why.

   > [A]ny attitude, action, social policy, or institutional structure that discriminates against a person or a group because of their color constitutes racism. Racism is specifically the subordination of people of color by white people because racism requires not only prejudice but power. "The history of the world provides us with a long record of white people holding power and using it to maintain that power and privilege over people of color, not the reverse."[20]

4. Write a short dialogue between you, Ellen Goodman, and Peter Schrag in which you listen to their points of view about the definition of "sexual

harassment" and offer your own point of view. (See the "Readings for Analysis" section.)

5. Write a short argument recommending an action. Enhance your argument by defining one of the key words in your argument.

6. Write about whether this chapter and your class discussions complemented, conflicted with, supported, or left out any of your previous ideas about the usefulness of definitions.

Notes

1. Gordon Allport, "The Nature of Prejudice," in Annette Rottenberg, *Elements of Argument*, 3rd ed. (Boston: St. Martin's Press, 1991) 92. Reprinted from the Seventeenth Claremont Reading Conference Yearbook, 1952.
2. Allport 93.
3. "Madame," *American Heritage Dictionary*, 1983 ed.
4. Paraphrases of a definition by Martin Luther King, Jr., in "Letter from Birmingham Jail," reprinted in Sylvan Barnet and Hugo Bedau, eds., *Current Issues and Enduring Questions* (Boston: St. Martin's Press, 1990) 502.
5. Inspired by Martin Luther King, Jr.
6. Bessie Head, *A Question of Power*, quoted in *Ms* Jan./Feb. 1993.
7. "Prejudice," *American Heritage Dictionary*, 1983 ed.
8. "Prejudice," Walter W. Skeat, *A Concise Etymological Dictionary of the English Language* (New York: Putnam, 1980).
9. James Thurber and E. B. White, *Is Sex Necessary? Or, Why You Feel the Way You Do* (New York: HarperPerennial, 1990) 64. First published by Harper & Row, 1929.
10. "Prejudice," *American Heritage Dictionary*, 1983 ed.
11. Allport 93.
12. "Prejudice," *American Heritage Dictionary*, 1983 ed.
13. The definitions and stories are from Jean O'Gorman Hughes and Bernice R. Sandler, " 'Friends' Raping Friends: Could It Happen to You?" Project on the Status and Education of Women, Association of American Colleges.
14. "Gender," from *Dictionary of Behavioral Science*, comp. and ed. Benjamin B. Wolman (New York: Academic Press, 1989).
15. "Gender," Rosalie Maggio, *The Bias-Free Word Finder: A Dictionary of Nondiscriminatory Language* (Boston: Beacon Press, 1991).
16. "Jealous," *American Heritage Dictionary*, 1983 ed.
17. Frances Moore Lappé, *Rediscovering America's Values* (New York: Ballantine Books, 1989) 21.
18. Lappé 99–101.
19. Lappé 193–94.
20. "Racism," from Maggio. The quote in the definition is from Paula S. Rothenberg, *Racism and Sexism*.

5 🖋

Attending to Language

CHAPTER GOALS

- To improve your ability to recognize ambiguity, irony, and misleading qualifiers.
- To learn to distinguish enlivening language from deadening language.
- To learn to identify language that evokes stereotypes and other associations.
- To use your understanding to avoid being misled by language, especially the language used in ads and political campaigns.
- To use your knowledge to enhance your arguments with precise and lively language.

YOUR THOUGHTS ABOUT LANGUAGE

What kinds of things about language do you find it useful to pay attention to? Jot down your ideas; then read this essay and answer the questions that follow.

At the time this book review was published in the *Dartmouth Review*, Dan Garcia-Diaz was a freshman at Dartmouth. This is a review of *The Common Sense Guide to American Colleges*, edited by Patty Pyott.

Colleges and Common Sense

Dan Garcia-Diaz

Ask the typical high school senior what college guide he reads and he will answer, *The Insider's Guide to Colleges* or *The Fiske Guide to Colleges* or both. . . . Although *Fiske* and *Insider's* give the reader a thorough appraisal of college life, they fail to go beyond that. With political correctness . . . running rampant in colleges and universities, today students must be wary of their opinions and beliefs lest college authorities take action against them. . . .

In order to fulfill this need, The Madison Center for Educational Affairs has published *The Common Sense Guide to American Colleges*—the politically *incorrect* guide. *Common Sense* . . . cites America's leading bastions of politically correct thinking, and tells the prospective college student where he is most likely to get a solid liberal arts education. For many students and parents who are bewildered by the media's mixed responses to P.C. on campuses, this publication is essential. . . .

Although what is happening to college curricula in America is unfortunate, one cannot study the absurd nature of political correctness without finding some humor in it. This humor is evident in the selected excerpts from course description bulletins of each college that was critiqued. For example, from Princeton University, Afro-American Studies 262—Rap Music 1990: "Rap Music 1990 is a study of the place of Rap in Afro-American musical life. The conflicting tendencies and directions, the diverse ideologies, and the custom threads, which link the entire rap community will be investigated. The historical genesis of these trends will also be studied." Intellectually deficient courses, like this one, are proliferating at American colleges, especially in the so-called "oppression studies" departments.

Perhaps the most delightful part of this guide is its dictionary, which defines some of the new and commonplace P.C. buzz words that dilute the English language's precision and power. Usually P.C. words are a roundabout way to say something, e.g. "differently abled" for handicapped or disabled. These words are designed to obfuscate reality under the shroud of meaningless and ambiguous words: unless one is well-versed, these words make absolutely no sense. P.C. words can also be an alternative, albeit distorted, definition for traditional words; for example, Conservative: "One who supports or contributes to the suppression of minorities, women, and the poor . . ."

The Common Sense Guide is conservative, yet it is not overbearingly so. . . . It confronts the conflict and lets the reader decide. Charles Horner, Executive Editor for the guide, does an excellent job of keeping pace with the mainstream public for whom this may be the first exposure to running controversies on college campuses. While this book is not intended to replace the traditional college guides, in light of the turmoil on college campuses today, it should be on the book shelves of every aspiring college student right next to the *Fiske* and *Insider's* guides.

Questions

1. What does Garcia-Diaz mean by "political correctness"? Do you have a similar definition? Explain.

2. What departments does Garcia-Diaz use the term "oppression studies" to describe? Would you use "oppression studies" to describe these departments? Explain.

3. What is Garcia-Diaz's critique of the phrase "differently abled"? Do you agree? Explain why or why not.

4. What other points or questions would you like to discuss about Garcia-Diaz's essay?

"A rose by any other name," Shakespeare tells us, "would smell as sweet." In a sense, things are as they are, independent of how we describe them. Yet what we *perceive* about things (what becomes salient to us) is affected by our words. We bring an audience in close with a detailed description or create distance with an unfamiliar technical term.

Our word choices also affect our audience's attitudes. A new rose named "skunk plant" may smell as sweet as other roses, but how many people would want to take a good whiff to find out?

Also, some members of the world conform to our labels. Roses may remain the same regardless of what we call them, but people do not. Children, for example, who are labeled "achievers" become achievers.[1]

Language—as advertisers, propagandists, and politicians know—has many effects. It can mislead, distract, and demoralize as well as inform, delight, and empower. No wonder the public debates language use. Whoever can control language can control audiences too—but only if those audiences remain inattentive to the powers of language.

This chapter introduces some primary types of language and their effects to help you select language for precise and engaging communication and to help you avoid being misled and controlled by others.

NOTICING DOUBLE MEANINGS

This section describes how authors use double meanings to their advantage and, sometimes, to the reader's disadvantage.

Deliberately Ambiguous Language

Ambiguity occurs, as we saw in Chapter 4, when words or phrases have more than one meaning. We've discussed how ambiguity undermines communication when an audience doesn't know which meaning the author intends.

Now we're going to look at how to use ambiguity to enhance communication.

We can use ambiguity to say more with less. Consider, for example, the title of this chapter, "Attending to Language." With one short phrase, it implies that the chapter is about paying attention to, or noticing, language as well as about tending, or taking care of, language.

Authors also use ambiguity to intrigue an audience. Consider, for example, the following title of a book about Richard Pryor's life: *Pryor Convictions and Other Life Sentences*.

By "convictions" does the author mean "being found guilty of crimes," and if so, what sorts of crimes—crimes against the state or crimes against one's own personal morality? By "convictions," does the author mean "strong beliefs"? And what "life sentences" does the author have in mind? Are we supposed to think of prison sentences here?

THE FAR SIDE   By GARY LARSON

Cartoonists choose ambiguous language to amuse their audience.

"Oh, wonderful! Look at this, Etta — another mouth to feed."

The title raises more questions than it answers, but in raising questions, it captures audience attention. I'd like to read the whole book now; wouldn't you?

Irony

When we use **irony,** we say the opposite of what we mean in order to express a more or less subtle criticism. With irony, our words have one meaning and our intentions express another. When we say, "Thanks for letting in some fresh air," to someone who has left the door ajar in weather that is 20 degrees below zero, our "thanks" is not genuine; our comment is ironic.

To understand our ironic message, our audience must figure out that we do not *really* mean what our words say. Sometimes we show by means of a raised eyebrow or tone of voice that we don't mean our words literally. At other times, the context makes our meaning clear. In the example above, the person who left the door ajar can tell from the ice cold draft that fresh air is not welcome.

Irony poses special problems for the reader who cannot see the look on the author's face or hear the author's voice. Background information about authors sometimes contains clues that they do not mean what they say. If we know that an author opposes laws outlawing marijuana, we will take her words of support for increased penalties for marijuana possession as ironic. Other times—as with Jonathan Swift's "modest proposal" that babies be killed and eaten—an alert audience finds the words too outrageous to be taken at face value.

Let's consider the following letter to the editor published in the *Press Democrat* on Saturday, July 13, 1991.

> Dear Editor: I was relieved to see that, according to your front page of July 5, a teen-ager accused of murdering two innocent people has confessed to the horrible deed and is jailed.
>
> However, I was pleased to see that a mere double murder did not give you any qualms about featuring, within inches of the murder story, the wonderful teen role model, Arnold Schwarzenegger, wielding a glamorous weapon with which he solves all his problems in the movie, "Terminator 2." After all, actors and theaters need money, and teens need role models.
>
> Thank you for your contribution to the quality of our community.[2]

I do not know the person who wrote this letter, so I have no background beliefs about her to give me clues about what she really means. But I am confident nonetheless that she does not mean literally what she says in the second and third paragraphs.

I inferred that she does not mean what her words say because I would not expect anyone to describe a double murder as "mere" or consider a man wielding a weapon a wonderful teen role model.

When using irony, be sure to give your audience some clues to indicate that you do not strictly mean what you say. Ask someone who doesn't know you well to listen to your speech or read your writing to see whether you've put in enough clues for your audience to discover your ironic meaning. And be sure to turn on your irony antennae when you're the audience, so you can pick up any ironic messages sent your way.

♦ 1. Do you find any ambiguity in the following titles of chapters from this book? Explain.

    a. "Deciding on Definitions"

    b. "Breaking up Arguments"

    c. "Evaluating Arguments"

♦ 2. Do you find any irony in the following? Explain.

    a. Wasn't that a great movie! The images were so dreamlike, in lovely muted colors.

    b. The movie was great all right. How many movies do you go to where half of the audience walks out and the other half falls asleep?

    c. The opening lines of *Pride and Prejudice* by Jane Austen:

It is a truth universally acknowledged, that a single man in possession of a good fortune must be in want of a wife.

However little known the feelings or views of such a man may be on his first entering a neighbourhood, this truth is so well fixed in the minds of the surrounding families, that he is considered as the rightful property of someone or other of their daughters.[3]

Weak Claims That Look Strong

When we use irony, we hope and expect that our audience will read between the lines of our language to discover our actual meaning. But authors do not always have such generous intentions. Some authors hope to deceive us into doing or buying something, yet they don't want to be held accountable for telling a lie. One popular way of achieving this goal is to use **weasel words.**

When a weasel eats an egg, it makes a small hole and sucks the egg through the shell. What remains looks like an egg but has no content. Some words and phrases treat sentences in the same way. When added to a sentence, they suck the strength from it. Consider, for example, the following sentences:

Aspirin reduces pain.

Aspirin helps reduce pain.

Everything in the store is discounted 75%.

Everything in the store is discounted up to 75%.

Scientists have discovered that eating animal fats causes breast cancer.

Scientists have discovered that eating animal fats may cause breast cancer.

new
up to
helps
virtually
perhaps
may
improved

Advertisers use weasel words to make weak claims that look strong.

In the examples above the words "helps," "up to," and "may" suck the strength out of the sentences they are in. Of course, we *should* suck the strength from our claims when we don't have sufficient evidence to make strong claims. When we're being open about the weakness of our claims, there's nothing misleading about using these words.

But some people using these words hope you won't notice that they're weakening their claims. Advertisers are particularly prone to using weasel words. They want to impress you with their products, but they are prevented by law from lying about them. Thus, when advertisers have no information to tell you about their products that is both impressive and completely true, they try to mislead you by using weasel words.

Newspapers too use weasel words to make events sound more dramatic than they are in fact. A bold front page headline "Scientists discover eating fats may cause breast cancer" at first glance appears to relate an important scientific discovery. Otherwise, why put it in bold and on the front page? But when looked at closely, the claim appears as empty as the egg the weasel sucked dry. You can see the emptiness of the headline when you realize that the newspaper might just as well have written "Scientists discover eating fats may not cause breast cancer." If the newspaper had found a scientific study that supported a causal link between breast cancer and eating fats, the newspaper would not have used the word "may."

Although weasel words weaken claims, they work to confuse because they are inserted into sentences with strong-sounding words to convey a false sense of certainty. In "With These Words I Can Sell You Anything," William Lutz calls "help" the number-one weasel word advertisers use. Other common weasel words include "virtually," "new," and "improved." As Lutz points out, " 'help' . . . does not mean conquer, stop, eliminate, end, solve, heal, cure, or anything else. . . . But . . . the claim that comes after the weasel word is usually so strong and so dramatic that you forget the word 'help' and concentrate only on the dramatic claim."[4] Similarly, unsuspecting people overlook the weasel word "virtually" in claims that something is virtually spotless or virtually 100% effective, because of the strength of the words "spotless" and "100%."

Besides making weak claims appear strong with strong-sounding words, advertisers also take advantage of the ambiguity of language to mislead consumers into thinking they are making stronger claims than they are. When a consumer hears the word "improved," the consumer might reasonably expect the product to work better; according to Lutz, however, advertisers call such things as a change in the scent of a detergent an improvement, although the change in scent has no effect on the effectiveness of the detergent.[5]

Lutz offers the following advice for reading ads: "[F]igure out exactly what each word is doing in an ad—what each word really means, not what the advertiser wants you to think it means."[6]

Sometimes what a word "really" means is what the federal law governing advertising says. For example, an advertiser may not call a product "new" for longer than six months. To get around this law, Lutz points out, manufacturers typically make minor, insubstantial changes in their products periodically so they can advertise their products as "new" again and again.

Sometimes what a word "really" means is what the dictionary says. Lutz describes a case in which a woman lost a suit against a birth control company for getting pregnant after taking a pill that was advertised as offering "virtually 100% protection."

> [T]he court ruled that there was no warranty, expressed or implied, that the pills were absolutely effective. . . . [T]he court pointed out that, according to *Webster's Third New International Dictionary*, "virtually" means "almost entirely" and clearly does not mean "absolute."[7]

If you learn to read advertisements and the "information" that comes with the drugs you take, you will be able to protect yourself from weasel language. As Lutz says, "Your only defense against advertising (besides taking up permanent residence on the moon) is to develop and use a strong critical reading, listening, and looking ability."[8]

Weasel words are effective because we tend to ignore them. To protect yourself from weasel words, practice highlighting them. Eventually, instead of lulling you into a false sense of security, weasel words will alert you to trickery.

◆ 1. Do you see any weasel words in the following?

Imagine a future that comes with a guarantee. It can happen. Simply qualify for the Army's Delayed Entry program, and training in one of over 250 different skills will be waiting for you when you graduate from high school. Best of all, that training is guaranteed in writing up to a year in advance. So, whether your dream is to do police work or drive tanks, direct aircraft or work in a lab, the Army can help to make it a part of your future. And that's not just a promise—it's a guarantee. For additional information, please see your Army Recruiter. . . . **Army. Be all you can be.**[9]

◆ 2. If you find any weasel words, explain why they are likely to be misleading in the context of this ad.

AWAKENING THE SENSES WITH LANGUAGE

This section focuses on the use of metaphors and descriptions to awaken the senses. As you will see, using language that awakens the senses can sometimes help achieve clarity and understanding; at other times, it misleads, distracts, or overwhelms an audience.

Metaphorical Language

Metaphorical language, as we saw in Chapter 4, identifies one thing with another that is quite different from it. Metaphors often awaken our senses and reveal things about our subject we wouldn't otherwise perceive, but sometimes they distort our vision.

Lively Metaphors   When we talk about abstract things, such as thought or learning, we can awaken our audience's senses and imaginations by using metaphorical language. In my classes, I use metaphorical language to describe degrees of understanding. I draw a pool on the board with a shallow end and a deep end and ask students to describe where they are: getting their feet wet, wading in shallow water, floating, swimming happily in the deep end, thrashing about, gulping for air, or sinking like a rock to the bottom.

Some metaphors are more lively than others. When they're new and surprising, they have lots of life. But after repeated use, a metaphor, such as "putting to sleep" for "killing," evokes no precise image. But tired metaphors, like tired people, come to life again when they get a break from routine. In *More Than Cool Reason* George Lakoff and Mark Turner give an example of how Shakespeare perks up the "death is sleep" metaphor by extending it:[10]

To sleep? Perchance to dream! Ay, there's the rub;
For in that sleep of death what dreams may come?

To get the most from the metaphors you use, ask how long they've been around. If they've been around a long time, try replacing them with a new metaphor or freshening them by extending them.

Misleading Metaphors   Metaphors sometimes conceal things we need to know or distort our understanding of a situation. In "War Is the Wrong Metaphor," Ellen Goodman argues that war is the wrong metaphor for responding to the problem of drugs. She writes,

> War simplifies the complex. It draws sides, us and them, good and evil. War demands a human enemy, people that in time become dehumanized. It eventually wipes out the differences between the coca farmer and the drug baron, the street dealer and the user. The pregnant woman and the pusher can lose their distinction in the process of becoming simply enemies.
>
> War has only one set of responses to a myriad number of situations: violence. It has only one approved pattern of behavior: power. Once begun it can only respond with more.
>
> And, of course, war, especially a "just war," demands sacrifice, even of our liberties. The one end it can see or accept without humiliation is total victory—zero tolerance—or abject surrender.
>
> Where imagery leads, policy follows. And the way we label things, talk and think about them, inevitably has an effect on how we behave. So the military cast to this declared War on Drugs easily becomes a disastrous way of thinking and planning.[11]

When talking about war itself, people sometimes use metaphors that disguise the real dangers of war. Carol Cohn gives some examples in "Nuclear Language and How We Learned to Pat the Bomb":

> A former Pentagon target analyst, in telling me why he thought plans for "limited nuclear war" were ridiculous, said, "Look, you gotta understand that it's a pissing contest—you gotta expect them to use everything they've got." This image says, most obviously, that this is about competition for manhood, and thus there is tremendous danger. But at the same time it says that the whole thing is not very serious—it is just what little boys or drunk men do.[12]

To avoid being misled by metaphors that limit your perception, you must first become aware of metaphors. You've got to stay alert, because tired metaphors won't jump out at you; you have to find them. Once you've identified metaphorical language, ask yourself what it reveals and what it conceals.

Descriptive Language

Vivid descriptions are concrete descriptions that awaken the senses. Pallid descriptions use more abstract terms and create fewer sensory images. Strong arguments use both vivid and pallid descriptions.

Vivid Descriptions   Vivid descriptions lead your audience to see, hear, taste, smell, or touch what you are talking about. Often, vivid descriptions evoke emotion. We use vivid descriptions to provide precise descriptions of problems and, at the same time, capture our audience's attention. We also use vivid descriptions when offering definitions by example. In the following, the second description is more vivid than the first:

1. Animals caught in the trap suffer.
2. A fox kit whose leg has been crushed by the force of the closing trap suffers such excruciating pain that it will chew its paw off to escape.

The second example evokes a visual image of an animal suffering in the trap, and you can almost feel the animal's pain.

We can tell how vivid our description is by watching our audience when we speak. Are their eyes glazing over, or are they shining brightly back? And we can look at our own reaction when reading our writing. Do our words create precise pictures in our minds?

Generally, vivid descriptions use concrete rather than abstract language. In each of the following examples, the descriptive language goes from the concrete to the abstract. Notice that the more concrete the description is, the more easily we can visualize precisely what the writer is talking about.

Fire-engine red. Red. A color.

The woman had a Mona Lisa smile. She was smiling. She had a pleasant facial expression.

Pallid Descriptions   Pallid descriptions are pale and wan, rather than vivid. They do not evoke precise pictures. We choose pallid descriptions for several reasons.

First, though vivid descriptions are useful for evoking images, they are not as efficient for referring to a wide range of things. We can describe the disaster in the garden more efficiently by using general terms instead of more specific ones. "The deer ate all of the plants in the garden," covers the ground more quickly than "The deer stripped the lower leaves from the six-foot-tall hollyhocks, ate the buds of the cream-colored roses, nibbled the flowering strawberries, and topped the blueberry plants."

We also save time and space with abbreviations. By using the acronym SWIP for the Society for Women in Philosophy we trade the descriptive power of the longer title for eleven syllables of breath.

Second, we choose pallid descriptions to avoid unwanted emotions. Witnesses, for example, might describe a fatal motorcycle accident in general terms to spare themselves and others the image of brains splattered across the roadway.

In times of war, the acronyms and abstract language used by the military distance us from the painful reality of death and destruction. In "When Words Go to War," Bella English describes some of the terms used in military briefings during the Persian Gulf War.

"Today, our troops executed BDAs in the KTO." Translation: Allied forces did bomb damage assessments in the Kuwaiti Theater of Operations, or, in simple English, surveyed how badly we bombed 'em. . . .

. . . The bombing of civilian areas such as schools, hospitals, and homes, has become "collateral damage." You're never "killed in action," but you're KIA. . . . And when military commanders speak of NBCs, they're not talking about the network; they're talking about nuclear, biological and chemical weapons.

We "engage" the enemy instead of creaming him. There is a "weapons delivery" instead of blanket bombing. Tanks are "neutralized" instead of being blown to kingdom come.[13]

Although pallid descriptions save time and emotion, they sometimes prevent an audience from perceiving the problem before them. To avoid being misled by an author's pallid description, translate the abstract terms into more concrete descriptions, as Bella English did above.

YOUR TURN C

◆ 1. Do you find any metaphors in the following? Are they lively or tired? Explain.

   a. "Screw" used to mean "sexual intercourse."

   b. Thomas Jefferson's words on slavery: "We have a wolf by the ears, and we can neither safely hold him, nor safely let him go."[14]

◆ 2. Is the above metaphorical language revealing? Is it concealing? Explain.

◆ 3. Which description do you find more vivid? Explain.

   a. It was really, really cold in my house this morning.

   b. It was so cold in my house this morning that even though I had on a down jacket, sheepskin boots, and a wool hat and was sitting next to a crackling wood stove, I was still chilly.

QUESTIONING ASSOCIATIONS

People associate images, experiences, and emotions with words that aren't strictly implied by their connotative meanings. If we don't learn to question these associations, we can draw false conclusions about the things the words label.

Positive- and Negative-Sounding Labels

Labels can sound positive or negative, depending on the associations we attach to them. One negative-sounding label is "terrorist." An associative definition of "terrorist" might include such things as images of a father being shot on his way out the door to work, vacationers confined for days in airplanes, and children screaming at the scene of a knifing.

Since "terrorist" has such negative associations, people generally prefer not to call themselves "terrorists." Recognizing that a terrorist by another name could bring approbation rather than fear, persons who use terror for political purposes adopt more positive-sounding labels.

At one time, the United States government supported the political agenda of a group that used terror to undermine the government of Nicaragua. President Reagan compared this group to the founding fathers of the United States and called them "freedom fighters." People who believed that differences between the United States and Nicaragua should be addressed nonviolently used the word "terrorists" to refer to the same group.

There was little disagreement about what these fighters did. No one disputed that they knowingly killed farm workers, school children, and mothers. But from one point of view, this killing was justified for a higher political goal; from the other point of view, the goal was a more oppressive, less democratic form of government. These different points of view gave rise to the two labels.

Positive- and **negative-sounding words** are frequently used during war. They're also used in times of peace. Advertisers link positive-sounding words to their products: "Fly the friendly skies of United." Politicians link negative-sounding words to their opponents: "bleeding-heart liberals" and "heartless conservatives." Both hope you'll be swayed by the feelings you have when you hear the words and won't look any further into the activities of the persons labeled.

To avoid being misled by positive- and negative-sounding words, remember the advice given in Chapter 1: Question your emotions. Pay attention to the emotions and attitudes you experience when you hear a word, then check to see if the author has given you adequate information to support those emotions and attitudes. Say to yourself, "That sounds bad, but what's really going on?" or "That sounds good, but what's really happening?" And when you're writing or speaking, be sure to provide your audience concrete information to support any positive- or negative-sounding words you use.

Language That Evokes Stereotypes

In "The Language of Prejudice," Gordon Allport points out that some labels, such as "blind" or "Chinese," carry strong, misleading **stereotypes**. As a result, these labels distort our perception of the individuals they describe. Allport calls these "labels of primary potency." [15]

These labels distort our perception of individuals and, as a result, influence our decisions. Suppose, for example, we want to hire a salesperson who is outgoing and communicates easily. Let's also suppose we associate reticence with Chinese people. If a friend suggests a Chinese woman for the job, we might be reluctant to give her an interview. We assume, because of the stereotype, that she'll be too quiet to make a good salesperson.

Allport noted that labels describing a person's disability, race, or ethnicity often carry stereotypes. We also associate stereotypes with descriptions of a person's gender, sexual orientation, age, and occupation. Some hear "woman" and think "emotional." Others hear "homosexual" and think "AIDS." Some hear "teenager" and think "wild." Others hear "lawyer" or "politician" and think "dishonest."

Some language actively promotes misleading stereotypes. To call a person with a disability a "victim" promotes the stereotype that persons with disabilities are helpless. To call a teenager "a bundle of hormones" promotes the stereotype that teenagers cannot make thoughtful decisions.

By drawing contrasts, we can imply that one group is more important than another. In a draft of the mission statement of the university where I teach, for example, the phrase "Western and non-Western" cultures was used. In a discussion at the Academic Senate about revising the mission statement to emphasize multiculturalism, one senator pointed out that rather than supporting multiculturalism, this phrase implies that Western culture is central. Another senator helped make the point by saying, "Yes, consider the phrase "Eastern and non-Eastern cultures."

Sometimes people use contrasting labels to give the false impression that certain groups are mutually exclusive and that one group is more respectable than another. Consider, for example, "Whereas scientists say . . . , environmentalists say . . ." or "Whereas scientists say . . . , peace activists say. . . ." These contrasts stereotype environmentalists and peace activists as unscientific and ignorant.

Language use also reinforces stereotypes about men and women. According to the University of Wisconsin-Extension Equal Opportunities Program Office and Department of Agricultural Journalism,

> Routinely using male nouns and pronouns to refer to all people excludes more than half the population. There have been many studies that show that when the generic "he" is used, people in fact think it refers to men, rather than men *and* women. Making nouns plural to ensure plural pronouns can help you avoid using the singular "generic" male pronoun.[16]

In other words, using the word "he" to mean "he or she" and "man" to mean "human" promotes gender stereotypes because, in spite of how "he" and "man" are defined in dictionaries, "she" does not come to mind when "he" and "man" are used. Thus, "she" often gets left out of the reader's picture of the activities "he" does. Also, sometimes "she" is used in a way that excludes males.

Expressions such as "lady doctor" and "male nurse" emphasize the gender of the person labeled, as if to say, "The other gender is supposed to do this activity, but sometimes a member of this gender butts in."

We use language in other ways to reinforce gender stereotypes. If we want our daughter to stop practicing soccer in the living room and we say, "Settle down now and act like a lady," we are reinforcing the stereotype that women are not rambunctious. If we use "paternalism" to describe interference with the expressed wishes of others for their own good, we support the stereotype that males are more guilty of well-intentioned interference than are females.

Shedding Stereotypes

We can shed gender and other stereotypes by using gender-neutral language, adding another descriptive word to the label, dropping the label, or changing the label.

Use Gender-Neutral Language   One way to shed stereotypes is to replace sexist language with gender-neutral language.[17]

Here are some examples of how to replace the generic "he" and "man":

Instead of "If he studies hard, a student can make the honor roll," use "If students study hard, they can make the honor roll," or "A student who studies hard can make the honor roll."

Instead of "Each nurse determines the best way she can treat a patient," use "Each nurse determines the best way to treat a patient."

Instead of "congressmen," use "members of Congress," "representatives," or "congressmen and congresswomen."

Instead of "policeman," use "police officer" or "detective."

Here are some examples of how to replace restrictive titles:

Instead of "career girl," use "professor," "engineer," "mathematician," "administrative assistant."

Instead of "working wife/mother," use "worker."

Instead of "lady/woman doctor" and "male nurse," use "doctor" and "nurse."

The following are some examples of how to replace stereotypical adjectives and expressions:

Instead of "male ego," use "ego."

Instead of "Founding Fathers" use "pioneers," "colonists," "patriots," "forebears," "founders"

But not all stereotypes can be shed so easily. There are no nonstereotypical alternatives to the labels of primary potency Allport describes. In other words, though "woman" carries stereotypes, alternative ways of naming the group would not escape the stereotypes that are attached to the group.

Add Another Descriptive Word to the Label   To minimize stereotypes we can add additional descriptive labels, such as "blind teacher" or "Chinese activist." By adding more details about the person, especially details that counteract our unwarranted assumptions, we bring the individual person more fully into focus. With each label we add, we create a more precise, less stereotyped picture of the person.[18]

Drop the Label   In the case of labels that promote stereotypes ("girl" for "woman") we can *drop the label*. We can refer to a woman without calling her a "girl." We can also sometimes avoid using labels of primary potency. A friend once told me about a time her department was looking for a visiting professor. My friend knew of a particularly well qualified philosopher who happened to be female. Now, my friend suspected that any reference to the sex of her proposed candidate would call up negative stereotypes in the minds of enough of her colleagues to nix her proposal, so she introduced information about the candidate without using any word that indicated the candidate's sex. Only after her colleagues began to nod their heads in agreement that this person had unusually strong qualifications and expressed interest in hiring such a person did my friend offer the candidate's name— from which her colleagues could infer that the candidate was a woman.

By giving the list of qualifications first, my friend undermined the distorting power of the label "woman." With this particular woman's list of credentials firmly in their minds, my friend's colleagues were protected from the stereotype that women are unphilosophical.

Change the Label   Another way to shed stereotypes is to change the label used to name a group. "Black person" and "African American" are labels that have been selected to shed the stereotypes associated with "Negro." "Persons with disabilities" is a label selected to shake off the stereotypes associated with "handicapped."

Changing labels is not a new way to drop stereotypes. Back in 1924, Mewok Indians decided they wanted a change from the label "Digger," that label having been applied to them by settlers who had treated them with scorn and disrespect. The tribe developed an imaginative way of calling attention to the change. They gathered for a two-day festival, at the end of which "an effigy labeled 'Digger' and well soaked with gasoline, was touched with a lighted torch. . . . Indians danced and chanted indicating joy that a hated name had passed." [19]

But stereotypes, like barnacles that reappear after a boat has been scraped of them, eventually attach themselves to the new labels. Changing labels is only a temporary solution. To permanently prevent labels from taking on stereotypes, we need to stop thinking in terms of stereotypes.

YOUR TURN D

◆ 1. Does the following language evoke or promote stereotypes? What stereotypes?

    a. "Provincial" for narrow-minded

    b. "Cosmopolitan" for broad-minded

◆ 2. Is the following language positive or negative? What positive or negative associations do you have to these words?

    a. "Patriot"

    b. "Traitor"

This chapter introduced words and phrases with double meanings, words that awaken our senses, and words that carry strong associations. Now that you're aware of these types of language and their effects, you can write more effective arguments. Paying attention to language also helps you recognize and compensate for slanting, the topic of the next chapter.

EXERCISES

1. For each of the following, discuss whether you find any examples of deliberate ambiguity, irony, or misleading weasel words. Explain your answers.

   a. A letter to the editor in *Time* magazine:

   > Of course the Internet should be rid of all its disgusting cyberporn, and those purveyors—and collectors—punished to the full extent of laws (to be quickly written). It is, after all, horrible for innocent children to see unnatural images of naked human bodies. How better for them to watch tens of thousands of natural images of murder and mayhem on television and in the movies.[20]

   b. "End the Recession" used to describe a treatment for balding.[21]

   c. The following ad that appeared in *Popular Mechanics*:

   > **Be the Boss of Your Own Business**
   >
   > FREE opportunity kits tell you how to earn money in one of 7 expanding markets.
   >
   > How often have you dreamed of being your own boss . . . of owning your own successful business? Foley-Belsaw's unique training programs can make those dreams come true!
   >
   > The key to your success lies in providing a service that is in great demand. Foley-Belsaw can provide you training in 7 different career fields where the demand is growing and will continue to grow through the twenty-first century. . . . [For example,]
   >
   > *Small Engine Service & Repair*
   >
   > Even simple repair jobs cannot be performed by the average small engine owner. With over 65,000,000 small engines in use across the nation (and that number grows by 1,000,000 each month), it's easy to see why small engine repair and service is a golden career opportunity. With specialized skills and knowledge you can earn as much as $49.94 for a simple tune-up that will take about an hour of your time.[22]

   d. "Go to Pot, Save the World," the title of an article about the many uses of hemp.[23]

2. For each of the following discuss whether you find any examples of lively or tired metaphorical language or of vivid or pallid descriptions. Discuss whether you find any of these language uses potentially misleading.

   a. *Destiny Magazine: The New Black American Mainstream* as the title of a magazine directed at African Americans who are Republicans.

   b. Yesterday, a car came careening around the hairpin corner by our house, skidded on the pavement wet from the dripping eucalyptus trees, somersaulted down the ravine, and exploded in a ball of fire at the bottom.

c. Something upsetting happened yesterday.

d. "Cutting red tape" used to describe a change in a governmental regulation.

e. An excerpt from *1001 Things Everyone Should Know about American History*:

> *Impressment.* Under British law, any subject of the crown could be drafted into the Royal Navy in an emergency. In wartime, captains sometimes stopped even neutral ships on the high seas and carried off any British-born sailors aboard. Thousands of men were impressed in this manner during the Napoleonic Wars. Since many American sailors were of British origin and since the British operated on the principle "once an Englishman, always an Englishman," the impressment of such sailors from American vessels caused bitter resentment in the United States.[24]

f. An excerpt from an essay titled "Kicking the Big One":

> An evil grips America, a life-sapping, drug-related habit. It beclouds reason and corrodes the spirit. It undermines authority and nourishes a low-minded culture of winks and smirks. It's the habit of drug prohibition, and it's quietly siphoning off the resources that might be better used for drug treatment or prevention. Numerous authorities have tried to warn us, including most recently the Surgeon General, but she got brushed off like a piece of lint. After all, drug prohibition is right up there with heroin and nicotine among the habits that are hell to kick. . . .[25]

g. An excerpt from an essay:

> I am very fond of bread. I am an extremely adventurous eater and will try any dish from any ethnic cuisine, and nine times out of ten I will enjoy the food and try it again. Open as I am to new food, though, when I approach bread I become the obverse of myself. Instead of the easygoing Puerto Rican that I think I am, I become gravely suspicious when I approach bread—it must prove itself to me. Bread is an elixir that can turn me into Ferdinand the Bull, content and dreamy, or bring out the fierce Mr. Hyde in me.[26]

3. For each of the following, discuss whether you find any positive or negative words or any words that evoke or promote stereotypes. Explain your answers. Where possible, rewrite the language to change how it sounds or to remove the stereotype.

a. *Let Freedom Ring*, title of a United States history textbook.[27]

b. From an article titled "Care and Feeding of the Plus-Size Child":

> If you are a large-size person, your children stand a very strong chance of carrying the same thrifty gene.
>
> No matter how comfortable you are with your own size and shape, dealing with a plus-size child's weight may be another matter entirely. Knowing what you've gone through to reach acceptance by society and self, you naturally hope to make a plus-size child's journey an easier one. . . .[28]

c. "Minority" used to describe African Americans, Asian Americans, or Mexican Americans.

d. "Hunk" to refer to a man and "fox" or "skirt" to refer to a woman.

e. An excerpt from a book arguing in favor of animal experimentation:

> . . . [V]aluable information has frequently come out of experiments that strike the layperson, who usually gives them only passing attention, as the most odious. To decide whether such investigations are morally justifiable in relation to their resulting benefits for humans (or animals) is no easy matter. . . . Once we penetrate beyond superficial media reports, antivivisectionist outcries, and skeletal outlines of research procedures published in specialist scientific journals—for example, by listening to scientists explain their work or reading their books and by reading the more accessible science magazines—previously puzzling and jumbled bits of information often fall into place to form a coherent picture, helping us make a more reasoned and cautious evaluation.[29]

f. Quote from the *Los Angeles Times* after the Japanese attacked Pearl Harbor:

> A viper is nonetheless a viper wherever the egg is hatched—so a Japanese American, born of Japanese parents—grows up to be a Japanese, not an American.[30]

4. Using the points made in this chapter, discuss the language in the following passages.

The Declaration of Independence

Thomas Jefferson

When in the course of human events, it becomes necessary for one people to dissolve the political bands which have connected them with another, and to assume among the Powers of the earth, the separate and equal station to which the Laws of Nature and of Nature's God entitle them, a decent respect to the opinions of mankind requires that they should declare the causes which impel them to separation.

We hold these truths to be self-evident, that all men are created equal, that they are endowed by their Creator with certain unalienable Rights, that among these are Life, Liberty and the pursuit of Happiness.

That to secure these rights, Governments are instituted among Men deriving their just powers from the consent of the governed. . . .[31]

The Declaration of Independence in American

H. L. Mencken

When things get so balled up that people of a country got to cut loose from some other country, and go it on their own hook, without asking no permission from nobody, excepting maybe God Almighty, then they ought to let everybody know why they done it, so that everybody can see they are not trying to put nothing over on nobody.

All we got to say on this proposition is this: first, me and you is as good as anybody else, and maybe a damn sight better; second, nobody ain't got no right to take away none of our rights; third, every man has got a right to live, to come and go as he pleases, and to have a good time whichever way he likes, so long as he don't interfere with nobody else. That any government that don't give a man them rights ain't worth a damn; also, people ought to choose the kind of government they want themselves, and nobody else ought to have no say in the matter.[32]

Take Notice

Livingston County, Ky. Sept. 5, 1817

And beware of the swindler JESSE DOUGHERTY, who married me in November last, and some time after marriage informed me that he had another wife alive and before I recovered, the villain left me, and took one of my best horses—one of my neighbors was so good as to follow him and take the horse from him, and bring him back. The said Dougherty is about forty years of age, five feet ten inches high, round-shouldered, thick lips, complexion and hair dark, grey eyes, remarkably ugly and good-natured, and very fond of ardent spirits, and by profession a notorious liar. This is therefore to warn all widows to beware of the swindler, as all he wants is their property, and they may go to the devil for him after he gets that. Also, all persons are forewarned from trading with the said Dougherty, with the expectation of receiving pay from my property, as I consider the marriage contract *null* and *void* agreeably to law: you will therefore pay no attention to any lies he may tell you of his property in this country. The said Dougherty has a number of wives living, perhaps eight or ten, (the number not positively known,) and will no doubt, if he can get them, have eight or ten more. I believe that is the way he makes his living.

Mary Dodd[33]

"Piggies Get Piggy, But Piggy Gets Piggies"

Purple Kush, Southern Trinity County, Emerald Triangle Bioregion, Northern California

Pot hunting is not all that it was once choppered-up to be during the bud bloom of the late 70s and early 80s. In fact, for the local CAMP cops, it has become quite boring. This week in the quiet hills of Southern Trinity and bordering Humboldt counties it seems the pot cops, bored of watching nudes along the local waterways as they patrolled for the most evil of weeds, saw a pig snerfing around beneath their oppressive chopper blades. They must have had a severe case of the munchies because they swooped down with their helicopter and shot that pig.

Next, they landed their chopper of justice and scooped up the dead pig. These stalwart CAMP cops then flew with their prize to the Double Flying-A Ranch to have this piggy prepared for them. Who was the German philosopher that said "You are what you eat"?

The Double Flying-A Ranch has been the traditional depot for deputies shuttling confiscated pot to the L.A. markets. When the brave helicopter pot cops presented the newly harvested pig to the ranch for preparation, someone got offended and called the 800 Fish & Game snitch number.

Here the trouble began for these upholders of justice: They were arrested for illegally hunting from a flying vehicle, and to make matters even worse, Piggy was not wild, but was some citizen's domestic livestock. Hence, the further charge of rustling was added to the charges against these protectors of peace and justice. . . .[34]

5. Using the points made in this chapter, discuss the language in the following ads:

a. Ad from Toyota:

→ **IT SHOULD LOOK BEAUTIFUL.
OUR ENGINEERS HAVE SPENT THE LAST
28 YEARS POLISHING IT.** ←

At Toyota, we know trust and confidence are things that must be built over time.

That's why Toyota engineers have been perfecting Corolla for over 28 years now.

In fact, despite overwhelming customer satisfaction, our engineers have continued

to refine the Corolla. Including such advanced features as a liquid-filled engine

mount. Side-door impact beams. Available integrated child safety seat.* And a 20-point

engine management system that's almost like having a Toyota mechanic under the hood.

That's probably why so many people consider the Corolla to be one of the most innova-

tive, most trustworthy cars built in America.** All because our engineers can't leave

well enough alone.

TOYOTA COROLLA
I Love What You Do For Me

b. Ad from the U.S. Air Force:

The War Prayer

Mark Twain

"The War Prayer" was first published in 1923.

It was a time of great and exalting excitement. The country was up in arms, the war was on, in every breast burned the holy fire of patriotism; the drums were beating, the bands playing. . . . [I]n the churches the pastors preached devotion to flag and country, and invoked the God of Battles, beseeching His aid in our good cause in outpourings of fervid eloquence which moved every listener. It was indeed a glad and gracious time, and the half dozen rash spirits that ventured to disapprove of the war and cast a doubt upon its righteousness straightway got such a stern and angry warning that for their personal safety's sake they quickly shrank out of sight and offended no more in that way.

Sunday morning came—next day the battalions would leave for the front; the church was filled. . . . The service proceeded; a war-chapter from the Old Testament was read; the first prayer was said; it was followed by an organ-burst that shook the building, and with one impulse the house rose, with glowing eyes and beating hearts and poured out that tremendous invocation—

God the all-terrible! Thou who ordainest,
Thunder thy clarion and lightning thy
    sword!

Then came the "long" prayer. None could remember the like of it for passionate pleading and moving and beautiful language. The burden of its supplication was, that the ever-merciful and benignant Father of us all would watch over our noble young soldiers, and aid, comfort, and encourage them in their patriotic work; bless them, shield them in the day of battle and the hour of peril, bear them in His mighty hand, make them strong and confident, invincible in the bloody onset, help them to crush the foe, grant to them and to their flag and country imperishable honor and glory—

An aged stranger entered, and moved with slow and noiseless step up the main aisle, his eyes fixed upon the minister, his long body clothed in a robe that reached to his feet, his head bare, his white hair descending in a frothy cataract to his shoulders, his seamy face unnaturally pale, pale even to ghastliness. . . .

The stranger touched [the preacher's] arm, motioned him to step aside—which the startled minister did—and took his place. During some moments he surveyed the spellbound audience with solemn eyes, in which burned an uncanny light; then in a deep voice he said—

"I come from the Throne—bearing a message from Almighty God!" The words smote the house with a shock; if the stranger perceived it he gave it no attention. "He has heard the prayer of His servant your shepherd, and will grant it if such shall be your desire after I, His messenger, shall have explained to you its import—that is to say, its full import. For it is like unto many of the prayers of men, in that it asks for more than he who utters it is aware of—except he pause and think. . . .

"You have heard your servant's prayer—the uttered part of it. I am commissioned of God to put into words the other part of it—that part which the pastor—and also you in your hearts—fervently prayed silently. . . . Upon the listening spirit of God the Father fell also the unspoken part of the prayer. He commandeth me to put into words. Listen!

"O Lord, our Father, our young patriots, idols of our hearts, go forth to battle—be Thou near them! With them—in spirit—we also go forth from the sweet peace of our beloved firesides to smite the foe. O Lord, our God, help us to tear their soldiers to bloody shreds with our shells; help us to cover their smiling fields with the pale forms of their patriot dead; help us to drown the thunder of the guns with the shrieks of their wounded, writhing in pain; help us to lay waste their humble homes with a hurricane of fire; help us to wring the hearts of their unoffending widows with unavailing grief; help us to turn them out roofless with their little children to wander unfriended the wastes of their desolated land in rags and hunger and thirst, sport of the sun-flames of summer and the icy winds of winter, broken in spirit, worn with travail, imploring Thee for the refuge of the grave and denied it—for our sakes who adore Thee, Lord, blast their hopes, blight their lives, protract their bitter pilgrimage, make heavy their steps, water their way with their tears, stain the white snow with the blood of their wounded feet! We ask it, in the spirit of love, of Him Who is the Source of Love, and Who is the ever-faithful refuge and friend of all that are sore beset and seek His aid with humble and contrite hearts. Amen."

[*After a pause.*] "Ye have prayed it; if ye still desire it, speak!—The messenger of the Most High waits."

It was believed afterwards, that the man was a lunatic, because there was no sense in what he said.

Questions

1. Quote some vivid descriptions, metaphorical language, and ironic language you find in Twain's article. Describe the effects of the language in the passages you quote.
2. What types of language do you find in the following quote from Twain's article: "In every breast burned the holy fire of patriotism"?
3. Does Twain use any language that evokes or promotes stereotypes? How would you rewrite what he says to shed the stereotypes?
4. Does Twain use any positive- or negative-sounding language? What are some specific examples?
5. What is Twain's main point? Do you agree with it? Explain.
6. What other points and questions about Twain's story would you like to discuss?

President's Speech to U.S. after Bombing Libya
NEW YORK TIMES SERVICE

The following speech by President Ronald Reagan was published in the *Press Democrat* (Santa Rosa, CA) on Tuesday, April 25, 1986.

Following is a transcript of President Reagan's broadcast Monday night:

My fellow Americans, at 7 o'clock this evening Eastern time, air and naval forces of the United States launched a series of strikes against the headquarters, terrorist facilities and military assets that support Moammar Khadafy's subversive activities.

The attacks were concentrated and carefully targeted to minimize casualties among the Libyan people, with whom we have no quarrel.

From initial reports, our forces have succeeded in their mission. Several weeks ago, in New Orleans, I warned Colonel Khadafy we would hold his regime accountable for any new terrorist attacks launched against American citizens. More recently, I made it clear we would respond as soon as we determined conclusively who was responsible for such attacks.

On April 5 in West Berlin a terrorist bomb exploded in a nightclub frequented by American servicemen. Sgt. Kenneth Ford and a young Turkish woman were killed and 230 others were wounded, among them some 50 American military personnel.

This monstrous brutality is but the latest act in Colonel Khadafy's reign of terror. The evidence is now conclusive that the terrorist bombing of La Belle discotheque was planned and executed under the direct orders of the Libyan regime.

On March 25, more than a week before the attack, orders were sent from Tripoli to the Libyan People's Bureau in East Berlin to conduct a terrorist attack against Americans, to cause maximum and indiscriminate casualties. Libya's agents then planted the bomb.

April 4, the People's Bureau alerted Tripoli that the attack would be carried out the following morning. The next day they reported back to Tripoli on the great success of their mission.

Our evidence is direct, it is precise, it is irrefutable. We have solid evidence about other attacks Khadafy has planned against the United States' installations and diplomats and even American tourists.

Thanks to close cooperation with our friends, some of these have been prevented. With the help of French authorities, we recently aborted one such attack: a planned massacre using grenades and small arms of civilians waiting in lines for visas at an American Embassy.

Colonel Khadafy is not only an enemy of the United States. His record of subversion and aggression against the neighboring states in Africa is well documented and well known. He has ordered the murder of fellow Libyans in countless countries. He has sanctioned acts of terror in Africa, Europe and the Middle East, as well as the Western Hemisphere.

Today we have done what we had to do. If necessary, we shall do it again.

It gives me no pleasure to say that, and I wish it were otherwise. Before Khadafy seized power in 1969, the people of Libya had been friends of the United States, and I'm sure that today most Libyans are ashamed and disgusted that this man has made their country a synonym for barbarism around the world.

The Libyan people are a decent people caught in the grip of a tyrant.

To our friends and allies in Europe who cooperated in today's mission, I would only say you have the primary gratitude of the American people. Europeans who remember history understand better than most that there is no security, no safety, in the appeasement of evil. It must be the core of Western policy that there be no sanctuary for terror, and to sustain such a policy, free men and free nations must unite and work together.

Sometimes it is said that by imposing sanctions against Colonel Khadafy or by striking at his terrorist installations, we only magnify the man's importance—that the proper way to deal with him is to ignore him. I do not agree. Long before I came into this office, Colonel Khadafy had engaged in acts of international terror—acts that put him outside the company of civilized men. For years, however, he suffered no economic, or political or military sanction, and the atrocities mounted in number, as did the innocent dead and wounded.

And for us to ignore, by inaction, the slaughter of American civilians and American soldiers, whether in nightclubs or airline terminals, is simply not in the American tradition. When our citizens are abused or attacked anywhere in the world, on the direct orders of a hostile regime, we will respond, so long as I'm in this Oval Office. Self-defense is not only our right, it is our duty. It is the purpose behind the mission undertaken tonight—a mission fully consistent with Article 51 of the United Nations Charter.

We believe that this pre-emptive action against his terrorist installations will not only diminish Colonel Khadafy's capacity to export terror—it will provide him with incentives and reasons to alter his criminal behavior. I have no illusion that tonight's action will bring down the curtain on Khadafy's reign of terror, but this mission, violent though it was, can bring closer a safer and more secure world for decent men and women. We will persevere.

This afternoon we consulted with the leaders of Congress regarding what we were about to do and why. Tonight, I salute the skill and professionalism of the men and women of our armed forces who carried out this mission. It's an honor to be your commander in chief.

We Americans are slow to anger. We always seek peaceful avenues before resorting to the use of force, and we did. We tried quiet diplomacy, public condemnation, economic sanctions and demonstrations of military force—none succeeded. Despite our repeated warnings, Khadafy continued his reckless policy of intimidation, his relentless pursuit of terror.

He counted on America to be passive. He counted wrong. I warned that there should be no place on earth where terrorists can rest and train and practice their deadly skills. I meant it. I said that we would act with others if possible and alone if necessary to insure that terrorists have no sanctuary anywhere.

Tonight we have. Thank you, and God bless you.

Questions

1. Do you find any vivid descriptions, metaphorical language, or ironic language in Reagan's speech?
2. Does Reagan use any language that evokes stereotypes? How would you re-write what he uses to shed the stereotypes?
3. Does Reagan use any positive- or negative-sounding language? What are some specific examples? What connotative, expressive, and associative definitions would you give to these words? What effect does this language have?
4. Do you agree with Reagan's main point? Explain.
5. What other points and questions about this essay would you like to discuss?

2 Pilots Destroy Record 23 Tanks

Alexander G. Higgins
ASSOCIATED PRESS

The following was published in the *Press Democrat* (Santa Rosa, CA), February 27, 1991.

A U.S. AIR BASE IN EASTERN SAUDI ARABIA— Two American pilots who fly as a team reported destroying a record 23 Iraqi tanks in one day as Saddam Hussein's armor started moving to meet the allied ground assault.

Capt. Eric "Fish" Salomonson, 28, of Berthoud, Colo., and 1st Lt. John "Karl" Marks, 26, of Kansas City, Kan., said each hit four tanks of the elite Republican Guard on Monday deep inside southern Iraq.

On two more missions near Kuwait City later that day, Marks destroyed eight tanks and Salomonson seven. They fly A-10 Thunderbolt II tank-killer aircraft, nicknamed Warthogs.

"We've been looking for tanks since the war started," Salomonson said. "Yesterday we found a bunch."

Marks added: "It was exactly what we had hoped, that the Army advance would do exactly what it did—that is force the Republican Guards out of their prepared positions, out in the open and onto the roads."

Lt. Col. Gene Renuart, 41, of Miami, commander of the 76th Tactical Fighter Squadron, said the pair "had an extraordinary day" and their performance was "quite exceptional."

He and other officers at the air base said they had not been keeping a tally of which pilot team had the most tank kills, but that 23 was so high it easily was a single-day record for the gulf war.

Salomonson and Marks were on standby Monday morning to provide close air support for advancing allied forces.

"We had a report from a night squadron that they had discovered a lot of Iraqi tanks on the move," said Salomonson, the flight lead. "We launched out of here, didn't quite know what we were going to see, so we got up there about sunup, and sure enough, there's tanks all over.

"We found them . . . and had tanks burning in five minutes."

Salomonson described the kills with awe. "It's the biggest Fourth of July show you've ever seen. . . . It's wonderful."

Questions

1. Do you find the descriptions of the effects of war in this article vivid or pallid? From reading the above story, can you tell whether Captain Salomonson and Lieutenant Marks killed any Iraqi soldiers? Explain.

2. Imagine that you are Iraqi and that a member of your family was in one of the tanks "killed" by Captain Salomonson and Lieutenant Marks. Can you imagine describing the burning of the tanks as "the biggest Fourth of July show you've ever seen"? Explain whether you find this metaphor revealing or concealing.

3. How would you rewrite this story to more fully portray the full effects of "killing" tanks?

"White Male" Resents Term

Richard Cohen

Richard Cohen writes a syndicated column for the Washington Post Writers Group.

WASHINGTON—I am reading the *Village Voice*, the New York weekly, and in a column criticizing the writer Pete Hamill for an article he wrote on homosexuality, I come across the phrase "white-male."

The writer was describing the sort of people *Esquire* magazine is supposedly now edited for: "Increasingly a magazine of moist musing designed to gratify the (orthodox) yearnings of menopausal, white-male credit-card holders."

Yikes, that's me!

OK, I may not be menopausal, but I am white and male, and my wallet is stuffed with credit cards. . . .

That phrase—white male—grates on me. Much of the time it's used descriptively. But here and there, someone says "white male" in a pejorative way. A quick computer search turns up a letter to the editor that says an article trashing soccer was written by "the usual white, American, male suspects" who prefer baseball.

The phrase comes up again in a quote from Karen Finley whose work was rejected for a National Endowment for the Arts grant. Her critics, she says, are "trying to maintain the power structure of the straight white male."

• • •

I am not so much troubled by these reckless and sweeping generalizations as I am by the implication that by being white and male I am some sort of partner in the grand and mysterious enterprise that runs this country.

I think sometimes of my father—born in poverty, raised in an orphanage, retired on a paltry pension and Social Security in Florida. Here is the white American male in all his glory—powerless, running nothing, controlling nothing and yet, by virtue of skin color and gender, held responsible and accountable for all that ails society. . . .

• • •

But it is as a writer that I protest the loudest. I am being told to butt out, that since I am a member of the Oppressor Class, I may not comment. I don't know the work of Karen Finley, but let's assume I did and didn't like it. Would my criticism be mere white, male bigotry? . . .

To simply dismiss anyone as "white male" is just the latest, most trendy, way of making an ad hominem argument—about as sophisticated as "Your mother wears a mustache."

Well, she doesn't, but her son is a white male. Wanna make something out of it?

Questions

1. What stereotypes does Richard Cohen find associated with "white male"?
2. What does Richard Cohen do to shed the stereotypes associated with "white male"?
3. Would Richard Cohen call the expression "white male" a positive- or negative-sounding word? Explain.
4. How would you describe the main point of Cohen's article? Do you agree with it? Explain.
5. What other points and questions about Cohen's essay would you like to discuss?

WRITING IDEAS

1. Review a paper you have written for this class. Rewrite it to
   a. Add an ambiguous title.
   b. Freshen or remove tired metaphors, remove misleading ones, and add a lively and revealing one.
   c. Add vivid descriptions where useful, and remove or qualify vague or misleading pallid language.
   d. Provide ample details to support any positive- or negative-sounding language you've used.
   e. Shed any stereotypes you find.

2. Write an ironic response to a proposal or action you disagree with. Be sure to provide sufficient clues for your audience to understand your intentions.

3. Write an advertisement for a product of your choice, using deliberate ambiguity, metaphorical language, positive-sounding words, and weasel words.

4. Do you believe that sticks and stones can break your bones, but words can never hurt you? Write a short argument in which you support or

reject this claim. Include at least one counterconsideration along with the support for your conclusion.

5. Write about whether this chapter and your class discussions complemented, conflicted with, supported, or left out any of your previous ideas about types of language you find it useful to pay attention to.

Notes

1. Research described in Anthony Pratkanis and Elliot Aronson, *Age of Propaganda: The Everyday Use and Abuse of Persuasion* (New York: Freeman, 1992) 47.
2. Kathleen Harness, "Role Models," letter, *Press Democrat*, Santa Rosa, CA, 13 July 1991.
3. Jane Austen, *Pride and Prejudice*, in *The Complete Novels of Jane Austen* (New York: Modern Library, n.d.) 231.
4. William Lutz, "With These Words I Can Sell You Anything," *Exploring Language*, ed. Gary Goshgarian (New York: HarperCollins, 1992) 168.
5. Lutz 170.
6. Lutz 179.
7. Lutz 169. (Wittington v. Eli Lilly and Co., 333 F. Supp. 98.)
8. Lutz 180.
9. Army ad from *Cycle World* Sept. 1994.
10. George Lakoff and Mark Turner, *More Than Cool Reason: A Field Guide to Poetic Metaphor* (Chicago: U of Chicago, 1989) 67.
11. Ellen Goodman, "War Is the Wrong Metaphor," *Press Democrat*, Santa Rosa, CA, 12 Sept. 1989: B4. Syndicated. The *Boston Globe* and The Washington Post Writers Group.
12. Carol Cohn, "Nuclear Language and How We Learned to Pat the Bomb," Goshgarian 128. Originally published in *Signs: Journal of Women in Culture and Society* 12 (Summer 1987): 687–718.
13. Bella English, "When Words Go to War," Goshgarian 153–54. Originally published in the *Boston Globe* 27 Feb. 1982.
14. John A. Garraty, *1001 Things Everyone Should Know about American History* (New York: Doubleday, 1989) 27.
15. Gordon Allport, "The Language of Prejudice," *Language Awareness*, 3rd ed., eds. Paul Eschholz, Alfred Rosa, and Virginia Clark (New York: St. Martin's Press, 1982) 209–18. Reprinted from Gordon Allport, *The Nature of Prejudice* (Reading, MA: Addison-Wesley, 1954), Chapter 11.
16. Rhonda Lee, ed., *Guide to Nonsexist Language and Visuals* (U of Wisconsin-Extension, 1985). Some of this material was adapted from International Association of Business Communicators, *Without Bias: A Guidebook for Nondiscriminatory Communication*, 2nd ed. (San Francisco: IABC, 1982).
17. Many of the examples I list in this section come from Goshgarian 251–55.
18. Allport 212.
19. From *News from Native California*, Volume 6, Number 2, Spring 1992, 15.
20. Randy Wilson, letter, *Time* 31 July 1995: 11.
21. From an ad for Premier Group, *GQ* July 1995: 142.
22. From an ad for Foley-Belsaw Company, *Popular Mechanics* Nov. 1994.
23. Kathleen Moloney, "Go to Pot, Save the World," *California Magazine* 17.
24. Garraty 5.
25. Barbara Ehrenreich, "Kicking the Big One," *Time* 28 Feb. 1994.
26. Jack Agüeros, "Beyond the Crust" 216.
27. Richard C. Brown, Wilhelmena S. Robinson, and John T. Cunningham, *Let Freedom Ring* (Morristown, NJ: Silver Burdett, 1977).

28. Garrett North, research by Janice Rosenberg, "Care and Feeding of the Plus-Size Child," *Big Beautiful Women*, Summer 1995: 19.

29. Michael Allen Fox, *The Case for Animal Experimentation: An Evolutionary and Ethical Perspective* (Berkeley: U of California, 1986) 113.

30. Quoted in Ronald Takaki, *A Different Mirror: A History of Multicultural America* (Boston: Little, Brown, 1993) 380.

31. Thomas Jefferson, *The Declaration of Independence*. Reprinted in Lynn Z. Bloom, *The Essay Connection*, 2nd ed. (Lexington, MA: D. C. Heath, 1988) 450–51.

32. H. L. Mencken, "The Declaration of Independence in American," *A Mencken Chrestomathy* (New York: Knopf, 1949) 583–84.

33. Mary Dodd, "To Warn All Widows of the Swindler," printed in Ruth Barnes Moynihan, Cynthia Russett, and Laurie Crumpacker, *Second to None: A Documentary History of American Women, Volume I: From the 16th Century to 1865* (Lincoln, NE: U of Nebraska, 1993) 369.

34. Purple Kush, "Piggies Get Piggy, But Piggy Gets Piggies," *Sonoma County Peace Press* Sept. 1992: 19.

6

Slanting for Fun and Profit

CHAPTER GOALS

- To understand what slanting is and how to distinguish it from falsehood.
- To learn how to determine the dominant slant of an article or medium.
- To learn how to recognize the principal slanting techniques, including omission, repetition, placement, the use of vivid language, and the use of evocative sights and sounds.
- To use your knowledge to identify and compensate for slanting in advertising, historical accounts, and news reports.

YOUR THOUGHTS ABOUT SLANTING

What do you think of when you think of slanting? Jot down your ideas; then read this newspaper article and answer the questions that follow.

Rape Victim Puts Beliefs before Justice

Sandra Chereb
ASSOCIATED PRESS

RENO, NEV.—A woman jailed for refusing to testify against a killer who allegedly raped her 16 years ago said Wednesday her defiance was right because the death penalty is wrong.

Lisa Christensen-Adamu, 35, was sentenced to two days in jail Monday for not testifying against Andrew Jacobson at his sentencing hearing. He could be sentenced to death for murdering a woman.

Christensen-Adamu said she opposed capital punishment and didn't want to relive the trauma of her own case.

"It was hard for me to do, but at the same time it was the only choice I had," Christensen-Adamu said.

"I believe our courts and our government are not a holy entity," she said. "Nobody has the right to kill anybody."

Washoe district Judge Brent Adams ordered her released late Tuesday after an investigator testified about the rape case. The judge said Christensen-Adamu's testimony was no longer needed.

Jacobson, 44, was convicted Friday of first-degree murder for murdering Julie Stewart, a 29-year-old mother of four whose body washed ashore in Pyramid Lake on Aug. 15, 1990. His sentencing hearing continued Wednesday.

Christensen-Adamu told deputies in 1975 that Jacobson broke into her Virginia City home and raped her. Although initially charged with rape, the charges were later reduced to breaking and entering under a plea agreement.

Jacobson didn't serve time for the crime, she said, adding that she was never notified of the plea bargain by the courts. She said she heard about it from a rape-crisis counselor.

Christensen-Adamu, who allowed her name to be used, now lives near Santa Cruz.

She refused to testify when called to the stand Monday.

"The more I think about this . . . the more I feel that I cannot contribute to the murder you are asking me for," she told the judge. "I could not be another nail in his coffin."

Christensen-Adamu said she believed the judge was "legally correct" in sending her to jail, but added, "I think he's lost perspective of humanity."

Her attorney, Martin Wiener, accused the prosecution of ignoring the victim's rights.

Questions

1. What impression do you have of Lisa Christensen-Adamu after reading this story?

2. Do her actions seem heroic, foolish, or nothing special one way or the other?

3. Do you have any ideas about how to change the story—without telling a falsehood—to create a different impression of Ms. Christensen-Adamu?

This chapter is called "Slanting for Fun and Profit" because, as you will see, slanting has a variety of effects. Sometimes it makes us laugh, and other times it leads us to buy products and accept ideas that profit others more than ourselves.

This chapter begins by defining "slanting" and identifying the primary purposes of slanting. It also explains how to determine the slant of a publication or broadcast medium and how to remedy the effects of slanting techniques.

By learning how to recognize and compensate for misleading slanting, you'll be better prepared to get the whole picture of a problem you're trying to solve—or at least know when you don't yet have the whole picture. And you'll be less likely to pass along naively misleading information to others. Learning to be on the lookout for your own tendencies to slant will make you better prepared to listen and report back accurately what others have said during conflict resolution.

DEFINING "SLANTING"

The word "slant" is sometimes given a negative definition, such as *Webster's* "to warp from objective presentation."[1] Notice the evaluative words "warp" and "objective" used in this definition. "Warp" has negative associations; for example, warped boards are not good for building solid structures. "Objective" has positive associations; something that is objective is real, and we can rely on it. Thus, if "to slant" is "to warp from objective presentation," slanting is something negative. We are ruining something we could have relied on. "Slanting" understood as "warping from objective presentation" is a word with a built-in judgment.

Instead of building a negative evaluation into the definition of slanting, I prefer to give a neutral definition of slanting and then evaluate the effects of slanting. I offer the following definition:

> **Slanting:** providing a partial and unrepresentative presentation of a particular position, opinion, or phenomenon.

Positive and Negative Effects of Slanting

To understand this neutral definition of slanting better, let's look at some of the purposes of slanting.

We use slanting to interest our audiences. If a friend asks me what I did over the weekend, I do not list everything I did, nor do I provide a representative summary. Instead I describe the events I believe will interest her.

Media also slant news coverage to interest their audiences. They include only the news of interest to their audiences, even though that news is a partial and unrepresentative presentation of what is happening in the world. For example, the magazine *Minorities and Women in Business* selects from all of the possible news stories only those about minorities and women in business. By reading this magazine, we find stories about women and minorities that we rarely see in the mass media news.

As a rule, newspapers report unusual stories to capture readers' attention. The local paper does not report a representative sample of stories about people taking quiet walks; instead, it reports the one story about someone who slipped off a cliff and had to be rescued by helicopter.

We use slanting to inform an audience. If an audience has heard only one side of a story, we tell the other side to give them a full picture. We use slanting to amuse an audience; for example, cartoonists exaggerate the nose or eyes of a politician to make us laugh.

People also use slanting to mislead or misinform. If you want to mislead someone but do not want to say anything false, slanting is the way to go. By leaving out information, you can tell only truths and still mislead. Even children are adept at this. When Janie wants Mom to punish Jonnie, Janie reports accurately that Jonnie pushed her, but she leaves out that she stepped on Jonnie's toe first. If Janie's mom doesn't get Jonnie's story, she might draw a false conclusion, that Jonnie pushed Janie without provocation. The support

THE FAR SIDE   By GARY LARSON   *Slanting for a select audience.*

"Details are still sketchy, but we think the name of the bird sucked into the jet's engines was Harold Meeker."

Janie gave was true, but it was incomplete. The part Janie left out would lead Mom to a different conclusion.

Picture Janie, now Jane, twenty years later, writing press releases for the White House, Standard Oil, or your university. Because Jane is paid to make her organization look good in the public eye, she will not present the full range of her organization's activities in her press releases. Instead, she will accentuate the activities that show her organization in a positive light.

How we evaluate slanting depends on how we evaluate these effects. As a rule, people want to be interested, informed, and amused by authors, not misled by them. Sometimes, though, people prefer being misled to hearing the unvarnished truth, whether it's about their appearance or the state of the economy.

Distinguishing Slanting from Summarizing

Ideally, when we summarize, we do not slant. In **summarizing**, we try to produce a brief but representative presentation of something. Suppose I say I am summarizing an argument I have read. The argument contains supports and counterconsiderations, but I report only the points in favor of the conclusion. In that case, my report would be slanted, and I would not have achieved the goal of a summary: to produce a presentation that is both brief and

Two different presentations of the events of the day. Which would you say comes closest to summary?

"We drove all day in the car, petted a rabbit, and had ice cream!"

"We drove to Grandma's house, then visited the zoo, had lunch there, and came home."

representative. However, if I had said that I would summarize only the support for the conclusion, I would be summarizing, not slanting.

It is difficult to shorten what other people say, put what they have said in our own words, and still give an accurate representation. Sometimes I think it's impossible to summarize. Nonetheless, some attempts at summarizing are farther off the mark than others. When we summarize, we can try to make our presentation as representative as possible.

Distinguishing Slanting from Falsehoods

When we slant, we don't tell a falsehood; what we say is true (or an exaggeration of the truth). Yet slanting and telling a falsehood frequently have the same purpose and effect, for an unrepresentative truth can mislead an audience as effectively as a falsehood.

YOUR TURN A

1. Review the news story at the beginning of this chapter ("Rape Victim Puts Beliefs before Justice"). Then write three short paragraphs that attempt to do the following.

   a. Summarize the news story.

   b. Slant the news story.

   c. Tell a falsehood about the news story.

2. Ask a friend to tell you about a personal problem. Listen carefully. Try to summarize what your friend said. Ask your friend to critique your summary. (You might tape record the original speech so you can both refer back to it.) Work with your friend to come up with a summary that captures the meaning of the original as closely as possible.

DETERMINING A MEDIUM'S DOMINANT SLANT

One way to avoid being misled by slanting is to be aware of it. If you know that you are reading a publication that is slanted toward a particular audience, for example, you will realize that there is more going on in the world than that publication puts forward.

Fortunately, many magazines clearly identify the audiences they are slanted toward. For example, the *National Review* labels itself "America's Conservative Magazine," *Filipinas* calls itself "A Magazine for all Filipinos," the *Advocate* calls itself "The National Gay and Lesbian Newsmagazine," *Emerge* identifies itself as "Black America's Newsmagazine," *Skin & Ink* calls itself "The Tattoo Magazine That's *More* Than Skin Deep" and the *Utne Reader* calls itself "The Best of the Alternative Press."

Other magazines, newspapers, and broadcast media, however, are not so forthcoming. Though they speak from particular perspectives and for select audiences, they do not identify them. Some even present themselves as speaking from God's eye view. For example, the *New York Times* labels its news coverage as "All the news that's fit to print." And television newscasters modulate their voices to give the impression that they are God telling the objective truth about the events of the day.

Textbook writers typically use an impersonal style to give the impression that they have no particular point of view or ax to grind. Their disembodied words lull us into the mistaken assumption that we are getting the full or at least unslanted truth, if they don't put us to sleep first.

Although the mass media generally keep a tight lip about their slant, everyone else, it seems, has something to say. Conservatives writing for the *National Review* claim the mass media is dominated by liberals. FAIR (Fairness & Accuracy in Reporting), a national media watch group, identifies its goal as focusing "public awareness on the narrow corporate ownership of the press, the media's persistent Cold War assumptions and their insensitivity to women, labor, minorities and other public interest constituencies."[2] *Extra!*, a publication of FAIR, argues that even PBS is dominated by conservative perspectives. According to *Extra!*,

> **PBS** executives admit that their weekly current events lineup favors conservative commentators, but say they can't find funding for an opposing show. Given its list of experts from the political/economic establishment, **MacNeil/Lehrer** is assured of corporate underwriting and a long life. But programs offering a diverse guest list that includes tough critics of government or corporate policies—such as **PBS's Kwitny Report**—have been taken off the air for lack of funds.[3]

I am not going to try to resolve the question of who dominates the mass media. Different papers and broadcast media have slightly different slants. Instead, I will give you a list of questions to think about when you form your own opinion about the media you read, watch, or listen to.

In trying to decide what perspective dominates a particular news medium, ask yourself five questions:

1. *Who owns the news medium?* To quote a familiar cliché, "Freedom of the press belongs to the one who owns the press." If you own a newspaper, you have much control over what goes in the paper. You can hire people who will collect and edit information in line with your perspectives on the world.

2. *Who provides income to the news medium?* Unless you have enough money to pay all the bills yourself, you'll have to get support elsewhere. Most mass media are funded primarily by corporate advertising. They must print corporate-friendly news to stay in business. Media funded primarily by subscribers must keep their subscribers happy.

3. *Who writes and edits for the news medium?* Writers and editors can add their perspectives by the slant they put on information they receive. Even so, their jobs depend on writing stories that do not offend owners, advertisers, and readers.

News writers must also stay on good terms with their sources or they will not have stories to tell. In *From the President: Richard Nixon's Secret Files*, President Nixon writes the following memo to his assistant Bob Haldeman to exclude a reporter from his presence:

> There was a woman reporter from the *Washington Post* at the church service this morning who was obnoxious to everybody who was there. She is not to be included in any further events at the White House under any circumstances. . . .[4]

4. *What audience is the medium directed to?* Even the mass media are directed toward particular audiences. Some mass media audiences are regional; others are national. A few mass media audiences—for example, in Europe, where people from different countries watch each other's television programs—are international to some degree.

Audiences affect what goes into the news and how it is written. Mass media audiences tend to be put off by news that is irrelevant to their daily lives, inconsistent with their political or personal values, or written in a style that is over their heads.

Thus, you will find a disproportionate amount of European news in a European paper and a disproportionate amount of U.S. news in a U.S. paper. Also you will typically find more openly critical news of a particular country's policies in a *different* country's paper. Italians, Japanese, or Mexicans can calmly read news critical of U.S. foreign policy—the same news would make much of the U.S. mass media audience blanch. Finally, you will find most U.S. mass media papers written in a simple, easy-to-follow style, so as not to challenge people with limited reading ability.

5. *Who supplies information to the news medium?* People who supply information to a paper also affect what goes into the paper, though the information may be altered by reporters and editors. Investigative journalism is expensive, so the mass media rely heavily on government or corporate press releases.

Even when news sources submit to public questioning, they find ways to minimize critical questions. Consider, for example, this memo from President Nixon to his assistant John Ehrlichman:

> On an urgent basis I need the press list before the press conference on Thursday. I intend to start following the practice used by Roosevelt and Eisenhower—calling on those press men who are not anti rather than constantly calling on those who are trying to give us the hook. . . .[5]

Answering the above questions will help give you an idea of the direction or directions a particular medium is likely to slant the news, but they will not tell you whether a particular story is slanted in a particular direction. You will need to read the story itself and compare it to other media accounts of the story to determine its slant.

YOUR TURN B

◆ 1. Read this passage, and answer the questions following. The passage is the complete text of a story published in the *National Review*, "America's Conservative Magazine," under the heading "The Week."

The Administration proposes to do something or another for owls that will cost "only" 15,000 jobs. That's not nearly enough, say the critics.[6]

a. What point do you think the story is trying to make?

b. Is the story of particular interest to a select audience?

c. What additional information would you like to have about the story?

2. Look through a magazine or daily paper you read. How would you describe its slant?

SLANTING TECHNIQUES

Being aware of the general slant of the media you watch, read, or listen to will help you stay on the alert for slanting. You can refine your ability to identify specific instances of slanting by studying the following **slanting techniques**.

Including and Omitting

What's included and what's excluded make a big difference in whether an audience gets a full or slanted picture of what's happening around them. The media slant by omitting relevant information from particular stories, undercovering important stories, and leaving out the opinions of certain groups. The information, stories, and opinions that remain form the audience's impression of what's important about the world around them.

Omitting Information   Perhaps the most basic slanting technique is **omission**, simply leaving out relevant information. We have already seen how little Janie used this technique with her mother.

History textbooks make effective use of omission to present historical figures of questionable integrity in a positive light. From the accounts I read as a child, I thought of Christopher Columbus as a hero who risked life and limb to discover what lay beyond the Atlantic. I found out recently that Columbus was primarily concerned with discovering how to provide large returns to his financial backers. According to "Discovering the Truth about Columbus," Columbus attempted to raise the needed cash by enslaving and terrorizing the Indians of Hispaniola:

> On Hispaniola, each Indian over 14 was obliged to bring in a certain quota of gold every three months. Indians failing to meet their quotas were punished by having both hands cut off, and usually then bled to death. Since there was very little gold on the island, most either fled or were killed.[7]

When history books do tell us about European oppression of Native Americans, they typically misrepresent the women as passive victims. In "*Resist!* Survival Tactics of Indian Women," Victoria Brady, Sarah Crome, and Lyn Reese challenge portrayals of Native American women as victims by telling stories (that have been omitted from standard texts) about ways Native American women resisted oppression and cultural assimilation:

> Although Indian women's response has been overlooked by historians, it is apparent that women did not sit passively to suffer their fate; they managed to grow up, marry, raise and support families, and sometimes fight back. Aggressive forms of resistance can be documented—fighting, speaking out against injustice, and devising unique ways of maintaining traditions—but most women employed more passive forms of resistance, modes shared with women in other dispossessed minority groups. Through stealth, deceit, running away, or the simple act of ignoring or hiding from the overriding culture, women used their wits to deliberately obstruct the group that sought to dominate them.[8]

Martin Luther King, Jr., is yet another national icon whose public persona has been distorted through the omission of critical facts. In *Unreliable Sources*, Martin A. Lee and Norman Solomon describe "the Martin Luther King Jr. we don't see on television" as a man who urged people to "directly confront the connections between racism, poverty and militarism."[9] Instead, the footage of King typically shown on the national holiday celebrating his birthday focuses on his concern with desegregation (which is a safe topic now that desegregation has become a mainstream value). Lee and Solomon write,

> Corporate-controlled news outlets repeatedly show King's beautiful but general "I have a dream" oration, to the virtual exclusion of his later speeches—like the address in which he declared: "A true revolution of values will soon look uneasily on the glaring contrast of poverty and wealth. With righteous indignation, it will look across the seas and see individual capitalists of the West investing huge

sums of money in Asia, Africa and South America, only to take the profits out with no concern for the social betterment of the countries, and say: "This is not just." It will look at our alliance with the landed gentry of Latin America and say: "This is not just." The Western arrogance of feeling that it has everything to teach others and nothing to learn from them is not just.[10]

Undercovered Stories   Besides identifying slanting in individual stories, we can look at the mass media as a whole and see that some stories are given prominence while others are played down or not included at all.

Each year, *Project Censored*, directed by Carl Jensen of Sonoma State University, seeks out news stories about significant issues that are not covered or that are undercovered in the mass media. The top three "Best Censored Stories of 1995" are described as follows:

1. TELECOMMUNICATIONS BILL. The bill would eliminate virtually all regulation of the United States communication industry. Source: *Consumer Project on Technology*, (Internet newsletter), 7/14/95, "Federal Telecommunications Legislation: Impact on Media Concentration," by Ralph Nader, James Love, and Andrew Saindon.

2. BALANCING THE BUDGET ON THE BACKS OF THE POOR. The budget could be balanced by 2002 without slashing Medicare, Medicaid, education, and social welfare. Source: *Public Citizen*, July/August 1995, "Cut Corporate Welfare: Not Medicare," by John Canham-Clyne.

3. CHILD LABOR IS WORSE TODAY. Children in the U.S. are working in environments dangerous to their social and educational development, health, and even their lives. Source: *Southern Exposure*, Fall/Winter 1995, "Working in Harm's Way," by Ron Nixon.[11]

Underrepresented Voices   As I mentioned before, people see things differently from different perspectives. A full account of any event would include representative voices of everyone involved in or affected by the event. Instead, most historical and news accounts feature only a few of the voices, and these voices typically come from groups with economic and political power. These political and economic insiders are invited to voice their opinions; outsiders are ignored or downplayed.

Though women are in the majority they have less political and economic power than men, and their voices are heard far less frequently in the mass media than men's. Women's voices are excluded not only in news coverage of Wall Street and war, but also in news coverage of reproductive rights.

In "Abortion Coverage Leaves Women Out of the Picture," Tiffany Devitt reports that stories about abortion in the mainstream media rarely cite women affected by proposed restrictions. She writes,

For example, the Supreme Court decision that enabled states to require women under the age of 18 to get parental consent before getting an abortion was widely covered. However, while more than a million teenagers become pregnant each year, and thousands of them are affected by state legislation requiring parental consent, reporters almost never sought their reaction. A *Wall Street Journal* article entitled "High Court Says Minors Can Be Required To Tell a Parent Before

Underrepresented voices.

Getting Abortion" (9/26/90) was typical, reporting the change in legislation without consulting anyone in the group that it impacts.[12]

In the same article, Ms. Devitt reports that a database that indexes articles from all major dailies indicates that over half of the newspaper stories about abortion do not address the effects of abortion legislation on women. Instead, they address how the abortion debate affects *politicians.* She writes,

> Though former Gov. Bob Martinez of Florida will never have an abortion, a *Washington Post* headline (8/2/89) declared: "Governor at Risk on Abortion Issue." While it is individual women, not political parties, who confront the choice to terminate a pregnancy, a *Wall Street Journal* headline (10/20/89) announced: "Abortion Debate Proves Painful for Republicans."[13]

Voices of African Americans are also underrepresented in the mass media. A different perspective shows up in journalist Kirk A. Johnson's study comparing six of the largest news media in Boston with four small print and radio outlets with black ownership. Johnson's study is summarized as follows by Martin A. Lee and Norman Solomon in *Unreliable Sources*:

"In the major media," Johnson found in examining coverage about the city's two mainly-black sections, "most of the stories about these neighborhoods dealt with crime or violent accidents and, all in all, 85 percent reinforced negative stereotypes of blacks. Blacks were persistently shown as drug pushers and users, as thieves, as troublemakers, and as victims or perpetrators of violence."

But the black media provided a very different mix of news coverage. By contrast, "57 percent of the stories about the two neighborhoods suggested a black community thirsty for educational advancement and entrepreneurial achievement, and eager to remedy poor living conditions made worse by bureaucratic neglect. Many of these stories went unreported by the major media."

Same city. Same neighborhoods. Same profession (journalism). Very different depictions of reality.[14]

There is general agreement that some groups are underrepresented in the mainstream media, but there is not complete agreement about who these groups are. In a *National Review* editorial criticizing Representative Maxine Waters of Los Angeles for saying "Riot is the voice of the unheard," John O' Sullivan identifies the "respectable poor" as the true unheard voice.

> . . . (T)here is a tacit coalition between the underclass and the liberal overclass against the respectable, hardworking Middle. Far from being "unheard," the underclass has its resentments anticipated and amplified by the media, the academy, Congress, the civil-rights leadership, etc. We are told in advance why rioters will riot, and afterward why they have done so. If rioters really are "unheard," that can only be because their senior partners in liberaldom won't let them get a word in edgeways.
>
> The genuinely "unheard" voices in our society are those of the respectable poor, the main victims of liberal indulgence of crime. They popped up on our screens for a few moments during the riots, denouncing the looters as a hostile "them," lamenting the destruction of their homes and livelihoods, and making no mention of Ronald Reagan's part in all this.
>
> It will require a small nuclear explosion to get them on ABC News again.[15]

People tend to be more observant about the exclusion of a voice similar to their own than they are of the exclusion of a voice that differs from theirs. When you are trying to determine which voices are excluded or underrepresented, be sure to consider a wide range of possible voices. Look not only for liberal and conservative voices, black and white voices, male and female voices, but also for other political perspectives and voices of other ethnic and racial groups. Look also for voices from different age groups, different socioeconomic groups, and different regions of the country and world.

Remedies for Slanting by Omission   Here are some things to do to compensate when you suspect slanting by omission.

1. Ask yourself how you would evaluate the situation the story describes and question whether there may be other relevant information that would lead to a different evaluation.

2. Read books, magazines, and newspapers written from perspectives different from those you commonly find in the mass media's accounts of history and news.

3. Listen to college radio stations and other alternatives to commercial radio stations.

4. Watch noncommercial television, documentary films, small budget, and international films. These are often shown at universities, colleges, and alternative theaters.

5. Interview people from underrepresented groups about their experiences.

YOUR TURN C

◆ 1. The *New York Review of Books* sent out a postcard offering free issues. Potential customers were to return the postcard, using one of two stickers with the following messages printed on them. Do these stickers give the full range of possible options? What's omitted?

Yes! I'm an intellectual	**No! I don't like to think.**
and proud of it. Send me 3 free issues!	Give my 3 free issues to someone who does.

a. What impression do these stickers give of someone who doesn't accept the *Review*'s offer of free copies? Is it positive, negative, or neutral?

b. Do these stickers leave out any information relevant to forming an opinion about someone who chooses not to accept free copies? What is it?

◆ 2. Answer the following questions about the story at the beginning of the chapter, "Rape Victim Puts Beliefs before Justice."

a. What impression did you get of Christensen-Adamu's behavior from reading this story? Is your impression of her behavior positive, negative, or neutral?

b. Was anything omitted from this story that is relevant to evaluating Ms. Christensen-Adamu's behavior?

◆ 3. Read the following passage from *1001 Things Everyone Should Know about American History*, and answer the following questions:

The Open Door. The name given to the policy developed by Secretary of State John Hay in his "Open Door Notes." Concerned by the way Great Britain, France, and Germany were establishing spheres of influence in the crumbling Chinese Empire, Hay in 1899 asked the powers to agree to respect the trading rights of all nations in their spheres. Their response was noncommittal at best. Shortly thereafter the nationalist-inspired Boxer Rebellion broke out in China, and in July 1900 Hay dispatched a second round of Open Door Notes, stating that the United States believed in "the territorial and administrative entity" of China and in "the principle of equal and impartial trade with all parts of the Chinese Empire." The Open Door policy worked well enough so long as no power was willing to use force to obtain and maintain special advantages.[16]

a. What impression did you get of the Open Door policy from reading this description? Is your impression of this policy positive, negative, or neutral?

b. Was anything omitted from this description that is relevant to evaluating the Open Door policy?

Highlighting and Hiding

Besides including and omitting information, stories, or points of view, print media slant effectively in how they present information. Through language use, placement of information, print size and intensity, and repetition within a news story, newspaper, or magazine, print media **highlight** some things and **hide** others.

Using Language to Exaggerate or Minimize   In Chapter 5, we looked at a number of effects of certain language devices—including metaphors to reveal or conceal, pallid or vivid language to distance or draw the reader near, words that evoke stereotypes to distort, positive- or negative-sounding language to affect the reader's evaluation, and weasel words to give a false impression of a claim's strength.

As a rule, reporters—unlike editorial and headline writers—stick to straightforwardly descriptive language and steer clear of positive- and negative-sounding language and lively metaphors in their own writing. But they liberally quote others whose words evoke emotions and conceal useful information.

During the Gulf War, for example, the mass media repeatedly quoted U.S. military language on the events taking place in the Persian Gulf. The military had selected the labels "Desert Shield" to name the mobilization of U.S. troops in Saudi Arabia in 1990 and "Desert Storm" to identify the war that followed soon after. The military chose these metaphors for their strong positive associations. "Desert Storm," for example, conjures up an image of sand blowing in the wind—a far more pleasant image than that of young men and women being blown to bits by exploding steel.

In a letter to the editor, a disenchanted reader offered her own label:

> I haven't heard what the name of the next operation is, but after viewing the human, monetary, and environmental damage wrought by both sides, "Desert Shame" seems appropriate.[17]

Newspapers typically choose labels that catch our attention, even if they are not the most accurate labels. NBC news anchor Faith Daniels pointed out the use of the name "Kennedy" to describe the rape case against William Kennedy Smith, a nephew of Senator Edward M. Kennedy. "The rape case in Palm Beach, for example—they keep calling it the Kennedy rape case, and the guy's name isn't even Kennedy."[18] But would people be as anxious to read countless stories about some guy named Smith?

Moving from the news to the opinion pages, you'll find plenty of ways that people use language to slant, including one we haven't discussed so far: exaggeration. Social critics frequently use exaggeration to get us to see something they think we may have overlooked. In "The Tedium Twins," Alexander Cockburn highlights the narrow points of view expressed on the "MacNeil/Lehrer News Hour" with the following mock interview:

Robert MacNeil (voice over): Should one man eat another?

(Titles)

MacNeil: Good evening. Reports from the Donner Pass indicate that survivors fed upon their companions. Tonight, should cannibalism be regulated? Jim?

Lehrer: Robin, the debate pits two diametrically opposed sides against each other: the Human Meat-Eaters Association, who favor a free market in human flesh, and their regulatory opponents in Congress and the consumer movement. Robin?

MacNeil: Mr. Tooth, why eat human flesh?

Tooth: Robin, it is full of protein and delicious too. Without human meat, our pioneers would be unable to explore the West properly. This would present an inviting opportunity to the French, who menace our pioneer routes from the north.

MacNeil: Thank you. Jim?

Lehrer: Now for another view of cannibalism. Bertram Brussell Sprout is leading the fight to control the eating of animal fats and meats. Mr. Sprout, would you include human flesh in the proposed regulation?

Sprout: Most certainly, Jim. Our studies show that some human flesh available for sale to the public is maggot-ridden, improperly cut, and often incorrectly graded. We think the public should be protected from such abuses.

MacNeil: Some say it is wrong to eat human flesh at all. Mr. Prodnose, give us this point of view.

Prodnose: Robin, eating people is wrong. We say . . .

MacNeil: I'm afraid we're out of time. Good night, Jim. . . .[19]

Placement   If you expect your audience to follow all the way to the end of your essay or speech, you can highlight information by putting it last. When writing for a newspaper, however, reporters use a different technique. People often read only the headlines or, at most, the first three paragraphs of news stories. Also, most people do not read the entire newspaper. They look at the front page, check out the sports section or Ann Landers, glance at the editorials and letters to the editor, and call it a day.

Knowing the reading habits of the average reader, a newspaper can create a slanted impression by *where it places a story in the newspaper* and *where it places information within the story*. An editor can highlight a story by putting it on the front page or hide it by placing it on an inside page. A writer can highlight information in a story by putting it in the headline or first few paragraphs of the story or hide it by placing it in the middle or end of the story.

Print Size, Print Intensity, and Repetition   Information that's written in large or bold type stands out and catches audience attention. Information that's repeated stays in the audience's memory. Authors highlight information by writing it in large or bold print and by repeating it. They hide information by writing it in small or normal print and by saying it only once.

In an ad for flatware in a Fingerhut catalogue, the largest, boldest type blares **$4.89.** If you look closely, you'll see that's the *per month* price. You have to turn to a different page of the catalogue and read small print to learn that you'll make those monthly payments for nine months and pay a total of $44.01 for the silverware. If you pay in full up front, the flatware costs $29.99.[20]

What a different effect that ad would have if the **$44.01** were in bold print!

Headlines—Slanter's Delight   Headlines provide an opportunity to use all of the above highlighting/hiding techniques. They catch our attention by their larger and more intense print. They highlight information in the story that is not always central to the story. They use words with built-in judgments when they want to exaggerate or sensationalize an event. They use pallid descriptions when they want to distance the reader. Most importantly, headlines are placed at the beginning of the story. Even if we don't have time to read the whole story, there's a good chance we will read the headline.

Consider the following *Press Democrat* headline: "Bloody Land Battle One of Largest Ever."[21] This headline was written only a few hours after the start of the Persian Gulf War before anyone knew how bloody or large the battle would ultimately be. A more apt title might have been "Battle in Persian Gulf Begins," but this title would not have captured the reader's attention as effectively as the headline the *Press Democrat* used.

Headlines often exaggerate the events described in a story. Here's another example from the *Press Democrat*: "Managed Care Forcing Demoralized Physicians to Quit."[22] The story is about physician burnout. The authorities quoted in the article point out that physicians are frustrated with the effects of managed care on their practices. The story also reports a study showing that physicians are applying for disability in greater numbers than before. However, none of the experts or studies quoted conclude that managed care forces physicians to quit.

Sometimes headline writers quote the judgmental language of partisan sources. A story in the *Christian Science Monitor* about the murder of a Colombian woman is headlined "The Death of a 'Crafty Little Blond.'" The woman reportedly was planning to give the United States Drug Enforcement Agency information damaging to Colombian president Ernesto Samper Pizano. In the story we find the label "crafty little blond" used by those taking responsibility for the woman's murder and by President Samper.[23]

Newspapers consider headlines so important that they hire headline writers to write them. Sometimes you'll find that the headline of a story slants the story in a slightly different way from the other slanting techniques used in the story. Editors and headline writers do this when they want to emphasize something different from what the reporter wanted to emphasize.

Highlight		Hide
Vivid language		Pallid language
Exaggeration		Weasel words
Place at the beginning		Place in the middle
Large print		Small print
Bold print		Normal print
Warm colors		Cool colors
Repeat		Do not repeat

Remedies for Highlighting and Hiding   Here are some ways to compensate for highlighting and hiding in the print media.

To remedy slanting with language:

Watch for exaggerations, metaphors, labels for groups, positive- or negative-sounding words, and pallid descriptions.

Replace language that conceals, sugarcoats, distances, or otherwise misleads with more fitting language.

To remedy slanting by placement:

Read through the newspaper, looking for short, out-of-the-way articles.

Read articles in their entirety, looking carefully for points of view that conflict with points highlighted in the headline and introductory paragraphs.

Read the opinion pages and letters to the editor for alternative views.

To remedy slanting by print size, intensity, and repetition:

Question whether the large, bold, or repeated points are the ones *you* want to remember.

Read the article or advertisement in its entirety, looking carefully for points you want to attend to.

Reformat the article or advertisement, accentuating the points you want to attend to.

YOUR TURN D

1. Read the two articles below and answer the questions following.

Kid to Be Caned for Car Caper

Michael Fay, an 18-year-old American from Dayton, Ohio, has been convicted of vandalism in Singapore. His punishment: a $2,230 fine, 4 months in prison, and six strokes of a cane. The American government has asked for clemency, but talk shows report that the majority of their callers favor the punishment. "I think they should whip his butt," one man said.[24]

Torture in Singapore

Michael Fay, an 18-year-old American from Dayton, Ohio, is the latest victim of Singapore's harsh criminal laws. Fay's crime: spray painting and throwing eggs at cars. His punishment: a $2,230 fine, 4 months in prison, and six strokes of a three-foot long, half-inch cane. For caning (called "torture" by Amnesty International) a prisoner is "tied to a rack shaped like an X. A practiced professional then dips the rattan in a chemical and strikes the prisoner with all his might. The first stroke breaks the skin. By the third stroke, the prisoner has usually passed out and must be revived. The scars are usually permanent." Talk shows—which don't always measure public opinion accurately—report that their callers support Fay's punishment. The American government has asked for clemency.[25]

◆ a. Does your impression of caning change when you read the second story? Explain.

◆ b. Explain whether either story uses any of the following slanting techniques:

- Omitting information
- Highlighting or hiding with language use
- Highlighting or hiding with placement
- Highlighting or hiding with repetition, print size, or print intensity.

c. Does one of the headlines better express your impression of the events described in the stories?

◆ 2. Review the news story at the beginning of this chapter ("Rape Victim Puts Beliefs before Justice").

a. What is highlighted or hidden in this story by:

- Language use
- Placement
- Repetition, print size, or print intensity

b. Rewrite the headline of the story, highlighting hidden aspects.

3. Suppose your teacher had two copies of a paper you'd written. On one copy the teacher wrote all positive comments in bright red pen and all negative comments in pencil. On the other copy the teacher did the reverse. Would you have the same or different reactions when reading the comments?

To remedy slanting with headlines:

Question whether the headline highlights or hides information you find important in the story.

Find information in the story that you would like to highlight.

Write your own headline expressing your view of the events the story describes.

Slanting with Sights and Sounds

Visual and audio media use many of the same slanting techniques that print media use. However, they use these techniques with images and sounds as well as with words.

Including and Omitting   People leave out sights and sounds they don't want their audience to see or hear. For example, suppose a travel agency wants to encourage people to tour Guatemala. The agency could show pictures of the beautiful Mayan women wearing colorful traditional clothing and leave out images of street children in rags. The agency could play a recording of the pat, pat, pat of women making tortillas and leave out the sobs of mothers of the disappeared. The agency could show tropical flowers and leave out images of buses spewing diesel exhaust into narrow city streets. On the other hand, if an organization wanted to raise funds for poor Guatemalan children, it would focus on images and sounds the travel agency left out. Consider, for example, the advertisement on page 29 of Chapter 1.

Ads for products typically leave out unpleasant sights that would discourage customers. You'll never see a person dying of cancer in a cigarette ad or someone passed out from recycled airplane air in an airline ad. Instead, you'll see happy smokers and safe, comfortable flyers.

Visual and audio media also include images and voices of people from some groups and exclude images and voices of people from other groups.

Highlighting and Hiding   Media apply the same or very similar highlighting and hiding techniques to sounds and visual images as they apply to printed words.

EVOCATIVE SIGHTS AND SOUNDS   Like language, images and sounds express as well as represent. Pictures of hungry children pull at our heart strings. Peppy tunes make us feel cheerful about buying pointless products that pinch our pocketbooks. Military marches create pride in country.

PLACEMENT   Media place images in key spots to highlight or hide. Newspapers put big, attention-getting pictures on the upper half of the front page to draw passersby to the newsstand. Cigarette advertisers place appealing pictures in the center of the eye's visual field (and put the warning off to the side).

REPETITION   Media also repeat images and sounds to highlight. During the Persian Gulf war, television news programs showed an image again and again of a bomb entering the center of a building and destroying it. Bombs like this one were labeled "smart bombs." After watching the precision of this bomb strike and hearing the bombs labeled "smart," many viewers stopped worrying about civilians getting caught in the crossfire. But, as Tom Wicker reported, 70% of the 88,500 tons of bombs dropped on Iraq and Kuwait in 43 days of war missed their targets.[26]

Remedies for Slanting with Sights and Sounds   Here are some things to do to compensate for slanting with sights and sounds.

1. Look and listen carefully to see what emotions and evaluations the images evoke.
2. Question whether the image maker has presented sufficient factual information to support the image's impression.
3. Find information about the event or story you find relevant.
4. Create a sight or sound to illustrate the information.

YOUR TURN E

1. Select an advertisement from a magazine of your choice; then answer the questions that follow.

   a. What emotional or evaluative impressions do the images evoke?

   b. Does the factual information you know about the product support the emotions and evaluations evoked by the images?

   c. What image would highlight information you find important about the product?

2. Watch a television commercial, and jot down the emotions and associations the images and music evoke.

This chapter has introduced slanting techniques to help you become more aware of slanting and less likely to fall prey to shared ignorance spread by the mass media. By questioning the assumptions we have held in the past and by questioning new information that we see, read, and listen to, we have a better chance of developing decisions we can live by.

Though I have focused on how to avoid getting misled by *others*, we also need to be on the lookout for *our own* slanting. We can avoid unintentional slanting by becoming aware of the perspectives from which we see the world and informing the reader of them. And we can listen to a variety of points of view to develop broader perspectives.

When writing this book—and this chapter, in particular—I think about the perspective from which I see the world and the sights and sounds that are readily available to me from my perspective. I see the grassy hills of northern California from my window, feel the moist, cool fog on a summer evening, and—after a short drive—hear the steady splash of the surf. I find myself automatically using these familiar images in my examples before I stop to think that many of you may find other images more familiar.

My physical surroundings form part of my point of view, and my social and political values and interests form other aspects of my point of view. My mailbox is filled with magazines, journals, and requests for funds related to women's issues, animal rights, and politically and economically oppressed people in Central America. But I know there are other worthy concerns, so I make periodic trips to libraries and news vendors to broaden the limited perspective my mailbox provides.

In spite of my efforts to broaden my perspectives, I realize that no matter what I do I will not develop God's eye view, and so I have chosen a writing style for this text that presents me as a person with particular cares rather than as an anonymous "objective" author.

By attempting to broaden my perspective and by presenting myself as a person with particular concerns, I hope to avoid misleading you about the subjects I discuss.

EXERCISES

1. For each of the short articles and ads on the following pages, would you say that the article or ad is directed toward a select audience? How would you describe that audience?

   a. The following item is from *Filipinas* ("A Magazine for All Filipinos") June 1995.

      ### Our Father in the Vatican

      While Jaime Cardinal Sin may be the best-known Philippine prelate, the highest-ranking Filipino priest in the Vatican is Fr. Jose Cardinal Sanchez. He is part of the Pope's Cabinet and had traveled with the pontiff during the latter's visit to the Philippines in January. The little-known Filipino cardinal was back in the country attending the 400th anniversary festivities of the Archdiocese of Cebu, as Special Envoy of His Holiness Pope John Paul II.[27]

   b. The following was printed under "International News" in *Ms.* magazine July/August 1995.

      ### Lesbian, Anglican, and Proud

      United Kingdom

      "I'm an out dyke," declared the Reverend Roz Hunt of Cambridge, England. The statement made Hunt the first openly lesbian Anglican priest in England. One of the first wave of female Anglican priests, Hunt told the *Times* of London, "I don't want there to be a furor, but I think it gets to the point where you just can't be bothered to be 'in.'"

      Most likely to be bothered is the Right Reverend Stephen Sykes, the Bishop of Ely, who ordained Hunt last year. Sykes's spokesman says the bishop doesn't believe the "current policy on sexuality should be changed"—which says that priests can be gay in theory, as long as it doesn't translate into practice. So while straight priests are permitted sexual relationships, the church says celibacy is Hunt's only option if she wants to keep her job.[28]

c. The following is from "Around the Nation" in *Destiny* ("The New Black American Mainstream") April 1995.

> WASHINGTON, D.C.—Coming soon to a college near you are classes in Gay, Lesbian and Bisexual culture. Along with Women's and African American studies, new courses in *Victimology* will be offered in universities around the nation. Under the heading of *Queer Studies*, courses will include *Sexism & Homophobia*, *Gay Men & Homophobia* and a full curriculum designed to "educate" the public about the deeper issues of homosexuality.[29]

d. The following is from "Hispanic Agenda" in *Hispanic*.

Sanctions against Legal Immigrants

> Part of the welfare reform package passed by the House, H. R. 4, the Personal Responsibility Act, would deny all non citizens benefits such as Medicaid, food stamps, Aid to Families with Dependent Children (AFDC), Supplemental Security Income (SSI), and access to block grant programs. In addition, all immigrants will be restricted from participating in all federal, state, and local programs for the poor, such as scholarships, and school lunches, if the legislation passes in the Senate and is signed into law by the president.
>
> In response, the Hispanic Caucus announced its bipartisan opposition to these measures. "The current wave of immigrant bashing has reached an all-time high," said Rep. Ed Pastor (D-Ariz.), Hispanic Caucus chair. "Immigrants make substantial contributions to the U.S. economy and do not come here for hand-outs." According to the latest estimates from the Urban Institute, legal immigrants paid more than $63 billion in taxes but received $34 billion in government services in 1992.[30]

e. The following is from "Dateline: U.S.A." in the June 1992 issue of *Emerge*, "Black America's Newsmagazine."

BLACK BROADCASTERS MAD

> NEW YORK, NY—Black broadcasters have voiced their displeasure over the recent FCC decision to deregulate radio ownership. The National Association of Black Owned Broadcasters told a congressional committee that its members were opposed to the commission's new rules.
>
> The FCC increased limits on individual broadcast ownership to 30 AMs and 30 FMs and instituted a new rule that allows an operator to own three to six stations in the same market, depending on market size. Previously, individual owners could have only one AM and one FM station in the same market.
>
> The African American broadcasters, whose position is being supported by AHORA, a Hispanic broadcast-ownership group, say minority media owners will be unable to compete with large broadcast groups, which can now afford to buy more stations and monopolize individual markets.[31]

f. The following is from *1001 Things Everyone Should Know about American History*.

> **Truman Doctrine.** President Harry S. Truman's response to a British Government message that it was no longer financially capable of supporting anti-Communist forces in Greece. In March 1947 Truman asked Congress for $400 million "to support free people who are resisting attempted subjugation by armed minorities or by outside pressures." This was an early sign of the Cold War.[32]

g. The following is from Howard Zinn, *A People's History of the United States*.

The Truman Doctrine

In Greece, which had been a right-wing monarchy and dictatorship before the war, a popular left-wing National Liberation Front (the EAM) was put down by a British army of intervention immediately after the war. A right-wing dictatorship was restored. When opponents of the regime were jailed, and trade union leaders removed, a left-wing guerrilla movement began to grow against the regime, soon consisting of 17,000 fighters, 50,000 active supporters, and perhaps 250,000 sympathizers, in a country of 7 million. Great Britain said it could not handle the rebellion, and asked the United States to come in. As a State Department officer said later: "Great Britain had within the hour handed the job of world leadership . . . to the United States."

The United States responded with the Truman Doctrine, the name given to a speech Truman gave to Congress in the spring of 1947, in which he asked for $400 million in military and economic aid to Greece and Turkey. Truman said the U.S. must help "free peoples who are resisting attempted subjugation by armed minorities or by outside pressures."

In fact, the biggest outside pressure was the United States. The Greek rebels were getting some aid from Yugoslavia, but no aid from the Soviet Union, which during the war had promised Churchill a free hand in Greece if he would give the Soviet Union its way in Rumania, Poland, Bulgaria. . . .

The United States moved into the Greek civil war, not with soldiers, but with weapons and military advisers. In the last five months of 1947, 74,000 tons of military equipment were sent by the United States to the right-wing government in Athens, including artillery, dive bombers, and stocks of napalm. Two hundred and fifty army officers, headed by General James Van Fleet, advised the Greek army in the field. Van Fleet started a policy—standard in dealing with popular insurrections—of forcibly removing thousands of Greeks from their homes in the countryside, to try to isolate the guerrillas, to remove the source of their support.

With that aid, the rebellion was defeated in 1949. United States economic and military aid continued to the Greek government. Investment capital from Esso, Dow Chemical, Chrysler, and other U.S. corporations flowed into Greece. But illiteracy, poverty, and starvation remained widespread there, with the country in the hands of what Richard Barnet (*Intervention and Revolution*) called "a particularly brutal and backward military dictatorship."[33]

h. Ad from the U.S. Army:

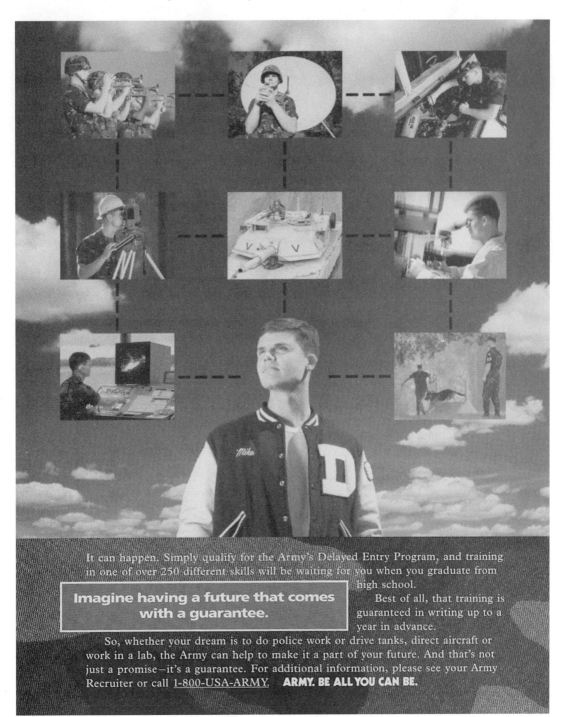

It can happen. Simply qualify for the Army's Delayed Entry Program, and training in one of over 250 different skills will be waiting for you when you graduate from high school.

Imagine having a future that comes with a guarantee.

Best of all, that training is guaranteed in writing up to a year in advance.

So, whether your dream is to do police work or drive tanks, direct aircraft or work in a lab, the Army can help to make it a part of your future. And that's not just a promise—it's a guarantee. For additional information, please see your Army Recruiter or call 1-800-USA-ARMY. **ARMY. BE ALL YOU CAN BE.**

i. Ad from Chevron:

j. Ad from Jordache:

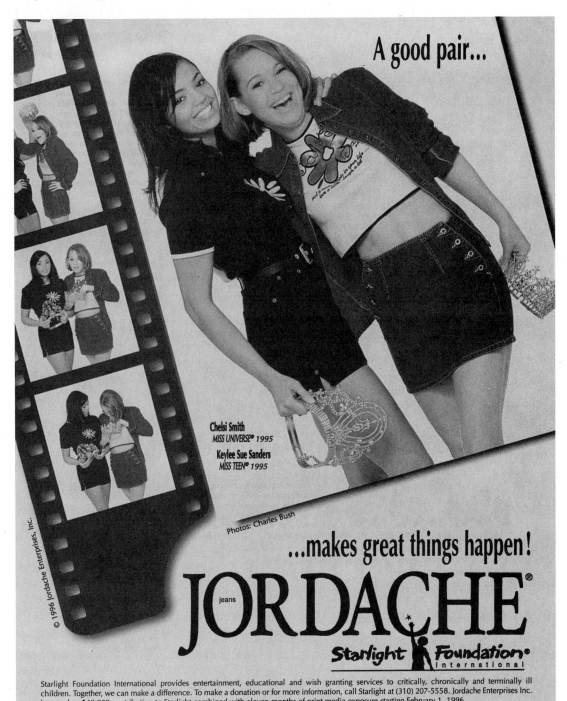

A good pair...

Chelsi Smith
MISS UNIVERSE® 1995

Keylee Sue Sanders
MISS TEEN® 1995

© 1996 Jordache Enterprises, Inc.

Photos: Charles Bush

...makes great things happen!

JORDACHE® jeans

Starlight Foundation International

Starlight Foundation International provides entertainment, educational and wish granting services to critically, chronically and terminally ill children. Together, we can make a difference. To make a donation or for more information, call Starlight at (310) 207-5558. Jordache Enterprises Inc. has made a $40,000 contribution to Starlight combined with eleven months of print media exposure starting February 1, 1996.

2. What general impression do you get about the persons, events, organizations, or products described in each article or ad listed under exercise 1? Is it positive, negative, or neutral?

3. Are any of the following slanting techniques used to create this impression?

Omitting information, points of view, or images

Highlighting or hiding by using language or evocative images

Highlighting or hiding through the placement of information or images

Highlighting or hiding through repetition or the size or intensity of printed information or images

Your other ideas

4. For each article or ad under exercise 1, what alternative headline and image would you use to create a very different impression? (Note: Except for item g, the articles are presented in their entirety with their original headlines.)

READINGS FOR ANALYSIS

College Students Abusing Plastic

Gene Yasuda
ORLANDO SENTINEL

If you thought saying no to sex or drugs was difficult, try walking away from credit cards.

For college students these days, it's easier to get a good parking space on campus.

From every corner of the campus lawn, sorority sisters and fraternity brothers offer you your very own plastic (Mom and Dad's OK not needed). Visa sends you a personalized letter promising a $500 credit line just because the company believes in your future.

And for signing up, the folks at Master-Card will send you Soul Asylum's newest CD for free. If that isn't enough, MasterCard will sell you tickets on the cheap to the rock band's next show—brought to your campus, of course, by MasterCard.

But what begins as a chance to pick up freebies, students say, is becoming one of their biggest problems on campus: plastic abuse.

Horror stories of students amassing five-figure debts are rare because lenders don't usually give sizable credit lines to students, who typically don't have steady or full-time employment.

Yet, students say nearly everyone has an undergraduate friend or two who have charged up $5,000 of debt.

"They've got three or four cards and they've maxed out on all of them," said Wendy Wesley, describing some of her friends' financial fixes. The 22-year-old advertising major at the University of Central Florida isn't immune from credit-card debt either: Her balance recently hit $1,300, which included an outlet mall shopping spree.

Wesley's friend Mike Johnson has charged himself deep into the red too. During his five years at UCF, the 22-year-old senior found himself the owner of more than 20 credit cards and $5,000 in bills.

"I've cut up some, but I still have plenty," said Johnson, who has three Visas, seven gasoline credit cards and a MasterCard remaining in his collection.

Credit trouble on campus shouldn't come as a surprise, given the number of cards in use.

Roughly 61 percent of all undergraduate students at four-year colleges and universities own at least one credit card, said Christian Donahue at Roper CollegeTrack, a marketing research company in New York. That translates into a conservative estimate of 3 million collegiate cardholders nationwide, he said.

It's a market that has exploded in recent years.

Although many students say they get plastic just for emergencies, good intentions often give way to temptation. Whether they're paying for pizza or tuition, students use credit cards as a preferred means of payment on campus.

At a time when college costs are spiraling, cash-strapped students say it's hard to resist the aggressive come-ons of credit-card vendors.

Their persistence is understandable: Courting college students has the makings of a serious relationship, not a one-night stand.

"It's what we call the first-card marketing syndrome," said Steve Apesos, a MasterCard representative. "We've discovered that our customers are very brand loyal.

"The first credit card they ever got, the one they got when they were back in college,

is the one they stick with," Apesos said. "They may change banks, move around the country, but when it's time to request another one they go with the brand they've always had."

Along with their savvy marketing campaigns, MasterCard and other credit-card companies—sensitive to growing complaints about how plastic abuse is saddling students with debt—are teaching students how to use credit wisely.

Like beer company campaigns advising drinkers to imbibe in moderation, the educational programs teach college students and high school seniors how credit cards work and how compounded interest inflates the price of products over time. "We think credit education is just as important as sex education," Apesos said.

Questions

1. What general impression does the article give you of college students using credit cards? Is it positive, negative, or neutral?
2. Does the language used contribute to this impression? If so, how?
3. Describe whether the placement of information in the article contributes to this impression. If so, explain how.
4. Do the sources quoted represent a variety of opinions on the topics?
5. Does the author leave out any information relevant to making an evaluation of college students using credit cards? Explain.
6. Rewrite the headline to create a very different impression.

Cuba Accused of Gouging Families of U.S. Exiles to Raise Cash
KNIGHT-RIDDER NEWSPAPERS

WASHINGTON—Cuban President Fidel Castro's government is raising hundreds of millions of dollars in desperately needed cash by taking advantage of the family ties of U.S. exiles,

charges a report released Tuesday by the Cuban American National Foundation.

Jorge Mas Canosa, chairman of the conservative anti-Castro foundation, accused the

Castro government of taking in nearly $235 million last year through what he said was a policy of "extortion" that overcharges exiles for airfares, shipping, humanitarian parcels and securing travel visas for relatives on the island.

"The Cuban government is exploiting the love of the Cuban-American community toward their relatives in Cuba," Mas Canosa said at a press conference. He called on the Bush administration to increase enforcement of the 30-year economic embargo against Cuba and narrow humanitarian exceptions.

An official at the Cuban Interests Section, Jorge Ruiz, called Mas Canosa's charges "outrageous." Rejecting claims that Cuba seeks to profit from divided families, Ruiz said the economic blockade has distorted the simplest transactions—including air travel and mail—and driven the price up.

He called Mas Canosa's statements "just another pretext to try to strangle the Cuban government economically."

Announcing the findings of a report released to the White House last week, Mas Canosa estimated that Cuba's economic benefits from humanitarian loopholes in the embargo last year included: $84 million from "overcharges" on parcels to the island, $49 million in cash and goods carried by travelers returning to Cuba, $40 million in cash remittances from exiles, $28 million in visas and fees for Cubans to visit the United States, $17 million for Cuban permission to extend their U.S. visits, $14 million for visits to Cuba by exiles, U.S. officials and journalists.

"The $235 million figure is considerably higher than the amount of transfers which the Treasury Department monitors," U.S. diplomats said.

The Treasury Department estimates Cuba took in a total of $48 million in cash transfers, gifts and travel costs.

Questions

1. What general impression does the article give you of Cuba's policy? Is it positive, negative, or neutral?
2. Does the language used contribute to this impression? If so, how?
3. Describe whether the placement of information in the article contributes to this impression. If so, explain how.
4. Do the sources quoted represent a variety of opinions on the topics?
5. Does the author leave out any information relevant to making an evaluation of Cuba's policy? Explain.
6. Rewrite the headline to create a very different impression.

Managua Rally Cheers Jeane Kirkpatrick

Stephen Kinzer
NEW YORK TIMES

At the time of this news story, President Ronald Reagan had designed U.S. foreign policy to support the Contras, a group trying to overthrow the democratically elected government of Nicaragua. Jeane Kirkpatrick was a strong advocate for President Reagan's policy supporting the Contras.

MANAGUA—Jeane J. Kirkpatrick drove a wildly cheering crowd of Nicaraguans to the brink of delirium here Sunday.

Cries of "Viva Kirkpatrick!" filled the air when the former chief American delegate to the United Nations stepped from a white

Cadillac. As she approached the speaker's podium, the crowd rose and began clapping rhythmically.

No one could recall the last time an American visitor to Nicaragua had received such a fervent reception. It began at Augusto Cesar Sandino Airport on Saturday, where Kirkpatrick was greeted by admirers who behaved as if they were welcoming a film idol.

If the visit seemed incongruous to some, it was because Kirkpatrick advocates the violent overthrow of Nicaragua's Sandinista government. She has campaigned for continued U.S. financing for the Contras, and Contra leaders consider her one of their most valuable allies. She is the only living American to have a rebel military unit named after her.

Photos of her arrival were featured in all three Managua daily newspapers. The pro-government paper Nuevo Diario described her as "one of the leading defenders of President Ronald Reagan's ultra-rightist policy towards Nicaragua."

A formal public speech by such a prominent Contra supporter is unparalleled in Nicaragua. Other Contra supporters, such as Senator Robert Dole, R-Kansas, have visited but have not spoken publicly.

The American Embassy distributed invitations to opposition political parties and other anti-Sandinista groups. Virtually every prominent opposition leader was in the crowd, which numbered more than 1,000.

"We love Kirkpatrick because she is strongly against the Sandinistas," said Jose Cruz Garela, a member of the Conservative Party. "We want what she wants for Nicaragua."

The government's response to her speech was, predictably, far different. Reuters reported that the Nicaraguan foreign minister, the Rev. Miguel d'Escoto Brockmann, lashed out at Kirkpatrick yesterday, saying: "She was sent here by the man who invented the war against Nicaragua—Ronald Reagan. She is an envoy of death."

The government maintains that only a few misguided or resentful Nicaraguans sympathize with the Contras and that all patriots oppose them.

In Managua, Kirkpatrick visited editors of the opposition newspaper La Prensa, which reopened two weeks ago after having been shut since June 1986. She also met with leading opposition figures, including Carlos Huembes, president of the principal anti-Sandinista coalition, Lino Hernandez, a human rights lawyer, and Mario Rapaccioli, head of a militantly anti-Sandinista faction of the Conservative party. She did not meet with any Sandinista officials.

The adulation that anti-Sandinista leaders heaped on Kirkpatrick matched their scorn for the other prominent American who visited Managua over the weekend, Senator Christopher Dodd, D-Conn. Some in the opposition consider him excessively tolerant of the Sandinistas.

Questions

1. What general impression does the article give you of Jeane Kirkpatrick and Nicaragua's reaction to her? Is it positive, negative, or neutral?

2. Does the language used contribute to this impression? If so, how?

3. Describe whether the placement of information in the article contributes to this impression. If so, explain how.

4. Do the sources quoted represent a variety of opinions on the topics?

5. Does the author leave out any information relevant to making an evaluation of Jeane Kirkpatrick and Nicaragua's reaction to her? Explain.

6. Rewrite the headline to create a very different impression.

WRITING IDEAS

1. Write two differently slanted reports about an incident that took place in one of your classes. Identify the impression you tried to create with each report (as positive, negative, or neutral) and the slanting techniques you used.

2. Create a political commercial, complete with photos, for a candidate of your choice. Identify the impression you tried to create and the slanting techniques you used.

3. Write an essay identifying the slant of this book. Describe the slanting techniques used.

4. Rewrite one of the essays for analysis or an article of your choice with a very different slant. Describe the slanting techniques you used.

5. Research the dominant slant of a newspaper, television station, or radio station in your area. Write a report of your research.

6. Write about whether this chapter and your class discussions complemented, conflicted with, supported, or left out any of your previous ideas about slanting.

Notes

1. "Slant," *Webster's*, 1986 ed.
2. "What's FAIR?" *Extra* March/April 1991: inside cover.
3. "PBS Tilts Toward Conservatives, Not the Left," *Extra* June 1992: 15.
4. Bruce Oudes, ed., *From the President: Richard Nixon's Secret Files* (New York: Harper & Row, 1989) 34.
5. Oudes 33.
6. "The Week," *National Review* 8 June 1992: 12.
7. "Discovering the Truth about Columbus," *Utne Reader* March/April 1990: 24.
8. Victoria Brady, Sarah Crome, and Lyn Reese, "*Resist!* Survival Tactics of Indian Women," *California History* Spring 1984: 142.
9. Martin A. Lee and Norman Solomon, *Unreliable Sources* (New York: Carol Publishing Group, 1991) 251–52.
10. Lee and Solomon 252.
11. *Project Censored*, "The 10 Best Censored Stories of 1995," (Rohnert Park, CA: Sonoma State University, 1996) 2.
12. Tiffany Devitt, "Abortion Coverage Leaves Women Out of the Picture," *Extra* March/April 1991: 5.
13. Devitt 5.
14. Lee and Solomon 243.
15. John O' Sullivan, "The Respectable Poor," editorial, *National Review* June 1992: 6.
16. John A. Garraty, *1001 Things Everyone Should Know about American History* (New York: Doubleday, 1989) 14.
17. Mark McLay, "Desert Shame," letter, *Press Democrat*, Santa Rosa, CA, 10 Mar. 1991.
18. "People Page," *Press Democrat*, Santa Rosa, CA, 17 June 1991. (Note also that the newspaper wrote William Kennedy Smith's name as "**William Kennedy** Smith.")
19. Alexander Cockburn, "The Tedium Twins," *Selected Issues in Logic and Communica-*

tion, Trudy Govier, ed. (Belmont, CA: Wadsworth, 1988) 39. Originally published in *Harper's* August 1982.

20. Fingerhut Catalogue, Fingerhut Corporation, 4404 Eighth Street North, St. Cloud, Minnesota 56395. Example from Virginia Flakne.

21. "Bloody Land Battle One of Largest Ever," *Press Democrat*, Santa Rosa, CA, 24 Feb. 1991: A1.

22. "Managed Care Forcing Demoralized Physicians to Quit," *Press Democrat*, Santa Rosa, CA, 9 Feb. 1996: A12.

23. "The Death of a 'Crafty Little Blond,'" *Christian Science Monitor*, 6 Feb. 1996: 6.

24. Information from Ellen Goodman, "Spare the Rod, Spoil the Child?" *Press Democrat*, Santa Rosa, CA, 14 April 1994: B4. Originally appeared in the *Boston Globe*.

25. Quote and information from Goodman B4.

26. Tom Wicker, "The First Amendment—A Casualty of War," New York Times Service, San Francisco *Chronicle*, 22 Mar. 1991.

27. "Our Father in the Vatican," "Brown Bag," *Filipinas* May 1995: 11.

28. "Lesbian, Anglican, and Proud," "International News," *Ms.* July/August 1995: 14.

29. "Around the Nation," *Destiny* April 1995: 13.

30. "Sanctions against Legal Immigrants" under "Hispanic Agenda" in *Hispanic*, June 1995: 10.

31. "Dateline: U.S.A." *Emerge* June 1992: 9.

32. Garraty 23.

33. Howard Zinn, *A People's History of the United States* (New York: Harper & Row, 1980) 417–18.

7

Evaluating Arguments: An Overview

CHAPTER GOALS

- To learn how to recognize a strong argument—that is, one that establishes its conclusion—by evaluating the acceptability, relevance, and sufficiency of its supports.
- To become more aware of the ways we commonly support arguments, such as referring to personal experience, citing an expert or authority, and relying on "common knowledge."
- To learn to distinguish relevant from irrelevant supports and to recognize instances of the straw person fallacy.
- To learn the difference between sufficiency in a deductive argument—called validity—and sufficiency in an inductive argument.
- To use your knowledge to evaluate arguments for decisions in personal, social, and political contexts.

YOUR THOUGHTS ABOUT EVALUATING ARGUMENTS

What comes to mind when you think of evaluating arguments? Jot down your ideas; then read this essay and answer the questions that follow. This passage is an excerpt from "Journal of a Voyage," written by 20-year-old Benjamin Franklin on his voyage to Philadelphia from London in the summer of 1726.

Mr G—n's Punishment
Benjamin Franklin

FRIDAY, AUGUST 19

. . . Yesterday, complaints being made that a Mr G—n, one of the passengers, had, with a fraudulent design, marked the cards, a court of justice was called immediately, and he was brought to his trial. . . . A Dutchman, who could speak no English, deposed by his interpreter that, when our mess was on

The
Main
Top

shore at Cowes, the prisoner at the bar marked all the Court cards on the back with a pen.

I have sometimes observed, that we are apt to fancy the person that cannot speak intelligibly to us, proportionably stupid in understanding, and, when we speak two or three words of English to a foreigner, it is louder than ordinary, as if we thought him deaf, and that he had lost the use of his ears as well as his tongue. Something like this I imagine might be the case of Mr G—n; he fancied the Dutchman could not see what he was about because he could not understand English, and therefore boldly did it before his face.

The evidence was plain and positive, the prisoner could not deny the fact, but replied in his defence, that the cards he marked were not those we commonly played with, but an imperfect pack, which he afterwards gave to the cabin-boy. The attorney-general observed to the Court, that it was not likely he should take the pains to mark the cards without some ill design, or some further intention than just to give them to the boy when he had done, who understood nothing at all of cards. But another [witness said] that he saw the prisoner in the main-top one day when he thought himself unobserved, marking a pack of cards on the backs, some with the print of a dirty thumb, others with the top of his finger, etc. Now, there being but two packs on board, and the prisoner having just confessed the marking of one, the Court perceived the case was plain. . . . [T]he jury brought him in guilty, and he was condemned to be carried up to the round-top, and made fast there, in view of all the ship's company, during the space of three hours, that being the place where the act was committed, and to pay a fine of two bottles of brandy. But the prisoner resisting authority and refusing to submit to punishment, one of the sailors stepped up aloft and let down a rope to us, which we, with much struggling, made fast about his middle, and hoisted him up into the air, sprawling. . . . We let him hang, cursing and swearing, for near a quarter of an hour; but at length, he crying out Murder! and looking black in the face, the rope being overtort about his middle, we thought proper to let him down again; and our mess have excommunicated him till he pays his fine, refusing either to play, eat, drink, or converse with him.

THURSDAY, AUGUST 25

Our excommunicated shipmate thinking proper to comply with the sentence the court passed upon him, and expressing himself willing to pay the fine, we have this morning received him into unity again.

Questions

1. What support does Ben Franklin report for the jury's conclusion that Mr. G—n had marked the playing cards "with a fraudulent design"?

2. Does the support Franklin reports convince you of Mr. G—n's guilt? Explain why or why not.

3. What support does Franklin offer for the decision to let Mr. G—n down after fifteen minutes of remaining hoisted up in the air?

4. Do you find Franklin's support convincing? Explain why or why not.

We have, in a sense, already begun the process of evaluating arguments. A good argument succeeds in communicating the author's meaning to the audience; it defines key terms and chooses language that entertains and informs. It also does something more. A good argument also achieves its primary purpose: to establish the acceptability of its conclusion.

Though arguments have one primary purpose, argument makers, like other communicators, sometimes aim to achieve several goals at once. They may be trying to figure out something, or explain something they've already figured out, trying to negotiate with someone, or resolve a conflict.

Whatever other purposes they may have, argument makers often are also trying to convince an audience to believe or do something. In the Ben Franklin story at the beginning of the chapter, for example, the jury didn't merely want to establish that Mr. G—n was guilty and deserving of punishment. They wanted to convince Mr. G—n to accept the punishment. Failing to convince him to go along to the round-top for his punishment, they used force against him.

To keep in mind this distinction between establishing a conclusion and convincing an audience, let's use the term **strong argument** to describe an argument that succeeds in establishing its conclusion and **weak argument** or

fallacious argument to describe an argument that fails to establish its conclusion. Let's call a **persuasive argument** one that succeeds in convincing its audience to believe or do what the conclusion says.

This chapter focuses primarily on how to evaluate the strength of an argument. By using the guidelines presented, you can help resolve disagreements with others by determining who has the strongest support for a position. You can also use these guidelines when writing papers and preparing speeches to develop the strongest possible support for your conclusions.

When determining an argument's strength, ask yourself three questions:

1. Are the supports acceptable?
2. Are the supports relevant to the conclusion?
3. Are the supports sufficient to establish the conclusion?

The rest of this chapter explores ways of answering these questions.

SEEKING ACCEPTABLE SUPPORT

If you want your support to establish that your conclusion is acceptable, the support itself must be acceptable. In other words, you can't base a solid argument on quicksand. Your supports must be steady and firm to hold up your conclusion.

The standard ways we arrive at **acceptable support** include personal experience, ecstatic experience, self-evident truths, inferential knowledge, authority, and common knowledge. These ways are not necessarily exhaustive; there may be others I have not covered. I invite you to see whether you can add to my list.

I believe that you will find these ways a helpful starting point for questioning support that you might otherwise have taken for granted. By learning to question whether support is acceptable, you will be less likely to be persuaded by a weak argument.

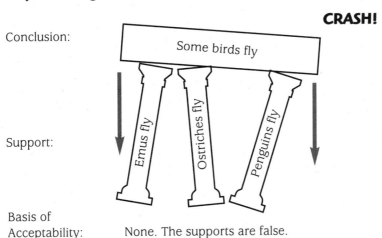

CRASH!

Conclusion: Some birds fly

Support: Emus fly / Ostriches fly / Penguins fly

Basis of Acceptability: None. The supports are false.

Unacceptable support.

Personal/Witness Experience

When you have **personal experience** of something, you witness it. You see, hear, taste, touch, or smell it. By means of these senses, we gain knowledge about the world around us. This knowledge is, in a sense, public. For example, many others may have also been eating popcorn at the movies along with you. They, too, will have seen, heard, tasted, touched, and smelled the popcorn. Like you, they can answer a question from their personal experience about whether the popcorn was unsalted or burned that evening.

We also have personal experiences of our internal landscapes. Besides the five senses listed above, we have a kinesthetic sense. We sense the movement of our bodies from the inside, so to speak. We feel the pain of a headache, pleasure from endorphins released during exercise, and the heartache of jealousy. These experiences, too, are not necessarily unique to you. Other people have headaches, released endorphins, and painful emotions. But this knowledge seems more private to us because others do not directly experience our pains and pleasures.

Questioning Personal Experience Although personal experience is one way to gain knowledge, our personal experiences do not always tell us the full or accurate story about what's happening around us. First, we may not have been in the best position to use our senses well. If we sit behind a tall person at the movie, we don't see everything that happens on-screen. If people are crunching their popcorn loudly in our ear, we miss a piece of dialogue.

Second, our sense organs don't always function at full capacity. We may be near-sighted, be hearing impaired, or have numbness in our fingers and toes.

Third, if we have taken medications, not slept for days, or have a high fever, we may see and hear things that are not present.

Fourth, as we saw in Chapter 1, we can be confused about our internal landscapes. When we try to adjust our emotions to what we think we should feel, we sometimes get out of touch with what we really do feel. We have to reflect on and question our emotions to know what they are.

Questioning Reports of Personal Experience Even when our personal experience was originally sound, our reports do not always constitute **reliable personal experience**. First, our memory may fail us over time. The name of the fishing boat fades from our memory; the fish we caught grows larger.

Second, people are not always fully candid about what they experience. They politely tell a weekend hostess they slept well, when they tossed and turned all night on a back-breaking sofa. They intentionally describe their internal landscape falsely, calling lust "love" to persuade a reluctant guest to stay overnight.

Third, people frequently make claims that go beyond their personal experience without giving additional support for those claims. We saw, for example, in Chapter 1 that people make claims about another person's intentions, as if they have direct sensory experience of a person's internal landscape. We rely on other people's reports to know what they are thinking or feeling, or we make inferences from what we perceive.

Finally, even when our reports are reliable, they are not always expressed effectively. Some people choose clear and effective language to express their experiences. Others use vague and confusing language when speaking and writing. We may also have difficulty understanding a report from a witness who does not speak our language with proficiency.

These points give us three basic questions to think about when we hear the testimony of a witness:

1. Is there any reason to think the witnesses' personal experiences do not give a full or accurate account of what happened?

2. Is there any reason to think the witnesses misremember, are not fully candid, or make claims that go beyond their personal experience?

3. Is there any reason to think you might not fully understand what the witness was saying?

Remember that your critically thinking audience will be asking these questions about claims you base on your own personal experience and on witness reports. So be prepared to inform your audience—either in the body of your paper or talk, in footnotes, or in a question-and-answer session—why you found the witness you quoted reliable.

Provided that we are aware of the limitations of our senses, we can use our personal experience to gain knowledge about the world around us and our internal landscapes. Also, well-told accounts of personal experience can enliven our essays or speeches and convey our knowledge of a subject.

Personal experience, however, cannot serve to support all claims, simply because not all knowledge is sensory. Moreover, none of us can be everywhere at all times, so we cannot have personal experience of everything that happens in the world. We need, then, to supplement our personal experience with other ways of attaining knowledge.

YOUR TURN A

◆ 1. The following are examples of reports of personal experiences. Explain whether you could easily understand the author's writing and whether you have any reason to question the reliability of the author's experiences or reports.

  a. Elena Albert's report of an event that happened to her when she was a child, quoted in Chapter 1, page 27.

  b. Dannie Martin's story about the death of Mr. Squirrel, quoted in Chapter 1, page 32.

  c. Ben Franklin and the people giving testimony in the story at the beginning of this chapter.

2. Review an argument you have written for this class. Are any of your supports acceptable on the basis of personal experience?

Ecstatic Experience

When people have an **ecstatic experience,** they lose a sense of themselves as individuals. People from many different religious and philosophical traditions, from Hinduism to Christian mysticism, from Plato to Alice Walker, have described these experiences. Some report having these experiences when giving birth; others report having them in the wilderness or when listening to music. Here's one fictional portrayal from Alice Walker's *The Color Purple*:

> [Shug] say, My first step from the old white man was trees. Then air. Then birds. Then other people. But one day when I was sitting quiet and feeling like a motherless child, which I was, it come to me: that feeling of being part of everything, not separate at all. I knew that if I cut a tree, my arm would bleed. And I laughed and I cried and I run all round the house. I knew just what it was. In fact, when it happen, you can't miss it. It sort of like you know what, she say, grinning and rubbing high up on my thigh.[1]

These experiences, as the philosopher William James pointed out almost a hundred years ago, show that there is more to consciousness than sensory awareness, and they may also give us knowledge of Divinity. They are, in any case, transformative for those who experience them.[2]

People use their experiences from ecstatic states to guide their actions. You would treat a tree differently if you felt that if you cut it your arm would bleed. Support derived from mystic states, however, will probably not persuade an audience who has never experienced one or who does not trust your mystic experience.

YOUR TURN B

1. Have you ever experienced an ecstatic state or known someone personally who has? Can you give directions for what another person might do to experience a mystical state?

2. Do you believe mystical states provide one with knowledge about the Divine and correct guidelines for action? Explain.

Self-Evident Truths

Some truths are said to be **self-evident truths;** that is, as soon as you hear them, you simply know them to be true. You need no sensory or ecstatic experience to know them, nor do they require logical proof.

Certain principles of logic are self-evident. Here are some examples: "If something is the case, then it is the case"; for instance, if something is a circle, it is a circle. "It's impossible for something to be what it is and not be what it is at the same time and in the same respect"; for instance, it's impossible for something to be a circle and a square. It's simply impossible to imagine these truths being false.

Some guiding moral principles have been called self-evident. Thomas Jefferson begins *The Declaration of Independence* with claims he offers as self-evident.

> We hold these truths to be self-evident, that all men are created equal, that they are endowed by their Creator with certain unalienable Rights, that among these are Life, Liberty and the pursuit of Happiness.[3]

Although many people accept the truths that Jefferson lists, other people might not find them self-evident.

YOUR TURN C

◆ 1. Would you say that any of the following claims are self-evident? Explain.

    a. All of my sisters are female.

    b. 2 + 2 = 4.

    c. Pain is undesirable.

    d. Goldfinches eat thistle.

    e. Being treated with respect is desirable.

2. Are any of the supports you've used for an argument you've given this semester acceptable as self-evident? Which ones?

Inferential Knowledge

Inferential knowledge is knowledge that we derive from other knowledge. In other words, we gain inferential knowledge by drawing a conclusion from acceptable support. Much of our knowledge is inferential. We derive our knowledge that our sister is angry, for example, from our knowledge that she's slamming the door now and that she slams the door whenever she's angry.

Not all of our inferences yield knowledge. As we saw in Chapter 1, we sometimes jump to conclusions without sufficient evidence. Whenever we use an inference to support a conclusion, we must therefore check whether it is both relevant and sufficient. We'll discuss the terms "relevant" and "sufficient" later in this chapter.

To determine whether a support is acceptable as inferential knowledge, ask yourself three questions:

1. Is the support (or should the support be) a conclusion of a subargument?
2. Is the evidence for the support sufficient to establish the support?
3. Is the evidence for the support itself acceptable?

Authority

The word **authority** has two senses: it can be defined as one who has expertise or one who has the right to command obedience in virtue of a role the person performs. We use both of these types of authority as bases for support.

Don't rely on experts until you know their credentials.

Drawing by P. Steiner; © 1993 The New Yorker Magazine, Inc.

"On the Internet, nobody knows you're a dog."

Expertise   When you thoroughly study a particular subject, whether it's criminal law, internal medicine, philosophy of science, gardening, building, basketball, or anything else, you develop **expertise** in that subject. As part of your formal schooling in the subject, you read about the experiences of others and learn the methods of making reliable inferences in your field. As a practitioner, you add personal experience to your theoretical and book knowledge. As your knowledge increases, you become an expert or an authority, someone other people call on for reliable information about your subject.

As we saw in Chapter 2, we rely on experts for our knowledge about areas where we have no expertise. The claims we base on authority or expertise are acceptable only if those authorities or experts are reliable. To make a thorough evaluation of an argument, therefore, we must question experts and their reports. Here are some guidelines.

First, consider the person's **degree of expertise.** The expert's training and experience in the field are two indicators of the degree of expertise. A poorly trained doctor, for example, won't serve you as well as a well-trained one, and even well-trained doctors need plenty of experience to fully develop their expertise.

Second, consider the person's **scope of expertise.** Some authorities are generalists, whereas others are specialists. Generalists have a wide range of knowledge, but they do not always have well-developed expertise in each area. Specialists have well-developed knowledge in a particular area but may be unable to provide expertise outside their areas. For medical treatment, for example, you typically go to a generalist for routine medical care and to a specialist for medical problems requiring advanced techniques or knowledge.

Also, take care not to rely on an expert in one area for expertise in another. Your doctor may well be an expert in how to cure a particular condition, but not in whether the cost of the cure is worth it to you.

Third, check whether an expert's claims are **controversial.** If you look beyond the first expert you consult, you'll sometimes find another expert who disagrees. If you ask a question that has no settled answer, experts sometimes let you know that; other times, they will not, so you need to ask.

Fourth, be aware that authorities are not always fully candid about what they know. Doctors sometimes withhold information from dying patients, for example, or exaggerate the need for certain types of lucrative medical treatments. In general, authorities are just as susceptible to slanting or lying as anyone else.

Fifth, remember that expertise has nothing to do with looks. This may sound obvious to you, but researchers have found that people tend to agree more readily with people they find attractive.[4] So guard against accepting a claim merely because you find the expert who makes it attractive. And just in case your audience hasn't learned to disregard looks, you might try combing your hair before giving your speech.

Sixth, be sure that an authority's report is useful to you. Some reports may use language you can't easily understand. When selecting a doctor or an attorney, for example, you need to find one who not only is knowledgeable and candid but also can explain technical information in everyday language.

These points give us six questions to think about when evaluating experts:

1. Is the expert's degree of expertise sufficient for your purposes?
2. Is the expert's scope of expertise sufficient for your purposes?
3. Is the expert's claim controversial?
4. Is there any reason to think the expert might not be fully candid?
5. Are you paying attention to how the expert looks rather than to whether the expert is reliable?
6. Is there any reason to think you might not fully understand the expert's report?

Once again, remember that your critically thinking audience will be asking these questions about you when you answer questions based on your expertise. And they'll be asking these questions about the experts you quote. So be prepared to inform your audience—either in the body of your paper or talk, in footnotes, or in a question-and-answer session—why you found the expert you quoted reliable.

But if you are not an expert yourself in a field you want information about, how do you answer these six questions? You can ask other experts. If you know someone who's a surgical nurse and good at what he does, you might ask him about surgeons he's worked with. If you want to know how much expertise a research scientist has, check reviews of her research to see how other scientists have responded to her work.

You can also get as much general knowledge about the subject as possible before you consult with an expert. Read a book about wills, for example, before selecting an attorney to drawn your own will. By getting some basic information, you will be able to pose more intelligent questions. In the end, you have to use your own judgment. If you can't understand what the recommended expert says, you'll want to keep looking.

Authority of Role Parents, teachers, police officers, judges, and employers are all authorities. They all have the right to command obedience in virtue of their roles (**authority of role**). As a result, we sometimes base our acceptance of an action on the fact that they commanded it.

However, we can use an authority's command to justify our actions only if the command is within the authority's scope. A teacher does not have the right to command anyone to do what she asks, only her students. Nor does she have the right to command anything of her students, only things relevant to their learning the subject she teaches. An English teacher cannot, for example, command a student to balance her checkbook or cook her dinner. Parents, police officers, judges, employees, and even military commanders also have limited **scopes of authority.**

Because we frequently make decisions in the presence of authorities directing us to do things, we need to know when to question an authority's direction. These points lead to two questions to ask when someone commands you to do something:

1. Does the person have the right to make commands?
2. Is the command within the scope of the person's authority?

YOUR TURN D

◆ 1. For each person described below, is the person described an expert, a witness, or both? Is there any reason to doubt that the expert or witness has the appropriate expertise or personal experience for his or her tasks and your purposes? Do you have any reason to doubt whether the expert or witness will be fully candid about his or her knowledge?

a. A talented and critically acclaimed biographer writing a biography of her father

b. A left-wing reporter covering a rebellion against a left-wing government

c. A scientist who works for a drug company that manufactures birth control pills, discussing the risks of birth control pills

(continued)

◆ 2. Suppose that you have agreed to be part of an experiment in learning. You are the "teacher," and another person is the "student." The scientist directing the experiment teaches you how to use an electric shock machine that is attached to the student. He tells you to give the smallest shock for the first wrong answer and to increase the shock slightly for each additional incorrect answer. The experiment begins. The student gives several right answers. Then the student gives a wrong answer. Would you shock the student? If the scientist told you that you must proceed, would you? Would you continue to increase the shocks if the student began crying out that they were becoming unendurably painful?[5]

3. Review an argument you've written for an earlier assignment. Did you provide any support based on expertise? If not, name someone with relevant expertise on your topic. How did you establish the extent and scope of your authority's expertise?

Common Knowledge

Some claims are so settled that we don't need to explain how we know them. We accept these claims on the basis of **common knowledge.** Here are some features of common knowledge.

First, common knowledge is noncontroversial: everyone who knows anything about the subject agrees. Anyone with even a minimal knowledge of United States history knows that Columbus sailed west across the Atlantic in 1492, for example. Everyone who knows anything at all about robins knows they fly. Everyone who knows anything about killing innocent people knows that it is undesirable. (Although soldiers and others sometimes do kill innocent people, they do not endorse the killing of innocents as a good thing in general.)

Second, if someone doubted something that is common knowledge, you could explain how you know it. You could show a flying robin to someone who doubted that robins fly. If someone doubted that killing innocent persons is wrong, you could say that it is self-evident and also that all of the world's major religious authorities hold it to be true.

In the examples I've given, the knowledge is very general knowledge. There's also common knowledge within special fields of knowledge. When you start researching an unfamiliar topic, everything will be new to you, but when you read more about the topic, you will see that some of the information is agreed on by everyone who knows anything about the topic.

Though commonly known supports are acceptable, we sometimes mistake mere assumption or **shared ignorance** for common knowledge. In other words, not all commonly believed claims are true. For example, at one time many American school children were taught that Columbus was the first European in America, so this belief became commonly held. Yet, Columbus was not *in fact* the first European to set foot on the North American continent. So the school children's commonly held belief was not common knowledge, but shared ignorance.

Here are some questions to ask to help you ascertain whether a claim is really common knowledge or simply the product of shared ignorance.

Is there general agreement—beyond my usual circle of acquaintance—about this claim?

Is the claim acceptable on the basis of personal experience, ecstatic experience, self-evident truth, inferential knowledge, or reliable authority?

Being attentive to the difference between common knowledge and common assumption or shared ignorance can help you in your speaking or writing. First, you'll be less likely to pass along shared ignorance as knowledge. Second, you can capture your audience's attention by starting your paper by questioning some common assumptions about the topic of your study.

YOUR TURN E

◆ 1. Can any of the following claims be accepted as common knowledge?

    a. The death penalty is the best form of punishment for murder.

    b. Hanging has been used as punishment for murder.

    c. People disagree about whether the death penalty is acceptable.

    d. No one should be subjected to torture or to cruel, inhumane, or degrading treatment or punishment.

2. Review an argument you have written. Are any of your supports acceptable as common knowledge? If not, what are some commonly known things about your topic? Check to make sure you aren't confusing common assumption or shared ignorance with common knowledge.

SEEKING RELEVANCE

Once we have assured ourselves that our support is acceptable, we can then move on to question whether it is relevant to our conclusion. What is relevant depends on our purpose. If we're trying to amuse our audience, then jokes are relevant. If we're trying to communicate effectively with our audience, then clarifying and expanding on our claims is relevant. If we're trying to establish a conclusion, then information that helps establish or undermine our conclusion is relevant.

In this chapter we're focusing on how to establish a conclusion. In this context, a **relevant support** provides some reason to accept the conclusion. A relevant counterconsideration provides some reason to reject the conclusion. This concept of relevance isn't new to you, since we used it in Chapter 3

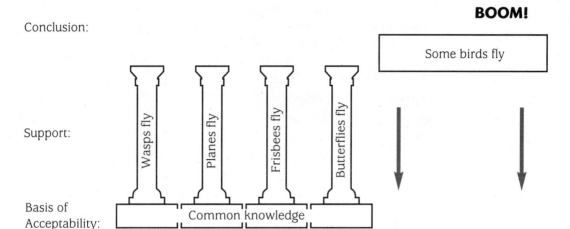

Irrelevant support.

to distinguish among support, counterconsiderations, argument enhancers, and support avoidance.

An argument's strength, then, depends on both the acceptability and the relevance of its supports. Support that is not relevant to the truth of its conclusion cannot possibly help establish that the conclusion is true. In other words, no matter how solid (acceptable) the support is, if it does not connect with the conclusion, it cannot hold the conclusion up. Similarly, for a counterconsideration to undermine a claim, the counterconsideration must be relevant to discrediting the claim it attempts to undermine.

In the following short argument, the supports offer relevant reasons for the conclusion, and the counterconsideration offers a relevant reason against the conclusion:

Conclusion:	Carol left the milk out Saturday night.
Support 1:	Carol typically leaves the milk out.
Counterconsideration:	Carol usually spends Saturday night with her parents.
Support 2:	Carol's parents were away on Saturday, so she stayed here.

The fact that Carol typically leaves the milk out gives some evidence that she is the person who left the milk out on Saturday. And the fact that Carol usually spends Saturday night with her parents gives some evidence that she didn't leave the milk out.

As a rule, we identify a statement as a support because we see some evidential link between it and the conclusion. Similarly, we recognize a counterconsideration as a counterconsideration because we see that it works to undermine the conclusion.

But watch out; don't assume that just because you see no evidential link between a support and the conclusion there is none. Sometimes we can't tell right away whether a statement is relevant to a conclusion. We need additional information to help us see the link. Here's an example of a speaker giving an audience background information to help the audience see the relevance of the speaker's support.

> *Judy*: Jane will get a prize today.
>
> *Beth*: Why do you say that?
>
> *Judy*: She came in the door at 10:00 A.M.
>
> *Beth*: What's coming in at 10:00 A.M. got to do with getting a prize?
>
> *Judy*: Oh, I forgot, you weren't here last time. The teacher said she'd give Jane a prize if she got to class on time. And Jane did!

Also, sometimes it's hard to tell whether an author is offering irrelevant support or no support at all. Whether something is support depends on an author's intentions, and authors frequently do not make their intentions explicit.

When in doubt, give the author the benefit of the doubt. In other words, use the principle of charity. If the author provides information that can function as relevant support, go ahead and assume the author means to offer the information as support. But if the author's information has no clear evidential link, think about whether the author may be trying to achieve some other purpose of communication, such as to tell a joke or to explain the meaning of a term. And remember, the problem may be with you instead of with the author. You may not understand what the author intends because you may lack background knowledge about the author and the topic.

Answers to Counterconsiderations

In order for a support to be a relevant response to a counterconsideration, the author must understand the counterconsideration. As we saw in Chapter 2, decision makers sometimes mischaracterize an alternative so that they can dismiss it more easily. But when an author responds to a misinterpretation of a claim, the author's response is irrelevant to the claim. The dismissal leaves the original claim untouched. This mistake in reasoning is called "straw person."

Let's look at an example. Annie, a sharp-shooter and gun control opponent, opposes a bill that requires a waiting period before gun purchase; she interprets this bill as a prohibition of gun ownership. Annie then points out the dangers and unconstitutionality of prohibiting citizens from owning guns. In doing so, Annie substitutes a straw person (prohibiting gun ownership) for the real person (requiring a waiting period) and then knocks down the straw person, leaving the real person standing.

You'll find many examples of the straw person fallacy in political debates and talk shows. Battling couples and roommates also use it. You yourself have probably had the experience of someone twisting something

It's easier to win against a straw person than a real one, but when you defeat a straw objection to your position, you leave the real, live one standing.

you've said in order to reject it. Exaggerated instances of the straw person fallacy are easy to recognize; more subtle ones are harder to spot. Here's one example.

In his argument in favor of the death penalty (Chapter 3), Edward I. Koch interprets those who call the death penalty "state-sanctioned murder" as claiming that "the state has no rights that the private individual does not have."[6] He then counters that claim by saying that the state *does* have rights that the private individual does not have—the state has the right to collect taxes, for example. Koch is surely correct that the state has rights that individuals do not have. But he hasn't yet addressed the position of those who believe that although the state does have some rights the individual does not have, capital punishment is not one of them.

We also commit the straw person fallacy when we present a weak part of a position as the whole position or a weak spokesperson's representation of a position as the best or only representation of the position. We commit the straw person fallacy, for example, if we reject libertarianism after listening to someone who is very committed to libertarianism but who doesn't yet know very much about it.

To avoid committing the straw person fallacy yourself, employ the **principle of charity.** Be generous when trying to understand the claims of others, giving their words interpretations that make their claims as plausible as possible. Practice active listening, especially when listening to positions you expect to disagree with. To eliminate the straw person fallacy from your papers, ask someone who's sympathetic to the positions you criticize to read your writing.

When looking for the straw person fallacy in the work of others, keep in mind that authors writing satire try to amuse and enlighten an audience through exaggerated representations of a position. Sometimes there's only a very fine line between political satire and the use of straw person reasoning practiced in political debates. But as a rule, authors who write political satire intend their audience to see that they're exaggerating, whereas political candidates hope their audiences will take their exaggerations as truth.

Audience Needs, Goals, and Values

If you want to support a recommended action with needs, goals, and values, make sure your audience holds those needs, goals, and values. Argument makers sometimes attempt to motivate an audience with support that's irrelevant to the audience's needs, goals, or values. Here's an example.

> Suppose someone has a garden that is well protected from deer, with ample water and plenty of flowering plants in cool colors, such as blues, lavenders, and greens. The person goes to a nursery to shop for some red and yellow flowering plants to complement the cool colors. The shopper is browsing through the nursery, when the nursery salesperson comes along and says, "We've got a special on lavender this week. You should get some of it. It's drought tolerant, has beautiful lavender flowers, and is even deer resistant."

The salesperson offers acceptable support: Lavender is commonly known to be drought tolerant, has lovely lavender flowers, and is deer resistant. However, this information is irrelevant to the shopper's goals. The nursery salesperson needs to find out what the shopper is looking for to provide relevant support for a purchase recommendation.

Here's another argument with irrelevant support:

> *Jane*: You should give me an A on this paper. I worked very hard all semester long.
>
> *Teacher*: I'm sorry, Jane. I know you've worked hard. But I'm grading on the quality of your paper, not on how hard you worked on your paper.

Jane's support may well be acceptable; perhaps she did work very hard on that paper. But Jane's teacher isn't persuaded by Jane's argument because the support Jane gives is irrelevant to how her teacher evaluates papers. To improve her argument, Jane could provide some relevant support. She could, for example, point out that her teacher overlooked some A-quality characteristics of her paper. (Or Jane could provide reasons why her teacher should change her grading criteria.)

Background Beliefs

Whether support is relevant depends on **background beliefs** the author relies on to link the support to the conclusion. If the author makes a true assumption about the meaning of a counterconsideration, the author can provide a relevant response to that counterconsideration. If the author makes a true assumption about the audience's needs, wants, or values, the author can provide information relevant to those needs, wants, and values. The straw person fallacy and the failure to provide information relevant to an audience's needs, wants, or values can result from false background beliefs.

Ben Franklin's story provides another example of how a false background belief can lead to an irrelevant conclusion. Mr. G—n concluded that the Dutchman would not understand why he was marking the cards because the Dutchman didn't speak English. But there is no real connection between not speaking English and not figuring out that someone's trying to cheat at cards. People play cards in many parts of the world, not just in English-speaking countries. As a result, Mr. G—n's support was irrelevant to his conclusion. In contrast, had Mr. G—n noted that the Dutchman was blind and could not see him writing on the back of cards, that information would have been relevant to Mr. G—n's conclusion that he could mark the cards in front of the Dutchman without the Dutchman figuring out what he was doing.

Let's look at a few more examples of relevant support with true background beliefs linking them to the conclusion:

Argument:	It's likely to rain. Look, there are dark clouds in the sky.
Background belief:	Dark clouds are a sign of rain.
Argument:	You'll get a good grade on your test. You studied every day.
Background beliefs:	Studying helps us learn a subject, and tests try to measure what we learn.

Because recognizing and establishing relevance depends on background knowledge, the greater your background knowledge about your subject and your audience, the more likely you will produce support that is relevant to your conclusions. For these simple examples about rain and studying, we can use our common knowledge to establish relevance. But when you are trying to reason about a subject unfamiliar to you, you'll need to research the subject fully to increase your chances of distinguishing relevant from irrelevant support.

Here are some questions to ask when checking support for relevance.

Does the author's intended support provide evidence for the conclusion, or does it just expand on the conclusion?

Does the author understand the counterconsiderations?

Does the author understand the audience's needs, wants, and values?

Does the author use true background beliefs to link the supports to the conclusion, or are the background beliefs false ones?

YOUR TURN F

◆ 1. For each of the following short arguments, discuss whether you find the support relevant to the conclusion. Use the above summary questions about relevance to guide your discussion.

   a. Jane is one of those rare people who are happy with their present income, but she doesn't have a companion and would like someone to go on country walks with. She and her friend Judy go to a bar to look for dates. Judy points to someone across the room and says, "Look, there's Beth. You should go out with her. She loves to go for walks, and besides that, she's got plenty of money."

   b. Freudian theory doesn't work to describe human nature. A main tenet of Freudian theory is that little girls wish they had a penis, but there's no solid evidence of this claim. Besides, if little girls have anything to envy, it's not the penis but the fact that little boys get to go out to play when little girls must stay in to wash the dishes.

   c. John should take this class. It'll help him pass the CPA test.

   d. Hemp should be legalized. It's useful for making paper and clothing, and besides, it's natural.

2. Review a paper you've written in which you recommend an action. Check to see whether your support is relevant to your audience's needs, goals, and values. Check to see whether you've committed the straw person fallacy when describing counterconsiderations. Check to see whether you could explain to a questioning reader how your supports provide evidence for your conclusions.

SEEKING SUFFICIENCY

Sufficient support establishes the acceptability of the conclusion (provided that the support is itself acceptable). When you have sufficient (and acceptable) support, you need look no further; you have enough to show that your conclusion is acceptable. In other words, when your support is sufficient, there is enough of it to hold up the full weight of your conclusion.

Your support has to be relevant to be sufficient, because irrelevant support cannot hold up a conclusion at all. But support can be relevant without being sufficient. "There are black clouds in the sky" is relevant to the conclusion that it will rain, but it is not sufficient to establish that it will rain. Adding additional evidence, such as "The temperature is dropping," improves the sufficiency of the support.

Although support must be relevant to be sufficient, it does not have to be acceptable to be sufficient. Of course, if you know that the support is **unac-**

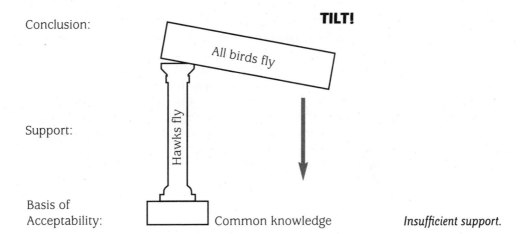

Conclusion: All birds fly **TILT!**

Support: Hawks fly

Basis of Acceptability: Common knowledge *Insufficient support.*

ceptable support you already have a good reason to question the conclusion. Consider the following argument:

> My cat is fluent in English. Thus, when I say, "Please don't kill the bluebirds," she will understand me.

The support in this argument is clearly unacceptable. Cats might understand some English expressions, but they are not fluent in English. So we've already got a good reason to call this argument weak. However, the support is sufficient to establish the conclusion. Why? Because if the support were acceptable, it would be enough to establish the conclusion. Let's look at another example.

> The temperature on the porch is below zero. Water freezes at 32 degrees or below. The water in the cat dish, which is on the porch, will freeze.

The support in my argument is sufficient to establish its conclusion. If the support were true, the conclusion would be true. But I'm in California. The temperature is not below zero; it's about 50 degrees and raining. The water in the cat dish isn't going to freeze.

Strong and Weak Conclusions

Whether your support is sufficient or not depends on the degree of certainty you're trying to establish for your conclusion. For example, in a criminal case the jury must conclude that a defendant is guilty "beyond a reasonable doubt." In a civil case, the jury need only conclude that there is a "preponderance of the evidence" against the defendant (that is, more evidence against than for the defendant). In effect, a higher degree of certainty is required in criminal cases than in civil cases; thus the same support can be sufficient to support a civil judgment against a defendant and insufficient to support a criminal judgment against a defendant.

In other words, whether support is sufficient or not depends on how strongly the conclusion is stated. "The defendant is guilty beyond a reasonable doubt" requires more support than "There is a preponderance of the evidence against the defendant." Similarly, the conclusion "It will certainly rain in the next ten minutes" requires more support than "It is likely to rain soon." "There are big black clouds in the sky, and the air is turning cooler" is sufficient to establish the second conclusion, but not the first.

Sometimes argument makers assert that the conclusion of an argument absolutely must be true if the support is true. They claim that if the support is true, it's impossible for the conclusion to be false. These arguments are called **deductive arguments.** The other arguments we make, ones in which we claim that our conclusion is possibly acceptable, very likely acceptable, probably acceptable, or true beyond a reasonable doubt on the basis of our support, are called **inductive arguments.**

Some Inductive Arguments

There are no set rules we can apply to every inductive argument to determine whether the support is sufficient. The following sections introduce some of the common types of inductive arguments we use in everyday life and the problems for establishing sufficiency that arise. Later chapters go into more detail about how to establish sufficiency in these types of arguments.

Argument from Analogy   In the argument from **analogy,** we assert that because something is true of A, it is true of B. We justify our inference by saying that A and B are analogous. We predict, for example, that Jane will like the movie *Manhattan* because she liked *Annie Hall*. We justify making this move by saying that *Annie Hall* is like (analogous to) *Manhattan* because they're both Woody Allen comedies.

Conclusion:	Jane will like *Manhattan*.
Support:	Jane liked *Annie Hall*.
Support (Subconclusion):	*Annie Hall* is like *Manhattan*.
Subsupport:	They're both Woody Allen comedies.

For an argument from analogy to be effective, the similarities you point out must be relevant to the conclusion you want to draw. If Jane is a particular fan of Woody Allen comedies, pointing out this similarity between the movies is relevant to establishing your conclusion. However, there are many other possible similarities between the two movies, including that they both last longer than an hour and a half. This similarity doesn't provide any evidence for your conclusion, unless Jane doesn't like a movie unless it's over an hour and a half long.

Also, there must not be any overriding relevant *dissimilarities* between the two things being compared. If Jane can't abide a particular actor who appears in *Manhattan* but didn't appear in *Annie Hall*, chances are she won't like *Manhattan* after all.

In the argument from analogy, you determine the sufficiency of the inference from the support to the conclusion by weighing the **relevant similarities** and dissimilarities. The stronger the similarities and the weaker the dissimilarities, the more sufficient the inference. The stronger the dissimilarities and the weaker the similarities, the less sufficient the inference.

There is no formal rule or procedure for weighing relevant similarities and dissimilarities. You use background knowledge about the subject to guide you. So the more you know about a subject, the better prepared you are to figure out the relevant similarities and dissimilarities.

We'll continue practicing evaluating arguments from analogy in Chapter 8.

Generalizing from a Sample In generalizing from a **sample,** we assert that because something is true of part (a sample of) a group, it is likely to be true of the whole group. We justify our inference by providing evidence that the sample is similar to, or representative of, the whole.

Suppose that Ben Franklin wanted to know which cards were marked and which were not but that he didn't want to check each card in the whole group of cards. He could select some of the group of cards and look at them. If he found that all of the face cards and none of the other cards were marked in the sample he looked at, could he conclude that the rest of the face cards and none of the other cards were marked? He could, if the cards he looked at were representative of the whole group of cards.

But how would he know whether the cards were representative? Shuffle the cards, of course. The more thoroughly Ben shuffled the cards, the more likely he would get a representative sample. What might prevent the small group from being representative? Anything that prevents the cards from being thoroughly and randomly rearranged, for example, jelly on some of the cards that kept them stuck together during the shuffle.

In making a generalization from a sample to the whole group, you determine the sufficiency of the support by weighing evidence that the sample is representative against evidence that the sample is not representative. The more things you do to ensure that the sample is representative, the stronger the inference. The more evidence that the sample is not representative, the weaker the inference.

Statisticians have developed a number of procedures, including random selection, to ensure that samples are representative. In questioning whether a sample is likely to be representative, then, we can question whether the person who selected the sample used one of the reliable procedures for developing representative samples. We'll study these procedures in more detail in Chapter 9.

Reasoning to an Explanation   When reasoning to an **explanation,** we attempt to rule out alternative explanations. Let's go back to an example we've looked at before. In Chapter 2, you read about Martin Levine's attempt to find out why his dryer wasn't working. He considered the explanation that the dryer was old and broken beyond repair, but he also considered the possibility that there could be some other, as yet unknown, explanation of why the dryer wouldn't go on.

He began by looking for relevant information. He opened the back of the dryer and found lots of lint. He then proposed a new explanation, namely, that the lint prevented the dryer from going on. He then tested his hypothesis by vacuuming out the lint and trying to turn on the dryer again. The dryer went back on. He concluded that the lint in the back of the dryer stopped the dryer from functioning. In other words, the lint caused the dryer to stop functioning.

By flipping the dryer switch before and after removing the lint, Levine performed an experiment to test his hypothesis that the lint stopped the dryer from functioning. An experiment of the sort Levine performed is one way to provide sufficient support for a causal claim. By performing his experiment, Levine ruled out the hypothesis that the dryer was broken beyond repair and established that it was the lint that prevented the dryer from going on.

Now let's consider some insufficient support for causal claims, again by going back to a previous chapter, this time Chapter 1. False fault finding is one example of providing insufficient support for a causal conclusion. In false fault finding, we jump from insufficient support to the conclusion that we are responsible for (the cause of) something we are at most only marginally responsible for (a partial cause of).

Suppose Jim concludes that he's fully responsible for the class getting into an uproar because he had unknowingly asked a question that had already been answered. In making this inference, Jim fails to provide evidence to rule out other possible explanations of the class's behavior. He doesn't consider, for example, what other members of the class were doing when he asked his question. Was anyone making a face when he spoke, for example? If so, that person's antics may have contributed to the uproar. By failing to rule out other possible explanations of the uproar, Jim fails to provide sufficient evidence that he was the sole cause of it.

When you reason that one causal explanation is better than others, your support is sufficient if it rules out the other possible causes. Scientists have designed some methods for generating sufficient support for causal claims. We'll study these methods in more detail in Chapter 10.

◆ 1. For each of the following passages indicate whether you see an argument from analogy, generalizing from a sample, or reasoning to an explanation.

    a. The students I've talked with so far like the math class I'm taking, so it's likely that all of the students in the class like the class.

    b. I suspect there's something wrong with my computer's hard drive. The computer turns on, but there's no hard drive icon. I thought I might fix the problem by reinstalling the system software. But when I put in the system install disk, it acts as if there's no hard drive to install onto. Also, I've tried inserting the tools disk to check for disk problems, but it doesn't find the hard disk.

    c. Mom, to her daughter who's putting her brother down: "Don't talk about your brother like that. You wouldn't want him to talk about you like that, would you?"

2. Review a paper you have written for this class. Identify any arguments from analogy, from a sample to a generalization, and to an explanation.

Using Emotion to Support Action

As we learned in Chapter 2, people sometimes take shortcuts when deciding how to act. Instead of gathering all of the relevant information, they jump to a conclusion, sometimes on the basis of emotion. Although we want to avoid acting from emotional impulse when making an important decision, we shouldn't avoid emotions altogether. Emotions often lead us to right action.

Consider, for example, Ben Franklin's explanation of why the ship's passengers thought it proper to lower Mr. G—n from the hoist. They decided to lower Mr. G—n because they feared that if they didn't, some great bodily harm would come to him. Ben Franklin helps his audience see the seriousness of the possible harm with his vivid emotion-evoking description: "he crying out Murder! and looking black in the face, the rope being overtort about his middle."

Here are some things to keep in mind to help you generate strong arguments with emotion-evoking support.

First, you'll want to make your emotion-evoking support relevant to the action you recommend. For example, if you're trying to convince people to keep their houses locked, you can provide evidence about the number of burglaries in their neighborhood. Don't use some sort of support avoidance, such as name calling, to try to persuade your audience to act. And make sure the information is relevant to your audience's needs, values, or goals.

Second, remember that relevant emotion-evoking support is not by itself sufficient to establish a conclusion. In other words, try not to act impulsively from emotion. Otherwise, you may be persuaded by insufficient support.

For example, suppose a person I meet on the street tells me she is hungry and asks me for money. Her hunger is relevant to her request for money. I feel sorry for her, and my impulse is to give her the money she asks for. To avoid being persuaded by insufficient support, I need to stop and think. Are there are other, more compelling, demands for the money I have? Are there other ways for her to get the food she needs? The facts that she is hungry and that I am concerned about her are relevant to my giving her money, but they are not sufficient. If I have hungry children at home, I may give the woman directions to the nearest soup kitchen instead of giving her my grocery money.

To avoid acting from impulse, remember to ask these questions:

Are there alternative ways to serve the goals, needs, and values relevant to this problem?

Which of the alternative ways is the best way to meet these goals, needs, and values?

The closer you can get to an answer to these questions, the more sufficient your support becomes.

Checking the Fit between Support and Conclusion

In a sense, sufficient support fits its conclusion. There's enough of it to hold up the conclusion. When working with inductive arguments, you can improve the fit of weak support to a strong conclusion by adding additional support and ruling out counterpossibilities.

You can also improve the fit by weakening your conclusion. In other words, if your support isn't sufficient to hold up your conclusion, cut your conclusion down to size. Say your conclusion is possibly acceptable rather than acceptable beyond a shadow of a doubt, when you have insufficient support to hold up the more strongly stated conclusion.

In some cases, you may need to strengthen your conclusion if you have been unduly skeptical about the strength of your support. If there are big black clouds, cooling air, thunder, and lightning, don't say it might rain soon and waffle about whether to shut your windows. Be bold. Say it will definitely rain, and slam those windows shut.

But remember, fitting your support to your conclusion won't solve all your argument troubles. If your support is unacceptable, you've got a weak argument, no matter how closely your conclusion fits your support. And remember to watch out for misleading your audience with weasel words. Don't try to pass off a weakly stated conclusion as stronger than it is, as advertisers do.

YOUR TURN H

◆ 1. For each of the short arguments listed below, does the support evoke emotion? Is the emotion likely to be intense enough to be distracting?

    a. You are a wonderful, special person. We have a close bond like none I have had with anyone else. This is a magical moment. Let's make love.

    b. The house is burning quickly. There's a chimney fire. Let's get out of here now!

◆ 2. For each argument in question 1, is the support relevant to the conclusion?

◆ 3. Would you like any additional information before deciding on the conclusion? If so, what?

4. Review an argument you have written in which you used emotion-evoking support to recommend an action. If you haven't written such an argument, do so now.

    a. Identify your emotion-evoking support.

    b. Is it relevant to your conclusion?

    c. Is it consistent with alternative actions that you have not yet ruled out?

Deductive Arguments

Deductive arguments, remember, assert that if the support is true then the conclusion must be true. If you have studied geometry, you are familiar with deductive arguments. When proving a geometric theorem, the geometry student asserts that if the premises of the geometric proof are true, the conclusion must also be true.

We also use deductive reasoning when using arithmetic. Consider the following:

> Oops, Jane says to the waitress. You owe me another dollar in change. Look, I gave you a $20 bill. The total check was $14.50. You gave me $4.50 in change. You should have given me $5.50. That leaves me a dollar short.

If the waitress agreed with Jane's supports but then said she possibly didn't owe Jane the dollar, Jane would be surprised. The rules of subtraction justify Jane in asserting her conclusion with certainty.

In the story at the beginning of the chapter, the jury used deductive reasoning to conclude that Mr. G—n had marked the cards they'd been playing with.

> Mr. G—n marked one set of cards on the back with a pen.
> Mr. G—n marked another set of cards on the back with fingerprints.
> There were only two sets of cards on the boat.
> We were playing cards on the boat.
> Therefore, Mr. G—n marked the cards we were playing with.

Rules with no exceptions or with very explicitly defined exceptions give us the opportunity to make deductive arguments. Here's an example.

> A batter comes up, the pitcher pitches a waist-high ball directly over the plate, the batter swings and misses, the umpire calls, "Strike one." The pitcher sends another fast ball flying, the batter misses it, too, and the umpire calls, "Strike two." The pitcher throws a wild-looking curve ball, and the batter doesn't move. At the last moment, the ball crosses the plate, and the catcher catches and holds onto it. The umpire calls, "Strike three."

Now, does the umpire need to weigh the merit of various alternative possibilities about what to do at this point? No. The umpire says, "You're out!" There's a rule here for the umpire to follow, namely, "When a batter makes three strikes and the catcher doesn't drop the third ball, the batter is out." Period.

No one would question the umpire on this point. The fans might disagree vociferously about whether the third ball actually curved back over the plate. But they would not utter a peep about the ump's inference from the three strikes to the conclusion that the batter was definitely, unequivocally, without question, out.

Sometimes we follow absolute rules off the baseball field. If you accept a moral principle that admits of no exceptions, then you can reason deductively from that moral principle to guide your action. Here's an example.

> You should never lie, no matter what the circumstances.
>
> Telling your parents you came home at 10:30 when you actually came home at 2:00 A.M. is an example of lying.
>
> You should not tell your parents you came home at 10:30 when you actually came home at 2:00 A.M.

Here the argument maker asserts that there are no exceptions to the rule about lying. We should never lie, no matter what. The argument maker can then move directly from the support (that in telling your parents you came home at 10:30 when you did not, you are lying) to the conclusion that you shouldn't tell your parents you came home at 10:30 when you didn't.

We also use deductive reasoning to challenge claims that are asserted to be exceptionless. Consider, for example, the claim that we should never lie, no matter what. Here's a deductive argument challenging that claim.

> If we should never lie, no matter what, then it's not acceptable to tell a lie to protect your life or the life of another from a crazed killer. But it's clearly acceptable to tell a lie to protect your life or the life of another from a crazed killer. So it's false that we should never lie, no matter what.

We use the same pattern of deductive reasoning to challenge scientific theories that claim to be exception-free. By finding an exception to the theory, we show deductively that the theory is not exception-free after all.

Valid and Sound Arguments   In everyday life, we often use the word "valid" to mean "acceptable," as in "That's a valid point." Logicians use the word "valid" to refer to the sufficiency of deductive arguments. Because deductive argument makers assert a very strong claim about the relation between the support and the conclusion, deductive arguments are held to a very high standard of sufficiency. A deductive argument is **valid** if and only if it is impossible for the supports to be acceptable and the conclusion to be unacceptable.

The conclusion of a deductively valid argument follows with necessity from the supports because the conclusion is, in a sense, already contained in the premises. In other words, the conclusion adds no new information to the supports. In inductively strong arguments, in contrast, the conclusion adds information not contained in the supports.

Deductive validity differs from inductive sufficiency in another way. Inductive sufficiency admits of degrees. It increases as we add additional supports, including answers to counterconsiderations. Deductive validity does not admit of degrees. An argument is either valid, or it is not. Period.

Each of the previous deductive arguments is valid. Assuming their supports are true, their conclusions follow with necessity. Here are some more examples of valid deductive arguments:

Stu: I got a B+ on my paper.

Lauren: How do you know?

Stu: The grading scale for a B+ is 87% to 89%. I got an 88% on my paper. So my paper grade must be B+.

If John is bigger than Sarah and Sarah is bigger than Sam, then John is bigger than Sam.

There are only five roses in my garden. One is 3 feet tall, two are 4 feet tall, one is 4½ feet tall, and one is 6 feet tall. Therefore, all of the roses in my garden are 3 feet or over.

The type of sufficiency between the supports and conclusion in a valid deductive argument is the strongest possible type of sufficiency an argument can have. But valid deductive arguments are frequently no stronger as a whole than inductive arguments. Why? Remember, the strength of an argument as a whole depends not only on sufficiency but also on acceptability. Valid arguments are just as susceptible to unacceptable supports as are other arguments. Here's an example of a valid argument with unacceptable support:

If computers are dogs, then computers bark. My computer is a dog. Therefore, my computer barks.

This argument is valid. That is, if its supports were acceptable, its conclusion would have to be acceptable. But its support isn't acceptable. Logicians call a valid argument with at least one unacceptable support *unsound*. A valid argument whose supports are all acceptable is called a **sound** argument.

Identifying Invalid Arguments   A deductive argument cannot be valid if it has true support and an unacceptable conclusion. Therefore, if a deductive argument has acceptable supports and an unacceptable conclusion, we can safely conclude that the argument is **invalid**. But invalid arguments don't always have acceptable supports and an unacceptable conclusion. How do we determine invalidity then? Here are a couple of tactics you can use.

FILL IN THE STORY   Sometimes deductive arguments are written in very general language. By filling in the story, you can highlight the mistaken reasoning. Let's look at an example. Suppose you want to know if the following argument is invalid.

> John is bigger than Sam, and John is bigger than Sara. Therefore, Sam must be bigger than Sara.

Here's how we fill in the story. We try to find additional details that would make the supports true, but the conclusion false. Let's suppose that John is five feet tall, Sam is four feet tall, and Sara is four feet, six inches. In this case, Sam is not bigger than Sara. Sara is a full six inches taller. So Sam is not *necessarily* bigger than Sara. It is *possible* that the supports be acceptable and the conclusion unacceptable.

THINK UP A REFUTING ANALOGY   A **refuting analogy** is an argument that has the same structure as the argument whose validity you question and has acceptable supports and an unacceptable conclusion. Because the refuting analogy is invalid, the argument you are questioning is also invalid. Let's look at an example.

> All flowers bloom in the summer.
> All roses bloom in the summer.
> All roses are flowers.

Do you find this argument suspicious? It has an acceptable conclusion. Roses are flowers. But does the support provided prove the conclusion? Not really. Here's a refuting analogy.

> All lawyers graduated from college.
> All doctors graduated from college.
> All doctors are lawyers.

Notice that the lawyer/doctor argument has the same structure as the roses/flower argument and has acceptable supports and a false conclusion. The lawyer/doctor argument is a refuting analogy. It shows that the roses/flower argument is invalid.

When thinking about whether an argument is valid or invalid, pay special attention to arguments whose conclusion you know to be acceptable. People tend to assume that if the conclusion of an argument is acceptable, the argument is valid. But that's an unacceptable assumption. As we saw with the roses/flower argument, an invalid argument can have an acceptable conclusion. An invalid argument can even have an acceptable conclusion *and* acceptable support. Consider the following example:

> If turning the ignition key triggers the car engine to start, then turning the ignition key precedes the engine's starting. Turning the ignition key precedes the engine's starting. Therefore, turning the ignition key triggers the car engine to start.

Do you think this argument is valid? Does its conclusion follow with necessity from its supports? Many people would say yes. They're misled by the truth of the conclusion. Turning the key in the ignition of a car does trigger the car engine to start. However, it doesn't follow with necessity from the support given here.

We can use a refuting analogy to show the ignition key argument to be invalid.

> If the low fuel light triggers the car's running out of gas, then the low fuel light goes on before the car runs out of gas. The low fuel light does go on before the car runs out of gas. Therefore, the low fuel light triggers the car's running out of gas.

The low-fuel-light argument is a refuting analogy. It has a structure analogous to that of the ignition key example, and it also has acceptable supports with an unacceptable conclusion. Thus, the ignition key argument is invalid—even though it has an acceptable conclusion and acceptable supports.

YOUR TURN I

◆ 1. Use deductive reasoning to challenge the following generalizations.

    a. All birds fly.

    b. All cars require gasoline to run.

◆ 2. Are any of the following deductive arguments invalid? If so, show that they are invalid by filling in the story or thinking up a refuting analogy. If you think the argument is valid, try to explain why the conclusion follows with necessity from the supports.

    a. Mark is to the left of Sara.
    Sara is to the left of John.
    Mark is to the left of John.

    b. All fruit ripens in the summer.
    Peaches ripen in the summer.
    Peaches are fruit.

    c. Alli plays tennis with Marsha, and Marsha plays tennis with José. So, Alli plays tennis with José.

    d. Most cats have tails.
    Mandy is a cat.
    Mandy has a tail.

    e. If a teacher is a good teacher, the teacher keeps the students' attention.
    Li-Wen keeps the students' attention.
    Li-Wen is a good teacher.

3. Review an argument you have written for this class. Did your main conclusion or any of your subconclusions follow with necessity from your supports?

This chapter has introduced three concepts of argument evaluation: acceptability, relevance, and sufficiency. You can use these concepts to improve your own arguments and to question the arguments of others.

You can also use these concepts to help you resolve conflicts by determining which argument is stronger, yours or that of the person you disagree with. And when you do not reach agreement, you can still find these criteria useful for gaining a better understanding of your disagreement. Perhaps you and your audience have different background knowledge or weigh goals and values differently.

This chapter also provided general guidelines for evaluating arguments. To improve our ability to evaluate arguments, we need to look at types of arguments in more detail. We'll continue working on argument evaluation in the next three chapters.

EXERCISES

Note: Before evaluating an argument, you need to break it into its parts.

1. Indicate whether you find each of the supports acceptable, unacceptable, or questionable in the arguments listed below. Explain your finding, using the ways to arrive at acceptable support discussed in this chapter. For example, if you find a support acceptable on the basis of expertise, name the expert you rely on, and explain how you know the person to be a reliable expert on the topic in question.

   a. Exercise 1(a) in Chapter 3

   b. Exercise 1(b) in Chapter 3

   c. Exercise 1(c) in Chapter 3

   d. Exercise 1(d) in Chapter 3

   e. Exercise 1(e) in Chapter 3

   f. More from Ben Franklin's *Journal of a Voyage*:

   > Man is a sociable being, and it is for aught I know one of the worst of punishments to be excluded from Society. I have read abundance of fine things on the subject of solitude, and I know 'tis a common boast in the mouths of those that affect to be thought wise, *that they are never less alone than when alone.* I acknowledge solitude an agreeable refreshment to a busy mind; but were these thinking people obliged to be always alone, I am apt to think they would quickly find their very being insupportable to them. I have heard of a gentleman who underwent seven years' close confinement, in the Bastille, at Paris. He was a man of sense, he was a thinking man, but being deprived of all conversation, to what purpose should he think; for he was denied even the instruments of expressing his thoughts in writing. There is no burden so grievous to man as time that he knows not how to dispose of. He was forced at last to have recourse to this invention: he daily scattered pieces of paper about the floor of his little room, and then employed himself in picking them up

and sticking them in rows and figures on the arm of his elbow-chair; and he used to tell his friends, after his release, that he verily believed if he had not taken this method he should have lost his senses. One of the philosophers, I think it was Plato, used to say, that he had rather be the veriest stupid block in nature, than the possessor of all knowledge without some intelligent being to communicate it to.[7]

2. Indicate whether you find the support relevant to the conclusion in each of the arguments below. If so, explain why. If not, explain why not. Where appropriate, discuss whether the support evokes emotion and whether the author appeals to needs, goals, and values you hold.

a. Exercise 1(c) in Chapter 3

b. Exercise 1(d) in Chapter 3

c. Exercise 1(e) in Chapter 3

d. Exercise 2(a) in Chapter 3

e. Exercise 2(d) in Chapter 3

f. Exercise 2(e) in Chapter 3

g. Exercise 3(a) in Chapter 3

h. Exercise 3(b) in Chapter 3

i. Exercise 3(e) in Chapter 3

j. You should let me turn in my paper late. I've had to stay up with a sick child all night every night for the last week, and I haven't been able to think well enough to write.

k. From a letter to Sebastopol Pet Center:

> To the Owners of the Sebastopol Pet Center:
>
> The ornate box turtle my daughters bought for my son for Christmas died about a month ago from unknown-to-me causes. She looked like she died in mid-step on her way to the water dish. The turtle was purchased from you, along with the aquarium paraphernalia and a book about keeping turtles as pets.
>
> The book stated that even experienced reptile handlers have difficulty keeping ornate box turtles alive for any length of time. On one of the occasions that I called you to plead for help, I was told that you had never experienced that kind of problem. Perhaps because you didn't have them long enough, I don't know. What I do know is that we all suffered grief while watching our little turtle refuse food, refuse to stay awake in spite of our efforts with a bath every morning, respond to warmth, love, tidbits, attention, no attention, prayers. Still, she died one day.
>
> Shortly after that, I read about the capture and selling of these endangered reptiles, turtles among them. Human habitat is not conducive to any kind of longevity for many of the "pets" sold in pet stores, and the article urged the reader not to buy these threatened animals as pets. To take it a step further, I am asking you to consider not selling them either.

I am well aware that you are a Pet Center, and that you have to respond to public needs. Since I am part of that public I am responding in the only way I know how. I am sorry that I cannot find my copy of the article mentioned above to send on to you. If you have information to the contrary, or can give me insight from another source I am very interested.

Sincerely,
Jimalee Plank[8]

3. Indicate whether each of the following arguments is inductive or deductive. Explain.

a. Although Anita Hill says she was upset by Judge Thomas's alleged advances, she nonetheless continued working for him. It seems unlikely then that he did in fact sexually harass her.

b. Teachers should come to class on time. They expect students to come to class on time, and they should follow the same rules of conduct they expect their students to follow.

c. Impressing a date

Mark: But Dad, I really want to impress this woman. How can I do that without spending money?
Dad: With your sense of humor, Mark. And by showing her how responsible you are. That's how I impressed your mom.

d. The following is from Devotion 7 by John Donne (1572–1631):

No man is an *Iland*, intire of it selfe; every man is a peece of the *Continent*, a part of the *maine*; if *Clod* bee washed away by the *Sea*, *Europe* is the lesse, as well as if a *Promontorie* were, as well as if a *Mannor* of thy *friends* or of *thine owne* were; any mans *death* diminishes *me*, because I am involved in *Mankinde*; And therefore never send to know for whom the *bell* tolls; It tolls for *thee*.[9]

e. A few minutes ago, I saw Donna vacuuming the living room. Now I can still hear the vacuum cleaner down there, and I also hear notes sounding from the piano. The cats are outside, and the piano's not a player piano. Donna is probably vacuuming the piano.

f. We should take the chains with us. According to the weather report, snow is on the way. And the road will be slippery in a snow storm.

g. The following passage from a textbook on Western philosophy:

Every event in the world is caused by some event prior to it. Either (a) the series of causes is infinite, or (b) the series of causes goes back to a first cause, which is itself uncaused. But an infinite series of causes is impossible. Therefore, a first cause, which is God, exists.[10]

4. Indicate whether you find the support sufficient to support the conclusion in each of the arguments below. Explain your answer. If you find the support insufficient, explain what question the author's support leaves unanswered for you.

a. A passage from the novel *The Color Purple*:

> Dear Celie, . . .
>
> You've got to fight and get away from Albert. He ain't no good.
>
> When I left you all's house, walking, he followed me on his horse. When we was well out of sight of the house he caught up with me and started trying to talk. You know how he do, You sure is looking fine, Miss Nettie, and stuff like that. I tried to ignore him and walk faster, but my bundles was heavy and the sun was hot. After while I had to rest, and that's when he got down from his horse and started to try to kiss me, and drag me back in the woods.
>
> Well, I started to fight him, and with God's help, I hurt him bad enough to make him let me alone. But he was some mad. He said because of what I'd done I'd never hear from you again, and you would never hear from me.
>
> I was so mad myself I was shaking. . . .
>
> love,
> Nettie[11]

b. A letter to the editor:

> Editor: Yesterday I euthanized a large, beautiful purebred Akita for biting a young lady in the face. The wound required 18 stitches to close. A colleague had the tip of his nose removed by a German shepherd during a routine visit for vaccination.
>
> Recently I euthanized a young cat whose chest had been crushed by the family Rottweiler, the second family cat to die in this manner.
>
> When I consider the dogs I have been asked to destroy based on temperament, they are nearly all purebreds. If not dangerous, they are often hyperactive, anxious and paranoid. In addition these dogs can be medical nightmares. Their close-line breeding or outright inbreeding has accentuated traits that would stay diluted or recessive in crossbred dogs or even properly mated purebreds.
>
> People naturally ask my advice as a veterinarian about what breed I would recommend. I used to have an answer. Now I can only tell them what *not* to get. And the list is rapidly growing. The fact is in a society fixated on how things "look" and what's fashionable, people are buying dogs like they buy shoes.
>
> Unfortunately, they can't put their new dog in the closet with the shoes when the fad dies. Clearly, if one is to live with a dog as part of the family, the most important thing is his behavior—not how he "looks."
>
> Some of my favorite patients are purebreds and there certainly are many great pets out there with papers. At the same time the trend is frighteningly clear. Make sure you spend enough time with the puppy's parents and if you aren't completely comfortable with her/him, don't buy the puppy no matter how cute it is.
>
> Better yet, choose your new family member from one of the 70,000 unplanned puppies or kittens born every day. You could do each other a very big favor.
>
> Peter Henriksen, DVM
> Sebastopol[12]

5. Indicate whether any of the following deductive arguments are invalid. If they are, show that they are invalid by filling in the story or thinking up a refuting analogy. If you think the argument is valid, explain why the conclusion follows with necessity from the supports.

   a. If the refrigerator's unplugged, then the freezer is defrosting. If the freezer is defrosting, the ice cream will melt. But the refrigerator is not unplugged, so the ice cream will not melt.

   b. If an argument's support is unacceptable, then the argument is weak. The argument Jenny just made has unacceptable support, so the argument Jenny just made is weak.

   c. Either Juanita is in the kitchen, or Juanita is in the living room, or both. Juanita is in the kitchen, so Juanita is not in the living room.

   d. The radiator must be broken. The car is overheating, and if the radiator's broken, then the car will overheat.

   e. If Mario is at home, he's either in the kitchen making pasta or in the living room playing the fiddle, but not both. He's not in the kitchen making pasta, so he's not at home.

   f. If the desktop is three feet above the floor, and the computer is three feet above the floor, then the computer is on top of the desk.

6. Use deductive reasoning to challenge the following generalizations.

   a. No computer functions when it's not plugged in.

   b. Smoking always causes lung cancer.

   c. All advertisements evoke emotions.

   d. Every married physicist has a wife.

   e. All women want to be mothers.

   f. It's always wrong to break a promise.

   g. You should never do anything that causes another person pain.

   h. All arguments from analogy are inductive arguments.

READINGS FOR ANALYSIS

Drugs Should Not Be Legalized

Robert Coles

A growing number of political and cultural figures in this country, conservatives as well as liberals, seriously advocate legalization of drugs. They claim that enormous criminal excesses of various kinds will thereby be eliminated. I recently heard one law professor say, "Overnight [with legalization] we'll be rid of drug wars, and the crime rate will drop significantly, because people won't have to steal to maintain their habit."

Meanwhile, in the ghetto where I work, not to mention in every other kind of neighborhood across the nation, parents struggle on behalf of their children. Matters debated publicly by big-shot experts or politicians are also considered by ordinary parents.

In a Boston ghetto these words were recently uttered by a 35-year-old mother of four children:

"The other day on the news a man who's a professor said they should make drugs legal. He kept talking about 'the drug epidemic' and the 'teenage pregnancy epidemic,' and he had the answers—make the drugs legal, and give the kids contraception and abortions. I sat and wished he was right here in my living room, so I could talk with him. I'd ask him if he had any kids. I'd ask him if he'd want us to make the drugs legal for *his* kids. He's writing all of us off—we're below him. He doesn't give a damn about us—so long as we stay out of his way. Give them drugs and condoms and abortions and some welfare money! Just stay out of my way."

She had much more to say, but her remarks amounted to a pointed analysis of the way class and race affect our judgment as we contemplate certain important social and moral problems. For our own sons and daughters we want a decent, sturdy, solid life of no drug abuse. For others "below" us, quite another point of view applies: Stop their stealing or violence by making drugs legally available.

What children of *all* classes and races need is a social order that responds to and clearly evokes a firm moral tradition. Children need to know what is right, decent, and responsible—and also what is wrong, harmful to themselves and others, and not to be encouraged or allowed. Serious problems are not solved by repeated acts of moral surrender. The mother quoted above is crying for a world that helps her struggle against a range of troubles.

Questions

1. What witnesses or experts does Robert Coles quote in this article? Do you find their claims acceptable? Does he? Explain.
2. Suppose the law professor's claim that legalizing drugs will lower the crime rate is correct. Is this support for the legalization of drugs relevant to the concerns of the mother of four whom Coles quotes? Explain.
3. Coles criticizes the position that drugs should be legalized. Does he create a straw version of this position? Explain. (You may find reading the following essay helpful in answering this question. Does it raise some points—omitted by Coles in his description of the legalizing drugs position—that strengthen the position in favor of legalizing drugs?)
4. Do you find any emotion-evoking support for Coles's conclusion that we should not legalize drugs? Is it relevant to his conclusion? Is it sufficient to establish his conclusion? Explain.
5. Coles implies that legalizing drugs will not solve the problem the mother of four raises. Will keeping drugs illegal solve her problem? If not, does Coles offer another solution to her problem? If so, does he offer any convincing support for his solution? Explain.
6. What other questions would you like to discuss regarding Coles's essay?

Drugs Should Be Legalized

Eric Scigliano

When we reinstated alcohol after prohibition, we knew that it was a dangerous drug, but realized that the dangers of legal use were outweighed by the penalties of prohibition: crime and violence, corruption, poisoning from bathtub gin, the immoderation that goes with surreptitious indulgence. But at that time we failed to attach a suitable program of education and warnings about alcohol's dangers. We are now catching up and sending the right messages about alcohol and tobacco—with impressive results.

We can make a better start with any other drugs we allow into the legal market, through a conscientious system of consumer information and warning labels. We could ban *all* advertising of recreational drugs, including alcohol and tobacco. We could also institute severe laws against the sale to kids of all recreational drugs, including tobacco. In these ways, legalization can be coupled with serious efforts to cut down usage, paradoxical as that may seem on the surface.

In addition, by eliminating the illicit market, legalization would silence a terribly destructive and seductive message that's now getting through to inner-city kids: that drugs spell wealth and power. In the ghetto, they're now seen as the most (and sometimes the only) visible means of upward mobility.

Opponents of legalization say such a measure is elitist and racist; it would consign the underclass to a perpetual hell of addiction in order to be free of the threat of crime. But the inner cities are already awash in crack and other drugs, and all the violence and waste that goes along with the high prices for drugs. Inexpensive crack is not the solution in itself. But by freeing our attention and resources from futile enforcement, we can begin to attack the immense and complex problems of education, unemployment, family structure, and internalized racism that nurture a growing and entrenched underclass.

Questions

1. Does Eric Scigliano use any reasoning to an explanation here? Explain.
2. Does he use an argument from analogy here? Explain.
3. Does Scigliano provide support for his position that drugs should be legalized that's relevant to the concerns of the 35-year-old mother quoted by Coles in the essay above?
4. Do you find Scigliano's support sufficient for his conclusion that drugs should be legalized? (Does he answer all of the questions raised by thoughtful decision making to your satisfaction?)
5. What other questions would you like to discuss about Scigliano's essay?

Military Service: A Moral Obligation

Donald Kagan

At the time of writing this article Donald Kagan was a professor of history and classics at Yale University.

The killing of 239 servicemen in Lebanon and the invasion of Grenada have reminded Americans of the military's role in pursuit of the nation's purposes and once again have raised the question of the citizen's obligation to do military service when called upon. This question still is before us because of continuing controversy over a law requiring students seeking Federal aid to register for the draft.

It would seem obvious that in a world of independent and sovereign states that come into conflict and threaten one another's vital interests—sometimes even existence itself—citizens who choose to remain in a particular country are morally obliged to serve in its armed forces when the need arises.

Critics of this view appeal to a higher morality in which an individual may refuse to serve if such service violates his conscience. Some assert the right, even the duty, to refuse service when they do not approve the national policy that leads to the need for military action, even though they do not oppose serving when they approve the cause. To accept such a claim would be to destroy all governments but especially democracies, which rely on the willingness of their citizens to accept the decisions that duly elected and appointed bodies and officials arrive at, even if they are wrong.

That is not to say that citizens are morally obliged to accept the decisions of any country in which they live, no matter how wicked and despotic—only in legitimate ones. My definition of a legitimate state is one that permits the open advocacy of different opinions, the possibility of changing the laws by peaceful means and, most important, emigration without penalty. A regime that fails to meet these criteria imposes its will by force alone and has no moral claim on the obedience of its subjects.

On the other hand, a nation that meets them has every claim to its citizens' allegiance and especially to the service most vital to its existence. When a citizen has become an adult and has not chosen to leave the country, he tacitly approves of its legitimacy and consents to its laws. He benefits from their protection and has the moral obligation to obey them if he wants to stay. To enjoy the enormous advantages provided by a free society while claiming the right to ignore or disobey the laws selectively, especially those essential to its survival and most demanding of its citizens, is plainly immoral.

Some recusants are pacifists who refuse to fight regardless of the occasion. Their position, though it lacks the absurdity of claiming the right of each citizen to conduct his own foreign policy, is also deficient. Leaving the country would not solve their problem, since wherever they go they will find a state that will be prepared to use force in the national interest when necessary and will ask its citizens to do military service. One solution has been to refuse and accept the legal penalty without complaint. Another has been to accept auxiliary service, such as in the medical corps, which, though dangerous, does not require killing. These responses prove sincerity and courage, but they do not satisfy the moral demands of citizenship. Pacifists in this imperfect world can pursue their beliefs only in free societies and only because their fellow citizens are willing to fight and protect them. There were no protected pacifists in Hitler's Germany and Stalin's Russia; there are none in Yuri V. Andropov's.

Pacifists are not alone in hating the need to kill. Most American soldiers find it impossible to pull the trigger in their first combat experience and find it profoundly painful even later. Yet they do their duty, though there is no way to know if they dislike killing any less than those refusing to fight. A decent, free society is right to allow concern for personal conscience a place in its considerations and to afford special treatment to those who refuse to fight on plausible grounds of conscience. But those who accept such treatment must realize that they are getting a free ride and failing in their moral responsibility as citizens.

Questions

1. Donald Kagan argues that citizens have a moral duty to accept the decisions of a legitimate (democratic), but not an illegitimate (despotic) government. What support does he provide for his argument?

2. Do you find the following argument valid?

   Citizens' refusal to serve in a war they disapprove of destroys a democracy. It's wrong to destroy a democracy. Citizens' refusal to serve in a war they disapprove of is wrong.

3. Do you find the support for the argument in question 2 acceptable? If so, explain. If not, explain why not. (Try producing a valid deductive argument that would challenge the claim that questioning the laws of a democracy destroys the democracy.)

4. Kagan claims that citizens have a moral duty to accept the decisions of a legitimate government. He also writes, "A decent, free society is right to allow concern for personal conscience a place in its considerations and to afford special treatment to those who refuse to fight on plausible grounds of conscience." Do you think these claims can both be true? Explain.

5. Kagan writes, "Pacifists in this imperfect world can pursue their beliefs only in free societies and only because their fellow citizens are willing to fight and protect them." Do you find this claim acceptable? Explain. If you don't find it acceptable, assume it is acceptable for the moment. Is it relevant to the concerns of pacifists? That is, would a pacifist see this as a relevant reason to accept the moral duty to kill others in war? Explain.

6. What other questions would you like to discuss regarding Kagan's essay?

Rebuttal to "Military Service: A Moral Obligation"

Emily S. Guttchen

This letter in rebuttal of Donald Kagan's position appeared in the *New York Times*.

To the Editor:

The citizen who according to Professor Kagan is morally obligated to do military service is male and 18 to 26 years old. No other is asked to do service of any kind. All Americans, he indicates, are given the right to dissent, but the select group earmarked for military service must be willing to risk their lives, forfeiting their right to dissent.

Professor Kagan appears to believe that, since the United States is a democracy, all decisions are made in a democratic manner. Unfortunately, this is not the case, particularly in regard to foreign policy.

And he plays on the "love it or leave it" theme when he makes the assumption that citizens who choose to remain in this country consent to its laws. People support some laws, are opposed to others and still wish to remain in the United States. Leaving is a difficult thing to do because one's country is not just laws and policies but loved ones, a culture and a home.

I was also struck by the anachronism of Professor Kagan's arguments. It is nuclear war, not some invading horde, that threatens our country's survival. The moral obligation of all United States citizens is to insist that their Government pursue policies designed to lessen tensions between the superpowers and support those forces in the third-world nations that are working toward a better life for their people rather than supporting repressive forces and using the Soviet Threat as an excuse for doing so.

Americans must stop their Government from engaging in wars of intervention to protect vested interests—wars that carry the risk of escalating, by way first of tactical nuclear weapons and ultimately nuclear missiles, into all-out nuclear war. This is the highest moral obligation.

Emily S. Guttchen

Questions

1. Emily S. Guttchen is criticizing Kagan's position. Does she accurately represent his position? Explain.

2. Is the following a valid argument? Explain.

   The United States is a democracy. Therefore, all of the decisions made by the United States are made democratically.

   Guttchen claims that Kagan would reason in this way. Do you think she is correct?

3. Do you think that Kagan believes that all governmental decisions have to be made democratically in order for the decisions to be legitimate? Explain.

4. Kagan asserts that by staying in the country, citizens indicate that they support the government. Guttchen questions this interpretation. What alternative explanation does Guttchen give for why citizens stay in a country?

5. Does Guttchen find citizens' refusal to go to war a pressing problem for today? Explain. If not, what problem does she find more pressing today?

6. What other questions would you like to discuss regarding Guttchen's essay?

WRITING IDEAS

1. Review an argument you have written this semester. Write an evaluation of your argument. Discuss whether your support is acceptable, relevant, and sufficient to establish your conclusion.

2. Write a paper in two parts. In part 1, write a letter to a younger sibling or friend recommending a teacher you have taken. List several criteria of good teaching, and argue that the teacher you have taken meets these criteria. In part 2, evaluate your own reasoning. Include a discussion of which of your sibling's or friend's needs, interests, or goals you appealed to.

3. Review one of the readings for analysis in this chapter. Write a letter to the author evaluating the argument.

4. Write a short paper explaining the difference between deductive and inductive reasoning. Give examples to illustrate each type of reasoning, and include a discussion of any confusion you have about this distinction.

5. Write a short paper explaining whether you use a basis of acceptability that is not described in this chapter.

6. Write about whether this chapter and your class discussions complemented, conflicted with, supported, or left out any of your previous ideas about evaluating arguments.

Notes

1. Alice Walker, *The Color Purple* (New York: Harcourt Brace Jovanovich, 1982) 167.
2. William James, *The Varieties of Religious Experience: A Study in Human Nature* (New York: Viking Penguin, 1982) 422–29.
3. Thomas Jefferson, *The Declaration of Independence.*
4. From research done by Horai, Naccari, and Fatoullah (1974) reported in Werner J. Severin with James W. Tankard, Jr. *Communication Theories* (New York: Longman, 1988) 167.
5. For further information about how people have behaved when asked to do this, see Stanley Milgram, *Obedience to Authority* (New York: Harper & Row, 1974).
6. Edward I. Koch, "Can the Death Penalty Ever Be Justified?" *New Republic* 1985.
7. Ben Franklin, *Journal of a Voyage*, in Jonathan Raban, ed., *The Oxford Book of the Sea* (New York: Random House, 1950) 249–50.
8. Jimalee Plank, letter to Sebastopol Pet Center, May 10, 1991.
9. John Donne, Devotion 7.
10. Donald Palmer, *Does the Center Hold?: An Introduction to Western Philosophy* (Mountain View, CA: Mayfield, 1991) 192.
11. Walker 107.
12. Peter Henriksen, letter, *Press Democrat*, Santa Rosa, CA, 4 March 1996: B3.

8

Thinking through Analogies

CHAPTER GOALS

- To expand your knowledge of one type of reasoning introduced in Chapter 7—the argument from analogy.
- To learn how analogies can be used to explain and clarify abstract or complex subjects.
- To learn how analogies can be used to support predictions, evaluations, and legal decisions.
- To use your knowledge to evaluate and to write arguments from analogy.

YOUR THOUGHTS ABOUT ANALOGIES

What kinds of things do you find analogies useful for? Jot down your ideas; then read this argument and answer the questions that follow.

The Gorge

Sterling Bennett

When my brother and I were little, my father would take us for Sunday afternoon walks up into the gorge, a forbidden place because of a dammed up moss-sided dark pool in which, my father was sure, we could easily drown. When we had gone no more than a half a block, he would say to us—me being about six and my brother eight—"We should be smoking," and he would send one of us home to snitch the cigarettes that my mother had already carefully placed on the living room table. Of course, in due time, we were puffing down the middle of the town and were thoroughly sick long before we neared the dreaded gorge.

The same thing occurred with alcohol. We were offered a sip here or there whenever those liquids were poured. Consequently, I like to believe, neither my brother nor I was ever drawn to large amounts of smoke or fermentation, and perhaps because of this experience I have always believed that measured early introduction to these possible vices was a sure way to avoid future excesses. If in Europe, I reasoned, you can drink while still in diapers, certainly you should be able to drink here in the U.S. at eighteen, especially since at that age you can already vote, expose your chest as a soldier to the enemy's bullets, be tried as an adult for a crime, or have a baby.

The drinking law, as it exists, turns young people into criminals, when what the law—as a social instrument—should be doing is what my mother and father had in mind when they were conspiring to keep us out of the dark waters of the gorge, keep our lungs unsmoked, and our brains unfermented, as we staggered through the rest of life's potential dangers.

Questions

1. What conclusion does Sterling Bennett argue for in the above essay? Is it explicitly stated?
2. Does Bennett convince you of his conclusion?
3. Do you agree with the comparison Bennett makes between persons under 21 drinking in Europe and persons under 21 drinking in the United States?
4. Does your answer to question 3 take into account the death toll from teenage drunk driving in the United States and that a much smaller percent of European youth drive?
5. Do you find any reason to question other comparisons Bennett makes?

When we say two things are analogous, we are saying that one is like the other. An analogy, then, is a comparison. This chapter focuses on the role analogies play in explaining complex, abstract, or unfamiliar things and supporting predictions, evaluations, and legal decisions. The chapter also teaches you how to evaluate analogies. The chapter's title hints at this double goal: "Thinking through analogies" means both "thinking by means of drawing comparisons" and also "thinking carefully about the comparisons we draw."

By the time you finish the chapter, you will be better prepared to inform your audience with analogies that explain and clarify. You will also have improved your skills in reasoning analogically and in assessing the analogical reasoning of others, from friends to Supreme Court justices. Understanding analogical thinking will help you to reflect on and improve your own decision making and to be better equipped to understand and critique social policy and judicial decisions that affect all of us.

USING ANALOGIES TO EXPLAIN

Sometimes we use analogies to explain complex or abstract concepts or things. When our audience has a hard time grasping something we're talking about, we can compare it with something they can hold on to more easily. Let's look at some examples of using analogies in explanations.

Analogies are useful for explaining how intangible things work. A physics teacher who wants to explain sound waves can liken them to ocean waves or to the audience's wave at a sports event, where motion appears to move horizontally around the stadium as groups of people, one after the other, stand momentarily and then sit again.

Analogies also help us conceptualize large numbers. It's difficult, for example, to grasp fully the difference between a million and a billion. The words look a lot alike, and the difference in the numbers doesn't look all that great: just add a comma and three more zeros to $1,000,000 and you get $1,000,000,000. In *Innumeracy*, John Allen Paulos helps us understand the immense difference between these figures with the following analogy. "[I]t takes only about eleven and a half days for a million seconds to tick away, whereas almost thirty-two years are required for a billion seconds to pass. . . ."[1] A trillion is an even more mind-boggling number. If we traveled in time back a trillion seconds, we would arrive to see "the disappearance of the Neanderthal version of early Homo sapiens,"[2] some forty thousand years ago.

Analogies also help us explain the operation of complex or inaccessible physical things. For example, the human heart is sometimes compared with a pump. This analogy helps us get a sense of how the heart works so that we don't have to cut someone open to view the beating heart.

By providing analogies, we can also help an audience understand our experiences. In his book on social class, Paul Fussell uses an analogy to help the reader understand what it's like to talk about the touchy subject of class.

> You can outrage people today simply by mentioning social class, very much the way, sipping tea . . . a century ago, you could silence a party by adverting too openly to sex.[3]

We frequently use analogies to explain mental operations. For example, consider the following quote by the Tibetan Buddhist Tarthang Tulku:

> The purpose of visualization is to develop our awareness so that wherever we go or whatever we do, we become very mindful, and alert, like a deer's ear.[4]

Start with Something Familiar

Your analogy can't help your audience understand what you're talking about unless they understand the example you start with. If your audience doesn't know how a pump works, they won't be any closer to understanding how the human heart works after they hear the comparison. If Fussell's audience had no awareness of Victorian attitudes toward sex, his analogy wouldn't help them understand his experience of talking about class.

In some cases you can help your audience by giving them more information. For example, you can show your audience how a pump works to help them understand the mechanism of the heart. Other times you will have to replace your analogy with something more familiar to your audience. Fussell could compare talking about class to talking about race, an experience more familiar to many contemporary audiences than the Victorian attitudes toward sex.

Note Relevant Similarities and Differences

Sometimes comparisons and contrasts don't need to be drawn out; your audience will know immediately what to focus on in your analogy. Your audience isn't likely to think that a human heart is made of rubber and metal, like the pump you are showing them. But sometimes your audience might mistake a difference as a point of similarity and head off toward confusion. In such cases, you need to inform your audience of **relevant differences.** If you suspect that the analogy will make your audience think it's easy to replace the human heart, you might want to remind them that replacing the human heart is considerably more complex than replacing the water pump in your car.

YOUR TURN A

◆ 1. Alberto Alvaro Rios describes the shift he made in two college writing classes. Previously he had been able to complete assignments in other classes merely by giving back information that his teachers or books had given him. But in the writing classes, something different was expected of him. He writes:

I was asked almost simultaneously in both classes to now *go write one*. A poem. A prose sketch.

   There was no reference book, no biology teacher. I could copy things down, of course, but both teachers had expressed thoughts on that ahead of time. There was no place to go. At that moment, school changed for me—and life, if I may be so dramatic. School had always come *at* me; I was the back wall to a tennis player, and I simply let things bounce back. But now, for the first time, school would have to come *from* me, from the inside. From the flick of my wrist, my racquet.[5]

a. What analogy does Rios use to explain his new experience as a student?

b. Does his analogy help you understand his experience? Are you personally familiar with the example he starts with?

c. What additional information or alternative analogy would you recommend for an audience who doesn't understand Rios's example?

2. Review a paper you have written for this class. Are you talking about any abstract, complex, or unfamiliar subjects that analogies would help your audience understand? What are they?

SUPPORTING PREDICTIONS WITH ANALOGIES

Like boats taking passengers from starting points to destinations, analogies move us between times and places. When we make a **prediction** about a future event based on our past experience, for example, we need an analogy to take us from that past experience to the future. Consider the following argument:

Order your Gravensteins from us. Last year's apples were sweet and crisp, and this year's will be, too. They're picked from the same tree.

In the above argument, the implied analogy "This year's apples *are like* last year's" connects a statement about past experience—"Last year's apples were sweet and crisp"—to a statement about the future: "This year's will be sweet and crisp." The other sentence, "They came from the same tree," provides evidence supporting the analogy.

Make Implicit Analogies Explicit

When reporting on an island vacation to someone familiar with the territory, we need not mention that we got to the island by boat. A knowledgeable audience will know how we got to the island without our telling them. Similarly, when presenting an argument we frequently do not explicitly state the analogy that we rely on to move us to the conclusion.

In the argument above, the analogy was not explicitly stated. The author didn't have to say explicitly that last year's apples *are like* this year's apples because the reader will infer this from the statement that the apples came from the same tree.

Although authors frequently leave analogies implicit, it's a good idea for audiences to make them explicit. Making an analogy explicit puts us in a better position to determine whether we have sufficient evidence to support it.

Now let's break the above argument apart, making the unstated analogy explicit:

Conclusion:	You should order your Gravensteins from us.
Support 1 (Subconclusion):	They will be sweet and crisp.
Subsupport 1:	Last year's apples were sweet and crisp.
Subsupport 2 (Unstated):	This year's apples are like last year's apples.
Sub-subsupport:	They came from the same tree.

Start with an Acceptable Claim about the Past

If you use a past experience as a support for an argument about a future event, the claim about the past must be acceptable, or the analogy won't help you to knowledge of the future. If last year's apples weren't sweet or crisp, then a strong analogy won't make the prediction come true. Instead, this year's apples will most likely be as sour and soft as last year's.

Check the Strength of the Analogy

Although analogies allow us to move beyond our present or past experience, analogies, like boats, are sometimes full of holes. And determining the strength of an analogy, like determining the soundness of a boat, is tricky business. Even the soundest boats—as any experienced sailor knows—let in some water. The question then is not "Does the boat leak?" but "How *big* is the leak?" If it's gigantic, the boat will sink before leaving the dock. But if it's a very small leak, the boat can get you safely to a destination halfway around the world.

Similarly, with analogies there are always some differences between two things being compared. The question, then, is not "Are there differences between the things being compared?" but "Are any of the differences between the things being compared relevant to undermining the analogy's conclusion?" If the differences are relevant, the analogy can't get you to your conclusion. If the differences are not relevant ones, the analogy will take you there.

Consider, for example, possible similarities and differences between the apples from last year's harvest and those from this year's. Which are relevant to how the apples will taste?

Apples came from same/different trees.

Apples grew under same/different conditions: water, sun, nutrients.

Apples were infested/not infested with bugs/worms, and so on.

Apples were picked by same/different people.

Apples were picked on same/different day.

Apples were packed in same/different way.

Apples were shipped in same/different way.

Apples were picked using same/different methods.

Apples were picked in same/different stage of development.

Apples were held for same/different lengths of time before shipping.

The Role of Background Knowledge   To answer these questions, you have to know something about apples. The more you know about apples, the more you will be able to determine which of these similarities or differences will affect how the apples taste.

In some cases we can use common knowledge. We know, for example, that apples that have been sitting around a long time taste less sweet and have a less crisp texture than apples that have recently been picked. We also know, from common knowledge, that apples that have been dropped during picking get bruised and don't taste the same as apples that have not been dropped.

To answer other questions, we need expertise. Unless we are apple experts ourselves, we will have to consult others to find out whether differences in sun, water, and nutrients affect the way apples taste.

Fitting a Prediction to Its Support   When we aren't sure whether we've found all of the possible relevant differences in our analogy, we can admit the uncertainty of our predictions by adding modifiers like "probably," "very likely," or "might" to our conclusions. Using past experience of winter rains and summer dry spells in California, we can predict that "it will probably rain in California next January and will very likely not rain next July."

Although no analogical reasoning guarantees certainty about the future, some predictions are so likely to be true that we need not announce their infinitesimal degree of uncertainty with a probability modifier. Suppose a visitor calls on July 3 asking whether to bring a raincoat for the July 4 celebration. If there are no clouds in the sky and no satellite pictures of squalls heading east from the ocean, only an inveterate worrywart would say, "It will probably not rain tomorrow."

Predicting from Disanalogies

Sometimes we argue in the following way: "Yesterday they were fixing the bridge and we were late to school, but today the bridge will be fixed, so we won't be late to school." Here, we find a difference between yesterday and today (a **disanalogy**) and conclude that today will be different from yesterday in other ways also, namely, that we won't be late to school. This argument works only if everything else about yesterday and today relevant to when we arrive at school remains the same. There could be other differences between yesterday and today that will make us late to school—maybe we oversleep today or receive an important call just as we walk out the door.

YOUR TURN B

1. Ben and Roger are two surfing buddies who have gone to the mountains for the first time. Read their conversation below and answer the questions that follow.

   "How long will it take to cook the pasta?" Ben asks.

   "Eight minutes," Roger says.

   "Are you sure?" Ben asks.

   "Sure," Roger says. "I brought the pasta from home, and it's always taken eight minutes to cook before."

   a. What prediction is made in this conversation, and what support is offered for it?

   b. Does the prediction rest on an implicit analogy? What is it?

   c. Are there any relevant similarities offered to support the analogy? Can you think of any?

   d. Can you think of any relevant differences between the things being compared?

2. Quickly make a list of occasions when you were surprised by people behaving differently from the way you expected. Select an example in which you assumed that another person would behave the way you did. (For example, you thought a joke was funny, so you expected your friend to find it funny also.) Do you now think you ought to have questioned your analogical assumption more closely? Explain.

SUPPORTING EVALUATIONS WITH ANALOGIES

When making predictions, we use analogies to move between times and places, from the past to the present, for example. When supporting evaluations, we use analogies to move from one evaluation to another.

In Chapter 7, we used refuting analogies to check for validity. To show that an argument was invalid, we compared it with an argument we knew to be invalid. When we found that the suspect argument had the same structure as the argument we knew to be invalid, we concluded that the suspect argument was also invalid.

Here's an example to refresh your memory. Some people may think the following argument is valid:

All fruit ripens in the summer.
Peaches ripen in the summer.
Peaches are fruit.

But this argument is invalid because it has the same structure as the following invalid argument:

All finches fly.
All robins fly.
Finches are robins.

In this case I used the finch/robin argument, which is obviously invalid, to show that the peach/fruit argument is likewise invalid.

We also use analogies to evaluate situations and persons. We start with a situation (or person) we evaluate positively or negatively, find similarities between it and the situation (or person) in question, and conclude with a positive or negative evaluation of that other situation (or person).

Here's an example of using an analogy to support an aesthetic evaluation. Josh is praising his little sister's drawing:

"That's a great drawing, Sis. It looks like a Picasso."

In the above passage, Josh holds Picasso up as a model of one who draws well, compares his sister's drawing with Picasso's, and concludes that his sister's drawing is good.

We also use analogies to support negative evaluations. Suppose Josh's Uncle Ed embarrasses everyone in the family with his red Hawaiian shirts and green plaid pants. Josh could use the following analogy to criticize his older brother's clothes—a green Hawaiian shirt and yellow plaid pants:

"That combination of pants and shirt is ridiculous. You look like Uncle Ed."

In moral reasoning, too, we often use models to support our evaluative conclusions. We select a valued human being as a model, then compare others to the model to praise their character and behavior. Jesus Christ, Buddha, Gandhi, Martin Luther King, Jr., and Mother Theresa are all such models. Saintly great uncles, angelic grandmothers, wise mothers, respectful older brothers, and honorable family friends also serve as models for judging character and behavior. We judge ourselves positively by pointing out our similarities to these venerable persons.

When people have criticized us, we sometimes counter their criticism by showing that our behavior is similar to an admired model's. Audre Lorde uses this strategy in response to a nurse who told Lorde to wear a prosthesis to her doctor's appointments after breast surgery, saying, "Otherwise, it's bad for the morale of the office":

> [W]hen Moshe Dayan, the Prime Minister of Israel, stands up in front of parliament or on TV with an eye patch over his empty eye socket, nobody tells him to go get a glass eye, or that he is bad for the morale of the office. The world sees him as a warrior with an honorable wound, and a loss of a piece of himself which he has marked, and mourned, and moved beyond. And if you have trouble dealing with Moshe Dayan's empty eye socket, everyone recognizes that it is your problem to solve, not his.
>
> Well, women with breast cancer are warriors, also. . . . For me, my scars are an honorable reminder that I may be a casualty in the cosmic war against radiation, animal fat, air pollution, McDonald's hamburgers and Red Dye No. 2, but the fight is still going on, and I am still a part of it. I refuse to have my scars hidden or trivialized behind lambswool or silicone gel. I refuse to be reduced in my own eyes or in the eyes of others from warrior to mere victim, simply because it might render me a fraction more acceptable or less dangerous to the still complacent, those who believe if you cover up a problem it ceases to exist. . . .[6]

If we accept young people using fire extinguishers and air bags, should we also accept young people using condoms?

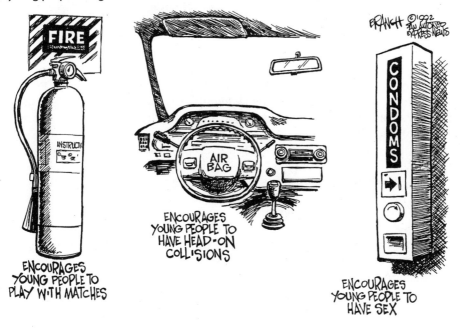

ENCOURAGES YOUNG PEOPLE TO PLAY WITH MATCHES

ENCOURAGES YOUNG PEOPLE TO HAVE HEAD-ON COLLISIONS

ENCOURAGES YOUNG PEOPLE TO HAVE SEX

In this argument, Lorde uses Moshe Dayan's wearing an eye patch as a model of proper behavior. She compares having breast cancer to fighting a war and not wearing a prosthesis to Dayan's not wearing a glass eye. She uses her analogy to support her conclusion that there is nothing morally suspect about not wearing a prosthesis—in fact, not wearing one has positive effects for others. People will be more likely to try to do something about breast cancer if they face its consequences.

YOUR TURN C

◆ 1. What two things are being compared in the following examples?

   a. *Sally*: Look, Juan, you think "women-only" colleges are acceptable. Therefore, you should think "men-only" colleges are acceptable.

   b. *Tyrone*: Jasmine, you shouldn't call women who have had a variety of sexual partners derogatory names, such as "slut." After all, you call men with a variety of sexual partners by positive labels, such as "stud."

2. Review your writing for this class. Have you written an analogy supporting an evaluation yet? If not, take a moment to do so now. What two things are you comparing in your argument?

Start with an Acceptable Model Case

Just as the claim about the past must be acceptable for us to reason safely from it to the future, so too our starting evaluation must be acceptable for our analogy to get us from it to an acceptable conclusion.

Let's look at some examples.

The starting point for the finches/robins–fruit/peaches argument is that the evaluation of the finches/robins argument is invalid. That evaluation is clearly acceptable. However, not all audiences may recognize this. For an audience that doesn't know how to identify invalidity at all, the argument maker could help by explaining that an argument that has true premises and a false conclusion can't be valid.

Josh's argument comparing Sis's drawing with Picasso's relies on the evaluation of Picasso's drawing as great. This too is an acceptable evaluation. Picasso is a recognized drawing master. However, once again, not all audiences may be familiar with Picasso. Josh could show pictures of Picasso's work to these audiences, pointing out the remarkable features of Picasso's drawing.

Lorde's argument relies on an evaluation of Moshe Dayan's wearing an eye patch. She points out that no one criticizes Dayan, which implies that the evaluation of Dayan is settled as common knowledge. The force of Lorde's argument depends on her audience's ability to picture the handsome and powerful Dayan with his eye patch. For an audience who didn't know of Dayan, Lorde could provide a picture.

Using Moshe Dayan as a model poses another potential problem of persuasion. His valor will be more appealing to audiences who supported his army's cause than to audiences who did not. Thus, Lorde would want to pick a different military leader if she were talking to an audience who had suffered from Dayan's army.

Fanciful Models   We've seen a similarity between reasoning from the past to the future and reasoning from one evaluation to another. In both cases, we must start with acceptable claims. But there is a difference, too. In reasoning from the past, we reason from actual experience, but in evaluative reasoning, we can start with a fictional case.

Audre Lorde, for example, didn't have to use a historical military leader to make her point. She could have made up a story of a powerful and handsome military leader who wore an eye patch instead of a glass eye. What matters is that her audience agree with her evaluation of the fictional general's patch.

Some of the most effective moral educators are science fiction writers. Consider, for example, the story about an advanced species of space people who came to earth to live. They were omnivores who found human flesh particularly tasty, so they started hunting humans for food. They also found human behavior delightfully peculiar and began caging humans behind bars. On their days off, space families would go watch the strange and funny behavior of the humans in their cages.[7]

Of course this is a fanciful story, but I think that most of you will agree on the evaluation: The space people's treatment of humans is morally suspect. The fact that they are a superior species doesn't justify them in caging and eating "lower" humans. One could use this story as the starting point of an argument from analogy.

> The space people's treatment of humans is morally suspect. Their treatment of humans is similar to human treatment of other animals. So, human treatment of other animals is morally suspect.

False Models   It's one thing to model ourselves on fanciful models. It's another to model ourselves on false models.

People sometimes mistakenly admire a false model. A teen may be impressed by a cool drug-pushing young adult; a college professor may consider it all right to stint on the time she puts into reading student papers because an older mentor did so.

According to some social critics, the mass media encourage us to develop false models. They create celebrities and then offer them as heroes. David Shaw, writing for the *Los Angeles Times*, gives several examples of media-created heroes:

Lorena Bobbitt, who cut off her husband's penis while he lay sleeping, was hailed as "a national folk heroine" by Vanity Fair. Earvin (Magic) Johnson, who says he contracted HIV from one of the large number of women he slept with, *sans* condom, during an epidemic, was hailed as a hero simply for having said publicly that he had the disease.[8]

Shaw's point is that we need to watch out for confusing celebrity with heroism. A person becomes a celebrity *merely* by staying in the public eye. Lorena Bobbitt and Magic Johnson were constantly in the public eye. The mass media put them there. They were clearly celebrities.

However, that they are heroes—moral exemplars for others to admire and emulate—cannot be determined by how frequently they appear on page one. Moral action, not popularity or notoriety, is the sign of heroism. It is up to each of us—not to news editors—to select persons who best exemplify the values we hold dear.

YOUR TURN D

1. Make a quick list of people you admire. Jot down some things they have done that you admire.

2. Select a person from your list. Write about something you have done that is similar to something that person did.

Check the Strength of the Analogy

Our analogies from evaluations take us safely to evaluative conclusions when there are no relevant differences between the arguments, situations, or people we compare.

When trying to determine whether differences are relevant, we need to remind ourselves of what the analogy is trying to establish. We then ask ourselves whether any differences we find would undermine the purpose of the analogy.

Let's look at some examples.

The finches/robins–fruit/peaches analogy was offered to show that the fruit/peaches argument was invalid. What we're looking for in this case are differences in structure between the two arguments. If the finches/robins argument has a different structure from the fruit/peaches analogy, then the finches/robins argument can't work to show that the fruit/peaches analogy is invalid. Any other difference besides structural difference is irrelevant. For example, although the finches/robins argument is about animals and the fruit/peaches argument is about plants, this difference is irrelevant to determining the validity of either argument.

Now let's look at Josh's comparison of his sister's drawing to Picasso's. Here are some possible differences. Which would be relevant, and which irrelevant?

Difference in subject: Sis drew Michael Jackson, and Picasso never drew Michael Jackson.

Difference in medium: Sis drew on her computer, and Picasso didn't own a computer.

Difference in style: Sis drew in a style Picasso never used.

To know which are relevant, we need to know something about Picasso. Was he known for drawing particular individuals—so that a drawing of a different individual just couldn't be like a Picasso? Was the medium crucial to making a Picasso a Picasso? From my knowledge of Picasso, I'd say not. What makes a Picasso a Picasso is its style of drawing, not its subject or medium. If Josh's analogy works, then there can't be any significant differences in style between his sister's drawing and Picasso's.

In the above excerpt by Audre Lorde, the author is tying to establish that there's nothing wrong with not wearing a false breast. For her analogy to work, we must find it no more harmful to others not to wear a false breast than not to wear a false eye. Because the analogy's strength depends on the likeness of these two points, other differences between the two cases are irrelevant.

Here's one difference between the cases. Dayan fought a war in the literal sense of the term. His war occurred between countries. Lorde participated in a metaphorical battle between her body and environmental pollution. But because this difference lies beyond the focus of her comparison, it does not undermine Lorde's conclusion.

Whether the battle is metaphorical or literal doesn't entail a difference in harm in showing the scars. In both cases people could be offended or demoralized. An eye patch could cause anxiety among recruits, if Dayan didn't wear it proudly. Similarly, a flat chest need not cause undue anxiety in a doctor's waiting room, if it is treated as a badge of honor rather than a symbol of failure. And Lorde points out that showing the effects of breast cancer will help people in the long run. We have to face the problem of breast cancer in order to take steps to do something about it. Lorde establishes, then, that going without a false breast isn't any more harmful than going without a glass eye.

YOUR TURN E

◆ 1. Look back to question 1 in "Your Turn C." Can you think of any relevant similarities or differences between the things being compared in arguments (a) and (b)?

◆ 2. Can you think of any possible similarities or differences between Josh's brother's green Hawaiian shirt and yellow plaid pants and Uncle Ed's red Hawaiian shirts and green plaid pants?

Invidious Contrasts

When we make an invidious contrast we find a difference between ourselves and a model and conclude that because we are not like the model, there's something wrong with us. This type of reasoning is fallacious because there is inadequate evidence to support the conclusion. It may be true that we are not like this model, but we may be like some other, equally worthy, model. Therefore, it does not follow that there is something wrong with us. Consider the following:

Will: "Sis's drawing is lousy. It sure isn't a Picasso."

Here Will argues from a disanalogy to a conclusion. But a disanalogy between Sis's drawing and Picasso's would suffice to support the conclusion that Sis's drawing is lousy only if Picasso were the only good model of artistic merit there is. Otherwise, Sis's drawing could be great, but in a different way from Picasso's. For example, Sis's drawing might resemble those of Mary Cassatt.

Advertisements invite us to make invidious comparisons by presenting a narrow range of beautiful men and women—as though there were no other aesthetic ideals. When people view ads and feel unattractive because they don't look like the images in the ads, they succumb to the fallacy of invidious comparison. Of course, this is exactly what the advertisers want. If you feel insecure about your looks, you're more likely to buy the products they're selling.

A decision about modeling oneself after images in ads should also include research into what makes the models look the way they look. Was it just the makeup that created the "natural" and "youthful" look? Maybe the photographer used a special lens or touched up the photo. Or perhaps the model looked like that to begin with.

Let's look at another example of an invidious contrast. In her book *The*

Mom becomes subject to the fallacy of the invidious contrast.

"Gosh, I never realized that Mom was so fat!"

Mismeasure of Woman, Carol Tavris critiques an invidious contrast of women to men. When men's behavior is used as the yardstick for women's behavior, women come up short and turn to self-help books to cure their ills. Tavris helps her audience recognize this invidious contrast by cleverly turning the tables. She produces descriptions of self-help books that men would be reading if society modeled men's behavior on women's behavior:

> *The Superman Syndrome* explains that because men are physically less hardy than women throughout their lives, men find it difficult to combine work and family. They would live as long as women do if they would scale down their efforts to seek power and success.
>
> *Erratic Testosterone Syndrome (ETS)—What it is and how to live with it* provides medical and psychological information to help George cope with his hormonal ups and downs. Because men do not have a visible monthly reminder of hormonal changes, they fail to realize that their moodiness and aggressive outbursts are hormonally based. A special concluding chapter helps the wives of men with ETS learn to live with their husbands' unpredictable mood swings.[9]

Notice that these examples are parodies of self-help books written for women to cope with "the superwoman syndrome" and "premenstrual syndrome." Many of us take these "syndromes" for granted in females. Analogous male syndromes seem funny because we do not typically characterize a common male behavior as an illness or deficiency. Why? Because the way men commonly behave is taken as the norm of behavior.

Tavris's analogy is a particularly clever use of the refuting analogy. First she points out that people have been reasoning in the following way:

> Women aren't like men; therefore, there's something wrong with women.

She then offers a refuting analogy:

> That line of reasoning is flawed. It's just as absurd as saying, "Men aren't like women; therefore, there's something wrong with men."

If you find the second argument flawed, Tavris is saying, you should also find the first argument flawed.

YOUR TURN F

1. Have you ever drawn any invidious contrasts between yourself and someone? Describe these contrasts briefly, and describe how they led to false and undermining conclusions about yourself.

2. Look through advertisements for models you find particularly attractive. Ask yourself the following questions:

a. Do you think the only way to be attractive is to look like one of these models?

b. Are these the only models of beauty there are? (Consider, for example, your family members and friends.)

c. Is their beauty in the lens of the camera? Is it make-up deep?

SUPPORTING LEGAL DECISIONS WITH ANALOGIES

Lawyers and judges frequently use the argument from analogy when supporting legal positions and decisions. In fact, according to the legal scholar Cass R. Sunstein, "Reasoning by analogy is the most familiar form of legal reasoning. It dominates the first year of law school; it is a characteristic part of brief-writing and opinion-writing as well." [10]

Analogical reasoning in the law has a structure similar to that of analogical reasoning in daily life. The reasoner starts with something thought acceptable and moves by means of an analogy to something that is not yet accepted. Sunstein offers the following example:

> We know that a speech by a member of the Ku Klux Klan, advocating racial hatred, cannot be regulated unless it is likely to incite, and it is directed to inciting, imminent lawless action; it is said to follow that the government cannot forbid the Nazis to march in Skokie, Illinois. [11]

In the above example, the reasoner starts with an acceptable support, namely, "a speech by a member of the Ku Klux Klan, advocating racial hatred, cannot be regulated unless it is likely to incite, and is directed to inciting, imminent lawless action" and concludes that "the government cannot forbid the Nazis to march in Skokie, Illinois." The assumed analogical support is that a speech made by a member of the Ku Klux Klan, advocating racial hatred, is like the Nazis marching in Skokie, Illinois, the largest community of Jews in America who survived the Holocaust.

Start with a Precedent

There is one notable difference between legal and everyday analogical reasoning. Legal reasoning typically starts with a previously decided case, called a **precedent**, whose acceptance is fixed by the legal doctrine of *stare decisis,* which means "let the decision stand." In other words, once judicial decisions are made, they stand firm. Lawyers are expected to use these judicial decisions as starting points in analogical reasoning—even if they personally disagree with them. Sunstein writes: "Consider, for example, the fact that lawyers must take *Roe v. Wade* [the Supreme Court decision guaranteeing the right to abortion] as authoritative as long as it stands, even if they think the decision is abhorrent." [12]

Questionable Precedents   The doctrine of *stare decisis* promotes stability in the law and a respect for the decisions of others. However, *stare decisis* is not the ultimate governing principle for making legal decisions. Sometimes, none of the past precedents apply to present circumstances. Other times, past precedents resulted from prejudice or other forms of injustice. In such cases, legal reasoners argue for new precedents. The law is not revolutionary, however, for judges still must use consensus of accepted past values when arguing for new precedents.

Conflicting Precedents   Sometimes legal reasoners start from different precedents and arrive at different conclusions.

To illustrate this point, Sunstein introduces the controversy about whether "hate speech" should be regulated. She notes that some people start with the precedent regulating physical assault. They argue that "hate speech" should be regulated because—like physical assault—it "has little or no connection to free speech values and produces severe and unique harm." [13]

Others start with a precedent preventing regulation of dissident political speech. They argue that "hate speech" should not be regulated because—like dissident political speech—"hate speech" is "merely a form of controversial expression, subject to a risk of censorship . . . by people who want to use the arm of the law to enforce a particular orthodoxy." [14]

To resolve the conflict, judges consider whether one precedent is more relevant to the case being determined than the other. Sometimes they agree that one precedent is more relevant, and other times they do not.

Check the Strength of the Analogy

To check the strength of the analogy, legal reasoners look for relevant similarities and differences between the precedent and the case being considered. Let's look at an example:

> [When trying to figure out the appropriate legal response to cross-burning, it] may be tempting to begin with the suggestion that cross-burning is action, not speech, and is therefore outside of the First Amendment altogether. . . . We know, however, that flag-burning qualifies as speech. If this is so, it seems difficult to claim that cross-burning does not.[15]

Notice the precedent stated in the support of the argument:

Conclusion: It is difficult to claim that cross-burning does not qualify as speech.

Support: Flag-burning qualifies as speech. (precedent)

Support (Unstated):   Cross-burning is similar to flag-burning.

To check for relevance, we need to think about why flag-burning would be identified as speech. Flag-burning has been used to communicate opinions. Protesters during the 1960s sometimes burned the flag to show their strong disapproval of the Vietnam war. Cross-burning, too, is used to express strong opinions. The fact that flags are typically made of fabric and crosses typically made of wood is not relevant. You can communicate as effectively by burning wood as by burning fabric.

Though cross-burning and flag-burning are similar enough to call both speech, Sunstein warns against concluding that both are *protected* speech. She writes, "It is possible that cross-burning is materially different from flag-burning, not because it is less speech, but because it is more or differently harmful."[16] Thus, comparing cross-burning with flag-burning can help us take one step toward a conclusion about whether cross burning can legitimately be regulated, but it cannot move us all the way to the conclusion. Other considerations—such as the potential harmfulness of the cross-burning—need to be explored first.

When checking for relevance, then, remember to pay particular attention to the claim the analogy is offered to support. An analogy may be strong enough to support one claim and not strong enough to support another claim.

YOUR TURN G

◆ 1. Sunstein provides an example of how the law can go wrong when analogies are not sufficiently questioned. Read the example and answer the questions that follow.

Consider, for example, Justice Holmes's notorious argument on behalf of compulsory sterilization of the feeble-minded in *Buck v. Bell*. Holmes suggested that if people can be conscripted during wartime, or can be forced to obtain vaccinations, it follows that the state can require sterilization of the "feeble-minded." But this is a casual and unpersuasive claim. . . . Holmes does not explore the many possibly relevant similarities and differences among these cases.[17]

a. What analogies does Holmes use?

b. What similarities do you find between the things compared?

c. What relevant differences do you find between the things compared?

d. What additional information would help you decide the strength of Holmes's analogies?

e. Do you agree with Sunstein that Justice Holmes's argument is poor?

◆ 2. Evaluate the following argument.

Society forbids juveniles of 16 and 17 to vote, drink, or serve on a grand jury and generally does not allow them to marry without their parents' permission. Therefore, society should not hold juveniles to the same standards of criminal responsibility as they hold adults, and juveniles of 16 and 17 should not be executed for murder.

This chapter has focused on the role analogies play in explaining complex, abstract, or unfamiliar things and in supporting predictions, evaluations, and legal decisions. Learning to identify and question analogies is also crucial for developing strong reasons for generalizations and causal claims, the subjects of the next two chapters.

1. Identify the things being compared in the following items.

   a. The following passage is from a book by the Tibetan Buddhist Tarthang Tulku:

   > In Tibet there is a certain kind of deer that yields a musk which is very valuable for making perfumes and medicines. Hunters go to great lengths to obtain this substance, caring nothing for the life of the deer. Likewise students sometimes seem to value the teacher only for what he can give them—they think they can buy his head. But this attitude upsets the learning process, as the development of a wholesome relationship of mutual respect and appreciation is essential for both the student and the teacher. It is especially important for the student, because there is no way to attain genuine understanding except through direct experience—and this learning process needs the guidance of a teacher.[18]

   b. In *Islands in the Street: Gangs and American Urban Society*, Martin Sanchez Jankowski describes a number of methods gangs use to increase membership. Sanchez calls one method the "fraternity type of recruitment" and describes it as follows:

   > In the fraternity type of recruitment, the gang adopts the posture of an organization that is "cool," "hip," the social thing to be in. Here the gang makes an effort to recruit by advertising through word of mouth that it is looking for members. Then many of the gangs either give a party or circulate information throughout the neighborhood, indicating when their next meeting will be held and that those interested in becoming members are invited. At this initial meeting, prospective members hear a short speech about the gang and its rules. . . . When one decides to join the gang, there is a trial period before one is considered a solid member of the group. This trial period is similar, but not identical, to the pledge period for fraternities. There are a number of precautions taken during this period to check the individual's worthiness to be in the group. If the individual is not known by members of the gang, he will need to be evaluated to see if he is an informant for one of the various law enforcement agencies (police, fire-arms and alcohol, drug enforcement). In addition, the individual will need to be assessed in terms of his ability to fight, his courage, and his commitment to help others in the gang.[19]

   c. The following is excerpted from a response Dr. Margie Go Singco-Holmes (a clinical psychologist) gave to a Filipino mother worrying about her 21-year-old son who was leaving home for the first time. The Filipino mother had written that she was "torn between the Filipino custom of nurturing children until they get married and the American custom of granting them independence at 18."

   > There is this analogy about eggs and families. American families, for example, are like hard-boiled eggs. There are boundaries, rather thick demarcation lines, that make family members very distinct from one

another. Each egg is so self-sufficient that there is no abiding need to connect with the rest of the family. This encourages independence, but it could also lead to loneliness and an inability to see another person's point of view.

Filipino families, on the other hand, tend to be like scrambled eggs. The lack of boundaries encourages closeness and empathy. What happens to one family member happens to the rest. However, it doesn't promote self-reliance. . . .

Healthy families are like "fried eggs" that have boundaries and connectedness. Members care for one another regardless of what happens because they are secure in their own lives. If a family member decides to separate from them for a while, this is accepted with equanimity and love. . . .[20]

d. The following words were spoken by Chief Tecumseh of the Shawnee to General William Henry Harrison in 1810:

Sell [our] country! Why not sell the air, the clouds, and the great sea? Did not the Great Spirit make them all for the use of his children?[21]

e. The following is from an interview with Charles Baron conducted by *Destiny Magazine*:

Destiny: So you believe in reparations?
Baron: Yes! I believe we should receive reparations. We can debate whether it should come in the form of money, programs or other kinds of material things, but just as the Japanese received reparations during the 40s and just as Germany is still paying reparations to the Jews, I think we [African Americans] are definitely entitled to reparations from America.[22]

f. The following is excerpted from "Stopping the Civil Rights Train" by Delbert Hawthorne:

I spent much of my twenties fighting for the right of blacks to live, prosper and pursue their own happiness as any other citizen of America. I fell to the ground and was arrested with blacks in a show of courage and commitment. I ate, slept and shared an outside latrine with fellow soldiers in what some of us came to know as the "Second Civil War." . . .

I am now 49 years old, and lay awake in a nebulous confusion as to how I could have arrived at a state of animosity for what used to be the most energetic purpose of my life. . . .

I can now no longer remember the [train ride from New York to Montgomery, Alabama] with fondness and now work to stop a Civil Rights Train out of control. What should have been a noble cause has become madness in the form of social policies that may have thrown us all several steps behind where we were prior to the '60s. . . .

. . . Preferences for whites which shut out blacks were wrong. And the nation's conscience knew it. We also know that today's policy to favor blacks is equally wrong. Fighting to overturn it isn't easy. But stop this train we must.[23]

g. The following is excerpted from Chang-Lin Tien, "Affirming Affirmative Action," published in *A. Magazine* June/July 1995. Chang-Lin Tien is chancellor of the University of California at Berkeley.

> I know there are Asian community leaders who argue that traditional academic criteria—grade point averages and SAT scores—should be the sole determinant for admission [to college]. I would point out that no major university admits students solely on this basis because such an approach ignores other factors that differentiate an excellent student from a good one. Elite private institutions routinely give special preferences to the children of alumni and of major donors. Yet no one argues that these practices have caused the academic quality of the Ivy League schools to decline.
>
> The fact remains that diversifying our student body is sound educational policy in a country undergoing profound demographic changes. Today's education student must be able to effectively teach in a multicultural classroom. The medical student who cannot comfortably interact with African American, Latino or Asian patients will fail to address modern society's medical needs. The business student who can't work in concert with colleagues from Hong Kong, Korea or Mexico will have a hard time climbing the corporate ladder.
>
> Our country has come a long way since the days of segregated buses. But if we fail to provide access to higher education for all minorities, major sectors of our population will not succeed in a society that increasingly mandates advanced academic skills. I fear that the net result will be a two-tiered society, divided like those old buses along racial and ethnic lines.[24]

h. The following is excerpted from Richard Wasserstrom, "Preferential Treatment":

> Someone might argue that what is wrong with [affirmative action] programs is that they deprive persons who are more qualified by bestowing benefits on those who are less qualified in virtue of their being either black or female.
>
> There are many things wrong with the objection based on qualifications. Not the least of them is that we do not live in a society in which there is even the serious pretense of a qualification requirement for many jobs of substantial power and authority. . . .
>
> But there is a theoretical difficulty as well, which cuts much more deeply into the argument about qualifications. . . . To be at all persuasive, the argument must be that those who are the most qualified *deserve* to receive the benefits (the job, the place in law school, etc.) because they are the most qualified. And there is just no reason to think that this is a correct premise. There is a logical gap in the inference that the person who is most qualified to perform a task, *e.g.*, be a good student, deserves to be admitted as a student. Of course, those who deserve to be admitted should be admitted. But why do the most qualified deserve anything? There is just no necessary connection between academic merit (in the sense of qualification) and deserving to be a member of a student body.

Suppose, for instance, that there is only one tennis court in the community. Is it clear that the two best players ought to be the ones permitted to use it? Why not those who were there first? Or those who will enjoy playing the most? Or those who are the worst and therefore need the greatest opportunity to practice? Or those who have the chance to play least frequently? . . .[25]

i. In *Furman v. Georgia* (408 US 238), the majority of the Supreme Court held that "as the statutes are administered . . . the imposition and carrying out of the death penalty [constitutes] cruel and unusual punishment in violation of the Eighth and Fourteenth Amendments."[26] The following is an excerpt from the majority opinion by Justice Stewart:

> These death sentences are cruel and unusual in the same way that being struck by lightning is cruel and unusual. For, of all the people convicted of rapes and murders in 1967 and 1968, many just as reprehensible as these, the petitioners are among a capriciously selected random handful upon whom the sentence of death has in fact been imposed. . . . I simply conclude that the Eighth and Fourteenth Amendments cannot tolerate the infliction of sentence of death under legal systems that permit this unique penalty to be so wantonly and so freakishly imposed.[27]

j. In the following, Columbia Law School professor Patricia J. Williams responds to efforts to prevent publication of *Live from Death Row*, a book written by Mumia Abu-Jamal, a radio journalist and Peabody Award–winning radio essayist who was convicted and sentenced to death for killing a police officer.

> There's hypocrisy in it [the attempt to prevent publication of *Live from Death Row*], you have to admit: If Sergeant Stacey Koon, convicted of directing the assault on Rodney King, can publish his rambling rationalizations for the glories of excessive violence in *Presumed Guilty: The Tragedy of the Rodney King Affair*, and if ex-con G. Gordon Liddy can stand on the steps of the Lincoln Memorial and rally gun rights supporters by shouting "just don't obey the damn law"—if the First Amendment protects all that, then it ought to protect Mumia Abu-Jamal's description of "Harry Washington," a death row inmate who
>
>> has begun the slide from depression, through deterioration, to dementia. . . . The conditions of most of America's death rows create Harry Washingtons by the score . . . solitary confinement, around-the-clock lock-in, no-contact visits, no prison jobs, no educational programs by which to grow, psychiatric "treatment" facilities designed only to drug you into a coma; ladle in hostile, overtly racist prison guards and staff; add the weight of the falling away of family ties, and you have all the fixings for a stressful psychic stew designed to deteriorate, to erode, one's humanity.
>
> Abu-Jamal's [book] is hardly an idle "book by a monster" [as some have labeled it] preaching death, teaching death or celebrating violence—it is a book of mourning for the condemned.[28]

2. In each of the passages in question 1, is the purpose of the analogy to explain something, to support a conclusion, or both? If the purpose is to support a conclusion, what is the conclusion?

3. Do you understand or accept the starting point of the analogies found in the passages? Explain.

4. Do you find any differences relevant to undermining the purpose of the analogies found in the passages? Explain.

5. For each of the analogies, can you think of a closer analogy that leads to a different conclusion or fuller explanation?

READINGS FOR ANALYSIS

Free Political Speech in Schools

The following is excerpted from *Tinker v. Des Moines Independent Community School District*.

MAJORITY OPINION BY
MR. JUSTICE FORTAS

Petitioner John. F. Tinker, 15 years old, and petitioner Christopher Eckhardt, 16 years old, attended high schools in Des Moines, Iowa. Petitioner Mary Beth Tinker, John's sister, was a 13-year-old student in junior high school.

In December 1965, a group of adults and students in Des Moines held a meeting at the Eckhardt home. The group determined to publicize their objections to the hostilities in Vietnam and their support for a truce by wearing black armbands during the holiday season. . . . Petitioners and their parents had previously engaged in similar activities, and they decided to participate in the program.

The principals of the Des Moines schools became aware of the plan to wear armbands. On December 14, 1965, they met and adopted a policy that any student wearing an armband to school would be asked to remove it, and if he refused he would be suspended until he returned without the armband. Petitioners were aware of the regulation that the school authorities adopted. On December 16, Mary Beth and Christopher wore black armbands

to their schools. John Tinker wore his armband the next day. They were all sent home and suspended from school until they would come back without their armbands. They did not return to school until after the planned period for wearing armbands had expired— that is, until after New Year's Day. . . .

. . . Our problem involves direct, primary First Amendment rights akin to "pure speech."

The school officials banned and sought to punish petitioners for a silent, passive expression of opinion, unaccompanied by any disorder or disturbance on the part of petitioners. There is here no evidence whatever of petitioners' interference, actual or nascent, with the schools' work or of collision with the rights of other students to be secure and to be let alone. Accordingly, this case does not concern speech or action that intrudes upon the work of the schools or the rights of other students. . . .

The District Court concluded that the action of the school authorities was reasonable because it was based upon their fear of a disturbance from the wearing of the armbands. But, in our system, undifferentiated fear or apprehension of disturbance is not enough to overcome the right of freedom of expression. . . .

It is also relevant that the school authorities did not purport to prohibit the wearing of all symbols of political or controversial significance. The record shows that students in some of the schools wore buttons relating to national political campaigns, and some even wore the Iron Cross, traditionally a symbol of Nazism. The order prohibiting the wearing of armbands did not extend to these. Instead, a particular symbol—black armbands worn to exhibit opposition to this Nation's involvement in Vietnam—was singled out for prohibition. Clearly, the prohibition of expression of one particular opinion, at least without evidence that it is necessary to avoid material and substantial interference with schoolwork or discipline, is not constitutionally permissible.

In our system, state-operated schools may not be enclaves of totalitarianism. School officials do not possess absolute authority over their students. Students in school as well as out of school are "persons" under our Constitution. They are possessed of fundamental rights which the State must respect, just as they themselves must respect their obligations to the State. In our system, students may not be regarded as closed-circuit recipients of only that which the State chooses to communicate. They may not be confined to the expression of those sentiments that are officially approved. In the absence of a specific showing of constitutionally valid reasons to regulate their speech, students are entitled to freedom of expression of their views. . . .

As we have discussed, the record does not demonstrate any facts which might reasonably have led school authorities to forecast substantial disruption of or material interference with school activities, and no disturbances or disorders on the school premises in fact occurred. . . . In the circumstances, our Constitution does not permit officials of the State to deny their form of expression. . . .

MR. JUSTICE BLACK, DISSENTING

. . . While the record does not show that any of these armband students shouted, used profane language, or were violent in any manner, detailed testimony by some of them shows their armbands caused comments, warnings by other students, the poking of fun at them, and a warning by an older football player that other, nonprotesting students had better let them alone. There is also evidence that a teacher of mathematics had his lesson period practically "wrecked" chiefly by disputes with Mary Beth Tinker, who wore her armband for her "demonstration." Even a casual reading of the record shows that this armband did divert students' minds from their regular lessons, and that talk, comments, etc., made John Tinker "self-conscious" in attending school with his armband. While the absence of obscene remarks or boisterous and loud disorder perhaps justifies the Court's statement that the few armbanded students did not actually "disrupt" the classwork, I think the record overwhelmingly shows that the armbands did exactly what the school officials and principal foresaw they would, that is, took the students' minds off their classwork and diverted them to thoughts about the highly emotional subject of the Vietnam war. And I repeat that if the time has come when pupils of state-supported schools, kindergartens, grammar schools, or high schools, can defy and flout orders of school officials to keep their minds on their own schoolwork, it is the beginning of a new revolutionary era of permissiveness in this country fostered by the judiciary. The next logical step, it appears to me, would be to hold unconstitutional laws that bar pupils under 21 or 18 from voting, or from being elected members of the boards of education. . . .

The true principles on this whole subject were in my judgment spoken by Mr. Justice McKenna for the Court in *Waugh v. Mississippi University*. . . . The State had there passed a law barring students from peaceably assembling in Greek letter fraternities and providing that students who joined them could be expelled from school. This law would appear on the surface to run afoul of the First Amendment's freedom of assembly clause. The law was attacked as violative of due process and of the privileges and immunities clause and as a deprivation of property and of liberty, under the Fourteenth Amendment. It was argued that the fraternity made its members more moral, taught discipline, and inspired its members to study harder and to obey better the rules of discipline and order. This Court rejected all the "fervid" pleas of the fraternities' advocates and decided unanimously against these Fourteenth Amendment arguments. The Court in its next to the last paragraph made this statement which has complete relevance for us today:

> It is said that the fraternity to which complainant belongs is a moral and of itself a disciplinary force. This need not be denied. But whether such membership makes against discipline was for the State of Mississippi to determine. It is to be remembered that the University was established by the State and is under the control of the State, and the enactment of the statute may have been induced by the opinion that membership in the prohibited societies divided the attention of the students and distracted from that singleness of purpose which the State desired to exist in its public educational institutions. It is not for us to entertain conjectures in opposition to the views of the State and annul its regulations upon disputable considerations of their wisdom or necessity.

It was on the foregoing argument that this Court sustained the power of Mississippi to curtail the First Amendment's right of peaceable assembly. And the same reasons are equally applicable to curtailing in the States' public schools the right to complete freedom of expression. Iowa's public schools, like Mississippi's university, are operated to give students an opportunity to learn, not to talk politics by actual speech, or by "symbolic" speech. And, as I have pointed out before, the record amply shows that public protest in the school classes against the Vietnam war "distracted from that singleness of purpose which the State [here Iowa] desired to exist in its public educational institutions." Here the Court should accord Iowa educational institutions the same right to determine for themselves to what extent free expression should be allowed in its schools as it accorded Mississippi with reference to freedom of assembly. . . .

Questions

1. What analogies do you find in the above Supreme Court opinions? Are all of the analogies you found explicitly stated? Are some of them implicit? Explain.
2. What are the authors' intended purposes in presenting these analogies?
3. Do the authors achieve their purposes? Are the things being compared relevantly similar?
4. Can you think of a more effective way for the authors to achieve their purposes?
5. Do you accept, reject, or remain neutral to the author's purposes? Explain why.
6. Are you aware of any attempts by school administrators to regulate clothing worn in schools today? If so, what similarities and differences do you find between the clothing in question and the arm bands worn to express disagreement with a governmental military policy?
7. What other points or questions would you like to raise about these readings?

The Constitutionality of Drug Testing

The following are excerpts from *National Treasury Employees Union, et al., v. William Von Raab, Commissioner, United States Custom Service.*

MAJORITY OPINION
BY JUSTICE ANTHONY KENNEDY

. . . We now affirm so much of the judgment of the court of appeals as upheld the testing of [Customs] employees directly involved in drug interdiction or required to carry firearms. We vacate the judgment to the extent it upheld the testing of applicants for positions requiring the incumbent to handle classified materials. . . .

. . . Employees of the United States Mint, for example, should expect to be subject to certain routine personal searches when they leave the workplace every day. Similarly, those who join our military or intelligence services may not only be required to give what in other contexts might be viewed as extraordinary assurances of trustworthiness and probity, but also may expect intrusive inquiries into their physical fitness for those special positions. . . .

We think Customs employees who are directly involved in the interdiction of illegal drugs or who are required to carry firearms in the line of duty likewise have a diminished expectation of privacy in respect to the intrusions occasioned by a urine test. Unlike most private citizens or government employees in general, employees involved in drug interdiction reasonably should expect effective inquiry into their fitness and probity. Much of the same is true of employees who are required to carry firearms. Because successful performance of their duties depends uniquely on their judgment and dexterity, these employees cannot reasonably expect to keep from the Service personal information that bears directly on their fitness. While reasonable tests designed to elicit this information doubtless infringe some privacy

expectations, we do not believe these expectations outweigh the Government's compelling interests in safety and in the integrity of our borders. . . .

The mere circumstance that all but a few of the employees tested are entirely innocent of wrongdoing does not impugn the program's validity. The same is likely to be true of householders who are required to submit to suspicionless housing code inspections, see *Camara v Municipal Court*, . . . and of motorists who are stopped at the checkpoints we approved in *United States v Martinez-Fuerte*. . . .

MINORITY OPINION
BY JUSTICE ANTONIN SCALIA

. . . The issue in this case is not whether Customs Service employees can constitutionally be denied promotion, or even dismissed, for a single instance of unlawful drug use, at home or at work. They assuredly can. The issue here is what steps can constitutionally be taken to *detect* such drug use. . . .

Until today this Court had upheld a bodily search separate from arrest and without individualized suspicion of wrongdoing only with respect to prison inmates, relying upon the uniquely dangerous nature of that environment. See *Bell v Wolfish*. . . . Today, in *Skinner*, we allow a less intrusive bodily search of railroad employees involved in train accidents. I joined the Court's opinion there because the demonstrated frequency of drug and alcohol use by the targeted class of employees, and the demonstrated connection between such use and grave harm, rendered the search a reasonable means of protecting society. I decline to join the Court's opinion in the present case because neither frequency of use nor connection to harm is demonstrated or even likely. In my view the Customs Service rules are a kind of immolation of privacy and human dignity in symbolic opposition to drug use. . . .

. . . It is not apparent to me that a Customs Service employee who uses drugs is significantly more likely to be bribed by a drug smuggler, any more than a Customs Service employee who wears diamonds is significantly more likely to be bribed by a diamond smuggler—unless, perhaps, the addiction to drugs is so severe, and requires so much money to maintain, that it would be detectable even without benefit of a urine test. Nor is it apparent to me that Customs officers who use drugs will be appreciably less "sympathetic" to their drug-interdiction mission, any more than police officers who exceed the speed limit in their private cars are appreciably less sympathetic to their mission of enforcing the traffic laws. . . . Nor, finally, is it apparent to me that urine tests will be even marginally more effective in preventing gun-carrying agents from risking "impaired perception and judgment" than is their current knowledge that, if impaired, they may be shot dead in unequal combat with unimpaired smugglers—unless, again, their addiction is so severe that no urine test is needed for detection. . . .

. . . In *Skinner* . . . we took pains to establish the existence of special need for the search or seizure . . . [W]e pointed to a long history of alcohol abuse in the railroad industry, and noted that in an 8-year period 45 train accidents and incidents had occurred because of alcohol- and drug-impaired railroad employees, killing 34 people, injuring 66, and causing more than $28 million in property damage. . . . In the present case, by contrast, not only is the Customs Service thought to be "largely drug-free," but the connection between whatever dug use may exist and serious social harm is entirely speculative. Except for the fact that the search of a person is much more intrusive than the stop of a car, the present case resembles *Delaware v Prouse*, . . . where we held that the Fourth Amendment prohibited random stops to check drivers' licenses and motor vehicle registration. The contribution of this practice to highway safety, we concluded, was "marginal at best" since the number of licensed drivers that must be stopped in order to find one unlicensed one "will be large indeed." . . .

Questions

1. What analogies do you find in the above Supreme Court opinions? Are all of the analogies you found explicitly stated? Are some of them implicit? Explain.
2. What are the authors' intended purposes in presenting these analogies?
3. Do the authors achieve their purposes? Are the things being compared relevantly similar?
4. Can you think of a more effective way for the authors to achieve their purposes?
5. Do you accept, reject, or remain neutral to the authors' purposes? Explain why.
6. What other points or questions would you like to raise about these readings?

WRITING IDEAS

1. Write an analogy that explains a complex or abstract concept or thing.
2. Make a list of new things you are doing or expect to do soon, such as attending college for the first time, studying a subject you've never studied before, getting married, having a child. Select one of them to explore. Reflect about past experiences you have had, and recall some that are

analogous to the new experience you want to know about. Discuss relevant similarities and potentially relevant differences between your past and future experiences. Draw a conclusion about what you can expect to happen in your new experience on the basis of your past experience.

3. Write a fictional story to critique an analogous real-life behavior.

4. Write an essay in which you give your reasons for supporting the majority or minority opinion in one of the essays for analysis.

5. Write about whether this chapter and your class discussions complemented, conflicted with, supported, or left out any of your previous ideas about thinking through analogies.

Notes

1. John Allen Paulos, *Innumeracy* (New York: Random House, 1990) 12.
2. Paulos 13.
3. Paul Fussell, *Class: A Guide Through the American Status System* (New York: Simon & Schuster, 1983) 15.
4. Tarthang Tulku, *Gesture of Balance* (Berkeley, CA: Dharma Publishing, 1977) 126.
5. Alberto Alvaro Rios, "Becoming and Braking: Poet and Poem, in Kathleen Aguero, ed., *Daily Fare: Essays from the Multicultural Experience* (Athens, GA: U of Georgia Press, 1993) 21.
6. Audre Lorde, *The Cancer Journals* (San Francisco: spinsters/aunt lute, 1980) 60.
7. Desmond Stewart, "The Limits of Trooghaft," *Encounter* (London, February 1972).
8. David Shaw, "Hunger for Heroes, Villians Rooted in American Psyche," *Los Angeles Times* 17 Feb. 1994: A19.
9. Carol Tavris, *The Mismeasure of Woman* (New York: Simon & Schuster, 1992) 15.
10. Cass R. Sunstein, "Commentary: On Analogical Reasoning" *Harvard Law Review* 106 (1993): 741.
11. Sunstein 744.
12. Sunstein 771.
13. Sunstein 773.
14. Sunstein 773.
15. Sunstein 759–60.
16. Sunstein 766.
17. Sunstein 757.
18. Tulku 157.
19. Martin Sanchez Jankowski, *Islands in the Street: Gangs and American Urban Society* (Berkeley, CA: U of California Press, 1991) 48.
20. Dr. Margie Go Singco-Holmes, "He's Leaving Home," *Filipinas* June 1995: 68.
21. John A. Garraty, *1001 Things Everyone Should Know about American History* (New York: Doubleday, 1989) 50.
22. From an interview with Charles Baron excerpted from "A Dissenting Voice: The Black Face of White Racism," *Destiny* April 1995: 27.
23. Excerpted from Delbert Hawthorne, "Stopping the Civil Rights Train," *Destiny* April 1995: 19.
24. Chang-Lin Tien, "Affirming Affirmative Action," *A. Magazine* June/July 1995: 87.
25. Richard Wasserstrom, "Preferential Treatment," *Philosophy and Women*, eds. Sharon Bishop and Marjorie Weinzweig (Belmont, CA: Wadsworth, 1979) 249.
26. *Furman v. Georgia* (408 US 238) quoted in *The Information Series on Current Topics: Capital Punishment Cruel and Unusual?* 1992 ed., 7.
27. *Furman v. Georgia* (408 US 238) quoted in *The Information Series*, 7–8.
28. Patricia J. Williams, "The Executioner's Automat," *The Nation* 10 July 1995: 60.

9

Generating Generalizations

CHAPTER GOALS

- To expand your knowledge of one type of reasoning introduced in Chapter 7—generalizing from a sample.
- To improve your ability to identify faulty generalizations, especially stereotypes.
- To gain an understanding of some of the basic concepts of statistical reasoning, from which many generalizations are derived.
- To learn how to draw acceptable conclusions from generalizations by learning the language and methods of sampling.
- To use your knowledge to suspend judgment about generalizations until you find they have sufficient support, as well as to generate acceptable generalizations of your own.

YOUR THOUGHTS ABOUT GENERALIZATIONS

When do you find yourself questioning generalizations? Jot down your ideas; then read these generalizations and answer the questions that follow. The sentences with asterisks are from a poll sponsored by Virginia Slims.[1]

1. Men are basically selfish and self-centered.*
2. Women are basically martyrs, unreflectively serving the needs of others.
3. Most men look at a woman and immediately think what it would be like to go to bed with her.*
4. Most women look at a man and immediately wonder whether he will be a good provider.
5. Most men think only their own opinions about the world are important.*
6. Most women cater to men and rarely publicly disagree with a view a man finds important.

Questions

1. Do you find these statements acceptable, unacceptable, or questionable?
2. If someone asked you to provide evidence to support or reject any of the above statements, what evidence would you provide?

3. Do you believe that the evidence you have is sufficient to establish the acceptability or unacceptability of any of these claims? Explain.

H. G. Wells once said, "Statistical thinking will one day be as necessary for efficient citizenship as the ability to read and write."[2] I agree. In order to make decisions we can live with, we need to understand statistics. Why? Because understanding **statistics** helps us recognize when someone is trying to trick us into believing a false **generalization,** and it helps us identify false generalizations and stereotypes we have absorbed unaware. Understanding statistics also helps us generate accurate generalizations.

Learning to separate accurate from faulty generalizations is important because we use generalizations when making predictions. In turn, we use predictions when deciding how to act. For example, if we know the *generalization* that roads tend to be slippery after a first rain, we can *predict* that the road may well be slippery during the first rain of this season. If we want to avoid a car accident, we will *decide* to drive more slowly than usual.

This generalization about slippery roads is part of our common knowledge. Other generalizations are more complicated to support, requiring time, money, and detailed knowledge of statistical methodology.

This chapter won't give you the time or money to do statistical research, nor will it give you a complete understanding of statistical methodology. But by introducing you to some of the basic concepts of statistical reasoning, this chapter can help you become more aware of your (and others') ignorance about generalizations. You will learn to question generalizations you previously would have assumed were true. And you will also be better able to question the experts you consult.

REASONING FROM A GENERALIZATION

To reason effectively from generalizations, we need to note the scope of the generalization, qualify the conclusion we make from our generalization, and make sure the generalization we began with was acceptable.

Noting the Scope of the Generalization

Before drawing a conclusion from a generalization, we need to determine how broad or narrow it is. That is, we need to ask whether the generalization is about the whole group or some part of it. For example, "All birds fly" is about the whole group of birds. It is a very **broad generalization.** We also make **narrower generalizations,** such as "Most birds fly" or "Some birds fly."

Statistical Generalizations Statistical **generalizations** are generalizations with numbers in them. Some statistical generalizations are stated very precisely. The exact percentage of the group is given, for example, "100% of birds fly," or "90% of birds fly," or "25% of birds fly." Other statistical generalizations are stated less precisely. For example, when we are sure that 25% of birds fly, but are not sure whether and how many more birds fly, we say: "At least 25% of birds fly." Or, if we know that 10% of birds do not fly, but we do not know how many more do not fly, we say: "At most 90% of birds fly." That statement indicates that the percentage of birds that fly could be as high as 90% or as low as 0%.

Sometimes people use less precise statistical generalizations to mislead an audience, as when businesses advertise that everything in a store will be on sale "at savings up to 75% off." The "75%" catches the unsuspecting buyer's eye, and the buyer expects everything to be 75% off. A smart shopper, however, notices the weasel words "up to" and realizes the savings may be slim.

Glittering, Sweeping, and Blanket Generalizations   Frequently, when making generalizations people do not describe the scope of the generalization in either words or numbers. Consider the following.

> Boys are better at math than girls.

Such broad generalizations are sometimes called **glittering generalizations, sweeping generalizations,** and **blanket generalizations.** This last label contains a clue about the effects of such broad generalizations. Broad generalizations cover the entire class like a blanket.

What impression did the sweeping generalization about boys and girls give you about the comparative math ability of boys and girls? You probably don't think that all boys are better at math than all girls, because you know from your personal experience that some girls are better at math than some boys. But you might still think that on average, the difference between boys' and girls' math abilities is fairly big; I did when I heard this sweeping generalization. But my ideas changed dramatically when I saw a more precise comparison: Graphs of girls' and boys' math abilities indicate that they are almost identical.[3]

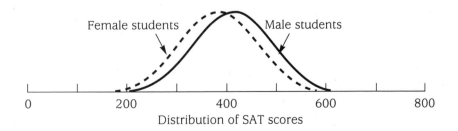

Distribution of SAT scores

YOUR TURN A

◆ 1. Are any of the following generalizations? Explain.

a. Seventy-five percent of the customers at Reliable Used Cars buy from Fred.

b. Fred sold 75 cars last week.

c. The cars at Reliable Used Cars are on sale at up to 75% off this weekend.

d. There are 20 trees in José's yard.

e. All of the trees in José's yard are pines.

◆ 2. Are any of the above generalizations statistical generalizations?

◆ 3. Do any of the generalizations above contain potentially misleading weasel words?

◆ 4. Are any of the statements listed at the beginning of the chapter glittering generalizations? Explain.

5. Review something you have written for this class. Have you made any generalizations? Were any of them overly broad?

Qualifying the Conclusion

We can make a prediction with certainty about whether an individual member of a group has a particular characteristic only if we start from a generalization that all, or 100%, of the group has that characteristic. Otherwise, we must add a qualifier, such as "very likely," "likely," "possibly," or "there's a slim chance" to indicate the degree of certainty the generalization we started with allows. Sometimes these qualifiers are stated with numbers, such as "There's a 90% chance of rain tomorrow."

Paying attention to qualifiers has important practical consequences. From the precise generalization about boys' and girls' math abilities, we can conclude only that there's some very small chance that of any two children, one boy and one girl, the boy will be better at math than the girl. But this chance is too small to be useful to us in everyday life. If we were hiring a math teacher, for example, finding out the sex of the applicant will be far less telling than finding out the applicant's math grades in college.

Acceptability of the Generalization

In order for the prediction from your generalization to be acceptable, your starting generalization must itself be acceptable. There are a number of ways to arrive at acceptable generalizations: use common knowledge, ask a reliable authority, take a census, and draw an inference from a representative group.

Use Common Knowledge   Many generalizations have become a part of our common knowledge. "Most birds fly," "Fish swim, " and "Humans laugh" are a few of the many generalizations about the world that we can safely take for

granted. Commonly known generalizations are acceptable. Remember, however, that although we have developed a lot of common knowledge over the
years, we have also developed a lot of shared ignorance. Commonly held
generalizations that have political significance, such as those based on race,
class, gender, age, disability, and nationality, should always be questioned
carefully. Stereotypes (false or questionable generalizations about humans)
are examples of shared ignorance passing for common knowledge.

Ask a Reliable Expert When we don't have common knowledge of a topic,
we can draw on the findings of experts. Biologists, anthropologists, sociolo-
gists, and other scientists specialize in making generalizations about the
world and its inhabitants. We can support generalizations by appealing to
their expertise. If the scientists we appeal to are knowledgeable and candid,
their generalizations are likely to be acceptable.

Probably the most common expert opinion on generalizations we
encounter in our daily lives comes in the form of polls and surveys. Especially during election years, we find constant front-page reports of voters'
attitudes toward propositions and candidates. Before relying on a report of a
poll or survey, ask these questions: "Who conducted the study, and who
sponsored it?"

WHO CONDUCTED THE STUDY? Was the study conducted by a reputable
polling agency, such as Gallup or Roper? Was it conducted by experts who
have studied statistical methodology and have conducted successful studies
in the past? If so, you have reason to believe the figures in the report. If those
conducting the study are not experts, you have reason to question whether
the figures are accurate.

WHO SPONSORED THE STUDY? The **sponsor** of a poll or survey is the individual or organization that pays to have it done. The sponsor decides whether to
release the conclusions or any part of them for publication. Some studies are
done for academic interest; others are done to promote the political or economic goals of the sponsor. Sponsors with vested political or economic interests are likely to release answers to survey or poll questions only if the
answers further the sponsors' interests and ideals.

Take a Census Experts sometimes support their generalizations by taking a
census, that is, by observing or interviewing each individual in the entire
group. We can sometimes take a census ourselves. For example, if you want
to know whether most of the students in your critical thinking class come to
class on Fridays, you can watch them all semester long to find out (assuming
you make it to class on Fridays yourself).

Study a Representative Group Frequently, however, we do not have the time
or money to survey the entire group of individuals we want information
about. There may be other reasons why we wouldn't want to observe

the whole class. If we ate every cookie during quality-control checks, for example, we wouldn't have anything left to sell. In such cases, we get information about a small group and then draw conclusions about the entire group. If the small group is analogous to, or **representative of,** the entire group, the generalization we draw from the small group will be acceptable. The next sections discuss this method for arriving at generalizations in more detail.

YOUR TURN B

◆ 1. Suppose you were reading reports about two studies regarding attitudes about cigarette smoking. One was sponsored by an academic institution; the other was sponsored by a cigarette company. Which sponsor do you think would be more likely to release a complete report of its study's findings? Explain.

2. Make a list of some commonly accepted claims about men and women or about some other group. Are these claims in fact acceptable, or are they examples of stereotypes (shared ignorance passing for knowledge)?

REASONING TO A GENERALIZATION

To be able to question experts and to question the inferences we make in everyday life from our own experiences, we need to understand the basics of how the experts arrive at generalizations. Experts use a multipart process to arrive at claims about everything from the percentage of whales that have parasites to the percentage of malfunctioning brakes in trucks on the freeway. We'll focus primarily on generalizations about people derived from polls and surveys.

The Language of Sampling

We begin learning how statisticians support generalizations by learning the language they use. In this section and the next, let's follow an example to see how statisticians use their special words.

Sample and Population Suppose that we want to know what percentage of Guatemalans speak fluent English. Instead of interviewing everyone in Guatemala, we could study a small group of Guatemalans and then draw a conclusion about the rest of the Guatemalans from this small group. Statisticians call the small group we select a **sample** and the entire group we want information about a **population.**

The spoon contains a representative sample of soup.

Representative Sample   In order for our inference from the sample to be reliable, it must be representative of (like or analogous to) the population; that is, we have to know that both groups, the small and the large, are likely to contain the same percentage of fluent English speakers. If both groups have the same percentage of English speakers, then once we find out the percentage of English speakers in the sample, we will know the percentage of English speakers in the population.

Sample Design

The question then becomes "How do we select a sample that is representative of (analogous to) the population?" Statisticians use several ways to design samples to achieve that goal.

Simple Random Sample   If you put the names of all Guatemalans in a hat, toss the names around until they are completely mixed up, then take some of them out one by one, you have a **simple random sample** of Guatemalans to study. Simple random samples provide high degrees of precision. However, they are not always practical to use. You may not *have* a list of the names of all Guatemalans, for example, to start with. And even if you did, sending interviewers around the country seeking the selected individuals is time-consuming and expensive.

Multistage Sampling Design   To avoid the problems of simple random design, researchers typically use a **multistage sampling design,** selecting areas of the country, then areas within the areas, then households within the smaller areas. This way, the researcher doesn't have to know the names of the individuals and can focus data collection in selected areas instead of points scattered about the country. The households are often selected by *systematic random sample*. The researcher selects a starting household at random, then selects every fifth or ninth household from that point.[4]

Stratified Random Sample   Researchers seeking information about specific groups (men and women; upper, middle, and lower classes; college, high-school, and grade-school graduates) within a larger population use a **stratified random sample.** You create a stratified random sample by dividing a population into groups, called *strata,* then selecting individuals from each stratum at random. When researchers know the percentages of the groups in the general population, they can ensure that their samples contain the same percentages by stratifying the samples. In such cases, the stratified random sample yields even greater precision than the simple random sample.

Researchers use various combinations of these and other methods to arrive at samples. Although we won't get into the details of reliable sample design, we can be on the lookout for some features of clearly unrepresentative samples.

Biased Sample   The question then becomes, "How do I know a sample is likely to be *un*representative?" or "How do I know a sample is biased?" A **biased sample** is a sample that is likely to fail to represent (be analogous to) the population. For example, suppose in our effort to find out the percentage of Guatemalans who speak fluent English we select college graduates in Guatemala as our sample. Because college graduates are more likely to speak fluent English than are other Guatemalans, our sample would be biased. Our sample contains a higher percentage of fluent English speakers than does the population as a whole.

The following sections describe some typical signs of sample bias.

SAMPLING BIRDS OF A FEATHER   If we want to know the eating habits of birds, we can't just look at the birds that munch away on black sunflower seeds at a nearby bird feeder. The commonalities we find among those birds will not serve to represent all birds. *They* may feed happily on black sunflower seeds, but that doesn't mean *all* birds will like black sunflower seeds.

The spoon contains a biased (unrepresentative) sample of soup.

Of course, I'm not likely to make a generalization about all birds based on the birds that come to my feeder, because I already know that penguins, for example, eat fish, not seeds. But we all too frequently make generalizations about things we don't know from the birds flocking near us. For example, people routinely generalize about human behavior from the humans they know. Because "birds of a feather flock together," you generally cannot use your friends and acquaintances as a sample (**sampling birds of a feather**) to build generalizations about people in general. Chances are that people in general will not have the same attitudes or beliefs your friends have.

Similarly, **man-on-the-street interviews** are unreliable representations of what people in general think. If you stand outside a pub and wait for people to interview, you will have a disproportionate number of people who favor drinking. If you wait outside a Baptist church for your interviews, you will find a disproportionate number of people who are opposed to drinking. And even if you pick more neutral locations for your survey, the people flocking to the street at the time of the interview do not represent the full range of humans, including those who live in a different place or have jobs that don't allow them to be wandering about the streets at the time of the interview.

Self-selecting samples are also unreliable for the same reasons. People who flock to be interviewed or surveyed—by calling in to answer a TV or radio survey question, for example—do not represent those who don't have the time or interest to make the call.

CRAFTY SAMPLE SELECTION   Sometimes people intentionally create biased samples to mislead others. A friend who was remodeling his house recently bought a large order of birch flooring on the basis of a small sample he was shown. The birch in the sample was uniformly light in color. The birch in the delivered order varied considerably from dark to light. The birch salespeople had intentionally selected a biased sample to give potential customers the impression that their birch floors would be uniform in color.

To avoid being similarly tricked by a **crafty sample selection,** always question whether the person who produces the sample has a vested interest in misleading you.

THE POWER OF VIVID SAMPLES   It's very important to be always on the lookout for sample bias in our everyday lives, because the samples that we collect ourselves—made up of our vivid personal experience—have a powerful effect on us.

One excellent example of a blindingly **vivid sample** is the placement interview. Studies have shown that interviews are "largely useless for predicting success in undergraduate or professional school, success in the Peace Corps, and performance in various jobs, including scientific occupations. . . ."[5] Why? A candidate's behavior in a stressful interview fails to provide a representative sample of the candidate's general behavior. Some people pull themselves together under stress; others fall apart. Test scores are far more telling about how the candidate will perform on the job.

Yet job interviewers—even ones who have learned that you cannot support a generalization with a biased sample—continue to be unduly impressed by a candidate's behavior during a job interview. Why do they regard the interview, rather than the test scores and letters of recommendation, as the best indicator of the candidate's ability? Because vivid data—the Technicolor sights of the job candidate before them—have much greater impact on them than pallid data, the comparatively dull test scores.[6]

We are unduly influenced not only by vivid personal experience but also by vivid writing and visual images. Graphic portrayals of violence we see in the newspaper and on television make more impact on us than do the pallid crime statistics we read. As a result, although crime is down, people believe that crime is increasing.

Because we are so unduly influenced by vivid data, Nisbett and Ross recommend that we avoid obtaining vivid data when there are other, less influential and more telling data available.[7] Instead of making a decision about buying a car on the basis of a test drive, read about the car in *Consumer Reports*. The relatively dull statistical information in *Consumer Reports* will be far more telling about the overall performance of the car than a lively ride around the block. And before making decisions about how to act on the basis of impressions of the world we pick up from the news, we need to check those impressions carefully against formal scientific studies.

Sample Size People sometimes scoff at the small samples used by Gallup and other experienced pollsters. These critics assume that larger samples lead to more accurate generalizations. But this assumption is not true. Once a sample is large enough to represent the full range of variables in the population, it doesn't really help to increase the size of the sample. In "Poll-lution: Coping with Surveys and Polls," Ralph Johnson notes that pollsters collecting election data use the same size sample (about 1,800) in Canada and in the United States even though there are about ten times as many voters in the United States.[8] He helps us see why the U.S. sample size need not be larger by drawing an analogy between sampling voters and tasting soup.

> Assume that two batches are in different size cauldrons: One pot is a five-gallon pot and the other holds one quart. Do you need to take a bigger spoonful of the bigger batch? Would you? Probably not. You are likely to use the same spoon and the same size sample for the bigger as for the smaller pot. Even though the pots are of different sizes, a spoonful of soup taken from a properly stirred pot could well provide an accurate sample in both instances.[9]

In order for a sample to represent the whole adequately, it has to have enough individuals in it to represent the variety of individuals (variables) in the whole. Let's look at the soup example again. If you are trying to figure out whether the soup has enough salt, one small teaspoon will be sufficient, but if you want to know whether the soup has the right percentage of carrots, beets, and potatoes you will have to spoon out a cup of the soup and study it. You can't fit all of the variables (carrots, beets, and potatoes) into one teaspoon.

Remember, too, that the cup of soup will work for you only if you have stirred the pot first. Otherwise your sample might contain only the vegetables that floated to the top.

If you haven't stirred the soup, even a fairly large sample will not be fully representative. Cups of soup taken from the top will not adequately represent the vegetables that sink to the bottom.

CUT FROM THE SAME MOLD   For some populations, any sample you select is likely to be like any other sample. In such cases, you can use a single individual to represent a group. If you want to know how cookies will turn out when you use a particular cookie cutter, all you have to do is bake one cookie to get the idea. The same is true for other things that are produced by a set method. You can get an idea of the shape of all 1994 Toyota Tercel hatchbacks by looking at the shape of one 1994 Toyota Tercel hatchback. You can also learn a lot about certain groups of plants and animals by looking at a few of them. If you have seen one California poppy, you have not quite seen them all, but the ones you have not seen are very much like the one you have seen.

We can also make some generalizations about the physical characteristics of humans by looking at only a few. For example, we don't have to slice open every human to learn that generally humans have hearts, stomachs, and livers.

Human behavior, in contrast, is more difficult to generalize about. Rarely can we generalize to all people from observing the behavior of a few of them. We can't, for example, assume that because our friends laugh at our jokes, everyone will; people laugh at different things. People differ not only from each other but also from themselves in different contexts. For example, some people are quiet at home and, surprisingly, the life of a party; others are outspoken at home and silent in a crowd.

DIFFERENCES BLURRED BY LANGUAGE   Though diversity of human behavior may seem obvious, our language, as we saw in Chapter 5, sometimes hides it from us. Once we name individuals by the same label—"Asian," "woman," "man"—we expect the individuals to be similar. And when we name individuals by different labels, we expect them to be different.[10]

This assumption—that the same name indicates uniform similarity and that a different name indicates essential differences—is harmless when we are seeking generalizations about classes of individuals cut from the same cookie cutters. Gingerbread boys and girls have set similarities and differences.

But when we are trying to learn about human social groups, this assumption gets us into trouble. Real people are far more variable than gingerbread clones. Thus, when you make generalizations, it's always a good idea to ask yourself whether you are expecting to find similarities because of the label you are using or whether you have reason to believe that the individuals are in fact all cut from the same mold.

Summary Questions about Sample Design When trying to decide whether a sample is likely to be representative of the population, ask yourself the following questions:

Was the pot stirred before you tasted it? (Was the sample selected at random?)

Are there any signs of sample bias?

Is the sample filled with floating vegetables? (Are the individuals in the sample "birds of a feather flocking together"?)

Did a soup salesman create the sample? (Is the sample likely to result from crafty sample selection?)

Is the tasting spoon large enough to contain all of the vegetables in the soup? (Is the sample large enough to contain the full range of variables in the population?)

Were all the cookies cut from the same mold? (Are the individuals in the population enough alike that one of them can represent the rest?)

YOUR TURN C

◆ 1. Suppose you wanted to know how many men in the United States wear felt hats. You obtain a list of the names of men in the United States, mix them up so that each name has an equal chance of being selected, then select the names to call to find out whether they wear felt hats.

   a. What is the population in the above example?

   b. What is the sample in the above example?

   c. What is the sample design? Explain.

◆ 2. Look again at the list of generalizations at the beginning of the chapter. Think about one of these that you agree with (or select any other generalization you have made).

   a. Was the generalization based on a sample chosen at random or by another design?

   b. Were there any signs of sample bias? Explain.

◆ 3. Read page one of your local newspaper or listen to the evening news. Do the stories there provide an unbiased sample of the stories of human life? Explain.

◆ 4. Suppose Ali is trying to decide whether to live on campus or off campus, and one factor in his decision is how good the dorm food is. When he comes to campus for summer orientation, he eats the dorm food and thinks it is very good. Ali also reads a survey that says most of the students are not happy with the dorm food. Do you think Ali will decide to live on or off campus? Explain why, making use of the distinction between vivid and pallid data.

Knowledge of the Sample

There's more to generating reliable generalizations than creating representative samples. We also have to make sure that we get acceptable information about the individuals in the sample. Researchers typically use observation and interviews to get to know the individuals in the sample.

Observation   In many scientific studies, scientists use observation to gather information about the individuals in the sample. They watch the rats in the laboratory to see how they behave; they taste samples of wine to see if it's ready for the next stage of fermentation. But observing individuals outside controlled environments can be difficult. Researchers spend hours waiting for a lion to appear from the jungle or a butterfly to wriggle free from its cocoon. And the study of humans is even more complex. Human couples would not smile upon a researcher waiting to observe their bedroom behavior. Researchers have to get permission from people to study them, and people often refuse permission for studies that would invade the privacy of their homes or disrupt their work.

Interviews   However, researchers need not rely solely on direct observations of human behavior. Because humans use language, researchers can ask them questions about their behavior rather than following them around with binoculars.

Compared with direct observation, getting to know the sample subjects by interviewing them saves time and interferes less with the subjects' daily lives. But interviews do not always yield the knowledge the researcher seeks. Many factors influence the completeness and accuracy of information from interview subjects. Below are some of them.

SUBJECT'S SELF-KNOWLEDGE   Sometimes the subjects do not know themselves well enough to answer the questions accurately. For example, in a study on prejudice conducted by the General Social Survey, a sample of 3,000 Americans were asked what they thought about various ethnic groups, including a group labeled "Wisian-Americans." In case you're wondering who they are, Wisian-Americans do not exist. The researchers added them to the list to check whether the people surveyed were paying attention. Apparently many were not; 39% of the sample *rated* the Wisians![11] These people apparently do not understand their own attitudes. For surely if they stopped and thought for a minute they would realize that they have never even heard of the Wisians.

SUBJECT'S CANDOR   Other times people do not answer questions candidly. People do not like to admit to things they or others disapprove of, even when things are fairly trivial—such as reading habits. Researchers found that people interviewed said they read such magazines as the *Atlantic Monthly* or *Harper's*. But when offered a free magazine for answering the interview questions, they selected *True Detective* or *Life*.[12]

NEUTRAL OR LOADED QUESTIONS   Because people do not like to admit to behaviors thought wrong or abnormal, researchers try to word questions in a way that makes the behaviors asked about sound neutral. For example, researchers studying sexual behavior found that when asked the question "Do you masturbate?" most of the subjects in their sample answered, "I never masturbate." But when they rephrased the question, asking, "About how many times a week would you say you masturbate?"—which implies that masturbation is a common and morally neutral behavior—the subjects began to respond to the question.[13]

Some questions are so effective in eliciting a particular answer that they are called **loaded questions.** The question is, in effect, loaded with the answer. Consider the following:

Do you accept murdering innocent babies in their mothers' wombs?

Even the most ardent pro-choice proponent would have a hard time saying yes to this question.

WHO ASKS THE QUESTION   Because people do not like to offend others, they are more likely to be candid with someone they do not worry about offending. In a study done during World War II, two staffs of interviewers went to a Southern city to interview African Americans about the outcome of the war. One staff was white; the other was African American. When asked whether African Americans would be treated better or worse if the Japanese conquered the United States, only 25% of those interviewed by *African-American* interviewers said that African Americans would be treated worse, whereas 45% of those interviewed by *white* interviewers said African Americans would be treated worse. Nine percent told African-American interviewers they would be treated better, and only 2% told white interviewers they would be treated better.[14] Apparently African Americans were more candid in their responses to African-American interviewers.

BREADTH OF QUESTIONS   Any list of questions is only a sample of the possible questions the interviewer could ask. An interviewer can fail to get complete information about some group's attitudes or behavior by failing to ask all of the relevant questions.

Consider, for example, the list of questions you are asked when evaluating your teacher at the end of the semester, such as "How well prepared was the teacher?" and "Did the teacher return the homework promptly?" There might well be specific things you think about your teacher that these questions do not ask you to report on. For example, you might believe your teacher had a good excuse for being late in returning homework, say because he was sick or wrote unusually thorough comments on each paper. But if no question asked you about whether you thought your teacher had a good excuse for turning back papers late, the person reading your evaluation would not know what you thought about your teacher's tardy paper returns.

Sometimes researchers ask open-ended questions, such as "Would you like to add anything to clarify answers you gave to this questionnaire?" or "Do you have any other comments to make about this topic?" These open-ended questions give interviewees an opportunity to add information that specific questions do not call for, thus rounding out the picture created by answers to the more narrowly stated questions.

PRECISE OR VAGUE QUESTIONS   In order for the interviewer to understand the subject's answer, the subject must interpret the question the same way the interviewer did. If the question is stated precisely, the subject and interviewer are more likely to understand the question to mean the same thing. However, if the question is vague, the interviewer and subject may have two very different things in mind.

Consider, for example, the question "How many times a week do you eat a healthy meal at dinner time?" If the interviewer interprets "healthy" as containing a small amount of or no animal products, and the subject considers meat and potatoes a healthy diet, the subject's answer of "Five times a week" will mislead the interviewer into thinking this subject rarely eats meat for dinner. In contrast, if the interviewer asked, "How many times a week do you eat meat, fish, or poultry for dinner?" there would be less opportunity for miscommunication.

YOUR TURN D

◆ 1. Suppose you want to find out whether men are basically selfish and self-centered and whether women are basically martyrs, unreflectively serving the needs of others. And suppose you created random samples of men and of women to interview. What challenges would you face in getting to know your samples?

◆ 2. If you could not rely on men and women giving knowledgeable and candid answers to these questions, is there some other way you could get the knowledge you seek about your samples?

◆ 3. Are any of the following questions loaded? What answer would the question tend to elicit? How would you reword the question to remove the load?

a. Do you favor a policy that requires judges to give life sentences to third-time offenders as a way of cutting down on violent crime?

b. Do you favor prison rehabilitation programs as a way of preventing offenders from returning to crime after they leave prison?

c. Do you favor giving judges the authority to consider special circumstances when sentencing third-time offenders?

d. Do you favor cutting back on prison rehabilitation programs as a way to cut the exorbitant cost of incarceration?

Qualifying the Conclusion

In all studies, even the most carefully constructed ones, statisticians do not know for certain that the sample is strictly analogous to the population. As a result, sample results tell us only more or less what to expect about a population. Statisticians qualify their conclusions from samples by stating the margin of error and the confidence level for their study.

Margin of Error   The **margin of error** tells you how far off the figures in the population are likely to be from the figures in the sample. Let's look at an example to see why knowing the margin of error is so important for drawing conclusions from a sample.

Suppose you want to know whether more registered voters are in favor of your candidate or in favor of the opposing candidate. You read a poll that says that 51% of randomly sampled registered voters are in favor of your candidate, and 49% are in favor of the other candidate. May you conclude that *exactly* 51% of *the population* of registered voters support your candidate? No. At best, the sample percentage indicates that *more or less* 51% of the population will support your candidate.

In order to draw a conclusion about whether your candidate is ahead in the population, you need to know how many more and how many less than 51% of the population are likely to support your candidate; that is, you need to know the margin of error for the study.

Suppose the margin of error for this study is ±3% (a typical margin of error for a well-designed survey). This means that the percentage of people in the population who support your candidate may be as high as 54% (51% + 3%) or as low as 48% (51% − 3%). The percentage of people in the population who prefer the opposing candidate may be as high as 52% (49% + 3%) and as low as 46% (49% − 3%).

Given the margin of error, it is just as likely that 52% of the population support the opposing candidate as it is that 51% support your candidate. Thus, your candidate is just as likely to be behind as to be ahead.

If you didn't know about the margin of error, you would have made a false prediction about the population. You would have assumed that because your candidate was ahead in the sample, your candidate would be ahead in the population.

Confidence Level   The **confidence level** tells you the statisticians' degree of confidence that the percentages sought for the population will fall within the reported margin of error. A confidence level of 95%, for example, with a margin of error of ±3% tells you that statisticians are 95% confident that the percentages for the population will fall within ±3% of the percentages for the sample. It's 5% possible, in other words, that the percentages for the population will be farther off than ±3% from the percentages for the sample.

YOUR TURN E

◆ 1. Can you conclude from the information given below that more residence hall students think the residence hall food is not nutritious than think it is nutritious? Explain.

Forty-seven percent of a randomly selected sample of residence hall students think the residence hall food is nutritious, and 53% think the residence hall food is not nutritious. Sup-

pose the margin of error is ±3% and the confidence level is 95%.

◆ 2. Can you conclude from the information in item 1 above that it's not at all possible that 59% of the residence hall students think the residence hall food is not nutritious?

◆ 3. Can you conclude from the information in item 1 that the residence hall food probably is not nutritious?

This chapter has covered how tricky it is to support generalizations and how easily people jump from insufficient evidence to generalizations. However you responded to the list of generalizations before reading this chapter, I suspect that you now find them highly questionable. At least I hope so. One of the main focuses for this chapter is to help people move beyond stereotypes, and the generalizations listed at the beginning of the chapter are all stereotypes.

All of us at one time or another hold common stereotypes. So if you accepted some of the stereotypes listed, you are not alone. In fact, a majority of women polled in 1990 by the Roper Organization held two of the cultural stereotypes about men listed at the beginning of the chapter. Fifty-four percent held that most men who look at a woman immediately think about what it would be like to go to bed with her, and 58% of women held that most men think only their own opinions about the world are important. A large minority (42%) held that men are basically selfish and self-centered. (The margin of error was ±2%.) This poll indicates that we have a way to go to remove cultural stereotypes. Understanding how to generate accurate generalizations is a step in that direction.

Although people are not constructed to generate perfect generalizations every time, there are some things we can do to enhance our chances of finding adequate support for generalizations. We can use the common knowledge that has developed over the years and rely on the experts who use sound statistical methodology for generating generalizations. And when we are developing generalizations of our own, we can continually check our conclusions with others. The more points of view we include, the more likely we are to become aware of things we have overlooked in our study.

Most importantly, we can remind ourselves of human limits, treat the generalizations we hear or make as provisional, and withhold judgment from ones that have clearly insufficient support.

EXERCISES

1. Which of the following are generalizations? Are they statistical generalizations?

   a. Most college students watch soap operas.

   b. At least 25% of college students watch soap operas.

   c. All college students watch soap operas.

   d. White college-aged women are more likely to think of themselves as overweight than black college-aged women.

   e. Up to 99% of the freshmen who enter our college will graduate in four years.

   f. Ninety-nine students attended the first meeting of the Frisbee golf club.

   g. Sara watched soap operas five times last week.

   h. People who have more autonomy at work report more satisfaction with their work than those who have less autonomy.

   i. Older people have weak memories.

   j. Aunt Sally has a weak memory.

   k. Women value being treated with respect at work.

   l. Men value wages and advancement at work.

   m. As few as 0.01% of the cookies from the local cookie manufacturer are broken.

   n. After House Speaker Newt Gingrich called New York City "a culture of waste," the New York *Daily News* wrote, "Stereotyping is dangerous— even by someone who comes from a state where people marry their siblings and think refrigerators are lawn decor."[15]

2. Are any of the generalizations listed above blanket generalizations, stereotypes, or likely to mislead through use of weasel words? Explain.

3. Identify the samples and the populations in the following.

   a. Social scientist Richard Nisbett, who lives in Ann Arbor, Michigan, reports that he once thought restaurants in Palo Alto, California, were better than restaurants in Ann Arbor because the restaurants that his co-author, Lee Ross, took him to when Nisbett visited Ross in Palo Alto were so good.[16]

   b. Civic leader: Charges of police brutality and deplorable prison conditions are unreasonable. I saw no evidence of them during my prison tour.[17]

   c. Suppose you want to determine the attitudes of college students about requiring students to own computers. You select the incoming class of Harvard to question. Everyone you select answers the questions you ask.

d. Suppose you want to know the attitudes of students at your university about the new president. You divide a list of the students into males and females, then select at random individuals from each group to question. Everyone you select answers the questions you ask.

e. Suppose you want to know whether college-aged women tend to see themselves as overweight. You do a random sample of the white sorority women on your campus. Everyone you select answers the questions you ask.

f. Suppose you want to know whether students on your campus believe that football should be funded in a tight budget. You stand at the football stadium, questioning students who come to the Saturday game. All of the students you approach answer your questions.

4. Were any of the following sample designs used to select the samples in the examples in item 3: simple random sample, multistage sample, stratified random sample? Explain.

5. Were any of the individuals sampled in the examples in item 3 birds of a feather or selected craftily? Are there other reasons to suspect sample bias? Explain.

6. Discuss the wording of the following questions. Consider, for example, whether any of them are loaded; encourage candid answers about potentially embarrassing topics; are open-ended, allowing for more individual answers; or are vague or ambiguous. Explain your answers.

a. About how many times a week would you say you watch soap operas?

b. Do you watch soap operas frequently, rarely, or not at all?

c. Do you think foreign students should watch fewer soap operas so they'll have more time to study for their classes?

d. Do you think foreign students should watch more soap operas to help them learn English?

e. What do you think about students watching soap operas?

f. Do you think critical thinking should be a required class?

g. About how many times have you waited until the last minute to do your critical thinking assignment?

h. Do you think critical thinking should be required so students will make better decisions?

i. Do you use critical thinking in your major?

j. Do you think critical thinking should not be required so students will have more opportunity to take classes they believe will help them with their careers?

7. The following are some typical criteria on forms asking students to evaluate their teachers. Students are asked to select a numerical score ranging from 1 (poor) to 7 (excellent). How useful do you think these criteria are for finding out what students think about the class? Explain. (Consider, among other things, whether the students are all likely to understand the criteria in the same way.) What would you suggest a teacher do to get more information about what students think of the class?

   a. Presents material clearly

   b. Fair grading practices

   c. Intellectually stimulating

   d. Senses when students bored

   e. Encourages creativity

   f. Available for consultation

   g. Informs students of requirements

   h. Well prepared

   i. Course well organized

   j. Returns paper promptly

   k. Open to diverse opinions

8. Which of the following methods do you think would be most effective in helping a teacher find out how many students like the class? Explain.

   a. The teacher asks students individually in private.

   b. The teacher asks each student in front of the whole class.

   c. The teacher asks a few students who are doing well in the class.

   d. The students put their answers on anonymous questionnaires.

   e. The students tell another person, who will keep their names confidential.

   f. The teacher asks a few students who are not doing well in the class.

   g. The teacher asks a few students who tend to stay after class to ask questions.

9. Discuss whether you find sufficient information in each of the following to draw any reliable conclusions from the polls. In your answer, discuss whether you know the margin of error, confidence level, size of sample, who conducted the poll, and who sponsored the poll. Explain your answers.

   a. The attitudes of 18- to 29-year-olds and of those 30 and older.

   Poll question: Would you say that it is very important to . . .

	AGE 18–29	AGE 30+	DIFFERENCE
Work for the betterment of society?	58%	70%	−12%
Follow a strict moral code?	53%	62%	−9%
Have a nice home and car?	44%	40%	+4%
Have an exciting, stimulating life?	63%	46%	+17%

SOURCE: 1989 Gallup poll[18]

b. Descriptions of young people today and young people 20 years ago.

Poll question: Do the following words apply more to young people today or young people 20 years ago?   Response of all adults:

TRAIT	TODAY	20 YEARS AGO
Selfish	82%	5%
Materialistic	79%	15%
Reckless	73%	14%
Idealistic	38%	49%
Patriotic	24%	65%

SOURCE: 1989 Gallup poll[19]

c. The attitudes of blacks, whites, and hispanics on the American national character.

Poll question: Has the American national character changed in the last 20 years?

	BLACKS	WHITES	HISPANICS
Changed for the better	19%	12%	9%
Changed for the worse	41%	63%	51%
Stayed the same	34%	23%	32%

SOURCE: 1995 *Newsweek* poll[20]

d. Beliefs of blacks, whites, and hispanics about the continued existence of the United States as one nation.

Poll question: 100 years from today, will the United States still exist as one nation?

	BLACKS	WHITES	HISPANICS
Yes, will exist as one nation	41%	61%	54%
No, will not exist as one nation	48%	26%	38%

SOURCE: 1995 *Newsweek* poll[21]

10. Are the people polled in the examples in question 9 reliable authorities or witnesses on the subjects they are questioned about? Explain.

READINGS FOR ANALYSIS

Majority Opposes Clinton's Smoking Crackdown
ASSOCIATED PRESS

NEW YORK—Most Americans oppose some of President Clinton's aggressive efforts to shield teen-agers from tobacco advertising and promotion, an Associated Press poll found.

Fifty-eight percent reject a proposed ban on tobacco brand names on T-shirts or in sporting events such as auto racing's Winston Cup or the Virginia Slims Tennis Tournament. And 53 percent oppose allowing only black-and-white text—no color or pictures—on tobacco billboards and in cigarette advertisements in magazines read by many young people. . . .

The poll of 1,007 adults, taken Aug. 16–20, finds relatively weak support for the premise behind these regulations. Only 40 percent agree unequivocally that the tobacco companies actively use advertising and promotion to try to get youngsters to start smoking.

Questions

1. Which of the following states a conclusion the author draws from the poll?

   a. Most Americans oppose some of President Clinton's aggressive efforts to shield teenagers from tobacco advertising and promotion.

   b. Only 40% agree unequivocally that the tobacco companies actively use advertising and promotion to try to get youngsters to start smoking.

2. Is the population clearly defined?
3. What is the sample in the above?
4. Does the study as reported provide sufficient information to support the author's conclusions? Explain. (Consider, for example, whether the margin of error is reported, whether a reliable polling organization conducted the study, and whether the sample design was reliable.)
5. Does the Associated Press have any vested interest in the outcome of the study? Explain.
6. Are the people who were polled reliable authorities or witnesses on the subjects they are questioned about? Explain.
7. Discuss the headline of this article.

Poll: State Voters Back Execution 4–1
LOS ANGELES TIMES

SACRAMENTO—The verdict of California voters is nearly 4–1 that the state should execute Robert Alton Harris, sentenced to die in San Quentin's gas chamber for killing two San Diego teen-agers, The Los Angeles Times Poll has found.

Harris' execution, which had been scheduled for 3 a.m. Tuesday, was stayed indefinitely Friday by a federal appeals court judge to give lawyers for the death row inmate more

time to challenge the competence of his trial psychiatrists. But lawyers for the state have asked the U.S. Supreme Court to lift the stay and allow the execution to go forward as planned.

In the court of public opinion, the judgment is that Harris should die.

The Times Poll, in a survey ending Wednesday, inquired of those interviewed whether they favored Harris' execution Tuesday and noted that he would be the first to die in the gas chamber since 1967.

The response was: In favor of the execution 60 percent, opposed 16 percent, don't know 5 percent, "haven't heard enough to say" 19 percent.

Harris, who already had served a prison term for beating a man to death, was sentenced to the gas chamber in 1979 for murdering two teen-age boys he had kidnapped while stealing a car to use in a bank holdup.

The voters' verdict on his execution, as measured by The Times Poll, reflected the public's strong, long-standing support for capital punishment, an attitude that was reaffirmed in this survey.

Asked whether they generally favored or opposed the death penalty for convicted murderers, the voters' response was: In favor 78 percent, opposed 18 percent, not sure 4 percent. That is virtually identical to voter sentiments found by The Times Poll in 1985 and 1981.

In the latest survey, The Times Poll, directed by I. A. Lewis, interviewed 1,667 registered voters by telephone for six days. The margin of error is three percentage points in either direction.

People also were asked which sentence they favored more strongly for convicted murderers—"the death penalty or life imprisonment without the possibility of parole." The answer, by nearly 2–1, was the death penalty—60 percent to 32 percent with 8 percent not certain.

This response contrasted somewhat with the findings of a poll sponsored last December by Amnesty International and the American Civil Liberties Union.

That survey, conducted by the San Francisco-based Field Institute, asked a slightly different question and got a different answer. It found 67 percent of the public preferring that murderers be sentenced to life imprisonment without parole, if they also are required to work in prison to pay the victims' survivors.

Questions

1. Several surveys are mentioned in the above news article.
   a. What do you know about the ideals or values of those who sponsored the surveys (the *Los Angeles Times,* Amnesty International, and the American Civil Liberties Union)?
   b. Do you know whether the sponsors support or reject the death penalty?

2. Did the news article report the exact wording of the questions asked in the polls? Explain why knowing the exact wording matters.

3. How were the samples defined?

4. Consider the labels.
   a. Were the populations labeled in the same way the samples were labeled? Explain why it matters whether they have the same label.
   b. Did the headline use the same label? Explain why this matters.

5. Were the sample sizes given? If so, do you have any reason to believe the sample sizes were inadequate?

6. What information contained in the article appears to support the article's headline: "State Voters Back Execution 4–1"?
   a. Does this information continue to support the headline, if you take the margin of error into account? Explain.
   b. Is there any study reported in the article that is inconsistent with the headline? Explain.

7. Suppose you were writing an article for Amnesty International's newsletter in which you cited the same polls the *Los Angeles Times* article cites. How would you word the headline for your article?

8. Suppose you are a disinterested party reporting on the *Los Angeles Times* and Amnesty International polls. How would you word the headline of your article?

9. What other points would you like to discuss about this article?

American Self-Advertising

Jin K. Kim

Jin K. Kim was born and raised in South Korea. He has a Ph.D. in communication from Syracuse University and teaches in the Department of Communication, SUNY Plattsburgh.

[In Korea my] high school principal, K. W. Park . . . used to lecture, almost daily at morning assemblies, on the virtue of being modest. . . . His most frequently quoted verse from Lao-tzu's *Tao Te Ching* was:

> True words aren't eloquent;
>   eloquent words aren't true.
> Wise men don't need to prove their point;
>   men who need to prove their point aren't
>   wise.
>
> The Master has no possessions.
> The more he does for others,
>   the happier he is.
> The more he gives to others,
>   the wealthier he is.
>
> The Tao nourishes by not forcing.
> By not dominating, the Master leads.

The Taoist principal, Park, was a fervent advocate of "conspicuous subtlety" in presenting oneself. He was not subtle at all about instilling in our budding minds his "messianic" message that self-advertisement was the worst form to let others know about "my existence." One's existence, we were told, should be noticed by others in the form of our acts and conduct. One is obligated to provide opportunities for others to experience one's existence through what he or she does. Self-initiated effort for public recognition or self-aggrandizement was the most shameful conduct for a person of virtue.

This idea is interesting and noble as a philosophical posture, but when it is practiced in America, it will not get you anywhere in most circumstances. The lack of self-assertion is translated directly into timidity and lack of self-confidence. This is a culture where you must exert your individuality to the extent that it would make our high school principal turn in his grave out of shame and disgust. . . . Self-advertising is encouraged almost to the point of pretentiousness. Years ago in Syracuse, I had an occasion to introduce a visiting Korean monk-scholar to a gathering of people who wanted to hear something about Oriental philosophies. After taking an elegantly practiced bow to the crowd, this humble monk declared, "My name is . . . Please teach me, as I do not know anything." It took quite a bit of probing and questioning for us to extract something to chew on from that monk with the mysterious smile. Contrast this with an American colleague of mine applying for a promotion several years ago, who literally hauled in two cabinets full of documented evidence of his scholarly achievements. . . .

Questions

1. What generalizations does Jin K. Kim make about American culture?
2. Are any of the generalizations Kim makes overly broad? Explain.
3. What support does Kim offer for the generalizations he makes?
4. Is Kim an authority on the topic of American culture? Explain.
5. What decisions are the generalizations Kim makes relevant to?
6. What other questions would you like to discuss about this reading?
7. What other points would you like to make about this reading?

A Study of Prejudice toward University Student-Athletes

Catherine McHugh Engstrom and William E. Sedlacek

Catherine McHugh Engstrom is a former assistant director of Resident Life at the University of Maryland, College Park. William E. Sedlacek is assistant director of testing and research in the Counseling Center and professor of education at the University of Maryland, College Park. *Reading hint: You might get more out of reading this study report if you start at the end—with the appendix of survey questions.*

METHOD

Participants

Participants were a random sample of 293 freshmen entering a large eastern university with an NCAA Division I-A athletic program. A total of 51% were women: 94% were 17 or 18 years old. The racial-ethnic background of the participants was as follows: 76% White, 11% Asian, 8% Black, 3% Hispanic, and 1% other.

Instrument

The Situational Attitude Scale (SAS) has been shown to be a reliable and valid tool for measuring attitudes toward racial-ethnic minorities, varying age groups, women, and student-athletes (Carter, White, & Sedlacek, 1987; Engstrom & Sedlacek, 1989; Hirt, Hoffman, & Sedlacek, 1983; Minatoya & Sedlacek, 1983; Peabody & Sedlacek, 1982). . . .

The SAS has been designed to elicit both overt and less conscious feelings and to control for socially desirable responses. . . . (T)wo . . . forms have been developed that include the same situations, but in one form the group under investigation (e.g., Blacks, Arabs) is inserted into each situation. Participants are not aware that other forms exist or that comparisons are being made. . . .

Procedures

The data were collected during a summer freshman orientation program attended by approximately 95% of all entering freshmen.

Trained graduate and undergraduate students collected data.

The students were randomly assigned to either the neutral form (Form 1) or the student-athlete form (Form 2). . . . Participation was voluntary; none of the students refused to participate although five cases were rejected from the analysis because of incomplete data.

RESULTS

For the remainder of the article, the term *students* refers to those in the general student body.

Form Differences

. . . In Situations 4, 6, and 8, students had significantly more negative attitudes toward student-athletes than toward "students." They felt more suspicious, worried, and displeased when a student-athlete rather than a "student" received an A in class. They expressed significantly stronger feelings of disappointment, concern, worry, and annoyance when a student-athlete was assigned to be their lab partner than when a "student" was assigned to be their lab partner. The participants indicated they were less pleased and accepting and more indignant and disturbed when tutorial and advising services were expanded for student-athletes. In Situation 10, students seemed to be less concerned, embarrassed, disapproving, and sad when student-athletes left school than when "students" left school.

DISCUSSION

The results of this study indicate that students do possess some negative attitudes toward student-athletes, particularly in areas related to academic performance. The finding that students seem to be more suspicious and less trusting of student-athletes obtaining an A in class suggests that students simply do not believe student-athletes have the academic capabilities to obtain an A. This notion is reinforced by the data indicating that students are less disturbed or concerned when student-athletes leave school. In addition, the participants are worried and disturbed about having a student-athlete assigned to them as a lab partner. Their negative reaction to the situation involving the expansion of tutorial and advising services suggests students' lack of tolerance to different privileges and services being offered by the institution to athletes. It also may indicate that the participants' lack of awareness and appreciation that student-athletes' needs may differ from the general student body. Or perhaps they are aware of these different needs but resent the institution responding to them. . . .

A commitment to address institutional racism must include addressing adverse prejudice toward the many cultures found within the institution. This study confirms that the student-athlete group is a culture prone to prejudice in the campus community and confirms the types of situations eliciting negative feelings. . . .

Implications for Practitioners

Negative attitudes toward student-athletes can be expected from freshman students who think in dualistic [black and white] ways (Perry, 1970). Stereotypical thinking would be quite common with this population. The challenge for counselors and advisers, however, is to confront these attitudes and encourage students to think in more open-minded, nonjudgmental ways. In addition, research sug-

gests that stereotypes can create self-fulfilling prophecy effects with members of this stereotyped group (Hamilton & Trolier, 1986; Word, Zanna, & Cooper, 1974). Student-athletes, particularly freshman athletes who would be prone to dualistic thinking, would easily believe that they lack the academic skills and abilities to succeed and sense a feeling of alienation and lack of belonging in the classroom. . . .

Leppo and Lustgraaf (1987–1988) noted that the more information we have about a particular group, the more comfortable and safe we are talking about the group and its differences from the majority culture and associating with others who exhibit these differences. Our negative attitudes, unless confronted, will result in self-perpetuating patterns of misinformation, stereotypes, fear, and conscious and unconscious prejudicial attitudes and behaviors.

Student-athletes themselves should be educated to the "isms" they may be facing in the classroom and be supported to confront the dumb jock stereotype. In addition, the strong negative attitudes of the freshman sample indicate the need to initiate "ism" reduction and sensitivity training toward student-athletes and other nontraditional groups at the onset of students' entrance to college. . . .

APPENDIX 1: INSTRUCTIONS AND SITUATIONS FROM THE SITUATIONAL ATTITUDE SCALE

Instructions

This questionnaire measures how people think and feel about a number of social and personal incidents and situations. It is not a test, so there are no right or wrong answers. The questionnaire is anonymous so please *do not sign your name.*

Each item or situation is followed by 10 descriptive word scales. Your task is to select, for each descriptive scale, the rating that best describes *your* feelings toward the item.

Sample item: Starting school this spring

Happy   A B C D E   Sad

You would indicate the direction and extent of your feelings (e.g., you might select "B" by indicating "B" on your response sheet by blackening in the appropriate space for the word scale). *Do not mark on the booklet. Please respond to all word scales.*

Sometimes you may feel as if you had the same item before on the questionnaire. This will not be the case, so *do not look back and forth* through the items.

Do not try to remember how you checked similar items earlier in the questionnaire. *Make each item a separate and independent judgment.* Respond as honestly as possible without puzzling over individual items. Respond with your first impressions wherever possible.

Situations

1. A group of students gets in a fight at a local bar.
   A group of student-athletes gets in a fight at a local bar.
2. You meet your new roommate.
   You meet your new roommate who is a student-athlete.
3. A good friend of yours has a blind date with a student.
   A good friend of yours has a blind date with a student-athlete.
4. A student gets an A in a college class.
   A student-athlete gets an A in a college class.
5. A student has an expensive sports car.
   A student-athlete has an expensive sports car.
6. You are assigned a lab partner in a class.
   A student-athlete is assigned to be your lab partner in a class.
7. A student misses class.
   A student-athlete misses classes.
8. The university announced the creation of an expanded advising and tutoring program for students.
   The university announces the creation of an expanded advising and tutoring program for student-athletes.
9. A student cuts in front of you in line.
   A student-athlete cuts in front of you in line.
10. A student in your class leaves school.
    A student-athlete in your class leaves school.

Questions

1. What is the population that Engstrom and Sedlacek seek information about?
2. How did they select their sample?
3. Are any of the generalizations Engstrom and Sedlacek make overly broad? Explain.
4. What support do Engstrom and Sedlacek offer for the generalizations they make?
5. Are Engstrom and Sedlacek authorities on student attitudes? Explain.
6. What decisions are the generalizations Engstrom and Sedlacek make relevant to?
7. What other points or questions would you like to discuss about this reading?

WRITING IDEAS

1. Write a "letter to the editor" critiquing a news article reporting a poll or survey. You may use one of the articles under "Readings for Analysis."
2. Write a letter to a friend in which you critique a cultural stereotype.

3. Write an evaluation of a paper you have written in which you reasoned from or to generalizations.

4. Write two lists of survey questions on a topic of your choice. In one list, write questions that will most likely elicit full and candid responses about the subject's beliefs and attitudes. In the other list, write questions that will most likely elicit partial and uncandid responses.

5. Write about whether this chapter and your class discussions complemented, conflicted with, supported, or left out any of your previous ideas about generalizations.

Notes

1. Virginia Slims poll reported in Gary Langer, "Women's View: Men Are Mean, Lazy, Oversexed," *Press Democrat*, Santa Rosa, CA, 26 April 1990.
2. Quoted in Darrell Huff, *How to Lie with Statistics* (New York: Norton, 1952).
3. Carol Tavris, *The Mismeasure of Woman* (New York: Simon & Schuster, 1992) 42.
4. David S. Moore, *Statistics: Concepts and Controversies* 2nd ed. (New York: Freeman, 1985) 26.
5. Richard Nisbett and Lee Ross, *Human Inference: Strategies and Shortcomings of Social Judgment* (Englewood Cliffs, NJ: Prentice Hall, 1980) 290.
6. Nisbett and Ross 252.
7. Nisbett and Ross 291.
8. Ralph Johnson, "Poll-lution: Coping with Surveys and Polls," *Selected Issues in Logic and Communication,* ed. Trudy Govier (Belmont, CA: Wadsworth, 1988) 167.
9. Johnson 167.
10. Nisbett and Ross 293.
11. Clarence Page, "Those Rotten Wisians" *Press Democrat*, Santa Rosa, CA, 20 Jan. 1992: B4.
12. Johnson 171.
13. Bruce Berg, *Qualitative Research Methods for the Social Sciences* (Boston: Allyn and Bacon, 1989) 25.
14. Huff 24.
15. "Gingrich to New York: I'm Sorry," Times Wire Services, *Los Angeles Times* 20 Sept. 1995.
16. Nisbett and Ross 260.
17. Ideas for examples are from information in Nisbett and Ross 252.
18. This 1989 Gallup poll report was published in Neil Howe and Bill Strauss, *13th Gen: Abort, Retry, Ignore, Fail?* (New York: Random House, 1993) 188.
19. This 1989 Gallup poll report was published in Howe and Strauss 43.
20. "Has the American National Character Changed in the Last 20 Years?" *Newsweek* 10 July 1995: 21.
21. "100 Years from Today, Will the United States Still Exist as One Nation?" *Newsweek* 10 July 1995: 26.

10

Causal Reasoning

CHAPTER GOALS

- To expand your knowledge of one type of reasoning introduced in Chapter 7—causal reasoning

- To understand causality as a web rather than a chain of events; that is, to understand that causes have multiple effects and that effects can have multiple causes.

- To distinguish among different types of causes and to learn the basic steps of a causal study.

- To recognize two common fallacies in causal reasoning, the post hoc fallacy and the correlation fallacy.

- To use your knowledge to evaluate the causal reasoning of others and to improve your own causal reasoning.

What kinds of things do you do when you try to figure out the cause of something? Jot down your ideas; then read this essay and answer the questions that follow.

Medical Experts and the Ghost of Galileo

Peter Huber

TRAUMATIC CANCER

Anita Menarde's misfortune apparently began on the morning of May 16, 1949, when she was injured slightly while alighting from a Philadelphia streetcar. She sued. . . . For breast cancer.

The facts did seem powerfully suggestive. Immediately after her fall, Menarde was treated at a local hospital for scrapes and bruises to her left ankle, right knee, and both hands. Dr. Koebert, her family doctor, saw her in the early evening. Upon disrobing later on that day she noticed a discoloration on her right side and breast. She called Dr. Koebert again the next day about the bruised breast; he examined it, found no lumps, and prescribed hot compresses. He examined her periodically for the next two months; the breast seemed perfectly normal. At the end of July, however, Anita detected a lump in her breast "at the exact spot" of the earlier bruise. Dr. Beck, a cancer specialist, diagnosed cancer; the breast was removed.

In the trial against the streetcar company, Dr. Koebert provided key support:

Q. Could there possibly have been something else which contributed to this cancer?

A. I do not think we are able to say.

Q. Can we say that this particular bruising or injury, to the exclusion of everything else, caused this cancer?

A. I believe other conditions which had happened, and according to the highlights of the case as I examined her originally, and in that it arose in that immediate area, I believe that this cancer was caused directly by the injury.

Q. Is it not possible that something else contributed to it?

A. Within the knowledge of man, I think not. . . .

Q. Would you say that it is impossible that there was any other thing that could have caused this cancer other than the blow?

A. In this case I would say not. . . .

Q. Doctor, is there even the slightest idea of speculation in your mind as to the judgment you have come to in concluding that this accident caused this cancer in this girl's body?

A. I believe that this accident was the direct cause of this woman's cancer.

Q. And is that judgment based on any speculation whatsoever in this case?

A. Not in this case, no.

Dr. Beck acknowledged differences of opinion "among outstanding authorities" as to whether simple trauma could cause cancer. But in the end, he too agreed that in Menarde's case, at least, there was a connection. The jury awarded $50,000, a considerable sum at the time, which the trial judge cut to $25,000. A unanimous Pennsylvania Supreme Court affirmed.

Questions

1. In the above story, Anita Menarde's attorney convinced a jury that the bruise she received when "alighting" from a streetcar caused her breast cancer. Identify any support offered for the claim that Menarde's bruise caused her breast cancer.

2. Would you consider Dr. Koebert and Dr. Beck reliable authorities on the causes of breast cancer? Explain.

3. If you had been on the jury, would you have agreed with the jury's award? Explain why or why not.

Causal reasoning plays a role in many decisions. Juries decide whether to find a defendant guilty of murder based in part on their determination that the defendant caused the death of the victim. In our daily lives, we make decisions about whether to stop smoking based on whether we believe that our smoking will cause us to develop cancer or other illnesses. We decide whether to get a new car—or a fill-up—based on our determination of why our car won't start.

In making the above decisions, we use causal generalizations about human motivations, health, and auto mechanics. Many causal generalizations are now a part of common knowledge. We all know that cars won't run without gas, for example. But other causal generalizations are not universally accepted. Some people, for instance, think humans commit crimes because they are "bad" persons. Others attribute criminal activity to social conditions, such as poverty and racism. These different explanations have different implications for our social policies. If people commit crimes because they are "bad," all we have to do is get them off the streets. If they commit crimes because of poverty and racism, we need to address poverty and racism to respond to the problem of crime.

Because causal generalizations play such a central role in our decisions about how to act, we need to understand how to support them. As we found in Chapter 9, supporting generalizations is frequently a complicated business and best left to researchers who have the time and money for experiments and data gathering and who have training in research methodology. However, once again there are some basic things we can learn about research methodology that will help us when questioning the experts and when engaging in causal reasoning in our everyday lives.

REASONING FROM KNOWN CAUSES

The word **cause** means to produce or bring about. Striking a match causes the match to flame; the striking produces, or brings about, the flame. We also talk of causing things to not happen. Pouring water on a match causes it to not flame. In other words, pouring water on a match prevents it from flaming.

Because causes bring about and prevent things from happening, we can use our causal knowledge to figure out what's happened in the past, what's happening in the present, or what will happen in the future. And we can use our causal knowledge to prevent things from happening or to bring about things happening that we want to happen. But not all types of causes are equally useful for making secure predictions, so it's useful to have an understanding of types of causes and effects and then look at how we can use them to make predictions.

The Causal Web

We frequently talk as though an event such as a match flaming is caused by one other event, the striking of the match. This way of talking implies that causal relations form a **causal chain** of single events linked one to another, each one of which is sufficient to bring about the next. However, one event never produces or brings about another event entirely on its own. Had the match end not been dry or not had the correct combination of flammable material on it, it would not have burst into flame when struck. Also you have to strike the match against something appropriately abrasive for the match to flame.

Just as effects (the flame) result from a combination of causes, so too do causes have more than one effect. The striking of the match produces sound and smoke as well as flame and heat. Moreover, the effects of striking the match proceed far and wide into the future. Starting a fire in the fireplace contributes to the romantic mood that leads a young couple to decide to get married and have children, one of whose great-great-grandchildren becomes a scientist who discovers the way to travel to the edge of our galaxy. All resulting in part from the striking of the match.

The chain metaphor for causation fails to capture the full complexity of causal relations. Thinking of causality as a web is a closer analogy. Like causal events, any one spot in a web is linked to many other spots.[1]

Usually, in everyday life, we simply talk about "the cause" of an event, instead of talking of the full set of causes for any one effect. What we focus on as "the cause" varies from context to context. The district attorney in a murder trial focuses on a cause that's closest to the effect and identifies a person pulling the trigger of a gun as "the cause" of the death of the victim. A psychiatrist looks at the defendant's childhood to seek earlier causes of the killing. A sociologist studying the causes of crime in a society takes a wider view of the **causal web** and offers ongoing conditions such as poverty and hopelessness as the causes of violence.

What we call "the effect" also varies from context to context. When drug manufacturers speak of the "effect" of a particular drug, they mean the desired effect of the drug. But all drugs have more than one effect, some of which are unwanted. Drug manufacturers downplay the unwanted effects of a drug by calling them **side effects**. Drowsiness may be a side effect of an antihistamine you take for a dripping nose. The antihistamine stops the drip and also may make you drowsy. The phrase "side effect" is misleading. It implies that drowsiness is not as "real" or central as the dryness. The only difference between the effects is that one is a central selling feature of the drug and the other is not. In fact, if antihistamines were sold to help put people to sleep, the drying effect of the drug would be listed as a "side effect."

The Certainty of Predictions

Not all types of causes play the same role in the causal web. When you make predictions, it's particularly important to consider whether you are predicting from a necessary condition, a sufficient condition, or a contributing factor and to keep in mind that causes have more than one effect. Here's why.

From Necessary Conditions   A **necessary condition** is an event that must take place in order for another event to take place. Oxygen being present in a room is necessary in order for flame to appear. No matter how abrasive the surface I strike the match against, or how carefully I strike it, no flame will appear without oxygen. (And neither will I, because oxygen is also a necessary condition of human life.)

Knowledge of necessary conditions is very useful for making predictions, because if we know that the necessary condition does not obtain, we can predict that the effect definitely will not happen. I know, for example, that my match simply won't flame if there is no oxygen. This allows me to predict that if I remove oxygen, say by holding a glass over the flame, the flame will definitely go out (once it uses the oxygen remaining in the glass). Nevertheless, even if the necessary condition happens, we cannot conclude that the effect will happen. For example, there's plenty of oxygen in my study right now, but no fire; other contributing factors are needed to produce fire.

From Sufficient Conditions   A **sufficient condition** is the combination of events that together bring about the effect. You must have oxygen in the room, a dry match with combustible material on it, and an abrasive surface to strike against. Then you can strike the match to produce the flame.

I would also be able to make a secure prediction that something would happen, if I knew that the full set of conditions sufficient for that event were present. Although frequently we do not know whether we have a full set of causal conditions that are sufficient to bring about a particular effect, sometimes we do know we have sufficient conditions—at least with a high degree of probability. If I got my matches from a reputable match company, if the match I'm holding is not wet, if I have something appropriate to strike it against, and if there's plenty of oxygen, I can predict that the match will very likely light when I strike it.

From Contributing Factors   Most causal claims do not describe necessary or sufficient conditions. They describe contributing factors. A **contributing factor** is something that partially causes an event but is neither necessary nor sufficient by itself for the event to take place. Striking the match was a contributing cause of the flame: Together with a number of other factors, it brought about the flame. Striking the match was not sufficient for producing flame: The match had to be dry, among other things, before striking would produce the flame. Striking the match was also not necessary to produce a

This boy commits the slippery slope fallacy. Starting a fire in the fireplace doesn't inevitably lead to burning the neighborhood.

"Let's not have a fire in the fireplace tonight, Dad.
It'll get too hot and catch the chimney on fire, then spread
to the roof, catch the trees on fire, and burn
down the whole neighborhood."

flaming match: Had the match gotten hot enough, it would have burst into flame without being struck.

Claims about contributing factors yield less certain predictions. From the claim "smoking contributes to developing lung cancer," you cannot conclude that you definitely will get lung cancer if you smoke; you can conclude only that you are more likely to get lung cancer if you smoke than if you don't smoke.

Recognizing that most individual causes are contributing factors helps us avoid a basic mistake in causal reasoning: the **slippery slope fallacy.** Once we realize that most causes are partial causes that depend on many other factors to produce an event, we are less likely to assume that from any one contributing cause a specific remote effect will definitely follow. In other words, taking a step onto a slippery slope does not necessarily result in sliding all the way down the mountain. There may be a tree or a rock that stops you on the way. The young couple sitting by the fire will not inevitably get married and have children—no matter how romantic the fire. They may see each other differently in the clear light of the next day.

When There Are Multiple Effects   To complicate matters further, we need to think about the multiple effects of causes when we make predictions. Consider the blanket causal generalization:

> Penicillin makes people feel better when they have bacterial infections.

This blanket generalization obscures the fact that penicillin has more than one effect. It kills bacteria, and in some people it also contributes to allergic reactions. Because of these allergic reactions, some people feel worse after taking penicillin. You can't predict with certainty, then, that if you take penicillin you will feel better—unless you have learned that you are not allergic to penicillin. (Furthermore, penicillin and other antibiotics also kill "good" bacteria that aid in the digestion of food as well as the "bad" bacteria that are making you sick. As a result, even people who are not allergic to penicillin sometimes experience negative gastrointestinal effects of taking antibiotics.)

In sum, when you use causal generalizations to make predictions, state the causal claim as precisely as you can, indicating whether the cause is a necessary condition, a sufficient condition, or a contributing factor and whether the cause has multiple effects, some of which are unwanted.

YOUR TURN A

◆ 1. For each of the following causal statements, indicate whether you think the statement is trying to describe a necessary condition, a sufficient condition, or a contributing factor.

  a. Plants can't live without water.

  b. Feeding plants produces more blooms.

  c. The blender being plugged in, the electricity functioning, the blender motor and blender parts functioning correctly, and flipping the blender switch together cause the blender to go on.

  d. Hummingbirds fly to red flowers because they are looking for something to eat.

◆ 2. Do either of the following conclusions below follow with certainty? Explain why or why not.

  a. John just filled up his tank with gas. His car will start when he turns on the key.

  b. John's gas tank is empty. His car won't start when he turns on the key.

◆ 3. Do you think David commits the slippery slope fallacy in the following dialogue? Explain.

  Sue: David, would you like a beer?
  David: No thank you. I'm an alcoholic, and if I drink a beer, the next thing I know I'll be passed out on the sofa.

  4. Review a paper you've written for this class. Do you find any causal claims?

  a. Are they describing necessary conditions, sufficient conditions, or contributing factors?

  b. Did you make any predictions from them? What were they?

BEGINNING A CAUSAL STUDY

Causal claims are tricky to support. We can, of course, rely on common knowledge and reliable authority, but we will frequently find ourselves wanting to know something that is not yet part of common knowledge or that we have no expert opinion on. In such cases we need to know how to conduct causal studies.

We normally associate "causal studies" with the work of scientists in their laboratories, pouring one vial of liquid into another to see what will happen. But in everyday life we also engage in causal problem solving. Though there is no one process that scientists use when investigating causes, nor one process that we use in our daily lives, there are some basic steps that are useful for all of us to take when searching for causes: clarify the goal of the study; develop a list of possible, testable causes (hypotheses); and test the hypotheses.

Although all scientists use these steps in causal problem solving, they do not always take them in the order I have described them. The particular problem and the scientist's interpretation of the problem creates the order, much as the music and the dancer's interpretation of it creates the order of steps in improvisational dancing. Let's look at a simple example.

At a recent retirement celebration for a colleague, I wanted to make an announcement. I went to the podium, flicked on the switch, and tapped the microphone. Nothing happened. I waved to the academic vice president for assistance. He speaks at podiums all the time, and I thought he could show me how to turn the microphone on. No luck. He hadn't used that particular podium before. But, being a scientist by training and having an interest in causal problem solving, he stayed around to help me find a way to turn on the mike.

We put our heads together and came up with a number of hypotheses: the microphone cord was not plugged into the extension cord; the extension cord was not plugged into the wall socket; the microphone's on/off switch was broken. A colleague who teaches children's literature walked by and suggested, "Maybe a genie has cast a spell on the microphone."

We began testing our hypotheses. We looked and saw that the microphone cord was plugged into an extension cord. We also saw the extension cord plugged into a socket. We began to think that perhaps the on/off switch was broken, but we realized there were some other possibilities we had not yet considered. We needed to eliminate them before we could conclude that the switch was broken.

To see whether the socket into which the extension cord was plugged was working, we plugged in a light. It went on. Just as we were getting ready to give up on the microphone, the school photographer stumbled over the connection between the microphone cord and the extension cord. When her foot hit the connection, we heard the familiar crackle of a loudspeaker for a second. "The connection must not be tight enough," she said. She reached down and tightened the connection. We heard the crackle again. The microphone was on.

Clarifying the Goal

The success of an inquiry is measured by whether it meets its goal. In the microphone mystery, my goal was to figure out what prevented the microphone from going on. I wanted to be able to speak to the audience before me. Goals are not always so practical. Sometimes the goal of a study is to increase the amount of knowledge, regardless of whether that knowledge has any immediate practical application.

Sometimes goals change during the study. In the above example I wanted to get the microphone on to make my announcement before dinner. Before we figured out how to turn the mike on, dinner had begun. My goal changed. I wanted the mike on so the after-dinner speakers would be heard. And figuring out why that particular microphone wasn't working was secondary to providing some form of amplification for the after-dinner speeches. If we had not been able to figure out how to get the mike on before the after-dinner speeches, I would have given up searching for an answer to that problem and looked for another microphone.

Generating Hypotheses

In a causal study it's important to generate multiple, testable **hypotheses**.

Multiple Hypotheses   When it comes to generating hypotheses, there is only one strict rule: Don't stop with only one hypothesis. As we saw in Chapter 1, people frequently jump to conclusions about causation and misread others or find fault with themselves without sufficient reason.

People make these mistakes because they come up with one possible explanation and leave it at that. A student sees a teacher frowning when she

Why is this man's hat in the air?

raises her hand and decides the teacher frowns because he doesn't want the student to ask a question. Had the student considered even one other hypothesis—say, that the teacher had a headache—she would have been more likely to realize she didn't yet have adequate evidence for her first hypothesis.

Sometimes there is only one really likely hypothesis, and there's no reason to come up with a bunch of unlikely ones just because some book tells you not to stop with one. Frequently, we check the most likely hypothesis first—such as whether the microphone is plugged in—and start coming up with the less obvious ones only later in the inquiry. In fact, getting involved in testing can help us generate more ideas.

SOURCES OF HYPOTHESES   Here are some things to keep in mind to help you generate causal hypotheses.

Play is essential for creativity. Sometimes an idea as silly as the genie hypothesis triggers a more realistic idea. And even if no solution flows immediately from a playful idea, the mood created by play frees the mind to discover other hypotheses. In *Conceptual Blockbusting: A Guide to Better Ideas*, James L. Adams tells us that the attitude that "playfulness is for children only" is a block to creativity. He also lists other attitudes that block creativity:

Fantasy and reflection are a waste of time, lazy, or even crazy.

Problem-solving is a serious business and humor is out of place.

How to block creativity.

The Bored Room
*Please check your sense
of humor, playfulness,
individuality,
fantasy, intuitions,
and innovative ideas
at the door*

Reason, logic, numbers, utility, practicality are *good*; feeling, intuition, qualitative judgments, pleasure are *bad*.

Tradition is preferable to change.[2]

If you have trouble coming up with a number of ideas, you can always ask for help. When it comes to generating hypotheses, two heads are better than one. The more people you involve, the more likely you are to come up with a wide range of possible solutions.

How you work with those other people affects your chances of success in generating hypotheses. You need to work in a supportive context to come up with ideas. Adams lists a number of contextual factors that block creativity:

Lack of cooperation and trust among colleagues

Autocratic boss who values only his [or her] own ideas; does not reward others

Distractions—phone, easy intrusions

Lack of support to bring ideas into action[3]

Sometimes you don't need to come up with novel ideas. You can call up your background knowledge to solve the problem. In the microphone example, most of the ideas that the vice president and I had came from our past knowledge of how electricity works. We already knew many causal conditions of working electrical mechanisms: they have to be plugged in and switched on, and electricity must flow to the socket.

Analogies are useful for creating hypotheses. Newton generated a new idea about the causal effects of gravity on the moon by comparing the relation between the earth and the moon to the relation between the earth and a falling apple. American business people are generating ideas about how to make companies more productive by studying Japanese companies.

Sometimes you'll get some help generating an idea by chance. Even given our common knowledge about electricity, we didn't question the connection between the microphone cord and the extension cord until the photographer by chance stumbled over the extension cord connection. But even here, our prior knowledge about electricity helped us. We knew from previous experience that connections that look tight are sometimes not fully in place. This knowledge enabled us to understand the significance of the speaker static when the photographer stumbled over the connection. As Pasteur wrote, "Chance favors the prepared mind."[4]

When generating hypotheses, remember the causal web. The cause you are looking for may be a combination of factors. When you record on a tape recorder, for example, you typically have to press two buttons to make the machine record. Someone who tried to discover how to make the machine record by testing only one button at a time would never solve the problem.

These are some of the common ways we generate hypotheses, but you will no doubt discover others. That's fine, for with discovery anything goes.

SOME INDICATIONS OF POSSIBLE CAUSES Whether using your imagination, reviewing your background knowledge, or using some other way of arriving at causal hypotheses, here are some things to look for to help you identify possible causes.

Consider as a possible cause an unusual event that preceded the effect. When a friend got an upset stomach after drinking a coffee substitute she'd never had before, she considered the hypothesis that the coffee substitute caused her upset stomach.

Also consider as a possible cause a common event among different preceding activities. If a whole family gets sick after eating at a restaurant and the only thing they all ate in common was the chicken soup, they could consider the hypothesis that the soup made them sick.

When two things change together (correlate), consider the possibility that one of them causes the other. When a doctor in the late eighteenth century noticed that dairy maids who contracted cow pox were less likely than other people to contract smallpox, he developed the causal hypothesis that having cow pox contributed to preventing smallpox.[5]

YOUR TURN B

◆ 1. Suppose you have a co-worker whom you see only at work. She's been acting grumpy for the six months that you've known her. What possible explanations can you think of for her grumpiness?

◆ 2. Assume that a steel pipe is embedded in the concrete floor of a bare room. The inside diameter is 0.06 inch larger than the diameter of a ping-pong ball (1.5 inches) that is resting gently at the bottom of the pipe. You are one of a group of six people in the room, along with the following objects: 100 feet of clothesline, a carpenter's hammer, a chisel, a box of Wheaties, a file, a wire coat hanger, a monkey wrench, a light bulb. List as many ways as you can think of (in five minutes) to get the ball out of the pipe without damaging the ball, tube, or floor.[6]

3. Review a causal claim you have made in a paper you've written for this class. Generate a list of alternative hypotheses for the effect you describe. Remember to play.

Testable Hypotheses A hypothesis is **testable** when someone could in principle show the hypothesis to be true or false. The hypothesis that the cord was not plugged into the wall socket was clearly testable. We could confirm the hypothesis by checking to see if the speaker went on when the cord was plugged in. We could disconfirm the hypothesis by finding that the speaker went on in spite of the fact that the cord was unplugged.

The hypothesis that a fickle genie in the cord prevents the speaker from going on is untestable. The genie could change its mind at any moment, thus preventing any "test" from showing anything.

Causal hypotheses also need to be written in language that is precise enough for us to determine what we are looking for. When studying the causes of violence in the home, for example, a scientist will carefully define "violence," for it has a wide range of meanings, from emotional suffering to physical death. Advertisers sometimes intentionally write causal claims in very vague language so that we can't show them to be false.

YOUR TURN C

◆ 1. Are any of the following causal hypotheses untestable or questionably testable? Explain.

    a. "Plastic makes it possible." (Slogan on an ad sponsored by the American Plastics Council)[7]

    b. "You *can* do it. Whatever your goals in life, a healthy dose of inspiration works wonders. Our Success Stories—from women who have been there—reveal the secrets of a healthy lifestyle to help you take action and reap the rewards." (From an ad for *Shape* magazine)[8]

2. Review causal claims you have made in your writing this semester. Are any of them too vague to test? Can you rewrite them to make them more precise?

DEVELOPING SUFFICIENT EVIDENCE FOR CAUSAL CLAIMS

Now that you've been introduced to the preliminaries of a scientific study, it's time to think about how to provide sufficient evidence to establish that a possible cause is an actual cause. To help us learn how to develop sufficient evidence for causation, we'll look at some methods scientists use to test causal hypotheses. Studying scientific methods will help you avoid two common mistakes in causal reasoning: the post hoc and correlation fallacies. Let's start with these inadequate ways of establishing causation, then look at the more telling scientific methods.

Insufficient Evidence

When a cause produces an effect, the cause precedes the effect. In the microphone example, jiggling the plug into a tighter connection preceded the speaker static. Also, causes and their effects are correlated: The effect occurs or changes when the cause occurs or changes; likewise, when the cause does not occur or change, the effect does not occur or change. Whenever we jiggled the plug, we heard the speaker static; whenever we loosened the plug, we no longer heard the speaker sound.

We used these two clues for causality to help us solve the microphone mystery. We inferred that a loose connection prevented the microphone

Do you find sufficient evidence for causation here?

THE FAR SIDE By GARY LARSON

"Coincidence, ladies and gentlemen? Coincidence that my client just *happened* to live across from the A-1 Mask Co., just *happened* to walk by their office windows each day, and they, in turn, just *happened* to stumble across this new design?"

from going on because jiggling the connection into place preceded the speaker's going on and because tightening and loosening the connection correlated with the speaker's going on and off. However, although priority in time and correlation are clues for causation, they do not individually or together provide sufficient evidence to establish causation.

The Post Hoc Fallacy People who jump from priority in time to causation commit the **post hoc fallacy**. *Post hoc* is short for *post hoc ergo proter hoc*, which is a Latin expression meaning "after the fact, therefore because of it." In other words, just because you got sick to your stomach after eating shrimp for lunch, it does not follow that eating the shrimp caused your sick stomach. Maybe the salad tomatoes were moldy, or you got the 24-hour flu.

To avoid the post hoc fallacy, ask the following questions when you notice that one event (for example, you got sick) follows another event (you ate shrimp):

Did the same presumed cause ever happen without the effect? (Did anyone else eat the shrimp and not get sick?)

Did the same effect happen without the presumed cause? (Did anyone else get sick without eating the shrimp?)

Is there another possible explanation of the effect?

The Correlation Fallacy   It may be obvious to you that priority in time isn't sufficient to establish causation, but less obvious to you that correlation doesn't establish causation. To get a handle on this idea, let's look at an example of **correlated events** described by the scientist Stephen Jay Gould.

> Do Baptist preachers cause public drunkenness? I raise this unlikely inquiry because an old and famous tabulation clearly shows a strong positive correlation between the number of preachers and the frequency of arrests for inebriation during the second half of the nineteenth century in America.
>
> You don't need a Ph.D. in logic to spot the fallacy. . . . Correlation is not causality. The undeniable association of preachers and drunks might mean that hellfire inspires imbibing, but it could also, and more reasonably, suggest that a rise in public drinking promotes the hiring of more preachers. As another possibility—almost surely correct in this particular case—preaching and drinking may have no causal relationship, and their simultaneous increase may only reflect a common link to a third, truly determining factor. The steady rise of the American population during the late nineteenth century promoted an increase in thousands of phenomena linked to total numbers but otherwise unrelated—arrests for drinking and hiring of clergy, for example.[9]

In the above example, why couldn't we conclude causation from correlation? First, we did not know which came first. As a result, we could not tell whether the preaching caused the drunkenness or the drunkenness caused the preaching. Second, we could pretty much predict that not all of the other potential causes stayed exactly the same. And, as Gould points out, further research showed that one possible cause—the increase in the population as a whole—did not stay the same; the population increased, along with the number of preachers and the incidence of public drunkenness. Maybe other things were increasing also, such as the availability of cheap liquor. And some things could have been decreasing, such as the number of jobs, which may also have contributed to the effect.

Gould's example illustrates that we cannot establish that one thing causes another merely by pointing out that they are correlated. This seems clear enough when we look at the example Gould presents. Yet people jump to causation on the basis of correlation so frequently that this precipitous leap has come to be called the **correlation fallacy**.

To avoid the correlation fallacy, ask yourself the following questions when you notice a correlation between two events:

This boy commits the correlation fallacy. He concludes that shoe size causes math ability because they're correlated.

"Research has shown a strong correlation between
shoe size and math ability!"

Do I have any evidence that one of the events is more likely to cause the other? (Is the evidence that preachers cause drunkenness greater than the evidence that drunkenness causes preaching?)

Do I have any evidence that there is no third event that may cause both of these events? (For example, an increase in the total population, which led to the increases in public drunkenness and preachers.)

Do I have any evidence that there is no causal explanation of the correlation? (For example, an increase in the availability of cheap whiskey led to the increase in public drunkenness. The amount of preachers just happened to go up at the same time.)

If we don't have any evidence beyond correlation, the only way to avoid the correlation fallacy is to withhold drawing a causal conclusion. However, sometimes we do have additional evidence of causation.

To draw a causal conclusion from priority in time or correlation, we have to rule out other possible causes. Scientists use a number of methodologies to rule out other possible causes. The following sections describe three of them: strictly controlled experiments, randomized experiments, and natural experiments.

YOUR TURN D

◆ 1. Does the story at the beginning of the chapter contain a description of a correlation or a temporal ordering between two events?

◆ 2. Read these examples; then, for each example, answer the questions that follow.

Example A

For 20 years now, doctors have been debating whether ear creases—lines in the earlobe that tend to appear in middle age or later—are somehow linked to heart disease. William Elliott, a cardiologist at Rush Medical College in Chicago, originally thought the connection was "a big bunch of malarkey." But last year, he announced that in his eight-year study of 108 men—half with ear creases—those with lined lobes were eight times more likely to develop heart disease than crease-free men.[10]

Example B

A few winters ago a dozen investigators independently reported figures on antihistamine pills. Each showed that a considerable percentage of colds cleared up after treatment.[11]

a. Are any correlations described in either of the examples?

b. Are any temporal orderings described in either of the examples?

c. Does the information in example A establish that ear creases cause heart attacks? Explain why or why not.

d. Does the information in example B establish that taking the antihistamine pills made the colds go away? Explain why or why not.

e. Do you have any other points to make or questions to raise about either example?

3. Review a causal claim you made in a paper you've written. Did you (or an expert) discover a correlation or temporal order between the two events in your claim? Explain.

Strictly Controlled Experiments

Because there typically is a wide range of possible causes (**variables**) that could cause any one effect, the most accurate method to determine whether a possible cause is an actual cause is to control all of the other variables. An experiment that controls all of the possible causes is called a **strictly controlled experiment**. In solving the microphone mystery we did a strictly controlled experiment to test whether a poor connection between the microphone cord and the extension cord was our problem. We kept everything else the same: the switch on, the extension cord plugged in, and the electricity to the wall socket on. The only variable that changed was the jiggling of the microphone plug. Because the microphone went on when it was jiggled into place and went off again when the plug was jiggled slightly out again, we knew we had found the solution to our problem.

In other words, priority in time and correlation in the context of a controlled experiment provide sufficient evidence of causation. The controlled experiment rules out the other possible causes.

Strictly controlled experiments are possible only when we can control all of the variables. Sometimes it's simply not possible to keep all of the variables constant. Although a person lounging on a Sunday afternoon may look roughly the same for as long as an hour at a time to the casual observer, on the cellular level the human body is changing second by second as a result of complicated biochemical processes, and the mind is in action as well. It is impossible, then, to change only one variable of a living individual, keeping all other variables exactly the same, and then change the variable back again.

For this reason, we have very few opportunities for controlled experiments in life. What can we do when we can't control all of the variables? In many cases, we have to rely on the authority of scientists who have developed research methodologies to address the problem of multiple, changing variables. Let's look at a couple of these methodologies to give us some background for questioning scientific authorities.

Randomized Experiments

When you cannot eliminate variability through a controlled experiment, the next best thing is to take it into account. Researchers take variability into account with **randomized experiments,** in which a researcher compares groups whose members are selected at random. Let's look at an example.

> Professor Hernandez has recently heard that the publishers of the logic textbook she is using are now offering a computer program for homework. Students have to pay extra money to get the program, and Professor Hernandez would have to make sure there was plenty of computer lab time for the students. She would also have to learn how to use the program herself. But Professor Hernandez cares about learning. If students will learn more by using the logic program, Professor Hernandez will make using the program a requirement for her course.

Using a Control Group   How can Professor Hernandez test the hypothesis that students will learn more by using the computer program? She can form two groups of students. One group—the **control group**—uses only the logic textbook. The other group—the **experimental group**—uses the textbook and the computer program.

Professor Hernandez tests the students at the beginning of the semester and at the end of the semester to measure how much they have improved. She averages each group's progress. Suppose she finds a correlation between using the computer program and good logic scores; that is, suppose the group using the computer program had better scores than the group that did not use the computer program? May she conclude that using the computer explained the difference?

If the use of the computer is the only difference between the two groups, Professor Hernandez may conclude that it caused the difference in the amount of logic the students learned. But as we know, no two humans are exactly the same; some students learn more quickly than others. What if a greater percentage of quick learners got into the experimental group than into the control group? If they did, quick learning—not the use of the computer program—would account for the difference in scores.

Selecting Members at Random   This is where the randomized aspect of Professor Hernandez's experiment comes in. Professor Hernandez realizes that no two groups of students are exactly the same, so she randomly assigns volunteers to the two groups she is comparing.

By randomly assigning the students to the groups, Professor Hernandez does not eliminate differences; there will still be some students who learn more quickly than others. Instead, through random assignment Professor Hernandez spreads the differences in learning ability (and any other differences that may exist among the students) evenly between the two groups.

Even with the randomizing process, however, the two groups are probably not exactly alike. (Remember, statistical studies always carry a margin of error.) As a result, Professor Hernandez has to consider the possibility that the difference, if any, she finds between the two groups results from chance rather than from the use of computers. In other, more technical, words, Professor Hernandez must find out whether any difference she finds is statistically significant. She will have to consult a statistician to find out more precisely how big the difference in learning between the two groups has to be in order to be statistically significant.

Watching for Confounding Variables   Professor Hernandez has another problem: She must be on the alert for confounding variables. A **confounding variable** is a possible cause that is inadvertently introduced into the experimental group along with the possible cause that the experimenter intentionally introduces into the experimental group. In experiments with humans, the expectations of the experimenter and subject sometimes serve as confounding variables. If Professor Hernandez expects the students who are using the computer program to do better than the other students, they may do better—not because they are using the computer program, but because they are responding to her high expectations. They may also score better because they expect more of themselves. Consequently, if Professor Hernandez or her students have higher expectations of students using the computers, she cannot conclude that the difference in the scores are due solely to the use of the computer program.

In some studies, researchers can rule out researcher and subject expectations with a **double blind,** keeping the researcher and subjects from knowing which group is the experimental group and which is the control group. In tests of drugs, for example, subjects in the control group are given a **placebo,** which looks to the researcher and subjects just like the medication given to the experimental group but has no causal efficacy.

There are no placebos for computers, but Professor Hernandez could create several different experimental groups, some of whom use the computer program more than others. By comparing differences among those groups, she could determine whether computer program use improved logic skill.

Achieving External Validity Professor Hernandez faces one more problem: If she finds that the experimental group benefits from the use of the computer program, can she generalize from her study to the future? In technical terms, does Professor Hernandez's study have **external validity**? For her study to have external validity, the present setting, students, computer programs, and teachers in her experiment must be like future settings, students, computer programs, and teachers. If the software company, for example, makes significant changes in the computer program for the next year, Professor Hernandez's study will have questionable validity for next year.

YOUR TURN E

◆ 1. Dr. Quong, a clinician and medical researcher, wants to study the potential effects of a new drug on a group of adults with AIDS. Dr. Quong is quite hopeful about this new drug because he noticed a dramatic improvement in one of his patients who received the drug. Dr. Quong selects a group of adults with AIDS at random and from that group selects at random a control and experimental group. Dr. Quong gives the new drug to the experimental group and gives a placebo to the control group. Suppose Dr. Quong finds a statistically significant improvement in the experimental group? May Dr. Quong conclude that the patients in the experimental group improved because of the new drug? If so, what would you suggest that Dr. Quong do to improve his experiment?

◆ 2. Suppose Professor Hernandez's experiment revealed that students on average learned faster when using a computer than when not. Can you conclude that you will definitely learn logic faster if you use a computer? Explain.

3. Are any of the causal claims you have made in your writing this semester supported by randomized experiments?

Natural Experiments

In a **natural experiment,** the researcher studies groups that arise naturally rather than as a result of the researcher's creating them. Studying lung cancer rates among people who already smoke and among those who do not smoke is a natural experiment.

Researchers must be ready to question the correlations they find and provide evidence that helps them select among alternative hypotheses. Let's look at a successful natural experiment conducted 150 years ago.[12]

In the nineteenth century, major cholera epidemics broke out in Europe, the United States, and other areas. The symptoms of cholera include severe diarrhea, vomiting, and muscular cramps. The diarrhea frequently produces extreme dehydration and death within 48 hours.

An English doctor, John Snow, studied cholera and eventually established that cholera was spread through the inadvertent ingestion of infected human wastes—people contracted the disease either through handling such things as soiled bed linen and then failing to wash their hands thoroughly before eating or through drinking river or well water that had been contaminated by infected sewage. Dr. Snow made a number of recommendations to prevent future epidemics, including a clean water policy. That policy was adopted in London, and there were no further cholera epidemics in that city.

Questioning Correlations   When developing his hypothesis that ingesting human waste, especially through contaminated water, causes cholera, Dr. Snow found a correlation between different water sources and the incidence of cholera. He had gathered evidence that communities using some water sources had different cholera rates from those of other communities using other water sources.

However, Dr. Snow didn't draw the conclusion that the water source caused cholera because he noted that there were other differences among the people who did not contract cholera and those who did. The people who did not contract cholera tended to be wealthy. Among the poor, those who did not contract cholera typically had different occupations from those who contracted cholera. Thus the data he had so far gathered about the correlation between water supply and incidence of cholera did not rule out that some factor or factors related to wealth or occupation caused the cholera.

Finding Roughly Similar Groups   Finally, Dr. Snow happened upon the perfect conditions for a successful natural experiment. He found a large area of London where people from different occupations and incomes lived and which was supplied by two different water companies. Lambeth Company drew its water upstream from London sewage. Southwark & Vauxhall Company drew water downstream from the sewage. Neither company served primarily poor or wealthy clients, nor clients from a particular occupation. Dr. Snow wrote:

> Each Company supplies both rich and poor, both large houses and small; *there is no difference either in condition or occupation of the persons receiving the water of the different Companies.* As there is no difference whatever, either in the houses or the people receiving the supply of the two Water Companies, or in any of the physical conditions with which they are surrounded, it is obvious that no experiment could have been devised which would more thoroughly test the effect of water supply on the progress of cholera than this. . . .
>
> The experiment, too, was on the grandest scale. No fewer than 300,000 people of both sexes, of every age and occupation, and of every rank and station, from gentlefolks down to the very poor, were divided into two groups without their choice, and, in most cases, without their knowledge; one group being supplied with water containing the sewage of London, and, amongst it, whatever

might have come from the cholera patients, the other group having water quite free from such impurity.

    To turn this grand experiment to account, all that was required was to learn the supply of water to each individual house where a fatal attack of cholera might occur. . . .[13]

Dr. Snow found that there were between eight and nine times as many deaths in houses served by Southwark & Vauxhall Company as in those served by Lambeth Company. He now had strong evidence that cholera was spread through contaminated water. The differences in wealth and occupation were spread among the control and the experimental groups. Also, subject expectation could play no role, because the people did not know whether their water was contaminated or not.

Ruling Out Rival Hypotheses   When Dr. Snow studied cholera, the germ theory had not yet been discovered. The existing microscopes were not strong enough to detect bacteria, and many people thought contagious diseases were contracted by breathing in "effluvia" given off by diseased persons. To provide further evidence for his theory that contaminated water caused cholera, Dr. Snow ruled out the hypothesis that cholera was contracted through effluvia.

    Dr. Snow argued that the effluvia theory was inadequate to explain the relatively low incidence of cholera among doctors and undertakers, who would surely have contracted cholera if people could do so by breathing in effluvia.

    Dr. Snow also criticized the theory that living in areas above sea level makes one less prone to contracting cholera. He pointed out, on the one hand, that those who lived closer to sea level were more likely to drink contaminated river water than those who lived at higher altitudes, and he noted, on the other hand, that those who lived at low altitudes and drank from deep wells sometimes escaped cholera altogether.

    Natural experiments such as Dr. Snow's provide strong evidence for causality. However, their evidence isn't as strong as the evidence that comes from randomized or strictly controlled experiments. When variables aren't controlled or randomized, it's always possible that some unidentified variable, rather than the possible cause being studied, was the cause of the difference between control and experimental groups.

YOUR TURN F

◆ 1. Describe a natural experiment to test whether sustaining a bruise causes cancer.

◆ 2. Do you see any difficulties with using a natural experiment to obtain the information you seek? Explain.

3. Are any of the causal claims you have made in your writing this semester supported by natural experiments? Explain.

SOCIETAL CONSTRAINTS ON ACHIEVING CERTAINTY

As we have seen, the certainty of the outcome of research depends on the research methodology. Strictly controlled experiments achieve more certainty than randomized experiments. Randomized experiments—especially double-blind experiments—achieve more certainty than natural experiments.

Society imposes a number of constraints on scientific research, however. Some of these are moral; others are political and economic. These constraints affect how research gets done and what is researched. Because of these constraints we will never test many causal hypotheses or use the most telling methodology for those we do test.

Moral Constraints

Ethical considerations affect decisions about how to engage in research. Researchers may not select people at random from the general population and force them to do things they would not choose to do, no matter how much more accurate such a study would be than a natural experiment. Forcing people to become research subjects violates their human rights. To study the effects of smoking, for example, it would be immoral to select people randomly, randomly divide them into two groups, force one group to inhale cigarette smoke, and wait to see what happens.

There are also occasions when using a placebo is wrong, especially when the subjects of the research have no idea that they may be receiving a placebo. For example, to give women placebos instead of birth control pills would subject them to the possibility of unplanned pregnancies; giving people placebos instead of treatment for syphilis would subject them to the ravages of that disease.

Ethical reasons also sometimes prompt scientists to call a halt to causal studies before they gather enough information to establish certainty. Here's one example. Stanford psychologist Philip Zimbardo was conducting an experiment on the effects of roles on human behavior. In the experiment, students assumed the roles of prisoners and guards. When Zimbardo saw how quickly the students developed alienating and destructive behavior, he called a halt to the experiment out of concern for his subjects' welfare.[14]

Although there is much agreement now about the rights of research subjects, researchers have not always treated their subjects with respect and care. In Nazi concentration camps, prisoners were forced to become subjects of excruciating experiments. And in a study in the United States, Mexican-American women were given placebos instead of birth control pills and had unplanned pregnancies as a result.[15] In another study in the United States, researchers withheld treatment for African-American males who had syphilis so that the researchers could observe the disease's effects.[16]

Federal guidelines for research on human subjects have been established, and many professional organizations have established their own research codes of ethics. There are also guidelines for the use of animals in research. However, because many people believe that animals exist for human use, animals are not protected from pain or death—if the study is expected to benefit humans—nor are they given any choice about being studied.

Political and Economic Constraints

Causal studies are frequently very expensive. For this reason, what gets studied is determined in part by those who can afford to fund the studies.

As a rule, people tend to spend money to further their own values and interests. Drug companies pay for research that is likely to bring them profits. Governmental agencies pay for research that is most likely to benefit governmental goals, such as national defense and satisfying the demands of citizens. Private funding bodies, too, use funding to further their own ends.

The following two sections give examples of how the values and interests of those who make funding decisions determine what gets researched.

Effects of Prejudice on Research Decisions In *How We Know*, Goldstein and Goldstein report that research in the treatment of syphilis met with much public resistance because people viewed the disease as a punishment for sexual immorality. Cholera was also believed to be a punishment from the Almighty:

> A governor of New York State once stated during a cholera epidemic, ". . . an infinitely wise and just God has seen fit to employ pestilence as one means of scourging the human race for their sins, and it seems to be an appropriate one for the sins of uncleanliness and intemperance. . . ." A Sunday School newspaper for children explained, "*Drunkards and filthy wicked people of all descriptions* are swept away in *heaps*, as if the Holy God could no longer bear their wickedness, just as we sweep away a mass of filth when it has become so corrupt that we cannot bear it. . . . The Cholera is not caused by intemperance and filth in themselves, but is a *scourge*, a rod in the hand of God." [17]

This otherworldly explanation of cholera sounds strange now that we understand the physical causes of cholera. Yet even in contemporary times, people sometimes view an unexplained deadly disease as retribution from the Almighty—especially when the victims of the disease are already socially stigmatized. In the early stages of the AIDS epidemic in the United States, when a large percentage of those who contracted the disease were homosexual, some people described AIDS as God's punishment for homosexuality. And Senator Jesse Helms rejects funding for AIDS because he believes people could avoid AIDS if they would "just straighten up and fly right." [18]

Effects of Economics on Research Decisions The financial interests of the funders also play a role in what gets studied. For example, it's hard to find funding to study herbal remedies, such as *Echinacea purpurea*, an herb that some European researchers believe prevents and treats the common cold.

The United States has never done a clinical study of *Echinacea*, according to the *University of California at Berkeley Wellness Letter,* because herbal remedies can already be sold without being tested and "pharmaceutical companies are usually uninterested in studying herbals, since herbals can't be patented."[19] In other words, no pharmaceutical company can increase its profits by cornering the market on an herbal remedy.

EVALUATING REPORTS OF CAUSAL STUDIES

We should always question causal claims presented in advertisements. We should even read news reports of causal studies with a skeptical eye: Headline writers tend to slant the findings of studies, making them sound more dramatic than they are, and newspapers sometimes select studies more for their entertainment value than for their scientific merit. You should also put on your thinking cap when going to doctors, who may jump to causal generalizations from the small samples their patients make up. You also should question reports before using them in your own arguments.

Here are some questions to ask before you accept reported findings as "fact":

1. Who conducted the study? Were the people who conducted the study both knowledgeable and candid? Does the reporter give you the researcher's credentials and experience? Does the reporter give you any information you need to determine whether the researchers are likely to be fully candid?

2. Who sponsored the study? That is, who paid for the study? Does the sponsor hope to benefit from the study's findings? For example, has a cigarette company sponsored a study finding no link between cigarettes and cancer? Has a broadcasting corporation sponsored a study finding no link between the media and violence? Has a pharmaceutical company sponsored a study finding no serious "side" effects of a profitable drug? How much information does the sponsor allow to be released about the study? Is the sponsor likely to slant the study report to maximize positive effects and minimize negative ones?

3. What sort of study was done? As you now know, randomized studies generate more scientific certainty than natural studies, and strictly con-

trolled studies generate the most scientific certainty. Did the reporter tell you what type of study was conducted so you can determine how certain the results are? Did the reporter discuss any methodological complications of the reported study or studies?

4. What are the findings? To be able to make any predictions from the study, you need to know whether a contributing cause or necessary condition was established or whether a correlation was found. You also need to know what the exact findings were. Did the reporter give you specific percentages or summarize the study's findings in sweeping or broad generalizations?

5. Are there any other studies reported that agree or disagree with the featured study's findings? You want to know how controversial the findings of the featured study are. Did the reporter summarize any of the other studies with conflicting findings? If so, does the reporter give you any information that would help you decide which study was likely to be the most reliable one?

YOUR TURN H

◆ 1. Answer the following questions for the report on Dr. Snow's study of cholera.

   a. Who conducted the study?
   b. Who sponsored the study?
   c. What sort of study was done?
   d. What are the study's findings?

   e. Are there any other studies reported that agree or disagree with the featured study?

2. Did you get from reporters any of the causal claims in your writing this semester? Did their reports contain the information you needed to assess the causal claims reported?

As you can see from reading this chapter, substantiating causal claims is a tricky process, and we will never achieve scientific certainty for many of the causal questions we care the most about.

The human mind tends to abhor uncertainty; sometimes we accept any answer to avoid the discomfort of not knowing. But if we are to be ready for answers when they come, we must not fill in the vacuum of uncertainty with set opinions.

Fortunately, we already have much causal knowledge, and there are reliable experts creating more of it all of the time. Also, we can solve causal problems in our own lives, particularly when we keep in mind the basic pitfalls of causal reasoning: settling on the first hypothesis we think of, inferring that something that precedes an event must necessarily be its cause, and inferring that one thing causes another merely because the two are correlated.

By using the information in this chapter, you can put yourself in a better position to make decisions, because many decisions rely on causal problem solving.

EXERCISES

1. Do any of the conclusions in the passages below follow with certainty? Explain why or why not. Discuss whether the causes described are necessary conditions, sufficient conditions, or contributing factors. Discuss whether the causes have multiple effects.

   a. Eating chocolate causes an effect similar to falling in love, so you'll feel good after eating this chocolate candy.

   b. Petunias require water to survive, and my petunias haven't received water for a year. So my petunias are dead.

   c. I must hit "save" for my computer to save material. I didn't hit "save" during the last five minutes of typing. My computer just shut down by itself. So I have lost the last five minutes of typing.

   d. My stove requires gas to work. It's not working. It must be out of gas.

   e. Putting fish emulsion on my plants helps them bloom. I haven't put any fish emulsion on my plants this year. My plants won't bloom this year.

   f. Putting fish emulsion on my plants helps them bloom. I have been putting fish emulsion on my plants. My plants will bloom.

2. List as many explanations as you can think of for the following. Let your imagination soar!

   a. John Berry, a 19-year-old college student wearing a baseball hat with the bill in back, comes into Professor Andy Stern's office. John stays in Professor's Stern's office about 20 minutes and does not take off his hat. Professor Stern regards taking off one's hat as a sign of respect. Why doesn't John take off his hat?

   b. Fifty percent of all working artists are women, but only about 15% of the work shown by museums and galleries was created by women. Why?[20]

   c. Thirteen sea otters were found dead along the coast of Monterey Bay beach. There were no visible wounds, and at the time there was a "red tide," which sometimes kills the sea otter's main source of food. Why did the sea otters die?

3. Are any of the following causal hypotheses untestable or questionably testable? Can you think of any evidence that would count for or against them? Explain.

a. John doesn't take off his hat when he comes in a room because he is a disrespectful person.

b. The reason why John doesn't take off his hat is that unbeknownst to him, there is a magic force floating around him that controls all of his actions and prevents him from taking off his hat.

c. The reason why John doesn't take off his hat is that the last time he took it off, he placed it in wet tar without realizing it, and now it's stuck to his head.

d. Listening to Mozart during math quizzes improves students' scores.

e. Taking a critical thinking class improves critical thinking.

f. The hypotheses you generated in item 2 above.

4. Do any of the following passages contain causal conclusions that are based on insufficient evidence? Explain. Discuss, among other things, whether the reasoning expresses the post hoc or correlation fallacy. Also discuss whether the passages contain information relevant to generating a causal hypothesis.

a. Young women intellectually improve more when they attend all-female schools for a couple of years than when they attend co-ed schools exclusively. Therefore, attending all-female schools for a couple of years helps young women improve intellectually.

b. "[A] study in the *Journal of the American Medical Association* concluded that nonsmoking women exposed to a moderate amount of second-hand smoke at home face a 30% increased risk of lung cancer; those living with a heavy smoker, an 80% increased risk; and those exposed at work, a 39% risk."[21] This study shows that second-hand smoke contributes to developing lung cancer.

c. Sue dials Ginny's beeper number. A few minutes later, the telephone rings. It's Ginny. Sue thinks, "Ginny must have called because I beeped her."

d. Helmut's electric hot-air popcorn popper recommends running the popper for three minutes before putting in the popcorn. Helmut wants to know what would happen if he didn't follow the directions, so he puts in some popcorn immediately after turning on the popper. A bunch of the kernels don't pop. The kernels don't pop because Helmut didn't let the popcorn popper run for three minutes.

e. A study at Johns Hopkins School of Medicine in Baltimore found that the teen pregnancy rate dropped 30% in the three years that free medical and contraceptive services were offered through a local high school.[22] This study shows that the free medical and contraceptive services contributed to the drop in teen pregnancy rate.

5. Do any of the studies described in the passages below have questionable external validity? Explain.

   a. From a study on child development:

   > 128 children [from "white and middle-class neighborhoods" and "re-cruited from among church-affiliated kindergartens in a southern city"] between the ages of 5 and 6 years were shown 4 films depicting all possible combinations of female and male physicians and nurses. Results showed that when confronted with counter-stereotypical occupational portrayals, children were likely to relabel them into the typical instance of the male physician and the female nurse. There was a stronger tendency for the subjects to relabel the male nurse than to relabel the female physician. The children's relabeling of the roles presented was not due to inattention to the stimulus materials (videotapes). Neither sex, nor age, nor the number of physician visits in the last year were related to the frequency of relabeling. Maternal employment and exposure to real male nurses were related to correct identification of the male nurse and the female physician. The results suggest that the relabeling and its asymmetric character may be due to the differential exposure of children to female physicians and male nurses.[23]

   b. From another study on child development:

   > 36 5–6 year-old girls ["recruited through local parochial and Sunday schools"] viewed one of 3 television network cartoons, either high or low stereotyped or neutral. They were then tested for sex-role stereotyping on a 24-item measure, each item showing a male and a female and asking a question about them. Results indicate that girls who viewed the low-stereotyped program received significantly lower sex-role stereotype scores than did girls in the high and neutral conditions, who did not differ from each other.[24]

6. In the following passages an author criticizes a causal conclusion. State the author's criticism. Do you agree with the author? Explain.

   a. From a newspaper article on children's toys:

   > Many parents of toddlers are horrified by the idea of children playing with weapon toys. They believe that an inevitable, continuous line exists between the play of childhood and the proclivities of an adult. Today a lollipop-stick sword, tomorrow an AK-47. . . .
   >
   > We need to take a look at this assumption. . . . We need to distinguish between innocent play of healthy children and the dark deeds of warped and twisted souls.
   >
   > The former, properly guided, leads to healthy attitudes about one's capacity to be assertive, about one's power to act on the world.
   >
   > The latter type of behavior is a tragic tale of development gone terribly wrong, of minds haunted and tormented. . . .

Those of us in the mental-health community know what kinds of childhood experiences lead to violence. A violent adult has been exposed to violence as a child—not stick swords and cap guns, mind you, but real, actual violence. Emotional needs have been ignored and neglected. Bodies have been horribly beaten. Loved ones have been abused or killed by others. These kinds of experiences sow the seeds of violence.[25]

b. From an article on tattoos:

In an article entitled "Tattooing and High-Risk Behavior," Norbert Loimer and Elisabeth Werner tell us that they administered a standardized questionnaire that included "questions concerning tattoo behavior to 175 patients treated at a drug dependence outpatient ward." Not exactly the place where you'd expect to find stable and productive tattooed folks, but never mind that—as far as the doctors were concerned, they'd found themselves a representative sample of our community. . . .

. . . [A]ccording to the good doctors you've got one foot in the grave and another on a banana peel. "The HIV infection rate of tattooed subjects was 31.4% compared to 7.2% of the subjects without tattoos." Since there has never been even one case of HIV transmission due to tattooing (when performed by a professional artist) reported in any medical data base (yes, I checked), either we've got a particularly unlucky crew here or you have to wonder about the high rate of HIV found. Do tattooed junkies have more sex than everyone else? Unsafe sex? Are they "tattooing" themselves between fixes with their hypos? We'll never know. The good doctors just blamed it on tattooing, period, and didn't bother to investigate further.[26]

7. Are there any ethical constraints on modifying the methodologies described in the above passages? Explain.

8. Is there anything else that you would like to comment on regarding these passages?

9. The following argument reports several causal studies. Evaluate the questions discussed under "Evaluating Reports of Causal Studies."

Is Only Red Wine Fine?

We all hear a lot about red wine, but what about white wine, beer, and other alcoholic beverages—are they also good for the heart? Is it alcohol itself or certain chemicals primarily in wine that help keep the heart healthy? While some researchers—as well as a recent *60 Minutes* report on the "French paradox"—talk only about red wine, other scientists have found that moderate amounts of *any* alcoholic beverage have a similar effect on the risk of heart disease. The debate continues:

- **Only wine?** Last year, a large 12-year Danish study, published in the *British Medical Journal,* found that wine drinkers have lower death rates from cardiovascular disease and stroke than nondrinkers and that other kinds of alcoholic beverages do not have this effect.

- **All alcohol?** In November, researchers from Harvard Medical School reported (at the annual scientific meeting of the American Heart Association) that a drink or two a day of *any* alcoholic beverage cuts the risk of heart attack in half. Wine, beer, and liquor were equally effective.

- **White better than red?** A few years ago a study at Kaiser Permanente Medical Center in Oakland found that of 81,000 drinkers, those who drank *white* wine actually had the lowest risk of coronary artery disease. A new small study, presented at last year's American Chemical Society Conference in Chicago, put this to the test. Twenty men and women with high blood cholesterol levels were recruited at the nonprofit Jordan Heart Research Foundation in Montclair, New Jersey. For four weeks, half drank six ounces a day of red wine (cabernet), half drank white (chardonnay). Then after a four-week no-wine period, they switched colors for another four weeks. Though cholesterol levels didn't change significantly, blood levels of free radicals (which oxidize LDL "bad" cholesterol and thus turn it into an artery-clogging form) dropped when wine was consumed—15% with the red wine, 34% with the white. In addition, the blood's ability to clot (which can precipitate a heart attack) decreased 10% from this particular red wine and 20 from this white. The researcher suggested that white wine's advantage may be due to its higher levels of catechins, a type of polyphenol with powerful antioxidant properties. But the exact chemical content of wines can vary tremendously, even from batch to batch.

Bottom Line

Wine has several advantages that may make it *seem* healthier than other drinks. Wine drinkers may be better educated and more well-to-do than other drinkers, which may account for other traits (such as a better diet or better health care) that help keep them healthy. Wine also tends to be consumed with meals, which may be beneficial.

    The bigger picture. Over the past few years evidence has continued to accumulate about the potential benefits of *moderate* alcohol intake. It has reached the point that the scientific advisory committee for the 1995 U.S. Dietary Guidelines has advised dropping the current government conclusion that alcohol "has no net health benefit" and that its consumption is "not recommended." But the essential phrase is "moderate intake," defined as no more than one drink per day for women and two drinks for men (a drink is 12 ounces of beer, 5 ounces of wine, or 1.5 ounces of 80-proof liquor). Excessive alcohol intake can lead to dependency and can *cause* heart disease, as well as liver disease, strokes, accidents, and birth defects, and it accounts for thousands of deaths each year. Drink what you like, but only in moderation and never if you're pregnant, never if you're on certain medications, and never before driving. Despite the "French paradox," even the French have toughened their laws about drunk driving.[27]

10. Do you find any evidence in support of causal claims in the ads below? State the claims and the evidence and discuss whether the evidence is sufficient to establish the claims. Also discuss whether these causal claims are relevant to a decision the advertisers hope you will make.

a. Ad from AT&T:

b. Ad from Depo-Provera:

If you don't want the hassle of daily birth control, find out why over one million women now use Depo-Provera.

Some of the benefits of Depo-Provera.
Depo-Provera is an injection you get from your doctor or nurse, every three months. When taken as scheduled – just 4 times a year – it's more than 99% effective. So it's one of the most reliable contraceptives available. Because Depo-Provera is reversible, once you stop using it, you can usually become pregnant within one year. And it costs about the same per year as birth control pills.

Some of the side effects of Depo-Provera.
The most common side effects are irregular menstrual bleeding, cessation of menstruation, and weight gain. Also, use of Depo-Provera may be associated with a decrease in the amount of mineral stored in your bones, which may be considered among the risk factors for development of osteoporosis.

Depo-Provera is not right for every woman.
Women with breast cancer, blood clots, liver disease or problems, unexplained vaginal bleeding, a history of stroke, or those who think they might be pregnant, should not use Depo-Provera.

Depo-Provera may be right for you.
Although Depo-Provera does not protect against sexually transmitted diseases, it does provide highly reliable birth control. But before you consider any birth control method, you should discuss the risks and benefits with your doctor or other healthcare provider.

If you'd like more information about Depo-Provera, call
1-800-861-8618.

Depo·Provera®
Contraceptive Injection
sterile medroxyprogesterone acetate suspension

Birth control you think about just 4 times a year.

©1996 Upjohn Company   Please read the accompanying patient information and discuss it with your physician.

The Television Time Bomb: Violence on the Tube, a Public Health Issue

David C. Anderson

For the toddlers, it's gangs of cartoon mice dynamiting a menacing cat. Elementary schoolers sit rapt while superheroes wield special powers to dispatch evil. And by the time they're in junior high, American kids regularly witness barroom fistfights, knife-point rapes, drug-deal shootouts and terrorist attacks.

All on television, of course. But for years parents have worried about the effects of such violence, fanciful as it may be, on developing minds. Now a Seattle psychiatrist, Brandon Centerwall, offers a theory that, if corroborated by other researchers, suggests good reason to worry.

In a recent issue of the *Journal of the American Medical Association,* Dr. Centerwall describes how he sought to measure the relationship between television and violence by comparing the United States with South Africa, where an affluent Westernized white population remained without TV programming until 1975.

In the U.S., Dr. Centerwall writes, the homicide rate among white Americans nearly doubled between the introduction of television in the 1950s and 1975. The biggest surge in American homicides occurred after 1965, just as the first generation of children to grow up with television reached adolescence.

The psychiatrist asserts that he considered the effects of age distribution, urbanization, economic conditions, alcohol consumption, capital punishment, civil unrest and the availability of firearms. Yet "none provided a valuable alternative explanation for the observed homicide trends."

Thinking that the American civil rights movement or the Vietnam War might have had some effect, he looked at similar figures for Canada. It introduced television at the same time the U.S. did but never had a big civil rights problem and didn't send troops to Vietnam. The Canadian homicide and TV use statistics rose in striking parallel with those for the U.S. The homicide figures for white South Africans, meanwhile, remained flat between 1950 and 1975.

But by 1987, as South Africa's first television generation came of age, the homicide rate had more than doubled. In the U.S. and Canada, meanwhile, homicide rates among whites between 1974 and 1987 remained relatively stable.

Dr. Centerwall concludes that long-term childhood exposure to television is a causal factor behind half of the homicides committed in the United States, or about 10,000 homicides annually.

That's a sobering conclusion, yet Dr. Centerwall suggests possible responses that wouldn't raise any censorship issues: educating pediatricians and parents about the problem, rating TV shows for violence and requiring that all new TV sets be equipped with time-channel locks that would let parents block reception of violent shows in advance. The problem also argues for more day care and after-school programs, which would allow working parents to make less use of TV as a baby sitter.

Those are useful ideas in any case. However much television violence may serve the needs of the entertainment industry, it fully warrants treatment as an issue for public health and social policy, and a special challenge for parents.

Questions

1. In the above article, David C. Anderson reports a causal study. Does he give you any information about the researcher who conducted the study that is relevant to determining the researcher's reliability? Explain.
2. What sort of study was done? Was it strictly controlled, randomized, or natural? Did Anderson discuss any methodological complications of the study? Do you see any?
3. What are the findings? Did Anderson give you specific percentages? Or did he summarize the study's findings in sweeping or broad generalizations?
4. Did Anderson report any other studies that agree or disagree with the featured study's findings?
5. Do you believe the study supports a particular causal hypothesis? Explain.
6. Does Anderson recommend a particular policy in response to the problem of violence? If so, do you see any bad effects of following this policy? Do you have a policy to recommend? If so, what is it?
7. Do you want to raise any other points or questions about this reading?

Does Television Itself Nurture Violence?

Marie Winn

Marie Winn is author of *The Plug-In Drug: Television, Children and the Family* (New York, 1985).

The statistics David C. Anderson presents in "The Television Time Bomb" are indeed dynamite: a certain number of years after television's introduction, the crime rate surges.

It happened in the United States and Canada around 1965, just as the first generation to grow up with television reached adolescence. In South Africa, where television was not introduced until 1975, the crime rate remained flat until the 1980s. But by 1987, as South Africa's first television generation came of age, the homicide rate had more than doubled.

These figures make it hard to deny that there is a relationship between television-watching and violence in society. But why does Mr. Anderson assume that this relationship has anything to do with violent programs? That assumption, underlined by the subheading "Violence on the Tube, a Public Health Issue," is unwarranted by the evidence presented.

The statistics merely demonstrate that there is a relationship between watching television and violence, not between watching violent programs and subsequent violence.

I would propose two alternative hypotheses:

1. For great numbers of children, television viewing substantially reduces, and sometimes altogether replaces, that crucial set of experiences known as play. Several famous experiments by Harry Harlow et al. have shown that a major function of play in monkey social development is to mitigate aggression, and that monkeys deprived of play grow up to be aggressive and antisocial. Could this not be true for humans as well? Play depriva-

tion among young television viewers may lead to fewer checks on later aggression.

2. Parents of young children universally use television to solve their children's behavior problems. What did parents do to survive before the television age? They had to work on making their kids behave with endless little lessons—"Don't do that. No, no. Pipe down. I don't like your tone of voice." These all fall into the large category known as socialization. In the old days it might have been called the civilizing process. With television available as a plug-in drug, today's parents don't have to train their kids as much. This might have a detrimental effect, once those kids grow up; homicide, after all, is as uncivilized as you can get.

It's enticing to assume that the programs alone create the relationship between television and violence. Why, in that case, all you need to do is cut out the violent programs. It's more unpalatable to consider that the problem may be in the medium itself—in the fact that the time-consuming act of watching replaces some crucial child experiences, notably play and socialization.

Then the answer requires reducing or possibly eliminating television itself from the lives of our children. Nobody wants to face that unthinkable prospect.

Questions

1. Marie Winn presents an alternative hypothesis to explain the findings in the study David C. Anderson reported on. What is this hypothesis? What evidence does she offer for it?

2. How did Winn generate the alternative hypothesis she came up with?

3. Can you think of any additional hypotheses that are consistent with the information in this article?

4. Do you find the information in the article sufficient to confirm any of these hypotheses? Explain.

5. Does Winn recommend a particular policy in response to the problem of violence? If so, do you see any bad effects of following this policy? Do you have a policy to recommend? If so, what is it?

6. What other points or questions would you like to discuss regarding this reading?

Imagebusters: The Hollow Crusade against TV Violence

Todd Gitlin

I have denounced movie violence for more than two decades, all the way back to *The Wild Bunch* and *The Godfather*. I consider Hollywood's slashes, splatters, chain saws, and car crashes a disgrace, a degradation of culture, and a wound to the souls of producers and consumers alike.

But I also think liberals are making a serious mistake by pursuing their vigorous campaign against violence in the media. . . .

If today's censorious forces smell smoke, it is not in the absence of fire. In recent years, market forces have driven screen violence to an amazing pitch. But the question the liberal crusaders fail to address is not whether these violent screen images are wholesome but just how much real-world violence can be blamed on the media. Assume, for the sake of argument, that *every* copycat crime reported in the media can be plausibly traced to television and movies. Let us make an exceedingly high estimate that the resulting carnage results in 100 deaths per year that would not otherwise have taken place. These would amount to 0.28 percent of the total 36,000 murders, accidents, and suicides committed by gunshot in the United States in 1992.

That media violence contributes to a climate in which violence is legitimate—and there can be no doubt of this—does not make it an urgent social problem. Violence on the screens, however loathsome, does not make a significant contribution to violence on the streets. Images don't spill blood. Rage, equipped with guns, does. Desperation does. Revenge does. As liberals say, the drug trade does; poverty does; unemployment does. It seems likely that a given percent increase in decently paying jobs will save thousands of times more lives than the same percent decrease in media bang-bang.

Now, I also give conservative arguments about the sources of violence their due. A culture that despises and disrespects authority is disposed to aggression, so people look to violence to resolve conflict. The absence of legitimate parental authority also feeds a culture of aggression. But aggression per se, however unpleasant, is not the decisive murderous element. A child who shoves another child after watching a fistfight on television is not committing a drive-by shooting. Violence plays on big screens around the world without generating epidemics of carnage. The necessary condition permitting a culture of aggression to flare into a culture of violence is access to lethal weapons. . . .

. . . If Janet Reno cites the American Psychological Association's recently published report, *Violence and Youth*, to indict television, she also should take note of the following statements within it: "Many social science disciplines, in addition to psychology, have firmly established that poverty and its contextual life circumstances are major determinants of violence. . . . It is very likely that socioeconomic inequality—not race—facilitates higher rates of violence among ethnic minority groups. . . . There is considerable evidence that the alarming rise in youth homicides is related to the availability of firearms." The phrase "major determinant" does not appear whenever the report turns to the subject of media violence. . . .

The question for reformers, then, is one of proportion and focus. . . .

So let a thousand criticisms bloom. Let reformers flood the networks and cable companies and, yes, advertisers, with protests against the gross overabundance of the stupid, the tawdry, and the ugly.

But not least, let the reformers not only turn off the set, but also criticize the form of life that has led so many to turn, and keep, it on.

Questions

1. What hypotheses does Todd Gitlin discuss to explain the amount of violence in our society?
2. What evidence does he offer for or against any of these hypotheses?
3. Do you find his evidence sufficient to confirm or disconfirm any of them?
4. Does Gitlin recommend a particular policy in response to the problem of violence? If so, do you see any bad effects of following this policy? Do you have a policy to recommend? If so, what is it?
5. Do you want to raise any other points or questions about this reading?

Caution: Children Watching

Suzanne Braun Levine

Suzanne Braun Levine is editor of the *Columbia Journalism Review*.

. . . Dr. Deborah Prothrow-Stith of the Harvard School of Public Health is thinking of ways to use the best of [television] to combat the worst. She suggests the campaign against smoking as an analogy. "We went from thinking it was the most glamorous thing in the world to finding it offensive and unhealthy," she points out at the *TV Guide* symposium. "How did we do that? It was education in the classroom. It was working with the media. We banned the advertising of cigarettes on television." She thinks we can perform a similar change of attitudes about violence. So does Charren, who has an imaginative suggestion of her own, a "media-literacy merit badge" for Girl and Boy Scouts. "It's a way to teach kids that the violence you see on television is not the solution to problems." she says.

While such ideas are building toward a nationwide campaign to heal the bruised hearts and minds of our children, I take my hat off to one innovative father I have heard about. He would let his child watch *Teenage Mutant Ninja Turtles* cartoons, but only if the child would imagine a fifth turtle named Gandhi. Later they would discuss how "Ninja Gandhi" might get the turtles out of trouble without violence.

Questions

1. What solution does Dr. Prothrow-Stith suggest for changing attitudes toward violence?
2. How did she come up with her idea?
3. Do you consider Dr. Prothrow-Stith a reliable authority on the topic?
4. Do you think Dr. Prothrow-Stith's solution is a good one? Explain why or why not.
5. What do you think about the "Ninja Gandhi" solution?
6. What other solutions would you suggest for the problems posed by television violence?
7. What other points or questions would you like to discuss regarding this reading?

WRITING IDEAS

1. Write about a causal problem you have solved. Describe what you did to solve the problem.
2. Write an evaluation of the causal reasoning in one of the readings above.
3. Write an evaluation of causal reasoning you have used in a paper you've written.
4. Write a letter to the editor critiquing a news article about a causal study.
5. Write about whether this chapter and your class discussions complemented, conflicted with, supported, or left out any of your previous ideas about causal reasoning.

Notes

1. The idea of the causal web and the match example come from Robert C. Pinto and John Anthony Blair, *Reasoning: A Practical Guide* (Englewood Cliffs, NJ: Prentice Hall, 1993) 152–53.
2. James L. Adams, *Conceptual Blockbusting: A Guide to Better Ideas,* 3rd ed. (Menlo Park, CA: Addison-Wesley, 1986) 53.
3. Adams 53.
4. Louis Pasteur, quoted in Martin Goldstein and Inge F. Goldstein, *How We Know: An Exploration of the Scientific Process* (New York: Plenum Press, 1978) 250.
5. Peter Huber, "Medical Experts and the Ghosts of Galileo," *Law and Contemporary Problems* 54 (Summer 1991): 160.
6. Adams 54.
7. Plastic slogan from ad on back cover of *Harper's*, March 1995.
8. Quote from ad for *Shape* in *Shape*, July 1995: 137.
9. Stephen J. Gould, "The Smoking Gun of Eugenics: Should We—Can We—Take a Kindly View Toward a Hero's Faults?" *Natural History* December 1991: 8.
10. Doug Podolsky and Joanne Silberner, "News You Can Use: 20 Medical Stories You May Have Missed," *U.S. News & World Report* 3 Aug. 1992: 58–60.
11. Darrell Huff, *How to Lie with Statistics* (New York: Norton, 1954, 1982) 8.
12. My understanding of Dr. Snow's work on cholera comes from Goldstein and Goldstein 25–62. The Goldsteins took these quotes from John Snow, "On the Mode of Communication of Cholera," republished in *Snow on Cholera* (New York: The Commonwealth Fund, 1936).
13. Snow, quoted in Goldstein and Goldstein 43.
14. Philip G. Zimbardo, "Transforming Experimental Research into Advocacy for Social Change," in M. Deutsch and H. A. Hornstein, eds., *Applying Social Psychology* (Hillsdale, NJ: Lawrence Erlbaum Associates, 1975).
15. R. M. Veatch, " 'Experimental' Pregnancy," *Hastings Center Report* 1 (June 1971): 2–3.
16. Bette-Jane Crigger, "Twenty Years After: The Legacy of the Tuskegee Syphilis Study," *Hastings Center Report* 22.6 (Nov.–Dec. 1992): 29.
17. Goldstein and Goldstein 26. The Goldsteins got these quotes from Charles E. Rosenberg, *The Cholera Years* (Chicago: U of Chicago Press, 1962), quoted with permission of the publisher and Dr. Rosenberg.
18. William J. Clinton, "Excerpts of the President's Speech at Georgetown University," *New York Times* 7 July 1995: A8.
19. *University of California at Berkeley Wellness Letter*, vol. 10.2, (November 1993).
20. Nikki Meredith, "Factoring the 'Buddy Factor' " *Marin Independent Journal* 12 May 1991.
21. *University of California at Berkeley Wellness Letter* 10.11 (August 1994): 7.
22. "Why American Children Have Children," *University of California at Berkeley Wellness Letter* 7.7 (April 1991): 5.
23. Glenn D. Cordua, Kenneth O. McGraw, and Ronald S. Drabman, "Doctor or Nurse: Children's Perception of Sex Typed Occupations," *Child Development* 50 (1979): 590–93.
24. Emily S. Davidson, Amy Yasuna, and Alan Tower, "The Effects of Television Cartoons on Sex-Role Stereotyping in Young Girls," *Child Development* 50 (1979): 597–600.
25. Catherine Fuller, "Toy Guns Don't Produce Adult Killers," *Press Democrat*, Santa Rosa, CA, 23 Aug. 1995: B5. From the *Los Angeles Times*.
26. Devon Dee, "Seeing Ourselves as Others See Us: When It Comes to Tattoos, It's the Shrinks Who Are Flirting with Madness," *Skin & Ink* July 1995: 59–60.
27. "Is Only Red Wine Fine?" *University of California at Berkeley Wellness Letter* 12.5 (February 1996): 3.

Where Do We Go from Here?

In the introduction, I encouraged you to loop back through earlier chapters to see how the skills and information that you learned in later chapters have helped you attain the goals of the earlier chapters. Let's see how looping back to earlier chapters can further improve our critical thinking; then we'll look at how we can improve our critical thinking by moving beyond this book.

LOOPING BACK

Here are some connections I find between later chapters and earlier ones. When you loop back, you'll probably find more.

The chapters on argument evaluation, analogies, generalizations, and causal reasoning all help us develop emotions we can live with. As we saw in Chapter 1, some of our negative emotions result from hasty generalizations, false fault finding, and misreading others. And, in general, our emotions involve inferences we make about what we experience or hear about the world and ourselves. The more mistakes in reasoning we can avoid, then, the more likely we are to avoid emotions that involve fallacious thinking—assuming, of course, that we remember to practice emotional awareness. We cannot detect and repair fallacious thinking in emotions that we remain unaware of.

Our study of language and slanting also helps us question our emotions. Our emotions involve judgments about the world and ourselves, and we sometimes unreflectively pick up judgments because of concealing language or slanted reports. By analyzing language and identifying and compensating for slanting, we are better able to question our judgments and the emotions that arise with them.

The material in later chapters also helps us follow the advice in Chapter 2. Understanding slanting helps us be on the alert when gathering information for our decisions, and understanding causality helps us analyze problems and think through the consequences of alternative solutions. We're also better able to resolve conflicts if we can distinguish support for a conclusion from abuse and clarify the meaning of novel, vague, and ambiguous terms.

MOVING FORWARD

We can also improve our critical thinking by moving beyond the text. First, we can improve our thinking about a topic by gathering as much information as we can about that topic. Increasing our background knowledge about a topic benefits us in several ways. The more research we do, the more aware we become of different points of view about the topic and different emotional responses to it. We also become better prepared to include counter-considerations in our arguments. And if we find out that people have different definitions of key terms associated with the topic, we can be careful to define the terms we use in our arguments. Furthermore, we perceive slanting more easily, because we know what's left out. Finally, we recognize more easily what's relevant and irrelevant to establishing claims about the topic. In short, besides learning the critical questions to ask, we need to gather as much information as we can about a topic to provide thorough answers to those critical questions.

Second, we can improve our critical thinking by taking classes and reading other books on critical thinking. We can take courses on statistics and on scientific reasoning to improve our critical thinking in these areas. We can take courses in fiction writing and poetry to help us develop our imaginations. We can take courses in ethics and comparative religion to help us think more about our values and the values of others. And we can study anthropology to find out the methodologies that other cultures use when making important decisions.

To continue to develop our critical thinking, we must remember to stay open not only to new information but also to new ways of questioning information. However, we must also take care not to develop an undermining skepticism about the possibility of knowledge. Unreflective skepticism is just as inhibiting for making good decisions as dogmatism or one-sided thinking.

If we want to be successful problem solvers, we must remain optimistic about finding solutions to the problems that we face. Sometimes that's difficult, given the complexity of problems. When I get discouraged, I think of the Dalai Lama. A reporter once asked him how he could remain optimistic in the face of the many depressing conditions and injustices in the world. The Dalai Lama laughed heartily and then responded, "What else would you suggest?"[1]

I agree with the Dalai Lama. It may be difficult to find solutions to the problems troubling us, but we have no better option than to keep trying. And to remember, on occasion, to laugh.

Notes

1. Spaulding Gray, *Utne Reader* (May/June 1993): 96–97.

Sample "Your Turn" Answers

Chapter I

Your Turn A

1. The teacher perceived (heard) the student say, "I can't understand these numbers," and his tone of voice sounded "grating" to her. She interpreted this tone of voice as accusatory; that is, she took the student to be blaming her for his inability to understand his grade. Because she was motivated to "set him straight," she told him his grade in a brusque manner. The story does not describe the teacher's inner sensations when she was annoyed. Her body may have felt tight and hot.

Your Turn C

1. *Happy*: Wow. I got a lower grade on that test than I expected. That teacher is holding us to higher standards than I thought. I like being pushed to do well. Now I'm really motivated to work hard in this class. I know I'll get a higher grade next time.

   Sad: Oh, bummer. I got a lower grade on that test than I expected. Poor me. I tried so hard and I wanted a good grade so badly. I was looking forward to celebrating tonight, and now I've got to stay home and study.

   Angry: Rats. I got a lower grade on that test than I expected. That teacher's standards are too high. How dare she hold us to such high standards when we're only freshmen! She's unfair.

   Fearful: Oh, no. I got a lower grade on that test than I expected. Mom'll have a fit when I

tell her. She was expecting me to do well in this class. And now, who knows? I may not get a good grade. I don't know what to do to improve my score. But I have to improve my score, or Mom won't keep paying my tuition.

Your Turn E

1. a. *Denial*: The summer my cat died, everyone else was aware of her feebleness before I was. I didn't want to face that she was rapidly declining, and I began to realize how feeble she was only after other people pointed it out to me. I was denying the evidence right in front of me because I didn't want my furry friend of 22 years to die.

   b. *Blaming the victim*: A woman I know had a very hard time finishing her thesis in graduate school. She had a thesis adviser who was notorious for undermining his students, but she wouldn't listen to people who suggested she change advisers. She kept blaming herself, saying that he would approve her thesis if she wrote one that was good enough. She eventually stopped blaming herself, by the way, got a new thesis adviser, and finished within months.

   c. *Reinterpreting the outcome*: The woman who was treated poorly by her thesis adviser tends to focus on the bright side of her suffering. She notes how her bad experience helps her understand others who have been treated unfairly.

2. a. The denial kept me from feeling sad when I wasn't ready to feel sad.

b. By blaming herself, this woman wasted much time she could have put to better use working with a more helpful adviser.

c. By looking on the bright side, this woman gets something positive from her negative experience, but she also risks not taking injustice seriously enough. If there's always a bright side, why try to change unjust situations?

Your Turn F

1. These are the conclusions:

   a. I may as well not work on it at all.

   b. Sara will never have time to spend with me.

   c. My teacher doesn't respect me.

   d. It's all my fault that our group didn't finish our homework.

   e. That's the worst thing I can imagine happening to me.

2. a. This conclusion is questionable. If the student begins working, he or she can get something done. It's better to do some work on a paper than none at all.

   b. This conclusion is questionable. Sara may have time for tea another day.

   c. This conclusion is questionable. Maybe the teacher didn't see the student's hand go up. Or maybe she had called on the student earlier and wanted to give other students a chance to talk.

   d. This conclusion is questionable. Maybe the group didn't work very efficiently in the time they had.

   e. This conclusion is questionable. A ride not showing up is more likely to be an inconvenience than a disaster.

3. a. This thinker decides he has no time just because he doesn't have the full amount of time he would like. ALL-OR-NOTHING THINKING

   b. This thinker generalizes without sufficient evidence. HASTY GENERALIZATION

   c. This thinker "reads" the teacher without sufficient evidence. MISREADING OTHERS

d. This thinker takes full responsibility for something without sufficient reason. FALSE FAULT FINDING

e. This thinker judges an inconvenience to be a disaster. CATASTROPHIZING

Chapter 2

Your Turn A

1. a. *A problem*: I'm in love with my boyfriend, and I want to go out with him exclusively. My relationship with him is more important than anything else in my life. (This challenges the goal of maintaining a monogamous relationship with my boyfriend.)

   An opportunity: Although I love my boyfriend and want a monogamous relationship, I've been thinking that I'm not ready to make a lifelong commitment. I think I'll focus on my studies and my friends and put building a relationship with my boyfriend on the back burner for a while. (This supports two goals: reevaluating my priorities and focusing on my studies and friendships.)

   b. *A problem*: I'm glad my friend wants to recognize my birthday, but I don't believe in using computers. I don't want to disappoint my friend, but I believe in integrity. I'll have to tell my friend I won't use the computer. (This challenges the goal of not wanting to disappoint a friend.)

   An opportunity: My friend must not know me very well, otherwise, he would know I have decided not to use a computer. I don't want to disappoint my friend, but I want my friend to understand who I am and what I value. Also, this is a perfect opportunity for me to spread the word about the computer industry. (This supports two goals: informing my friend about my values and informing others about the computer industry.)

2. b. The goal of having children or not having children would change for me in different contexts. I may not want to have children

while I am still in school and unemployed but change my mind once I have finished school and have a sustaining income.

    c. I wonder to what extent my goal to lose weight is really mine and to what extent it is a product of the images of women I grew up seeing in the popular press.

Your Turn B

1. a. Yes, these are false alternatives. Other alternatives include renting a computer and sharing a computer with someone.

    b. Yes, these are false alternatives. Other alternatives include sharing the bill with my roommate, withholding money I owe my roommate until the bill is paid, and negotiating with the telephone company for more time to pay the bill.

Your Turn C

1. I might think about the legality of such a decision: I might see hanging the picture as an expression of freedom of speech and thus decide that I have the constitutional right to hang it if I choose. I might then think about the morality of my action: On the one hand, I might be concerned about whether the picture sensationalizes suicide or the use of weapons; on the other hand, I might think that the picture could lead an audience to think carefully about suicide and violence. I might consider the artistic merit of the photograph and raise aesthetic questions about it: Is it pleasing to look at? Are light and shadows balanced? I would certainly think of practical questions: How long will it take me to hang the picture? and How much time will I spend answering other people's objections or questions about it?

2. Yes, other students will expect similar pictures to be treated similarly in the future.

3. I'm not sure whether there are any predictable long-range consequences to viewing one photo. Maybe it will inspire someone to become a great artist. Maybe it will lead someone to point a gun at his or her head. It's very hard to say.

4. I would expect the student to emphasize the positive side of showing the photograph. I

would ask the student to brief me, but I would also ask someone who would be more likely to address the down side of showing the photograph.

Your Turn D

1. a. My value of avoiding hurting a friend's feelings would come into conflict with the value I place in respecting my own needs. In this case, I would put respecting my own needs above avoiding hurting my friend's feelings.

    b. My value of helping a friend comes into conflict with my value of not cheating. In this case, I would put not cheating over helping my friend, especially because I don't think that using my paper will ultimately serve my friend's interest. My friend could go to a tutor instead of using my paper, or I could help my friend myself.

2. a. I might fear punishment and so not want to approach the teacher with the problem.

    b. I might be embarrassed at "rocking the boat" and so not want to say I don't find the joke funny.

    c. I might want to put my own self-interest first and eat the cake before my brother notices.

    d. I might want to retaliate against Suzy for the sloppy apartment by screaming at her in front of her friends.

Chapter 3

Your Turn A

1. Yes: The second one and the last one.

Your Turn B

1. a. Consequently

    b. So, as a result

    c. No conclusion clue words here.

2. a. It's likely to rain soon.

    b. *Subconclusion*: Watching violent images causes children to play roughly.
    Main conclusion: Children should not

be allowed to watch violent images on television.

c. This passage is not an argument. The author is giving directions, not offering support for a conclusion.

Your Turn C

1. a. Since
   b. In as much as
   c. After all

2. a. *Support*: I feel like kissing Jane.
   b. *Conclusion*: I shouldn't try to kiss Jane again.
   Support (Subconclusion): Jane probably does not want me to kiss her.
   > *Subsupport a*: Jane turned her head away when I tried to kiss her.
   > *Subsupport b*: She changes the subject when I try to discuss our becoming romantically involved.
   c. *Conclusion*: John doesn't understand how to read my body language.
   Support 1: He keeps trying to kiss me, even though I turn my face away when he comes near.
   Support 2: If he understood how to read my body language, he wouldn't keep trying to kiss me.

3. a. *Unstated support*: I should do what I feel like doing.
   b. *Unstated support in the subargument*: Jane's turning her head away and changing the subject from romance are signs that (indicate that) Jane doesn't want to be kissed.

   Unstated support in the main argument: If Jane doesn't want to be kissed, I shouldn't try to kiss her.
   c. There is no unstated support in this argument.

Your Turn D

1. a. "True" precedes the counterconsideration, and "but" precedes the answering support.
   b. "Yes" precedes the counterconsidera-

tion, and "still" precedes the answering support.

c. There are no counterconsideration clue words here.

2. a. *Counterconsideration*: It hasn't rained in July for the last sixty years, which tends to indicate that it won't rain out the July 4 barbecue tomorrow.
   b. *Counterconsideration 1*: Eucalyptus are quick growing.
   Counterconsideration 2: They smell wonderful.
   Counterconsideration 3: There's nothing like the sound of the breeze in their leaves.
   c. *Counterconsideration 1*: Motorcycles don't protect you from rain or cold.
   Counterconsideration 2: Motorcycle accidents are more dangerous than car accidents.

   (For some people, these counterconsiderations would override the support given in this argument. Such people would put comfort and safety above the advantages the motorcycle offers, namely, saving money, having fun, and getting quickly through traffic.)

3. a. *Conclusion*: We should have a backup plan ready.
   Support: There are big storm clouds overhead.
   b. *Conclusion*: Let's not plant eucalyptus in our pasture.
   Support 1: They spread like weeds, crowding out California natives.
   Support 2: They're a fire hazard.
   c. *Conclusion*: Let's buy a motorcycle instead of the used car your Uncle offered us.
   Support 1: The motorcycle costs less.
   Support 2: It's more fun to ride.
   Support 3: It can get through traffic more easily than the car can.

Your Turn E

1. The first paragraph of the passage begins with communication enhancers. The author tells a joke and follows it with a personal story. In doing so, the author motivates the

audience to read on. At the end of that paragraph we find the author's conclusion: Students should learn a foreign language.

The second paragraph contains more argument enhancement. The author expands on the conclusion, explaining that learning a foreign language involves being able not only to read it but also to speak about complex issues.

The third paragraph introduces support: Students cannot understand their own language and culture without knowing a foreign language.

Your Turn F

1. a. Jed offers an argument and includes some support avoidance for good measure.
   Conclusion: Capital punishment is acceptable.
   Support: People who commit murder deserve to be killed themselves.
   Support avoidance (name calling to dismiss any opposition): You'd have to be a fool or some kind of liberal not to believe in capital punishment.

   b. *Sean's conclusion*: Your looking at (and copying) my homework isn't right.
   Support 1: You would be giving the teacher a false impression of what you had done.
   Goldie's conclusion: You should let me copy your homework.
   Goldie's support: I need a good grade in this class.
   Goldie's support avoidance (name calling): Calling Sean a "goodie two shoes."
   Sean's counterconsideration: You need a good grade in the class.
   Sean's support 2: You need to learn critical thinking.
   Sean's support 3: Copying my answers won't help you learn how to answer the questions yourself.
   Goldie's support avoidance (threat): I won't give you a ride over to your girlfriend's unless you give me those answers.
   Sean's attempt to stay on track:
   Acknowledges Goldie's concern: Look, Goldie, I understand that you are concerned about your grade.

Repeats his conclusion: It's not right for you to copy my work.
Adds additional support:
Sean's support 4: We could both get in trouble if you copy my work.

Chapter 4

Your Turn A

1. a. The word "good" has a number of possible meanings, and it's not clear to me which meaning the author has in mind. Is the latest Woody Allen movie *artistically* good—that is, is the acting and directing of high quality? Is the movie *morally* good—that is, will watching it make me a better person? Is the movie good for a laugh or a sob? I need some answers to these questions before I understand the author's meaning.

   b. The word "bank" does have a number of meanings, including a financial institution or the side of a river. It's clear which meaning is intended in the sentence.

   c. The word "religion" has a number of possible meanings. Two of them are: (a) devotion to God and (b) strong commitment to a way of life exemplified by a divine or human model, such as Christ or Buddha. Before I could figure out what the "Religions of the World" course was about, I would need to know whether the teacher had one of these meanings in mind or some other meaning of "religion."

Your Turn B

1. a. Connotative definition. This definition describes something Martin Luther King, Jr., considers common to just laws, namely, that they have the effect of lifting human personality.

   b. Definition by example. This definition gives a specific instance of an unjust law to help the reader understand the meaning of "unjust law."

   c. Definition by synonym. This definition offers a word that means roughly the same as "justice."

Your Turn C

1. a. expressive definition
   b. definition by metaphor
   c. definition by association

2. "Sexual infidelity" expresses and evokes disapproval and negative emotions such as jealousy and anger. No, I do not think everyone would give the same expressive definition of "sexual infidelity." Some people, for example, might enjoy "sexual infidelity"; for them, the phrase might evoke approval and positive emotions, such as hope.

Your Turn D

1. Sexual infidelity: 1. Sexual interaction (including flirtation or other typical patterns of sexual foreplay) with a person outside one's significant relationship. (This definition is an attempt to state the common features of examples 1, 2, 4, and 5.) 2. Any strong, ongoing emotional or sexual attachment with a person outside one's significant relationship. (This definition attempts to state the common features of examples 3 and 5.)

   Neither of these definitions expresses what I mean by "sexual infidelity." I would focus not only on whether one engaged in some sort of sexual behavior with another person, but also on whether one had promised one's mate not to. Thus, I offer the following definition of "sexual infidelity": 3. Any sexual activity with a person other than one's mate that one implicitly or explicitly promised one's mate not to engage in. Because none of the examples mentions whether the person who engages in the sexual conduct had explicitly or implicitly promised not to do so, none of these examples fully illustrates my definition of "sexual infidelity."

Your Turn E

1. a. "Gaining something one values" uses very general language and is vague. Some specific examples would help an audience focus. It is also a broader definition than definition (b). You can gain something you value without completing a plan, as, for example, when someone unexpectedly dies and leaves you a fortune. But is being left money "success"? If not, then definition (a) is too broad.

   b. This definition also uses general language. Adding some examples would help an audience focus. It's narrower than definition (a).

   c. This definition is circular. "Healthy" is used to define "health."

   d. This definition is broader than definition (e). It includes females as well as males. It also blurs a distinction between the class of males and the class of males and females. To keep the distinction clear, it's useful to avoid using this definition of "man."

   e. This definition is narrower than definition (d). It also blurs the distinction between "man" and "boy" because it does not restrict "man" to adult males.

   f. This definition is broader than definition (e) because it could include other species than the human species. An adult male frog could be a man, given this definition. But this definition is also narrower than definition (e) because it limits "man" to adults, whereas definition (e) does not.

2. According to this definition of "sexist decision," lesbians, gays, and heterosexuals all make sexist decisions when they date. I find this definition too broad for my purposes. I would want to use "sexist decisions" to refer to unfair decisions made on the basis of sex, and I don't believe that choosing dates on the basis of sex is unfair.

Chapter 5

Your Turn A

1. a. I didn't intend any ambiguity here, and I don't see any. I try to create interest by using an alliteration (repeating the "d" sound).

b. I meant this title to be ambiguous. It means (a) separating arguments into supports and conclusions and (b) stopping fights.

c. I didn't intend ambiguity when I originally wrote this title, but I now see ambiguity here. I had intended the title to refer to the process of evaluating arguments, but it can also mean "arguments that evaluate." Actually, when you go through the process of evaluating an argument, you are drawing evaluative conclusions about the argument (making arguments that evaluate).

2. a. I don't find any irony here.

b. I take this statement to be ironic. I wouldn't expect anyone to think a movie was good when half the audience walked out and the other half fell asleep.

c. I take the first sentence to be ironic. Austen does not mean what her words say. She herself would doubt that all single men with money are looking for wives. She's poking fun at the wishful thinking of people seeking husbands for their unmarried daughters. I'm helped by knowing that the nineteenth-century novelist Jane Austen excels at ironic social commentary. Also, Austen gives a clue in the second sentence by pointing out that people form this opinion of any man without knowing anything about him.

Your Turn B

1. The ad says the army "can help" to make your dreams a part of your future. "Can help" is a weasel phrase.

2. This phrase is misleading in the context of the ad. The ad uses the strong word "guarantee," but we have to read carefully to notice that it does not guarantee us any jobs or guarantee that our dreams will come true in the army. It only guarantees us "help." In other words, there's no guarantee at all that we will get the job of our dreams by entering the army. The guarantee is empty.

Your Turn C

1. a. Yes, "screw" is a metaphor. It's a familiar slang expression for sexual intercourse, and it is not very lively.

b. Yes, "holding a wolf by the ears . . ." is a metaphor for the relationship between the government and people of the United States and the institution of slavery. It's a very lively metaphor, producing strong visual imagery.

2. In (a), "screw" is a mechanical image and sounds painful, which intercourse can be when force is used. It conceals the joyful experience of sexual intercourse between loving partners.

In (b), Jefferson's metaphor highlights the complexities of the institution of slavery for the society in which it occurs. It suggests that the society is damaged by continuing to hold on to slavery and could also be damaged by abolishing it—if society doesn't take care when dissolving the institution of slavery.

3. The first is less vivid than the second. The second evokes more precise sensory images.

Your Turn D

1. a. "Provincial" promotes the stereotype that country people are narrow-minded.

b. "Cosmopolitan" promotes the stereotype that city people are broad-minded.

2. a. "Patriot" is a positive-sounding word. People typically use it to express approval. Some associations to "patriot" are "honorable," "wise," "self-sacrificing," "courageous."

b. "Traitor" is a negative-sounding word. People typically use it to express disapproval. Some associations to "traitor" are "evil," "sneaky," "self-interested." Sometimes a person who tries to change a country is considered a patriot by one group and a traitor by another, depending on whether the group believes the changes will improve or harm the country.

Chapter 6

Your Turn B

1. a. The point is to criticize people who seek the protection of owls for being insufficiently concerned about the resulting job loss. The meaning of the last sentence is cleverly ambiguous. "That's not enough" could refer to how much the administration is doing to protect the owls *or* to the number of jobs lost. The ambiguity leads the reader to consider the possibility that those who criticize the administration's environmental policy do so not because they think the policy fails to protect the owls sufficiently, but because the policy fails to eliminate enough jobs.

   b. I would expect this item to be of interest to conservatives, because it is published in the *National Review*.

   c. I would like to know what those who want additional protections say about job loss. I would also like to know what jobs are in jeopardy and whether these people can find other ways to make a living without causing environmental damage. I would like to know other positive and negative effects of protecting owls.

Your Turn C

1. a. They give the impression that the only reason you would not ask for the three issues is that you don't like to think. That leaves me with a negative impression of those who would not ask for the three issues.

   b. Yes. First, someone can like to think without being an intellectual; we can think about lots of things besides those that intellectuals think about. Second, reading *The New York Review of Books* is not the only source of ideas of interest to intellectuals.

2. a. The headline implies that Christensen-Adamu has done something wrong by going against justice, and the story as written does nothing to support Christensen-Adamu's stand as legitimate. Instead, it portrays her as a bit of an oddball, a "rape victim" who acts in "defiance" of a court order.

   b. Many responsible people question the justice of capital punishment, and Amnesty International considers it a human rights violation. Responsible people, including Henry David Thoreau and Martin Luther King, Jr., have gone to jail to protest injustice. If the story contained either of these pieces of information, it would leave the reader with a less negative view of Christensen-Adamu.

   I would like to know more about Christensen-Adamu. Who is she, besides a "rape victim"? Is she a college professor, an attorney, a mother, a musician? If the story included information about her that showed some of her strengths, it would leave the reader with a less negative view of her.

   I would also like to know more about her attorney's position that the prosecution ignored her rights as a victim.

3. a. From reading this description, I have a fairly neutral evaluation of the Open Door Policy.

   b. The responses of Great Britain, France, and Germany are described as "noncommittal at best," but we are given no information about China's response to the policy. We also aren't told whether there was any objection raised to the policy in the United States.

   In *A People's History of the United States*, Howard Zinn puts the Open Door Policy in the context of other questionable U.S. foreign policies to create a negative impression:

   > For the United States to step forward as a defender of helpless countries matched its image in American high school history textbooks, but not its record in world affairs. It had instigated a war with Mexico and taken half of that country. It had pretended to help Cuba win freedom from Spain, and then planted itself in Cuba with a military base, investments, and rights of intervention. It has seized Hawaii, Puerto Rico, Guam, and fought a brutal war to subjugate the Filipinos. It had "opened" Japan

to its trade with gunboats and threats. It had declared an Open Door Policy in China as a means of assuring that the United States would have opportunities equal to other imperial powers in exploiting China. It has sent troops to Peking with other nations, to assert Western supremacy in China, and kept them there for over thirty years. (p. 399)

Your Turn D

1. a. Yes. The second story includes information about the seriousness of the effects of caning. I'm more opposed to caning after reading this information.

   b. As I just mentioned, the first story omits the details about the caning and its effects, which are pertinent to making an evaluation of caning.

   The language (alliteration and slang words like "kid" and "caper") in the first story's headline is playful, hiding the seriousness of the situation. The second story uses "torture," a negative-sounding word, to highlight the seriousness of the situation. The second story also uses vivid language to highlight the effects of caning.

   The first story sandwiches the U.S. request for clemency in the middle of the story and follows this fact with two statements supporting the caning. In a story this short, you can expect readers to get to the end, if they get beyond the headline at all. The second story hides support for the caning toward the end of the story and includes a qualifier, "which don't always measure public opinion accurately," undermining the strength of the support.

   The first story features the playful language in the headline. The second story features serious language, "torture," in both the headline and the body of the story.

2. a. The headline uses language—calling her point of view a "belief" and contrasting it with "justice"—that hides the fact that Christensen-Adamu's point of view is about justice. It also labels her a "rape victim," which implies that she is helpless.

The first paragraph describes her act as one of "defiance." A less negative phrase would be "challenge to authority" or "civil disobedience."

The story hides Christensen-Adamu's attorney's criticism of her treatment in the final paragraph of the story.

The headline "Rape Victim Puts Beliefs before Justice" leads me to suspect that Ms. Christensen-Adamu did something unjust and therefore wrong. However, once I read the story, I found myself admiring Ms. Christensen-Adamu for refusing to participate in a death penalty proceeding that she views as unjust, especially given the expectation that she would want to retaliate against the man who raped her.

   b. I recommend the headline "Woman Puts Justice before Revenge."

Chapter 7

Your Turn A

1. a. Elena Albert uses clear and straightforward language to describe details of an incident that happened to her when she was a child. Although the event happened some time ago, she says she remembers it clearly, and it's the kind of event that would leave a strong impression. I see no reason to question her description or her integrity. I would accept her description of her experience.

   b. Dannie Martin gives a vivid account of his personal experience. Although Dannie Martin was an inmate in federal prison, he is not known as a con artist. I see no reason to question his integrity. I therefore accept his description of Mr. Squirrel.

   c. We could begin by asking these questions of Franklin himself. He's recounting his personal experiences of the trial and punishment of Mr. G—n. The biggest difficulty I see comes in understanding Ben Franklin's words. He uses language differently from the way we do today. However, he doesn't say anything to raise a doubt about the reliability of his experiences or his reports of them.

But what about the two witnesses who testified against Mr. G—n? Let's start with the Dutchman. We hear from Franklin that Mr. G—n marked the cards in full view of him. The Dutchman was then in a good position to gain personal experience of Mr. G—n's behavior. The Dutchman speaks no English, we find. But, as Ben notes, that doesn't prevent him from having reliably seen Mr. G—n mark the cards. However, unless the Dutchman had an excellent interpreter, something may have slipped between his lips and his audience's ears. Still, that seems unlikely; the events are simple enough to pantomime, if nothing else. And, besides, Mr. G—n himself admitted to marking the cards—further corroboration that the Dutchman's audience understood him correctly.

What about the second witness? This person claims to have seen Mr. G—n mark a pack of cards on their backs in the round-top, without being seen by Mr. G—n. I have some questions for this witness. For Mr. G—n not to have noticed him, he must have been far enough away from or in some way protected from Mr. G—n's view. Where, exactly, was he? Could he clearly see the cards and the marks on their backs?

Then, there is Mr. G—n himself. He admits to marking the first pack of cards but claims they weren't the cards the group commonly played with. He says he gave them to the cabin boy. Is there any reason to doubt his testimony? He's clearly got something to gain by creating the impression that he did not mark the cards with fraudulent intent: If the jury finds him innocent, he can avoid punishment.

However, we don't want to assume that a person charged with a crime cannot therefore be trusted. Defendants are to be assumed innocent until proved guilty. Still, it does seem a bit odd, as the attorney general observed, that Mr. G—n would mark the face cards for no particular reason at all and then give them to the cabin boy, who, according to the attorney general, doesn't play cards.

What about the attorney general? How does he know the cabin boy doesn't play cards? Perhaps we should ask the cabin boy himself. Maybe he has some other use for cards.

In sum, after questioning the witnesses in Franklin's story, we find we'd like more information before deciding to accept or reject the reports of the second witness and of Mr. G—n.

Your Turn C

1. a. Sisters are, by definition, female. This claim is self-evident to anyone who understands English.

   b. This claim is self-evident to anyone who knows how to add.

   c. This claim is self-evident to anyone who understands what pain is. I'm assuming the claim is NOT saying that one should avoid pain at all cost, but rather that pain generally is undesirable.

   d. Not self-evident. You need to witness the behavior of goldfinches (or rely on someone who has) to accept this claim.

   e. This claim is self-evident. Once you know the kind of thing respect is, you can see that it's good to be treated with respect.

Your Turn D

1. a. This person has expertise in the relevant writing skill and, assuming she lived with her father, plenty of personal experience to be a reliable witness as well. But I would question whether she's likely to be fully candid about her father. I'd want to know more about her relationship with him: Does she have any axes to grind? Conversely, does she have any reason to build him up? To form an opinion about him, I wouldn't rely on her account exclusively.

   b. Reporters generally act as witnesses to what they have seen or heard. Nothing is said about this reporter that indicates a physical impediment to gaining information. However, his political views may affect what he chooses to report and the language used. Like Edward Koch in his description of people who disagree with his views of capital punishment, the reporter may use words that subtly undermine those who disagree with him. I'd be on the lookout for that, and I wouldn't rely on this reporter's account exclusively.

c. I'd expect this scientist to have expertise about the methods of testing birth control pills and knowledge about experiments that he or she and other scientists have conducted. I'd question whether the scientist would be fully candid about this knowledge, because the scientist's job depends on selling the pills. I wouldn't base any claim on this scientist's account alone but would check it against other scientific reports.

2. The situation I've described here comes from an experiment conducted by Stanley Milgram. In that study (which was replicated around the world), the machine did not actually shock the "student," but the "teacher" did not know this. An actor played the role of the "student" and began crying out in pain when the "teacher" pushed the more intense shock buttons. A few people who played the role of teacher refused to shock anyone, and some people stopped after a few shocks. Most people, however, continued shocking the student until they reached the highest shock level possible on the machine—even though they felt bad about what they were doing. Some even cried in sympathy with the student being shocked.

If you thought you would not shock the student, think again. Would you have been one of the few who refused even to take part in the experiment? Have you ever questioned an authority's directive that went against your own sense of what was right? (Have you ever gone along with a crowd against your own sense of what was right?) We can improve our chances of acting in

accord with our own values if we remember to question authorities. The people in the Milgram experiment could have refused to begin until the scientist established that he had a right to direct them to cause pain to another person. We can do the same when an authority (or crowd) asks us to do something we believe is wrong.

Your Turn E

1. a. Not common knowledge. People disagree about this.

b. Common knowledge. People agree, and it's easy to document.

c. Common knowledge. People agree that there is disagreement, and the disagreement is easy to document.

d. Common knowledge. People agree. It's stated in Article 5 of the Universal Declaration of Human Rights, and it's self-evident.

Your Turn F

1. a. Some of Judy's support is relevant, and some is not. Judy's support that Beth likes to go for walks is relevant to Jane's values, but Judy's support that Beth has plenty of money is not; Jane isn't looking for someone with money. Both of Judy's supports may well be acceptable; remember, support can be acceptable without being relevant.

b. This is an example of straw person. The author takes one of Freud's more questionable claims and uses it to represent Freud's entire theory of human nature.

c. I don't have enough background knowledge to know whether the support is relevant. If John has already passed the CPA test, taking the course is not relevant to his needs, for example.

d. There are two supports here: that hemp is useful for making paper and that hemp is natural. That hemp is useful for making paper is relevant to legalizing it. That a product is useful provides some evidence that it should be legal. That hemp is natural is information about what hemp is.

But it's not clear to me how the fact that something is natural counts toward legalizing it.

Your Turn G

1. a. This argument generalizes from a sample. "The students I've talked to" is the part (or sample), and "all of the students in the class" is the whole group.

   b. This argument presents reasons for an explanation. After offering evidence to rule out the system software as the explanation (cause) of the problem, the argument maker concludes that the hard drive is the explanation (cause) of the problem.

   c. This is an argument from analogy. Mom is implying that sister's being put down by brother is analogous to brother's being put down by sister. So if Sis doesn't accept being put down by Bro, neither should she accept putting him down.

   If you've found these types of arguments easy to identify, great. If not, don't worry. You'll have no trouble after reading the chapters devoted to these types of reasoning.

Your Turn H

1. a. With the aid of a full moon, this support could evoke strong romantic feelings. And the feelings could be quite distracting.

   b. This support evokes fear, which could be intense enough to be distracting.

2. a. That depends on the values of the audience. If the audience values having a close bond with a sexual partner, then yes, the support is relevant.

   b. Yes, assuming the audience values life and safety.

3. a. Yes, I'd like to know, for example, whether the audience values safe sex. If so, the argument maker needs to add that precautions will be taken. I'd also like to know if the audience values fidelity. If so, I'd like to know if either member of the couple already has a committed relationship with someone else.

   b. Has anyone called the fire department? Where is the fire in the house? Is there time to make a phone call or grab a portable phone? Are there any people or pets who need help getting out of the house?

Your Turn I

1. a. If all birds fly, then emus fly. But emus don't fly. Therefore, it's false that all birds fly.

   b. If all cars require gasoline to run, then electric cars require gasoline to run. But electric cars do not require gasoline to run. Therefore, it's false that all cars require gasoline to run.

2. a. This is not a valid argument. From the information given in the supports, Mark could be to the left of John, but he's not necessarily to the left of John. If Mark, Sara, and John are sitting in a straight line and facing the same direction, then Mark would be to the left of John. However, if they are sitting at the points of a triangle, Mark would not be to the left of John.

   b. This argument is invalid. It has the same structure as the flower/roses argument. So we can use the same analogy to refute the argument:

   All lawyers graduated from college
   All doctors graduated from college.
   All doctors are lawyers.

   c. This argument is invalid. We can fill in the story to show why. Suppose that Marsha works in the city and lives in the country. She plays tennis with Alli in the country and with José in the city. Alli and José don't even know each other, much less play tennis with each other.

   d. Once again, we can fill in the story. Suppose Mandy is a Manx. Manx cats don't have tails.

   e. Let's fill in the story to show this argument to be invalid. Suppose Li-Wen keeps her students' attention by lighting fires to the books in the room. She's keeping her students' attention all right, but she's not being a very good teacher. We could also use a refuting analogy to show that this argument is invalid. It has the same structure as the argument about the ignition key and the low-fuel light.

Chapter 8

Your Turn A

1. a. Rios compares his first reaction to school to a back wall—school was the tennis player, and he was the wall. He then compares his response to school to the flick of the player's wrist. He moves from a passive role to an active one.

   b. Yes. I find his analogy useful. Although I've never literally been a back wall, I know what one is, and I have played tennis. I know the feel of flicking the wrist and using the racquet.

   c. For someone who's never played tennis or engaged in a physical activity like tennis, Rios might try another analogy. How about a cooking analogy? He could be a lump of dough molded by school or a baker molding the school to serve his educational needs.

Your Turn B

1. a. Prediction: The pasta will take eight minutes to cook (in the mountains).

   b. Implicit

   Analogy: *Cooking pasta this time will be like cooking pasta in the past. (analogical support)*

   c. Yes, the relevant similarity is that the pasta is the same.

   d. The atmospheric conditions in the mountains differ from those at sea level. This difference affects the length of time it takes pasta to cook.

Your Turn C

1. a. Women-only colleges are being compared to men-only colleges.

   b. Sexually experienced women are being compared to sexually experienced men.

Your Turn E

1. a. Whether women-only and men-only colleges are both acceptable depends on the social setting of the colleges. In a society in which women consistently have the same social and political opportunities as men, both would be acceptable. But in a society in which women have traditionally had fewer social and political opportunities than men have had, women-only colleges can be acceptable, but not men-only colleges. In such a society, women-only colleges help redress the socially created differences between men and women and give women a place where they can practice being leaders in and out of the classroom. Men do not need the same opportunities and typically have more resources allocated to their educations. In such a society, it is important for the men's-only schools to open their doors to women in order to redress the socially created differences.

   b. Calling a woman who has several sexual partners a "slut" and a man who has several sexual partners a "stud" seems like a double standard to me because it places higher expectations on women. Assuming that the sex was consensual, I do not see why one member should be degraded by it and the other not, merely because one party is female and the other is male. Do you? I'd say that if it's inappropriate to call a sexually experienced male by a derogatory name, then neither is it appropriate to call a sexually experienced female by a derogatory name.

2. Yes. They both wear clashing patterns. Color is the main difference, but it's not sufficient to undermine the comparison.

Your Turn G

1. a. Holmes compares the draft to the sterilization of the "feeble-minded." He also compares requiring people to obtain vaccinations to requiring the "feeble-minded" to be sterilized.

b. The situations being compared are similar in that the state is forcing someone to do something the person may not otherwise choose to do. And what the person is being forced to do is in part for the benefit of others as well as for the person. Defending one's country, for example, benefits all the citizens in the country. Obtaining a vaccination benefits oneself and others who might otherwise get sick and die from a contagious illness. Forcing the "feeble-minded" to become sterilized benefits their caretakers who would otherwise have to take care of a child as well as the "feeble-minded" person, and it protects the "feeble-minded" person from the discomfort and possible risks of pregnancy and childbirth.

c. There are some clear differences. Fighting in a war and obtaining vaccinations protect others from life-threatening events: enemy attacks and deadly diseases. Restricting someone's liberty makes sense under such circumstances. Sterilizing a "feeble-minded" person, in contrast, protects others from inconvenience but not from life-threatening circumstances. This difference is relevant to undermining the analogy, because it was the severe danger that made the limit to liberty seem justifiable.

d. I would like additional information about the circumstances in which people are forced to become vaccinated. I was assuming they could be forced to become vaccinated only during a deadly epidemic. Also, I would like to know when people may be forced into military service. Not all wars are fought to protect a country from deadly enemy attacks. In fact, few of them are. Thus, it's not clear to me that the precedent itself is a good one.

I would also like to know what Holmes means by the "feeble-minded." What types of mental and physical disabilities is he referring to? Until I know more precisely whom he is talking about, I cannot decide how harmful childbirth would be

for them and those around them. Also, I would like to know whether there are other, less invasive, ways of protecting vulnerable persons from pregnancy.

e. I agree with Sunstein that Justice Holmes's argument was poor.

2. (From *Stanford v. Kentucky* and *Wilkins v. Missouri* (LW 4973, 1989), where the majority held that juveniles of 16 and 17 could be executed for murder.) According to Justice Scalia, writing for the majority, the fact that juveniles are denied the right to drink or vote is irrelevant to whether a minor could understand and follow the law against murder. (Paraphrased from *The Information Series*, p. 21.) Justice Brennan, however, writing for the minority, held that juveniles are too immature to be held responsible for their actions in the way adults are. To Brennan, the fact that society forbids juveniles to vote, drink, or serve on a jury and generally does not let them drive or get married without parental permission indicates that society does not hold juveniles responsible in the same way they hold adults responsible. (*The Information Series*, p. 22.)

Chapter 9

Your Turn A

1. a. A generalization about the customers at Reliable Used Cars.

   b. Not a generalization.

   c. A generalization about the cars at Reliable Used Cars.

   d. Not a generalization.

   e. A generalization about the trees in José's yard.

2. Yes, (a) and (c) are statistical generalizations. They use numbers.

3. Yes, (c) uses the weasel phrase "up to." The cars could be anywhere from 1% to 75% off, and the generalization would be true. The buyer should beware here.

4. The first two claims are stated very broadly, with no qualifiers at all. Even the statements with the words "most" are overly broad; they

seem to be making claims about women and men all over the world at all times. They are not narrowed to a particular historical period or to a particular cultural or geographic location.

These claims fail to take into account differences among men and differences among women, and they exaggerate differences between men and women.

Because these claims are stated very broadly and because I do not know of any evidence strong enough to support them, I would call all of these claims stereotypes. However, I do not know that these claims are *false*. Still, it seems unlikely to me, for example, that most men look at a woman and immediately think what it would be like to go to bed with her. What about men in nursing homes? What about men visiting their mothers? What about gay men? And do most women look at a man and wonder whether he will be a good provider? Perhaps some jobless or underpaid heterosexual women consider whether potential mates would be good providers—but so might some jobless or underpaid heterosexual men.

Your Turn B

1. The academic institution would be more likely to release the full findings of the study than the cigarette company. The cigarette company has a vested interest in holding back any information that would inhibit sales of cigarettes.

Your Turn C

1. a. The population is men in the United States.

   b. The sample is the list of men selected at random.

   c. The sample design is simple random sample, because the sample was chosen at random directly from a list of the individuals in the population.

2. a. I have not created any random samples for the generalizations made at the beginning of the chapter, nor do I know of any. That's one reason why I say those generalizations do not have sufficient support.

   b. Suppose I sampled the men and women I know to test these generalizations. That sample would be biased, because my friends would be "birds of a feather." If I've met an unusual number of men who look at a woman and immediately think what it would be like to go to bed with her, the reason might be that I've spent an unusual amount of time in heterosexual singles bars. On the other hand, if I rarely meet any men who look at a woman and immediately think what it would be like to go to bed with her, the reason might be that I hang out mostly with men whose minds are occupied with philosophy. Both samples are biased. They cannot be used to establish either the truth or the falsity of the statement.

3. The newspaper fills the front page with terrible things happening in the world: child beatings, grisly car accidents, government scandals, and natural disasters. If we took the news to be representative of what's happening in the world, we'd be afraid to set foot in the street and cautious about remaining at home as well.

   But don't worry—news stories are not selected at random. They are selected to get the audience's attention and to sell newspapers. The world is not as bad as it looks in the papers.

4. Since surveys of student attitudes are pallid data and eating food oneself is vivid data, I would expect Ali not to pay much attention to the survey of student attitudes. As a result, I think he would not change his mind—unless he's studied critical thinking, that is. Then he might ask himself whether the food served during orientation is a biased sample of the dorm food. Maybe the cooks go all out for orientation when parents come to visit.

Your Turn D

1. Because people do not like to admit to attitudes and behaviors thought unappealing, I would expect that the persons I interviewed would be reluctant to admit to these behaviors. I would have to word the questions carefully to encourage candid answers.

2. I would have to watch them and see how they behaved. I would have to keep in mind that—unless I stay with them every minute from birth to death—I am sampling a small amount of their behavior. From a sample I would have trouble knowing whether the men I observed were *in general* selfish and the women *in general* martyrs or whether they behaved those ways only when I happened to be around them.

3. a. Loaded with the answer yes. To unload, write, "Do you favor a policy that requires judges to give life sentences to third-time offenders?"

   b. Loaded with the answer yes. To unload, write, "Do you favor prison rehabilitation programs?"

   c. Loaded with the answer yes. To unload, write, "Do you favor judges having the authority to determine sentences for third-time offenders?"

   d. Loaded with the answer yes. To unload, write, "Do you favor cutting back on prison rehabilitation programs?"

Your Turn E

1. No. 47% + 3% = 50%, and 53% − 3% = 50%, so it is possible that as many residence hall students think the residence hall food is not nutritious as think it is nutritious.

2. No. It's very unlikely, given the confidence level of 95%, but it is possible that more than 53% + 3% of the students do not believe the residence hall food is nutritious.

3. Not necessarily. That depends on how knowledgeable the sampled students are about nutrition. It's possible that they aren't very knowledgeable. If that were the case, even if 100% thought the food was not nutritious, it would still not follow that the food was not nutritious. Because I do not know how likely the sampled students are to have knowledge of nutrition, I would say I do not know whether the residence hall food is likely to be nutritious merely because a large percentage of them say it is. (The margin of error is not relevant to answering this question.)

Chapter 10

Your Turn A

1. a. This is an attempt to describe a necessary condition.

   b. This sounds like it's trying to describe a sufficient condition. Feeding plants is actually a contributory factor in producing blooms. Many other things besides food are necessary for plants to bloom. Most need light as well.

   c. This is an attempt to describe a collection of causes that together create a sufficient condition for a blender going on.

   d. This is describing what causes a hummingbird to seek out red plants. Again, though it sounds like it is describing a sufficient condition, it is describing a contributing factor. The bird's ability to identify red and the bird's inclination to associate red with food also play a role; otherwise, it would not seek out red flowers, no matter how hungry it was.

2. a. John's filling up his tank with gas is a contributing factor to his car's starting, and so is turning the key. Other things need to be working also for John's car to start. His starter, for example, has to function. The conclusion's not definite, but assuming John's car started before he filled up his tank, it will very likely start this time also.

   b. Having gas is a necessary condition for a car to start, so John's car definitely won't start if he has no gas in his tank.

3. Alcoholics do not inevitably end up on a binge if they take one drink of alcohol. However, David may be one of the alcoholics who has a hard time stopping after taking a drink, so the slope may be somewhat slippery in his case. On the other hand, if there is not very much beer or other alcohol in the house, and if David's friends stop him from driving to the store for more, he will end up sober by the end of the evening. How slippery David's slope is depends on these other background conditions. If David knows that there is plenty of beer in the house and his

friends aren't likely to interfere with his drinking, then he doesn't commit the slippery slope when he predicts that he'll end up passed out if he takes the beer.

Your Turn B

1. If you didn't stop by labeling her a "grumpy person" but were able to consider the possibility that she may not like her job or that she may be having a hard time at home, good for you. According to Nisbett and Ross, we are particularly susceptible to thinking of only one causal hypothesis when trying to figure out why people do what they do. We tend to attribute people's behavior to their characters and don't even consider the hypothesis that *the situation* contributes to their behavior. Thinking of only one hypothesis about human behavior has important negative consequences. Because we think of character as static, we assume there is nothing we can do to prevent the behavior. Nisbett and Ross write:

> Every day, people make harmful and damaging judgments about themselves, or harmful judgments about their spouses even to the point of severing marriages, because they wrongly attribute current crises to stable personal dispositions instead of to transient situational pressures. (*Human Inference: Strategies and Shortcomings of Social Judgment* [Englewood Cliffs, NJ: Prentice Hall, 1980] 252.)

If we consider the situation as a contributing cause of a person's behavior, we can find ways to change the behavior. If our coworker is taking on too much responsibility on the job, we can help out to improve her spirits.

2. James Adams, in *Conceptual Blockbusting: A Guide to Better Ideas* (Menlo Park, CA: Addison-Wesley, 1986) lists the following solutions: "[1] filing the wire coat hanger in two, flattening the resulting ends, and making tweezers to retrieve the ball . . . [2] smashing the handle of the hammer with the monkey wrench and using the resulting splinters to retrieve the ball . . . [3] having your group urinate in the pipe" (p. 53). Adams notes that the last solution is difficult to think of in mixed company, because it requires breaking a cultural taboo: urinating in front of the opposite sex.

Your Turn C

1. a. This sentence has a positive ring to it, but it is stated in such general terms I wouldn't know how to begin testing it.

   b. Once again, I'm not exactly sure what "wonders" to expect from my life if I subscribe to *Shape*. I would also like to know what specific action and rewards I can expect to be produced by my reading the success stories of *Shape*. Until I know these things, I can't tell whether my experiences after reading *Shape* confirm or disconfirm these causal hypotheses.

Your Turn D

1. The story at the beginning of the chapter describes a temporal ordering among the fall from the trolley, the bruise, and the cancer lump. The fall came first, the bruise second, and the cancer lump third. No information for a correlation is given. There is no information presented that says that cancer frequently occurs in bruised tissue and that cancer does not occur on unbruised tissue.

2. a. Example A describes a correlation between having ear creases and getting heart attacks: Among the people studied, those who had ear creases had eight times as many heart attacks as those who did not have ear creases. Example B does not describe a correlation. It gives only half of the information found in a correlation. It describes a "considerable percentage" of people whose colds went away after they took an antihistamine. But it does not describe what happens when people do not take antihistamines.

   b. In example A, no temporal ordering is given between heart attacks and ear creases. In the second example, a temporal ordering is stated. Taking the pill comes before the cold's going away.

   c. If I were to say the information in this example establishes that ear creases cause heart attacks I would be committing the correlation fallacy. The information in example A is not sufficient to establish that ear creases cause heart attacks, because correlation alone does not establish a specific causal relation between the two events. When two events are correlated, there are a number of possible explanations:

(1) Either of the two events could cause the other. So, heart attacks could cause ear creases.

(2) Some third event could cause both of them. Perhaps ear creases tend to increase more with age, as do heart attacks.

(3) The correlation could be coincidental.

We need additional information to account for the correlation. Among other things, we need to know whether the ear creases or the heart attacks occur first.

d. If I were to say the information in this example establishes that antihistamine pills cure colds, I would be committing the post hoc fallacy. The information in example B is insufficient to establish causation, because temporal order alone does not establish causality.

e. I question whether the researchers studied a large enough sample of people to draw a reliable correlation. The article that reports Dr. Elliott's study goes on to say,

> But epidemiologists in Framingham, Mass., who have scrutinized the inhabitants of that community for over 40 years, have not found the link in their subjects. (Doug Podolsky and Joanne Silberner, "News You Can Use: 20 Medical Stories You May Have Missed," *U.S. News & World Report* 3 Aug. 1992: 58–60.)

I also question how useful this information could be to any of us. Assuming there is a correlation between ear creases and heart attacks, I do not see how that correlation will help us find a way to prevent or treat heart attacks.

In *How to Lie with Statistics*, Darrell Huff reports a joke Henry G. Felsen made to highlight the importance of examining what happens if the treatment isn't given before drawing a conclusion about causation: "Proper treatment will cure a cold in seven days, but left to itself a cold will hang on for a week." In other words, the treatment had no effect on the cold's going away! It would have gone away on its own in any case. You can't find out whether a treatment has an effect, then, without comparing what happens when the treatment is given with what happens when it isn't.

Your Turn E

1. There's a possible confounding variable in Dr. Quong's experiment: his expectation that his patients will do well with the new drug. His is a single-blind experiment. His *patients* don't know whether they're receiving the new drug or something with no effects, but *he* does. And he may treat patients receiving the drug differently from those not receiving the drug. To improve his experiment, he could turn it into a double-blind experiment. He could have another doctor—one who does not know which group is the experimental group and which is the control group—give the pills to the patients.

2. Professor Hernandez's experiment does not give a particular student reason to believe that he or she will definitely learn logic faster by using a computer to do homework. Professor Hernandez has discovered at most a contributory cause: using a computer contributes to learning logic faster. First, because using a computer is not a sufficient condition for learning logic faster, it doesn't follow that you will definitely learn logic faster if you use a computer. The other effects for fast learning must be present. Second, using a computer has other effects in addition to helping people learn faster. Like penicillin, using a computer has negative effects for some people. If you are computer phobic, using a computer will not help you learn logic faster.

Your Turn F

1. We could gather information about women who have bruised their breasts and women who have not and see whether there is a difference in the incidence of breast cancer in these two groups.

2. Problems include the following:

   a. How are we going to find the women to study in the first place?

   b. A problem of memory. (How certain could the women be that they had never had a bruised breast?)

   c. Ruling out alternative hypotheses. Even if we find that there is a greater incidence of breast cancer among the women who remember sustaining bruises, how do we know that it was *the bruise* that led to the cancer? Perhaps women with bruised breasts are more likely than other women to suffer from abuse and it's *the abuse* that led to the cancer, not the bruise itself. We could get additional information by breaking down the group of women who had sustained bruises into two groups, those who sustained bruises because of spousal or other abuse and those who sustained bruises as a result of an accident.

Your Turn G

1. Selecting patients at random without obtaining their informed consent to be studied is unethical. Giving people with AIDS a placebo (and thereby allowing them to go untreated) is ethically troublesome. When researchers expect serious consequences from no treatment, they compare two or more treatments from which they expect improvement rather than comparing a treatment with a placebo.

2. If I had $100 million to spend on research, I would spend it to study the effects of diet on prevention. Knowledge about diet helps us to become more autonomous than knowledge about drugs does: We don't need prescriptions for food, but we typically need prescriptions for drugs. Also, many people can grow at least some of their own nutritious food, but rarely can we produce our own pharmaceuticals. As a result, we are more dependent on large corporations for medication than we are for food.

Your Turn H

1. a. I described the person who conducted the study as "John Snow, an English doctor." I did not give his credentials or experience, nor did I say anything about his character or personal interests that would indicate whether he was likely to be candid or not.

   b. I didn't say who sponsored (paid for) the study.

   c. I described the study comparing the incidences of cholera among residents in the neighborhood served by the two water companies as a "natural experiment."

   d. The study found that there were eight to nine times as many cases of cholera in homes served by water drawn downriver from sewage than by water drawn upriver from sewage. This is a correlational statement. From this correlation, Dr. Snow drew the causal conclusion that water contaminated by sewage contributed to the spread of cholera. His conclusion was a strong one, because though this was a natural experiment, there was a good chance that other potential causes (related to income or occupational differences) of the spread of cholera were more or less evenly spread among the two groups he compared. Also, Dr. Snow did not draw his conclusion from the correlation found in the natural experiment alone, but from other evidence that his hypothesis accounted for, such as that people contracted cholera *after* drinking contaminated water. Also, Dr. Snow gave evidence against other current hypotheses offered to explain the spread of cholera.

   e. I didn't report any other studies, but I did describe how Dr. Snow ruled out rival hypotheses.

Glossary

acceptable support Support that's self-evident, common knowledge, or based on reliable personal experience, reliable expertise, or reliable inference; true support.

active listening A listener giving full attention to a speaker and checking with the speaker to ensure that the listener heard what the speaker intended.

all-or-nothing thinking Claiming that something went totally wrong because it didn't go totally right (or vice versa).

ambiguous Having two or more meanings.

analogy A stated or implied comparison of two things.

analysis of a situation Interpretation of a situation, including claims about how the situation arose and predictions about what is likely to happen because of the situation.

analysis of an argument Breaking an argument into its parts; identifying the conclusion, support, and any counterconsiderations of an argument.

analytic skill The ability to divide something into its parts or elements; the ability to identify differences among similar things and similarities among different things.

argument 1. A series of statements at least one of which is offered to establish the truth or acceptability of another. 2. Abuse or strongly expressed disagreement.

argument extras Acts of communication that sometimes occur along with arguments, either to enhance the communication of arguments or to derail them. See also **communication enhancers** and **support avoidance**.

assumption See **unstated support.**

authority 1. One who has expertise. See **expertise.** 2. One who has the right to command obedience in virtue of his or her role. See **authority of role.**

authority of role One with the right to command obedience because of his or her job or position. For example, a police officer has the right to command a speeding motorist to pull over by virtue of the officer's authority of role.

background beliefs One's beliefs about the subject of an argument that affect how one evaluates the argument, including whether one sees the stated support as relevant or irrelevant.

biased sample A sample that is likely to be unrepresentative of its population.

blanket generalization See **glittering generalization.**

brainstorm Coming up with ideas in a group by quickly offering any idea for consideration, no matter how zany. During brainstorming, no criticisms of ideas are given.

broad definition A definition of a word that describes a relatively large number of the word's possible referents.

broad generalization A claim that something is true of all of the members of a group.

causal chain A metaphor that implies falsely that each effect has one cause, that each cause has one effect, and that from any one cause a specific distant event will inevitably happen.

causal web A metaphor that implies that effects

happen from multiple interlinking causes and that these interlinking causes have multiple effects.

cause Produce, bring about, prevent.

census Observing, interviewing, or collecting information about each member of a group to form a generalization about the group.

circular definition Using the word being defined or a version of it in the explanation of the word.

cognitive Having to do with thinking.

cognitive distortions Also called "thinking mistakes," "fallacies," or "thinking gaps," these involve jumping to conclusions from insufficient evidence. See also **fallacy.**

coincidence Two events that occur together but are not related to each other causally.

common knowledge Settled, noncontroversial claims for which support could be provided if necessary.

communication enhancers Acts of communication that enhance communication, including definitions, background information, and jokes.

conclusion 1. In an argument, the point an author is trying to establish, show, or prove; thesis. 2. In an essay or speech, the final section.

conclusion clue words Words that indicate a conclusion, including "thus," "therefore," "so."

confidence level A statistician's degree of confidence ($n\%$) that the percentages sought for the population will fall within the margin of error. See **margin of error.**

confounding variable A possible cause introduced to the experimental group other than the possible cause being tested.

connotative definition Explaining the meaning of a word by listing the common features or family resemblances of the things the word refers to. Avoid confusing a connotative definition with the connotations (associations) of a word: namely, any idea, image, or emotion that one experiences when one hears a word. See **definition by association.**

contributing factor An event that partially causes an effect to occur or fail to occur but is neither necessary nor sufficient for the effect to occur or fail to occur.

control group The group in a causal experiment that is not given the suspected cause but is watched to see if the effect occurs nonetheless.

controversial claims Claims about which informed people disagree.

correlated events Events that increase and decrease in the same direction (e.g., shoe size and math ability) or events that increase and decrease in opposite directions (e.g., number of people and the amount of oxygen in a room). Also, events that are present together and absent together.

correlation fallacy Drawing a conclusion that one event causes another because the two events are correlated; assuming falsely that correlation alone establishes causation.

counterconsideration A reason that goes against a conclusion.

counterconsideration clue words Words that signal a counterconsideration in an argument, including "although," "even though," "in spite of the fact that."

crafty sample selection Knowingly selecting members of a sample that are unrepresentative of a population in order to fool an unsuspecting audience.

critical thinking Activities of the mind crucial for making decisions we can live with, including becoming aware of and reflecting on emotions, identifying values, assessing information and authorities, analyzing and clarifying language, imagining solutions to problems, evaluating alternative solutions, and assessing and producing arguments.

deductive argument An argument about which the argument maker claims that the conclusion follows with necessity from the support, that is, if the support is true the conclusion must be true. Another definition (not used in this book) defines a deductive argument as an argument from the general to the particular.

definition by association Setting forth stereotypes and personal experiences that come to mind when one hears a word but that are not strictly implied by the connotative definition of the word.

definition by example Explaining the meaning of a word by telling detailed stories to illustrate the condition, concept, or activity the word refers to. Sometimes a definition by example names specific things that a more general word refers to, such as "Birds include such things as ducks and finches."

definition by metaphor Explaining the meaning of a word by equating it with something different.

definition by synonym Explaining the meaning of a word by offering another word or words with a similar meaning.

degree of expertise Depth of knowledge an expert has about a particular subject.

denial Refusing to let in or become aware of information that leads to a conclusion one does not want to hold; one of the psychological strategies, usually unconscious, that people use to maintain a false sense of security. See also **denigrating (blaming) the victim** and **reinterpreting the outcome.**

denigrating (blaming) the victim An attempt to justify abuse or injury by claiming that the injured party is at fault; one of the psychological strategies, usually unconscious, that people use to maintain a false sense of security. See also **denial** and **reinterpreting the outcome.**

disanalogy A stated or implied contrast between two things.

double-blind experiment An experiment in which the experimenter and the subjects do not know which group is the experimental group and which is the control group; a method used to prevent confounding variables because of experimenter and subject expectation.

ecstatic experience A sense of losing oneself as an individual; feeling one with the universe, other people, or God.

emotion A complex phenomenon including thoughts, feelings (inner sensations), and motivations to act. The thoughts and feelings of emotions are often occasioned by sensory perceptions. See **mood.**

emotional awareness The ability to notice all of the aspects of an emotion one is having; realizing that one is having an emotion when one is having one.

emotional expression Speech, such as "I'm angry!" or behavior, such as a frown, that communicates emotion.

emotional labor Modifying one's emotions or emotional expressions as a part of one's job.

evaluation A statement that something meets or fails to meet a standard or goal; a determination that something is desirable or undesirable or has or fails to have worth, merit, or beauty.

experimental group The group in a causal experiment that is given the suspected cause and watched to see whether the expected effect occurs.

expertise Relatively advanced knowledge of a field or subject, evidenced by advanced degrees and publications in a field of study or by years of successful practice.

explanation 1. A statement of the cause or causes of something. 2. A clarification of an abstract or complex subject.

expressive definition Describing the evaluations and emotions a word expresses or evokes.

external validity The relevance of the outcome of a study for situations other than the experimental situation; in an externally valid study, the effect will happen not only in the lab but also outside the lab.

fact A description or report that something is happening or did happen.

fallacious argument An argument that fails to establish its conclusion; an argument with unacceptable, irrelevant, or insufficient support. Some fallacious arguments include hasty generalization, all-or-nothing thinking, misreading others, false fault finding, false alternatives, straw person. See also **cognitive distortions.**

fallacy See **fallacious argument.**

false alternatives A fallacy in which a reasoner draws a conclusion about what to do from a false statement about the number of alternatives available, called "false dilemma" when the reasoner asserts falsely that only two alternatives are possible.

false dilemma See **false alternatives.**

false fault finding Finding oneself (or another) responsible for something without sufficient evidence.

family resemblances Identifying similarities among individuals in a group in which each member of the group shares at least one of the similarities with at least one other member of the group. For example, a member of a family may have the family eyes and nose but not the family ears, whereas another member of the family may have the family nose and ears but not the family eyes.

feeling The inner sensation, such as stomach dropping or chest pounding, of emotion. As this book defines "emotion," feeling is one aspect of emotion. In everyday discourse, "feeling" is sometimes used as a synonym for "emotion."

freewrite A writing exercise in which one writes whatever comes to mind without censorship or editing.

generalization A claim that something is true of all, most, some, or a specific percentage of a group.

glittering generalization An unqualified claim about a group that implies that a larger percentage of the group have the particular quality attributed to the group than do in fact have that quality; a generalization that distracts an audience from or hides the differences among individual group members; sweeping generalization or blanket generalization.

goal Something someone aims to achieve or have happen.

hasty generalization A claim that something will always happen because it has happened a few times.

hiding A category of slanting techniques in which one uses such things as small print, pallid language, and placement of information to minimize the likelihood that the audience will attend to one side of a multisided account.

highlighting A category of slanting techniques in which one uses such things as bold print, vivid language, and up-front placement of information to maximize the likelihood that the audience will attend primarily to one side of a multisided account.

hypothesis A statement that something might be a cause of something else.

implement Put a decision into action.

inductive argument An argument about which the argument maker claims that the conclusion follows from the support with some degree of probability or likelihood but not with necessity. Another definition (not used in this book) defines an inductive argument as an argument from the particular to the general.

inferential knowledge A statement that is based on reliable inference from acceptable support; the conclusion of a strong argument or subargument.

insufficient support Lack of enough support to establish the acceptability of its conclusion (even if the support is acceptable).

intuition A sense of awareness (seemingly without inference from evidence) that something is or may be the case; a hunch, a suspicion.

invalid argument A deductive argument in which it is possible that the support be acceptable and the conclusion be unacceptable; a deductive argument with insufficient support.

irony An act of communication in which an author says the opposite of what he or she means to express criticism.

irrelevant difference In an explanation using an analogy, a difference between the things being compared that does not hinder the audience from understanding the subject being explained. In an argument from analogy, a difference between the things being compared that does not undermine the claim that if something's true of the first thing it is also true of the second.

irrelevant support Support that fails to provide any reason whatsoever to accept its conclusion.

loaded question A question phrased to elicit a particular answer.

main argument An argument whose conclusion is not offered to establish, show, or prove another statement.

main conclusion The conclusion of a main argument.

man-on-the-street interviews Interviews in which individuals are selected from among whoever happens to be on the street at a particular time; an example of sampling birds of a feather.

margin of error A percentage range ($\pm n\%$) indicating how far off the percentages of the population are likely to be from the percentages found for the sample.

misreading others Making a claim about what another person is thinking or feeling without sufficient evidence.

mood A positive or negative feeling, often without any particular focus. Moods typically last longer than emotions and are less intense. Moods with particular thoughts as their focus develop into emotions. See **emotion.**

motivation A propensity or inclination to do something; one of the aspects of emotion.

multistage sample design A sample design in which areas of the country are selected and individuals are then selected within those areas.

narrow definition A definition of a word that describes relatively few of the word's possible referents.

narrow generalization A claim that something is true of some members of a group.

natural experiment An experiment in which the groups compared arise on their own (e.g., smokers and nonsmokers), not because they were created by a researcher.

necessary condition An event that must take place in order for another event to take place.

negative-sounding label A label (e.g., "terrorist") that evokes negative images, emotions, and judgments.

nutshell briefing A short list of the pros and cons of alternative solutions, sometimes one-sided or slanted when compiled by someone with a vested interest in one of the solutions.

omission Leaving out information or points of view crucial for creating a representative account; the most basic slanting technique.

ostensive definition Showing the meaning of a word by pointing to the thing or quality the word refers to.

pallid descriptions Descriptions that do not evoke strong sensory images.

perception 1. Taking in information using one of the five senses: seeing, touch, taste, hearing, smell. 2. An intuition or suspicion that something is the case.

personal experience An individual's awareness of things and events by means of the senses and awareness of the individual's own inner sensations and thoughts.

persuasive argument An argument that succeeds in convincing its audience to believe or do what the conclusion says; fallacious arguments are sometimes persuasive to uninformed or inattentive audiences.

placebo In drug testing, something given to the control group that looks like the medication given the experimental group but that has no causal efficacy.

population A group that a statistician is seeking information about, either through taking a census or by making an inference from a sample.

positive-sounding label A label (e.g., "peacekeeper") that evokes positive images, emotions, and judgments.

post hoc fallacy Drawing a conclusion that an event that happened before another event caused the second event simply because it happened before the second event; assuming falsely that priority in time is sufficient to establish causation.

precedent In law, a previously decided case used to guide decisions about future like cases.

prediction A claim that something will happen.

preventive measure An action designed to stop a problem from occurring or recurring.

principle of charity A rule of good argument manners in which one puts a position one disagrees with in the most positive light possible; useful for avoiding straw person reasoning.

questionably acceptable support Support that has not been established either as acceptable or as unacceptable.

randomized experiment An experiment using randomly selected control and experimental groups to test a causal hypothesis.

refuting analogy An analogy used to show that a deductive argument is invalid. A refuting analogy has the same structure as the argument in question and has acceptable support and an unacceptable conclusion.

reinterpreting the outcome An attempt to justify an insult or injury by claiming it has a silver lining or benefit; one of the psychological strategies, usually unconscious, that people use to maintain a false sense of security. See also **denial** and **denigrating (blaming) the victim.**

relevant difference In an explanation using an analogy, a difference between the things being compared that distracts an audience from understanding the subject being explained. In an argument from analogy, a difference between the things being compared that undermines the claim that if something is true of the first thing, it is also true of the second.

relevant similarities In an explanation using an analogy, the similarities between the things being compared that help the audience understand the subject being explained. In an argument from analogy, the similarities between the things being compared that provide evidence that if something is true of the first thing, it is also true of the second.

relevant support Support that succeeds in providing some reason to accept its conclusion.

reliable personal experience When the things an individual expresses awareness of actually exist and have the features the individual reports them to have, the individual's personal experience is reliable. Such things as impaired vision, impaired hearing, impaired touch, and dishonesty limit the reliability of an individual's personal experience.

representative Having similar features; like or analogous.

role-play Pretending to be someone else or oneself in a situation one hasn't been in before.

sample A small group selected for study from a larger group for the purpose of making inferences about the larger group.

sampling birds of a feather Selecting individuals for a sample from group members who resemble each other in significant ways but who do not necessarily represent the population; one way to achieve a biased sample.

scope of authority The area in which an authority of role has the right to command obedience. For example, a police officer's demand that a motorist go out to dinner falls outside the officer's scope of authority.

scope of expertise The breadth of knowledge an expert has.

self-evident truths Statements that are true in themselves, such as "If p is true, p is true"; truths whose denial is impossible to imagine or involves a contradiction.

self-selecting samples Selecting individuals for a sample on the basis of who offers to give information; an example of sampling birds of a feather.

shared ignorance Beliefs, assumptions, or claims that have questionable acceptability yet are accepted by a wide range of persons. Advertisements are a good source of shared ignorance.

side effect A term used by drug manufacturers to label any of the multiple effects of a drug other than the effects the advertiser uses as selling features of the drug.

simple random sample A sample whose members are selected at random from a population.

slanting Providing a partial and unrepresentative presentation of a particular position, opinion, or phenomenon. Slanting is often used by advertisers and others to mislead. But it also has more positive uses, such as to amuse or to reveal. Slanting is different from telling falsehoods and from summarizing. See **summarizing.**

slanting techniques Ways to give an audience a partial and unrepresentative impression of something.

slippery slope fallacy The faulty assumption that from any one contributing cause a specific remote effect will definitely follow.

sound argument A valid argument with acceptable support; a strong deductive argument.

sponsor With respect to studies, the individual or organization that paid to have the study done.

stare decisis In law, the doctrine that decisions about past cases stand firm and guide future similar cases unless the decisions are found to conflict with basic principles of justice.

statistical generalization A generalization about a specific percentage of a group.

statistics The process of gathering and analyzing numerical information about groups.

stereotypes False or misleading claims about groups; claims about groups that overlook individual differences among members of the groups.

stratified random sample A sample achieved by dividing a population into groups (strata)—say, of men and women—then selecting individuals from those groups at random.

straw person fallacy Attacking a weak, partial, or exaggerated version of a point of view or solution and concluding that the point of view or solution itself is flawed.

strictly controlled experiment An experiment that keeps all of the possible causes of an effect stable except the possible cause being tested.

strong argument An argument that succeeds in establishing its conclusion; an argument whose support is acceptable, relevant, and sufficient.

strong conclusion A conclusion that's asserted to be acceptable with a relatively high degree of certainty.

subargument An argument whose conclusion is offered to establish, show, or prove another statement.

subconclusion The conclusion of a subargument.

subsupport The support in a subargument.

sufficient condition A combination of events that together bring about an effect.

sufficient support Enough support to establish the acceptability of its conclusion (assuming the support is itself acceptable).

summarizing Producing a brief but representative presentation of something.

support A statement or series of statements offered to establish the truth or acceptability of another statement; premise, evidence, reason.

support avoidance Acts of communication that attempt to derail an argument, including loud repetition of a point, abuse, and distraction.

support clue words Words that typically introduce support, including "follows from," "in as much as," "after all."

sweeping generalization See **glittering generalization.**

systematic random sample Selecting a particular household at random as a starting point of a sample selection then selecting every nth household from that point.

testable hypothesis A hypothesis that can in principle be shown to be true or false.

thought Activity of the mind, including associating a present experience with something from the past, interpreting evidence, drawing a conclusion from support, and forming moral or aesthetic judgments.

unacceptable support Support that is inconsistent with a self-evident truth or common knowledge or that is inconsistent with a claim based on reliable personal experience, reliable expertise, or a reliable inference; false support.

unstated support Support for a conclusion that's not explicitly stated but is implied by the stated support; assumption.

vague definition Using language in the explanation of a word that is as unclear as the word being defined.

valid argument An argument in which it is impossible for the support to be acceptable and the conclusion to be unacceptable; a deductive argument with sufficient support.

variable In a population, a difference—such as sex, income, or ethnicity—among individuals. A representative sample includes all of the variables in the population and in the same percentages as in the population. In a causal study, a possible cause of an effect.

vivid descriptions Descriptions that evoke sensory images.

vivid samples Samples made up of an individual's personal experiences. Individuals typically form generalizations from these samples, although these samples tend to be unrepresentative of their populations.

weak argument An argument that fails to establish its conclusion; an argument with unacceptable, irrelevant, or insufficient support; fallacious argument.

weak conclusion A conclusion that's asserted to be acceptable with a relatively low degree of certainty.

weasel words Words such as "helps" and "up to" that weaken claims but are artfully placed alongside strong-sounding language to mislead an audience into interpreting the weak claims as strong.

wisdom Recognizing one's ignorance or the limits to one's knowledge.

world of ignorance All of the things a person doesn't know, including things one realizes one doesn't know, things one hasn't thought of yet, and things one assumes one knows but doesn't know.

Acknowledgments

Page 2   Buster Keaton, One Week photograph. Courtesy of The Douris Corporation (Columbus, OH).

Pages 20, 22, 27   Bob Blauner, excerpts from *Black Lives, White Lives: Three Decades of Race Relations in America*, copyright © 1989 The Regents of the University of California. Reprinted by permission of The Regents of the University of California and the author.

Page 28   California Department of Health Services, second-hand smoke public service ad. Reprinted by permission of California Department of Health Services (Sacramento).

Page 28   Health Letter Associates staff, excerpt from "Fish: How Safe?" Reprinted by permission from the University of California at Berkeley Wellness Letter, copyright © 1992 Health Letter Associates (NY).

Page 29   Children International ad, "In Her Eyes, You Could Be a Hero." Reprinted by permission of Children International, © 1995.

Page 30   FEMA ad, "I Never Thought It Could Happen to Me." Reprinted by permission of the National Flood Insurance Program, Federal Emergency Management Agency, Washington, DC.

Page 32   Dannie M. Martin and Peter Y. Sussman, "Requiem for Mr. Squirrel" from *Committing Journalism: The Prison Writings of Red Hog* by Dannie M. Martin and Peter Y. Sussman. Reprinted by permission of W. W. Norton & Company, Inc.

Page 34   Jonathan Kozol, from *Rachael and Her Children*. Copyright © 1988 by Jonathan Kozol. Reprinted by permission of Crown Publishers, Inc., a division of Random House (NY).

Page 38   Wendell Berry, "Why I Am Not Going to Buy a Computer" from *What Are People For?* by Wendell Berry. Copyright © 1990 by Wendell Berry. Reprinted by permission of North Point Press, a division of Farrar, Straus & Giroux, Inc.

Page 58   Tom Teepen, "Lying Holocaust Ads Corrupt the Campuses" from "Other Views" section of the *San Francisco Chronicle*, December 2, 1991. Reprinted by permission of Tom Teepen – Cox Newspapers.

Page 59   AP staff, news report. "Congress Focuses on Teen Moms" as appeared in the *Marin Independent Journal*, Sunday, Nov. 27, 1994, A9. Reprinted by permission of Associated Press (NY).

Page 64   Julie Loesch Wiley, excerpt from "She's Come for an Abortion: What Do You Say?" Copyright © 1992 by Harper's Magazine. All rights reserved. Reproduced from the November issue by special permission.

Page 66   Frederick Turner, excerpt from "She's Come for an Abortion: What Do

You Say?" Copyright © 1992 by Harper's Magazine. All rights reserved. Reproduced from the November issue by special permission.

Page 68   Nancy Mitchell, "Options in the Face of Abuse" from *Christian Science Monitor*, October 21, 1991, p. 18.

Page 70   Camille Paglia, excerpt from "Rape and Modern Sex War" from *Sex, Art and American Culture* by Camille Paglia. Copyright © 1992 by Camille Paglia. Reprinted by permission of Vintage Books, a division of Random House, Inc.

Page 80   Definition of "support" from *Webster's Third New International Dictionary*. Copyright © 1986 by Merriam-Webster, Inc., publisher of the Merriam-Webster® dictionaries.

Page 93   Bertrand Russell, "Why I Am Not a Christian," *Current Issues and Enduring Questions*, eds. Sylvan Barnet and Hugo Bedau, Boston: St. Martin's Press, 1990, pp. 665–666.

Page 95   Teresa Arnott and Julie Matthaei, "Comparable Worth, Incomparable Pay," *Current Issues and Enduring Questions*, eds. Sylvan Barnet and Hugo Bedau, Boston: St. Martin's Press, 1990, p. 166.

Page 96   Charles Krauthammer, "The Just Wage: From Bad to Worth," *Current Issues and Enduring Questions*, eds. Sylvan Barnet and Hugo Bedau, Boston: St. Martin's Press, 1990, p. 174.

Page 97   Jon Margolis, "Animals Have No Rights" as appeared in *The Press Democrat*, March 20, 1991. Reprinted by permission of Tribune Media Services (Chicago, IL).

Page 98   Serge Etienne, "Rights for Animals" editorial, as appeared in *The Press Democrat*, March 27, 1991. Reprinted by permission of Serge Etienne.

Page 99   Frances Byrn, "Death Penalty No Deterrent" as appeared in *The Press Democrat*, March 29, 1990. Reprinted by permission of Frances Byrn, former Chair of ACLU of Sonoma County, CA.

Page 100   Edward I. Koch, "Can the Death Penalty Ever Be Justified?" Reprinted by permission of The New Republic, © 1985, The New Republic, Inc.

Page 104   Mary Utne O'Brien, Ph.D., "Sexual Fidelity Today" as appeared in *Utne Reader*, July/August 1993. Reprinted by permission of the author.

Page 104   Gordon Allport, *The Nature of Prejudice*, © 1979 by Addison-Wesley Publishing Company, Inc. Reprinted by permission of Addison-Wesley Publishing Company, Inc.

Page 109   Definition of "madame," from *The American Heritage Dictionary*, Second College Paperback Edition, copyright © 1983 by Houghton Mifflin Company. Reprinted by permission.

Page 114   Definition of "prejudice" from *The American Heritage Dictionary*, Second College Paperback Edition, copyright © 1983 by Houghton Mifflin Company. Reprinted by permission.

Page 115   Walter W. Skeat, *A Concise Etymological Dictionary of the English Language*, NY: Putnam, 1980. Reprinted by permission of the publisher.

Page 124   Bernice Sandler and Jean O'Gorman Hughes, "Bob and Patty" story from *Friends Raping Friends: Could It Happen to You?* Reprinted by permission of the Center for Women's Policy Studies. For information on this publication, please call the Center at (202)872-1770 or write to 2000 P Street NW, Suite 508, Washington, DC 20036.

Page 125   Definition of "jealous" from *The American Heritage Dictionary*, Second College Paperback Edition, copyright © 1983 by Houghton Mifflin Company. Reprinted by permission.

Page 126   Frances Moore Lappe, excerpts from *Rediscovering America's Values*. Copyright © 1989 by Frances Moore Lappe. Reprinted by permission of Ballantine Books, a division of Random House, Inc.

Page 128   Ellen Goodman, "Sexual Bullying in Schools." Copyright © 1993 The Boston Globe Newspaper Co./Washington Post Writers Group. Reprinted with permission.

Page 129   Peter Schrag, "Bias, Harassment Reports Out of Focus: Girls Short-changed?" as appeared in *The Press Democrat*, Wednesday, June 9, 1993. Copyright, The Sacramento Bee, 1993.

Page 130   Jack D. Forbes, from "Only Approved Indians Can Play: Made in the U.S.A." in *Only Approved Indians* by Jack D. Forbes (University of Oklahoma Press, 1995). Reprinted by permission of the author.

Page 134   Dan Garcia-Diaz, from "Colleges and Common Sense" as appeared in *The Dartmouth Review*, Nov. 20, 1991, p. 14. Reprinted by permission of The Dartmouth Review.

Page 136   Mike Luckovich. Reprinted by permission of Mike Luckovich and Creators Syndicate.

Page 138   Kathleen Harness, "Role Models" from *The Press Democrat*, letter to the editor, Saturday, July 13, 1991. Reprinted by permission of the author.

Page 143   Ellen Goodman, "War Is the Wrong Metaphor." Copyright © 1989 The Boston Globe Newspaper Co./Washington Post Writers Group. Reprinted with permission.

Page 144   Bella English, excerpts from "When Words Go to War." Reprinted by permission of The Boston Globe.

Page 146   Gordon Allport, *The Nature of Prejudice*, © 1979 by Addison-Wesley Publishing Company, Inc. Reprinted by permission of Addison-Wesley Publishing Company, Inc.

Page 149   Heyday Books staff, "Mewuk Indian Tribe Burns 'Old Man Digger' in Effigy at Ione Festival" from *News from Native California*, Vol. 6, No. 2. Reprinted by permission of Heyday Books.

Page 150   Foley-Belsaw Institute ad, "Be the Boss of Your Own Business." Copyright © 1994. Reprinted courtesy of Foley-Belsaw Co.

Page 151   Barbara Ehrenreich, "Kicking the Big One" from *Time*, February 28, 1994. Copyright © 1994 Time, Inc. Reprinted by permission.

Page 151   Garrett North, from "Care and Feeding of the Plus-Size Child" in *Big Beautiful Woman*, Summer 1995, p. 19. Includes research conducted by Janice Rosenberg. Reprinted by permission of the publisher (Los Angeles, CA).

Page 153   Purple Kush, "Piggies Get Piggy, But Piggy Gets Piggies" as appeared in *Sonoma County Peace Press*, September 1992, p. 19. Reprinted by permission of Sonoma County Peace Press, a publication of Sonoma County Center for Peace & Justice (Santa Rosa, CA).

Page 154   Toyota ad, "It should look beautiful . . ." Copyright © 1996. Reprinted by permission of Toyota Motor Sales, USA, Inc. Contact Toyota via Saatchi & Saatchi DFS/Pacific (Torrance, CA).

Page 155   U.S. Air Force Recruiting ad, "Join the Air Force and soar without leaving the ground." Reprinted by permission of the United States Air Force Recruiting Service.

Page 156   Mark Twain, excerpts from *The War Prayer*. Copyright © 1923 by The Mark Twain Co. Reprinted by permission of HarperCollins Publishers, Inc.

the Nation" section of *Destiny*, April 1995. Reprinted by permission of Destiny (Lansing, MI).

Page 185   Emerge Communications staff, "Black Broadcasters MAD" as appeared in *Emerge*, June 1992, p. 9.

Page 185   Hispanic staff, "Sanctions against Legal Immigrants . . ." from *Hispanic*, June 1995. Reprinted by permission of National Council of La Russo (Washington, DC).

Page 186   Howard Zinn, "The Truman Doctrine" from *A People's History of the United States* by Howard Zinn. Copyright © 1980 by Howard Zinn. Reprinted by permission of HarperCollins Publishers, Inc. For territory outside the United States, contact The Balkin Agency, Inc., PO Box 222, Amherst, MA 01004.

Page 187   U.S. Army Recruiting ad, "Imagine having a future that comes with a guarantee." Reprinted courtesy of the U.S. Army.

Page 188   Chevron Corporation ad, "A Tip for Mother Nature" © 1994. Reprinted courtesy of Chevron Corporation.

Page 189   Jordache Enterprises ad, "A good pair . . . makes great things happen!" Copyright © 1996 Jordache Enterprises. Reprinted by permission of Jordache Enterprises.

Page 190   Gene Yasuda, "College Students Abusing Plastic" as appeared in *The Press Democrat*, December 14, 1993. Reprinted by permission of The Orlando Sentinel.

Page 191   "Cuba Accused of Gouging Families of U.S. Exiles to Raise Cash" (found in *The Press Democrat*, Wed., March 27, 1991), from KRT News Wire.

Page 192   Stephen Kinzer, "Managua Rally Cheers Jeane Kirkpatrick" from *New York Times*, October 13, 1987. Copyright © 1987 by The New York Times Company. Reprinted by permission.

Page 204   Peter Steiner, "On the Internet, nobody knows you're a dog" cartoon. Drawing by P. Steiner; © 1993 The New Yorker Magazine, Inc. Reprinted by permission of The New Yorker Magazine, Inc.

Page 227   Jimalee Plank, letter to Sebastopol Pet Center, May 10, 1991. Reprinted by permission of the author.

Page 229   Peter Henriksen, DVM, "Choosing Dogs" as appeared in *The Press Democrat*, March 4, 1996, B3. Reprinted by permission of the author.

Page 230   Robert Coles, "Drugs Should Not Be Legalized." Copyright © 1988 New Oxford Review. Reprinted with permission from New Oxford Review (1069 Kains Avenue, Berkeley, CA 94706) and the author, Robert Coles.

Page 231   Eric Scigliano, "Drugs Should Be Legalized" as appeared in *Seattle Weekly*. Reprinted by permission of Eric Scigliano, a senior editor at the Seattle Weekly.

Page 232   Donald Kagan, "Military Service: A Moral Obligation" from *New York Times*, December 4, 1983. Copyright © 1983 by The New York Times Company. Reprinted by permission.

Page 237   Sterling Bennett, "The Gorge." Courtesy of the author.

Page 240   Alberto Rios, excerpt from "Becoming and Breaking: Poet and Poem" in Kathleen Aguero, ed., *Daily Fare: Essays from the Multicultural Experience*, 1993, p. 21. First published in *Ironwood*. Copyright © 1984 by Alberto Rios. Reprinted by permission of the author.

Page 245   John Branch, "Fire, Air Bag, and Condoms" cartoon, as appeared in *Best Editorial Cartoons of the Year, 1993*. Reprinted by permission of John Branch/San Antonio Express-News.

Page 245   Audre Lorde, from *The Cancer Journals*, © 1980 by Audre Lorde. Reprinted by permission of Aunt Lute Books.

Page 248   David Shaw, excerpts from "Hunger for Heroes, Villains Rooted in American Psyche" as appeared in *Los Angeles Times*, February 17, 1994. Copyright © 1994 David Shaw. Los Angeles Times. Reprinted by permission of the Los Angeles Times.

Page 251   Carol Tavris, excerpt from *The Mismeasure of Woman* by Carol Tavris. Published by Simon & Schuster. Copyright © 1992 by Carol Tavris. Reprinted by permission of Lescher & Lescher, Ltd. as agents for the author.

Pages 252, 253, 254   Cass R. Sunstein, "Commentary: On Analogical Reasoning" from *Harvard Law Review*, Vol. 106: 741–791. Copyright © 1993 by the Harvard Law Review Association. Reprinted by permission of the author and Harvard Law Review Association.

Page 255   Margarita Holmes-Marinaccio, Ph.D., excerpts from egg/family analogy as appeared in *Filipinas,* June 1995, p. 68. Reprinted by permission of the author.

Page 256   Delbert Hawthorne, from "Stopping the Civil Rights Train" as appeared in *Destiny*, April 1995, p. 19. Reprinted by permission of Destiny (Lansing, MI).

Page 257   Chang-Lin Tien, "Affirming Affirmative Action" as appeared in *A. Magazine*, June/July 1995. Reprinted by permission of the author.

Page 257   Richard Wasserstrom, "Racism, Sexism, and Preferential Treatment: An Approach to the Topics." Originally published in 24 *UCLA Law Review*, 581. Copyright © 1977, The Regents of the University of California. All rights reserved. Reprinted by permission of the UCLA Law Review (Los Angeles, CA) and Fred B. Rothman & Co. (Littleton, CO).

Page 258   Patricia Williams, "The Executioner's Automat" from *The Nation*, July 10, 1995. Reprinted with permission from The Nation magazine. Copyright © The Nation Company, L. P.

Page 259   Tinker v. Des Moines Independent Community School District, from *The Supreme Court Reporter*, published by West Publishing Company. Reprinted by permission of the publisher.

Page 262   Cases, National Treasury Employees Union et al. v. William Von Raab, United Customs Service, from *The Supreme Court Reporter*, published by West Publishing Company. Reprinted by permission of the publisher.

Page 267   Robert Sapolsky, "Distribution of SAT Scores" graph from *Mismeasure of Woman* by Carol Tavris. Originally appeared in *Discover*, July 1987, pp. 42–45. Philip Scheuer/© 1987 Discover Magazine. Reprinted by permission of Discover Magazine.

Page 285   Gallup Organization staff, two graphs comparing attitudes of various age groups, © 1989 The Gallup Poll. Reprinted by permission of the Gallup Organization.

Page 285   Poll, "Has the American National Character Changed in the Last 20 Years?" From *Newsweek*, July 10, 1995. Reprinted by permission of Newsweek.

Page 285   Poll, "100 Years from Today, Will the United States Still Exist as One Nation?" From *Newsweek*, July 10, 1995. Reprinted by permission of Newsweek.

Page 286   AP staff, "Majority Opposes Clinton's Smoking Crackdown" as appeared in *The Press Democrat*, Wednesday, August 23, 1995, A7. Reprinted by permission of Associated Press (NY).

Page 286   Los Angeles Times staff, "Poll: State Voters Back Execution 4–1" from *The Los Angeles Times*, April 2, 1990. Copyright © 1990 Los Angeles Times. Reprinted by permission.

Page 288   Jin K. Kim, "American Graffiti: Curious Derivatives of Individualism" in Philip R. DeVita and James D. Armstrong, *Distant Mirrors: America as a Foreign Culture*, 1993, pp. 11–20. Reprinted by permission of Jin K. Kim, Ph.D. (SUNY).

Page 289   Catherine McHugh Engstrom and William E. Sedlacek, excerpts from "A Study of Prejudice toward University Student-Athletes" in *The Journal of Counseling and Development*, Sept./Oct. 1991. Reprinted by permission of American Counseling Association (Alexandria, VA).

Page 293   Peter Huber, "Medical Experts and the Ghost of Gallileo" as appeared in *Law and Contemporary Problems*, Vol. 54, No. 3, Summer 1991, p. 125. Copyright © Law and Contemporary Problems—Duke University School of Law. Reprinted by permission.

Pages 302, 303, 304   James Adams, from *Conceptual Blockbusting: A Guide to Better Ideas*, Third Edition. Copyright © 1986 by James L. Adams. Reprinted by permission of Addison-Wesley Publishing Company, Inc.

Page 307   Stephen Jay Gould, "The Smoking Gun of Eugenics: Should We—Can We—Take a Kindly View toward a Hero's Faults?" Reprinted with permission from Natural History, December 1991. Copyright © The American Museum of Natural History, 1991.

Page 309   Doug Podolsky and Joanne Silberner, "News You Can Use: 20 Medical Stories You May Have Missed" as appeared in *U.S. News and World Report*, August 3, 1992. Reprinted by permission of U.S. News & World Report.

Page 321   Catherine Fuller, excerpt from "Toy Guns Don't Produce Adult Killers" as appeared in *The Press Democrat*, Wednesday, August 23, 1995, B5. Reprinted by permission of the author. Dr. Fuller is a clinical psychologist in Pasadena, CA.

Page 322   Health Letter Associates staff, excerpt from "Is Only Red Wine Fine?" Reprinted by permission from the University of California at Berkeley Wellness Letter. Copyright © 1996 Health Letter Associates (NY).

Page 322   Devon Dee, "Seeing Ourselves as Others See Us" from *Skin & Ink*.

Page 324   AT&T ad, "Daughters Are Listening to Everything Their Mothers Say." Copyright © 1995 AT&T. Reprinted by permission.

Page 326   Pharmacia & Upjohn ad for Depo-Provera, "Things Are Crazy Enough Around Here . . ." Reprinted courtesy of Pharmacia & Upjohn, Inc.

Page 328   David C. Anderson, "The Television Time Bomb" from *New York Times* (Op-Ed), July 27, 1992. Copyright © 1992 by The New York Times Company. Reprinted by permission.

Page 329   Marie Winn, "Does Television Itself Nurture Violence?" Letter to the editor, appearing in the *New York Times*, August 9, 1992. Marie Winn is author of *The Plug-In Drug: Television, Children and the Family,* Viking/Penguin. Revised Edition 1985. Reprinted by permission of the author.

Page 330   Todd Gitlin, from "Imagebusters: The Hollow Crusade against TV Violence" in *The American Prospect*, Winter 1994. Copyright © New Prospect, Inc. Reprinted by permission from The American Prospect and the author.

Page 332   Suzanne Braun Levine, "Caution: Children Watching: When It Comes to Violence on TV, What's a Parent to Do?" from *Ms. Magazine*, July/August 1994. Reprinted by permission of Ms. Magazine, © 1994.

Page 352   James Adams, from *Conceptual Blockbusting: A Guide to Better Ideas*, Third Edition. Copyright © 1986 by James L. Adams. Reprinted by permission of Addison-Wesley Publishing Company, Inc.

Index

A page number followed by "n." indicates a note and includes the note number.